C000181404

Wednesday

Every day of the week

Wednesday Star

Every day of the week

Compiled by

Keith Farnsworth

Breedon Books
Publishing Company
Derby

First published in Great Britain by
The Breedon Books Publishing Company Limited
Breedon House, 44 Friar Gate, Derby, DE1 1DA.
1998

© Keith Farnsworth 1998

All Rights Reserved. No part of this publication may be reproduced, stored in
a retrieval system, or transmitted in any form, or by any means, electronic,
mechanical, photocopying, recording or otherwise without the prior permission in writing of the copyright holders, nor be otherwise circulated in any
form or binding or cover other than in which it is published and without a
similar condition being imposed on the subsequent publisher.

DEDICATION:
To Linda

ISBN 1 85983 131 1

Printed and bound by Butler & Tanner Ltd., Selwood Printing Works, Caxton
Road, Frome, Somerset.

Colour separations by Freelance Repro, Leicester.

Jackets printed by Lawrence-Allen, Avon.

Contents

Acknowledgements
The author wishes to thank all the people who have contributed memories to this book, and particularly Peter Pollitt for his help in research. Thanks to *The Star* for access to their library (where Susan Woods was most helpful) and for the loan of and permission to reproduce photographs to supplement pictures and illustrations kindly lent by Keith Bannister, Ivor Seemley, Brian Ryalls, Gerry Young, Duggie McMillan, Sam and Helen Ellis, Lily Shelton and Frank Ronksley.

An especial thanks to Steve Ellis, Wednesday's official photographer. Apologies to those with whom contact was made but then lost during research – a deadline meant that in a number of cases delays in communications were not overcome!

Introduction

WHEN I was growing up in the Newhall area of Sheffield's East End in the early 1940s, my father was always talking about football, and he filled my head with romantic images of Wednesday idols like Ronnie Starling, Mark Hooper and Jackie Robinson. Somewhere out there, at a place called Hillsborough, there was a wonderful world I couldn't wait to discover. Unfortunately, when it came to arranging a visit, father was full of promises, but never quite got round to it. By the age of eight, I was starting to get desperate, and one day in March 1947, I announced I was going to make the trip – alone.

It just happened we had an insurance man called Unwin, who was a Wednesday fanatic, and, when he made his usual Saturday call at our house and talked about being in a hurry because he was going to "see the lads play Tottenham", I knew the time had come to join him and the other 20,000 who were making the pilgrimage. If father preferred to stay at home, at least he could tell me how to get there – and cough up the money I needed for tram fares and admission! (I'm not too sure now, but I think it cost ninepence in old money at the boys' entrance to the Kop, while two tram-rides each way used up four half-pennies – total outlay less than 5p in modern currency).

That day, the Owls won 5-1 and Jimmy Dailey, who scored a hat-trick, became my first hero. It was the start of a passion which has lasted for more than 50 years and left me with an abundance of memories – too many to list now, although I must mention Dailey's five-goal show against Barnsley in 1947, and a wet afternoon in 1951 when Dooley repeated the feat, for they were moments I'll treasure in much the way, half a century from now, today's young fans will still be talking about the "wonder" goals they saw Paolo Di Canio, Benito Carbone and Francesco Sanetti score in 1997-98.

My early enthusiasm extended to games in which Hillsborough was a neutral venue, which reminds me of a morning when I lost our front door key (it disappeared forever as I dashed through Hillsborough Park!) in my haste to be up at before five o'clock one Sunday morning to reach the ground and queue for a ticket for the 1948 FA Cup semi-final between Manchester United and Derby County. The ticket, for the Spion Kop, cost 2s 6d (12½p), and, as you were allowed to buy two, a man in the queue gave me a threepenny bit for getting an extra one for him. I was too young to appreciate how much more I might have profited had I only been able to invest my own money in that second ticket, and re-sell it. But, then, those were innocent days when life seemed so simple and all the romance was in watching your heroes.

I especially want to mention Fred Stones, who was a Supporters' Club official for many years. Back in the late 1940s, Fred and his wife used to stand outside the South Stand before matches looking for youngsters who might not be able to afford the admission charge. They would loan them their shareholders' tickets. Having walked all the way from Paget Street without a penny in my pocket, intent on getting into the ground for the last ten minutes when the gates opened, it was a more than welcome bonus to benefit from Mrs Stones' generosity and watch the match in comparative luxury.

The only time my father ever took me to a match was when England played Switzerland in a midweek "B" international in January 1950. No floodlights then, so it was an afternoon kick-off, and it was the only occasion I recall when father said I could take time off school and he'd write me a "sick" note. The teacher at Newhall School, a lovely little Irishman called Frank Connelly, obviously knew me well, because the next morning, after reading the note which said I'd been poorly, he asked: "Did you enjoy the match?"

We can all recall similar experiences, and, whether you played for the Owls, worked for them, or simply followed the team with unstinting loyalty, everyone has his own fund of memories. And memories are what this book is all about. It's not so much remembering a certain match, a great goal or a particularly outstanding performance or incident – it's also the background and personal circumstances against which they were set which makes them special to the individual.

All the leading figures of the post-war era, most of the major matches and many memorable goals are featured here, but this is a slice of history rather than a comprehensive study. The idea is to recapture something of the essence of "the way it was" with the off-beat tale, the anecdote, touches of humour and drama, etc. These are the memories of players, backroom and other staff, and supporters whose stories tell you more about how things have changed in the game and at the club over the years than any formal history. It didn't always cost a fortune to watch your favourite team, and there was a time when players didn't earn as much in their entire careers as their modern counterparts collect in a week!

Around a hundred people have contributed to this book, and, had time and space permitted, one could have collected as many memories again; but those featured here – the famous and less familiar favourites, the people from behind the scenes, and the ordinary fans – represent better than most the different phases in the last 60 years.

It has been my good fortune to have been a writer on the local football scene for the past 35 years. For me, the real reward has been the involvement, the opportunity to work with so many players, managers and club officials, to have had their respect, trust and friendship. Of course, you can't please all the people all the time, and, over the years, there have been disputes and disagreements, because, as a journalist, you have to stick to your principles – and people are not always pleased when you insist on writing what you see rather than what they want you to see. Happily, in the long run being truthful strengthened friendships.

Of course, when I first started on the old *Morning Telegraph*, the local football writers still used to travel with the team. I can't explain what a thrill that was for someone who had grown up in Sheffield and always aspired to follow in the footsteps of such once-famous pundits as Richard A.Sparling and Fred Walters, respectively sports editors of the *Telegraph* and the *Star*. Some people might consider that reaction rather juvenile, but, in the context of my background, it was an experience I savoured – and it proved an important part of my education and progress, giving me an insight for which I have always been grateful.

Today football and the media are both very different, and, in a world which has changed so much, I don't think it is only the fact that one is older which has removed the sense of belonging which once seemed so natural. Part of the fun was knowing and being known by everybody from the chairman to the gateman, and having the kind of access and freedom of movement increasingly denied in modern times. It was all based on mutual respect, trust and goodwill. Circumstances only partially explain changes which have affected many loyal supporters.

A 20 per cent increase in ticket prices despite a disappointing 1997-98 season served to stress the truth that modern football is increasingly dominated by financial considerations, and the recent withdrawal of complimentary privileges previously granted long-serving ex-employees and former players highlighted changes in attitudes and structure as the club moves into a new era. Some might suggest the developments make this book of memories all the more relevant as a social as well as a sporting document.

However, whatever the future holds, you can be sure there will never be a shortage of Owls fans determined to maintain a Hillsborough tradition in which they look at the calendar and contend that it really is Wednesday every day of the week!

Part 1 – Playing for Wednesday 1933-1998

Jackie Thompson

Jackie Thompson was a talented inside-forward who scored more than 50 goals in some 140 games for the Owls between 1933 and 1946. It was the slightly-built Geordie's misfortune that the peak of his career coincided with the war years, although in that period he gave Hillsborough regulars plenty to cheer, and, as he recalled in this interview shortly before his death, he always remembered his Wednesday days with great affection. However, although for many years he lived in a house close enough to the ground to hear the fans cheering, he never went to another professional game after he hung up his boots. He died in November 1996.

It was around the time of my 18th birthday when I joined Sheffield Wednesday in 1933. It all came about after the club's North East scout persuaded Bob Brown, the manager, to travel up to look at me when I was playing for Blyth Spartans. I always remember Mr Brown and a Wednesday director talking to me one Saturday and, after some initial discussions, they invited me and my Dad to join them for a meal at their hotel in Newcastle on the following day.

Dad was a miner, and, being keen to ensure I got the best advice, he thought it would be a good idea to take my uncle along with us. As a pit deputy, my uncle was regarded as the brainy one in the family, so Dad was happy to let him do most of the talking on my behalf.

I shall never forget that when we sat down for the meal there was so much cutlery on the table I didn't know which to use for each course, but nobody took much notice and the main topic of conversation was what Wednesday were prepared to pay me. The figures they mentioned sounded very large to someone like me, earning 12s 6d [62½p] a week for working on the tubs with the pit ponies at the local colliery!

Mr Brown offered £5 10s [£5.50],

Jackie Thompson.

but I heard my uncle say: "Well, it's a good wage, but can't you give the lad another ten shillings? After all, he will have to send £2 home each week to help his mother and father."

In the end, they agreed on £6 a week, and I was eager to sign before they changed their mind. But Mr Brown explained that transfers couldn't be completed on a Sunday and said they would stay overnight and I should meet him again the next morning.

It was a lovely feeling because I had always hoped I might get the chance to be a professional footballer. That was every Geordie boy's ambition in those days, and lots of lads from that part of the world had gone on to play with some of the top clubs. The area was known as a natural breeding ground for footballers.

I had played with Cramlington Schoolboys and got into the Northumberland Boys team, and then when I left school, after a spell with a local junior side, I joined Blyth and soon got into their first team at centre-forward. There were always lots of scouts at the games, and there was much talk about my prospects after I scored four goals in six games and we reached the Final of a local cup competition.

The Final was played at St James's Park, the home of Newcastle United, and I think the thrill of playing there was almost as rewarding as the lovely medal I collected after the game. It must have been about this time that Mr Brown came to see me.

I think the return train fare from Newcastle to Sheffield was £1 1s 9d [about £1.08] when I first made the journey, and I recall I didn't feel too far from home when I started at Hillsborough because there were eight Geordies playing alongside me in the reserve team!

I hadn't been here long when Bob Brown resigned owing to ill-health. He was a famous manager and Wednesday had done very well under him, and I think one or two of the senior players felt he had been pushed out a bit suddenly. Joe McClelland, his assistant, took over, and he was the man who gave me my first-team debut at Sunderland

WEDNESDAY EVERY DAY OF THE WEEK

Sheffield Wednesday, League North War Cup Finalists 1943. Back row (left to right): Eric Taylor (secretary-manager), Russell, Ashley, Millership, Morton, Gadsby, Cockroft, Catlin. Front row: Reynolds, Robinson, Melling, Thompson. Swift, Powell (trainer).

in November 1933. I came into the side because Ronnie Starling, who had played for England the previous April, had been dropped, which at the time was a big sensation.

I only stayed in the team for a couple of games, and it was another two years before I was given another chance. In the meantime, Billy Walker took over as manager, and, of course, in 1935, Wednesday won the FA Cup. I was sorry not to see the Final at Wembley, but, if I'm not mistaken, I was playing for the Reserves at West Brom that day and scored a hat-trick in a 3-3 draw. My consolation was being chosen for the close-season tour to Denmark, and I played a few times in the Cup-winning side as a deputy centre-forward.

There was a lot of competition for places, and we had a lot of inside-forwards. As well as Starling, there was Jackie Robinson and George Drury – who were both in digs with me in Dorothy Road – and, later, Charlie Napier. I also had a few injury problems, so, one way and another, I think I managed under 40 first-team games in the six years before the war.

Fortunately, the war years coincided with a spell when I was pretty much an automatic choice when available, and I thoroughly enjoyed that period. I scored nearly 50 goals in just over 100 games, and, of course, we reached the League North War Cup Final in 1943, when we lost over two legs to Blackpool.

After the war started, I went to work at Shardlows, and, strangely enough, working on crankshafts strengthened my legs and made them more resistant to knocks. I had a long run free of problems. The only serious injury I suffered after that was a knee I damaged in a match against Bradford Park Avenue. It happened not long after I joined the army, and, at the time, the injury looked so serious that it brought an abrupt end to my soldiering. I was fearing my footballing days were over as well, but "Doc" Stephen, the club doctor, had a good look at the knee and promised he would get me fit – and he did.

The highlight of the war years was the run to the Cup Final in 1942-43. Eric Taylor had taken over from Jimmy

McMullan as manager, and we had a fair team. Jackie Robinson, Frank Melling and me shared over 76 goals that season, although I must admit my contribution was 14 while "Robbo" scored 35.

Robinson was brilliant. He was what I would call a second centre-forward. He didn't do any midfield work, and he was sometimes criticised for that, but he had the speed of lightning, a terrific body swerve and a wonderful scoring knack. The supporters saw him as an idol, but I must admit some of his team-mates felt Jackie was simply idle – or, at least, he didn't pull his weight if he didn't feel like it.

He certainly wasn't everybody's favourite in the dressing room. Joe Cockroft used to play at right-half, behind Robinson, until one day he went to Eric Taylor and said he wanted to switch to left-half because he was fed up of doing Jackie's legwork for him.

There were a lot of games in that Cup Final season when Jackie's brilliance brought us some great victories, and I've heard people say we would have won that League North Cup if he

10

had played for the team instead of for himself in the home return leg.

We drew the first leg at Blackpool 2-2, and, although we lost Ted Catlin with a serious injury in a clash with Jock Dodds, we were only denied victory by a goal two minutes from the end. In the second match, we didn't deserve to win. We never really got into the game, and Jackie didn't produce any magic.

I think the fact that we were without Catlin was partly to blame, but not so much because we missed him as that Walter Millership seemed to be more concerned with avenging Ted's injury. He spent most of the match trying to "do" Dodds. What Dodds had done in the first game was a wilful and unnecessary act, but it was silly to let it affect our concentration in return fixture.

We were all pleased to see the end of the war, but, unfortunately, by the time football got back to normal in 1946, my Wednesday days were over. I went to Doncaster Rovers and played about 90 games for them, and ended my playing days at the age of 37 after around 60 matches for Chesterfield between 1948 and 1952.

At Doncaster I was in the side that won the Third Division North championship in 1946-47. That was the year when Clarrie Jordan, the Rovers centre-forward, scored 44 goals, and, in the following season, I had a hand in getting Clarrie to Hillsborough. Eric Taylor came to ask me about Jordan, and I said: "Well, he's not brilliant with his head, but if you give him the ball on the floor he's fantastic. He has the speed and only needs half a chance to score a goal." I think Wednesday paid £6,000 and let Rovers have Arnold Lowes, and it was good business. It would have been excellent business if Clarrie had not been dogged by injuries.

After I gave up football I had a spell on a building site before going to work at Samuel Fox's steelworks, where I stayed until my retirement in 1980.

Frank Westlake

Frank Westlake made some 150 appearances for Wednesday between 1938 and 1950, but there was an eight-year gap between his first and second Football League games for the club. Moreover, when I spoke to him in November 1997, it emerged that even at the age of 82 he still remembered that his Owls debut was a match with a rather painful footnote.

It is all of 60 years ago, but I still recall the thrill of being told that Sheffield Wednesday wanted to give me a trial, and I'll never forget the pleasure and pride I felt when they decided to sign me as a professional in 1937.

Honestly, I couldn't believe my luck in getting paid to keep fit and entertain people by playing football. It was certainly better than earning a living down the pit, as I had been doing.

I was already turned 21 and captain of a local team called Thurnscoe Victoria when this chap came up to me after one game and said Wednesday would like to have a look at me. I travelled into Sheffield on a bus and obviously made an impression in the trials because they offered me terms without any hesitation.

I got my chance in the first team late in that first season, turning out at right-back at Luton in March 1938. All I remember now is that we drew 2-2, and I think Jackie Robinson got one of the goals.

Unfortunately, it transpired that Wednesday had failed to register me, and, while the club was fined by the Football League, I was suspended for the rest of that season. It was rather an embarrassing start to my career, and, although I can laugh about it now, I wasn't amused at the time because I felt I was innocent of any offence.

Curiously enough, I didn't play in the Second Division team again until 1946, and, by coincidence, that game was also at Luton. This time we lost 4-1, but at least my appearance was legitimate!

Of course, like so many of my friends, my football career was interrupted by the war, although I maintained peak fitness because I served in the RAF and eventually became a sergeant PT instructor. I also managed to get home to play in around 40 matches for Wednesday in those years.

I always prided myself on being the fittest player at Hillsborough, and, with me being something of a fitness fanatic, the training sessions were as enjoyable as the matches. It really was a wonderful life, and I had some marvellous times among some very good pals – people like Cyril Turton, Joe Cockroft and Eddie Gannon were particularly friendly and helpful.

I could play in either full-back position, and my most regular partner was Hugh Swift – a lovely man and a very good footballer who is probably best remembered for his sliding tackle. Hugh and me once had a run of 104 consecutive appearances together, and, with Roy Smith a regular in goal in those early years after the war, the first three names on the team sheet seldom changed.

It took two bus journeys, with a change in Sheffield, to get me from my home in Conisbrough to Hillsborough, but I would gladly have walked if I'd had to. However, there was a spell when I travelled in comparative style, because Roy Smith, who lived at Bentley, near Doncaster, acquired a two-seater MG, and he used to pick me up on his way in for training.

In more recent times, private transport is commonplace for most people, but in those days having a car was quite a luxury. When I eventually bought one myself, I felt I had really come a long way in the world!

It is always sad when something comes to an end, and I was disappointed about leaving Wednesday. But I was nearly 35, had lost my place, and the time had come for me to accept a move to Halifax. Of course, it wasn't the same. Anywhere had to be a let-down after Hillsborough. I didn't stay long at The Shay, and soon decided it was time to hang up my boots and look for another way of life.

So I became a greengrocer, and me and my late wife, Vera, ran our little business in Denaby for 25 years until the premises were demolished. Then we decided to retire to a bungalow in Conisbrough. I've not seen much football for many years, but I still sometimes think back to those good old days when I revelled in the life of a professional footballer.

Redfern Froggatt

Redfern "Ticker" Froggatt was an outstanding inside-forward, one of the biggest Hillsborough favourites of the early post-war years. He was a one-club man who made some 550 senior appearances for Wednesday between 1943 and 1960 and scored around 170 goals in all competitions. His tally of 140 in the Football League brought him the club's post-war scoring record until that honour passed to Johnny Fantham in 1968. Redfern played in four promotion teams, and won three Division Two title medals, and, when he captained the Second Division championship side of 1959, he emulated his father, Frank, who led the Owls to the same prize in 1926. Redfern's four England caps came between November 1952 and June 1953, with three of his international appearances being at Wembley.

Redfern Froggatt sees his attempt to get on to the end of Walter Rickett's cross thwarted as Spurs goalkeeper Ted Ditchburn gets to the ball first during the famous promotion clash of May 1950 when the Owls went up on goal-average.

I was always a Wednesdayite, but this wasn't particularly because my father played for and captained the club. In fact, he left to join Notts County when I was about three years old, so I never saw him play at Hillsborough. However, although we then moved from Burton Street to Nottingham for about four years, we subsequently returned home and lived near the Wednesday ground again at a time when I was starting to take notice of things. As much as anything, it was simply going to a school overlooking Hillsborough that inspired my dream of one day wearing the famous blue-and-white stripes.

When I was a boy, a lot of Wednesday players were in digs near our house in Lennox Road. Most were Geordies, and I remember often following them down the street, deliberately trying to imitate the way they walked. It sounds daft now, but I used to imagine that if I could walk like them, I might be able to play like them! Towards the end of my schooldays, my great hero was Jackie Robinson. He was fantastic and many was the time I saw him collect the ball on the halfway line and go through everybody before planting the ball in the net.

We kids spent all our free time kicking a ball around in Hillsborough Park, and I invariably pretended I was "The Great Robbo", never realising that one day I would actually play alongside him. There were many days when we camped in the park from dawn to dusk, footballing in the winter and cricketing in the summer. I was a very small boy among dozens of bigger lads, but somebody would always say: "Come on, Tich, you can play in my team."

I never played for Sheffield Boys at football, but I did achieve that honour at cricket, and I remember once taking five wickets for two runs. I mention this because it was actually through my cricketing abilities that I got the nickname "Ticker" which was so familiar to Wednesdayites. At the time, everybody's favourite Yorkshire cricketer was Arthur "Ticker" Mitchell, and my pals seemed to think his nickname suited me – although I was a fast bowler and he was a spinner!

It will be of interest to older supporters that, when I was playing for Hillsborough Council School, the most talked-about schoolboy in our district was Dennis Woodhead, who was at Wadsley Bridge. He was quick and skilful, one of the best left-wingers in Sheffield at his age. Our two schools had quite a few battles, and it was a happy coincidence that we ended up playing together for Wednesday.

After leaving school, I got into a local side, and an early turning point came after I had a good game against the YMCA. The man who ran the YMCA, "Pop" Bennett, said he was impressed and invited me to play for them. When I asked if that would mean me having to become a member and he said yes, I told him it was out of the question because times were hard and my parents couldn't afford the subscription. Mr Bennett promised he would make

himself responsible for my subs if I'd play for them. That was an act of generosity I appreciated.

It was while I was with the YMCA that a Wednesday scout called Cyril Hemmingfield spotted me. We won a tournament in Millhouses Park, and, after the Final, about eight scouts from professional clubs invited me for trials. The only one I was interested in saying "yes" to was Mr Hemmingfield – a man, incidentally, who became a Wednesday director in July 1946.

Joining Wednesday meant me training at the ground on Tuesday and Thursday evenings, and, as I was working full-time learning to be a jig-and-tool draughtsman, attending night school three times a week, playing football on Saturdays and doing my homework on Sundays, life was pretty hectic.

The war had started just over a week after my 15th birthday, but, when I reached 18 in August 1942, I didn't get called up because I was in a reserved occupation. It meant I was available to play football, and, in February 1943, I made my debut against Grimsby at Hillsborough. The previous week, Wednesday had beaten Sheffield United 8-2 and my hero Jackie Robinson had scored three. Now he wasn't available, so I replaced him. What a thrill for a teenager!

PLAYING FOR WEDNESDAY 1933-1998

I was slight in build, and my legs were rather thin, and I remember my lack of pounds was sometimes over-emphasised in those early wartime games because of the way the kit was issued. Of course, numbers weren't compulsory then. Someone would throw ten shirts without numbers, and 11 pairs of shorts, on to a table, everybody would make a grab, and, being the youngest and the last in the queue, I'd often be left with gear that was far too big for me. Sometimes the shorts I wore were big enough to fit two of us!

I played in about 90 games during the war, and my only regret was that my father's death at the age of 45 meant he didn't live to see me start to make the grade. Sadly, he died around the time I first got into the team. However, he was certainly in my thoughts when, after "normal" football resumed in 1946, the club offered me full-time terms.

Father had always told me to concentrate on a "proper" job in case I didn't progress as a footballer, and it was some while after the war before I allowed myself to be persuaded to become a full-time professional. In fact, I might not have done it when I did but for an experience which seems funnier in retrospect than it did when it happened.

When I saw a draughtsman's job advertised by Jessop's, a big firm in Sheffield's East End, I decided to go for it, and, after the initial interview, it seemed obvious from the boss's manner that I had as good as got the position. He said he'd show me round the drawing office. Having been at a small firm where there were just two of us, I was taken aback when I saw this huge room with 50 or 60 drawing boards all occupied by draughtsmen.

Yet I soon felt at home because, as I was being shown around, people kept shouting: "Hey up, Redfern!" This reaction to my presence puzzled the boss, and he suddenly asked: "What did you say your name was?" I told him:

"Froggatt." Then he said: "You're not Redfern Froggatt, are you?"

When I said I was, he told me: "Oh, I can't give you the job. If I do, all these blokes would never get any work done, they'd be wanting to talk football with you all the time! Sorry." I thought he was joking, but he wasn't, and the experience prompted me to accept Wednes-

day's offer. I didn't regret it, because a few months of full-time training made all the difference to my development as a footballer.

I spent 20 years with Wednesday and I can honestly say that I never wanted to play for anyone else. At the peak, around the time I was playing for England, I could have gone to Fiorentina in Italy, and top English clubs like Tottenham and Newcastle were also keen to sign me. Later, there was a spell when Sheffield United were said to be ready to take me to Bramall Lane, but it never got beyond the inquiry stage.

I think the United speculation came up halfway through the 1953-54 season. That was the only time I ever talked about asking for a transfer, but, really, there was never any real prospect of me leaving.

I suppose it was because I was a bit of a home bird that a myth grew to the effect that my father had made Eric Taylor promise never to transfer me. What really happened was my father had simply said to me: "If you ever get in with Wednesday, stick with them." And I was determined to do just that. Mind you, although I had my frustrations and knew times when I wasn't entirely happy, I think I had a better deal from the club over a longer spell than my father got.

Father had played for Wednesday from October 1921 to November 1927. He enjoyed his best run after he came in at centre-half around 1925 when George Wilson, an England international, made the mistake of refusing to re-sign and ended up playing in the Third Division North with Nelson. Father captained the 1925-26 Second Division promotion side, but, after only three games in the First Division, he was dropped and never got back. He asked for a transfer, the request was granted, and only when it was too late did he regret even having thought of leaving. He always said Wednesday was the best club in the world, and didn't want me to make the same mistake as him.

Hugh Swift, the team-mate with whom I was most frequently associated at Wednesday, was very similar in outlook to me. He was another local lad who never wanted to leave. His misfortune was that his career at the top was ended by injury. Hugh did not have the

same luck as me in terms of playing for England, as he certainly should have done, but he did play for England "B" and would have gone on from there but for a broken jaw.

That injury, at Coventry in early 1950, marked the beginning of the end. It was a pity because he was one of the best full-backs in the business, and there was no better exponent of the sliding tackle. He was so quick and his timing so good he always got the ball and never the man. He never caught anyone's ankles or brought them down.

We had our ups and downs in my time with Wednesday, but being a professional footballer was a smashing way of life, and, although it might sound corny to the modern generation, playing for the club you supported was special. I was lucky, and, frankly, I'd have played for nothing.

I think the most I ever earned was £15 a week, with a £4 win bonus. I can remember the 1958-59 season as if it were yesterday. The team was shaping into perhaps the best one I played in at Hillsborough, and we won about 28 League games in our promotion run. Roy Shiner used to come up as we left the field and say: "We've won again. Another four quid. Isn't it bloody marvellous!" We felt we were in clover. The irony was that going up meant the end of Shiner's run as first-choice centre-forward, and, although I didn't know it, my own days as a senior player were numbered.

Of course, it was sad when it all came to an end.

After we went up in 1959, I played in the first 12 games, and I can remember starting that season back in the First Division with a really good personal performance in a 1-0 win at Arsenal. I was 35 but felt much younger, and was really enjoying my football. Unfortunately, I developed some cartilage trouble, and when the manager signed Bobby Craig in November, it started the countdown to the final whistle.

I did get back in the side for four games towards the end of the season, but only as an emergency centre-forward, and for the next two years I had to be content with reserve-team football. Then, at 38, I was released and the big challenge was to find a new way of life. There was no pension after 20 years, and no question of getting the kind of new start modern players enjoy when they hang up their boots.

Of course, you survive, and I adapted. Also, for many years I saw a lot of football at Hillsborough, much of it as a voluntary commentator with the Hospital Radio, then subsequently as a guest of the club. Unfortunately, they stopped my ticket, which was disappointing. Perhaps they didn't want me because I couldn't score any more goals!

Cyril Turton

Cyril Turton, a centre-half from South Kirkby who made around 200 appearances for Wednesday between 1944 and 1954, is remembered as one of the Owls' great early post-war characters. Affectionately known by supporters as "Mother Turton", it was said he could run backwards quicker than he ran forwards! He has paid only two visits to Hillsborough in over 40 years after he left, but retained fond memories of his time at the club.

Whenever I meet anybody who saw me play for Wednesday, they invariably refer to my habit of running backwards at speed. For some reason it used to amuse the crowd, but it was quite a serious and deliberate tactic. I was always taught that it was important for a defender to keep his eye on the ball at all times, especially when retreating towards his own goal. So I taught myself to run backwards rapidly to be sure of never losing sight of my opponent and the ball.

Wednesday signed me from Frickley Colliery for about £200 in 1944 and I spent ten years with them. For the first four years I continued to work at the pit five days a week and played football as a part-timer, and I returned to the pit after I left Hillsborough in 1954. It was never a hardship combining playing and working, training two nights a week after a long shift underground; and I always considered myself very privileged in those six years when I enjoyed the luxury of being a full-time footballer.

As a youngster I played with South Kirkby Juniors until they were disbanded when the secretary was called up soon after the outbreak of war, and I remember my time with that team as among my happiest days. My pal in the

Cyril Turton.

team was Clarrie Jordan, who was later at Doncaster Rovers and eventually joined me at Wednesday.

Clarrie was a very good centre-forward and a wonderfully cheerful man. He always played for the team and many supporters did not recognise the donkey work he did for some of the stars like Quigley and Sewell. He led his line well and, as Dennis Woodhead used to say, Clarrie was best appreciated by team-mates who benefited from his instinctive football brain and his unselfishness.

If Clarrie had a fault, it was that he was too modest about his abilities. He never minded when others got the glory after he had done all the running and chasing to create chances for someone else. Chaps like Clarrie are the salt of the earth, not just in football but in

everyday life. His spirit and the strength of his character were never better illustrated than late in his life when he had to have both his legs amputated. That was a blow which would have defeated many men, but Clarrie remained as bright and cheerful as ever, and you never once heard him moan or complain.

I made my Wednesday debut in October 1944 in a game against Mansfield, when I stood in for Walter Millership. We lost 6-1 and two of the Mansfield lads got a hat-trick apiece, but I don't think I played badly, and, if I remember right, we were beaten because we had to play with an emergency goalkeeper. The only other thing I recall about that first season was I scored the only first-team goal I ever got for Wednesday in a match in which we beat Halifax. It was quite a thrill to be alongside Jack Lindsay and Charlie Tomlinson on the scoresheet!

Although I made my Football League debut in the first match of the 1946-47 season, it was in the following two seasons that I probably had my best run and missed only a few games. But the competition for places was always keen, and, with Edgar Packard being preferred at the start of 1949-50, I then endured a couple of seasons when I managed only four appearances.

I got back into the side during the Second Division championship campaign of 1951-52, the year when Derek Dooley had that marvellous scoring run, and I remained a regular to the end of 1952-53 when, ironically, I lost my place to Ralph O'Donnell.

I say it was ironic because I had known Ralph's father very well, and his old man, who was ill, had asked me to look after the lad. I would have helped Ralph anyway, but his Dad's request prompted me to concentrate on encouraging him. Ralph was a good player, always very quick, but, at the time, he was having some difficulty with his heading, and I spent hours sharpening up his timing.

The upshot was that Ralph was in the first team and I wasn't, but, as we were pals, his success at my expense never troubled me. Of course, I was disappointed when I realised my Wednesday days were at an end, but I didn't particularly fret about having to go back to life at the colliery. I worked there until I retired in 1981. After leaving Wednesday, I had a couple of years with Goole Town and then was trainer and later manager back at Frickley. But I didn't stay in it for long, and, to be honest, for many years after that I lost all interest in the game.

As a lad I could never have imagined life without football, but a time did come when the game passed me by. Not that I ever forgot the good years I'd had, and I was always proud to have played with Wednesday.

Vin Kenny

Vin Kenny, a Shirecliffe product who made 152 League and Cup appearances for Wednesday between 1946 and 1955, *played at right-back in the promotion side of 1949-50 and was left-back in the Second Division championship team of 1951-52. Always known as "Mick", he belonged to a tough and fearless breed of defenders, and playing for the club he had supported as a boy was the fulfilment of a dream.*

I started my working life just before the war in the engineering tools department of Firth Brown's in Carlisle Street, where I worked on a universal milling machine. As the firm had a very good sports club, Atlas & Norfolk, I was soon an enthusiastic member of the football section, and it was while playing in works' football that something happened which was to prove beneficial when I became a professional.

Obviously, being very keen, I was happy to play anywhere I was asked, and it was pleasing when the team's trainer noticed I could use both feet. But he said he'd spotted I was stronger on the left, and encouraged me to work on strengthening my "weaker" right. It meant that by the time I joined Wednesday I was comfortable at both right and left-back, and it never made any difference to me where I played.

There were always scouts from lots of big clubs at our games, and I could have gone to Arsenal, Everton and Huddersfield Town – Town, by the way, were in the old First Division then. Of course, I always hoped Wednesday might want me, because I'd been supporting them since I was eight years old. My dad introduced me to the delights of watching such idols as Mark Hooper and Tommy Walker some time in the 1932-33 season, and I never dreamed then that old Tommy would still be around and on the coaching staff when I joined the club.

I'll never forget the day Wednesday finally came for me. It was sometime in 1942, and I was at work when I got this message to say the firm's welfare officer wanted to see me. The welfare man was a chap called Ernest Kangley, who later became very well known in local football circles as the secretary of the Sheffield & Hallamshire FA.

I went to Kangley's office and found Eric Taylor, Wednesday's secretary-manager, there. He said he'd come to sign me and our team's centre-half, Reg Stewart. Naturally, neither of us needed asking twice. I subsequently signed full-time professional forms at 18 because, as I was about to be called up into the army, Wednesday didn't want me to be attracted to another club while I was serving with the Royal Engineers. There wasn't much chance of that happening in my case because I couldn't wait for the war to end to be able to get home to Hillsborough to start my football career properly.

When the war ended, I remained in khaki for quite some time. There was a dock strike on, and, as we were a dock operating company, we were brought back from Europe in a hurry to work on the ships at Purfleet. It was while I was there that Eric Taylor started phoning to ask when I might be available to play.

That's how I made my first-team debut at Leicester in September 1946 while on leave. I think I stood in for Frank Westlake, but played at left-back with Hugh Swift switching into Frank's role on the right. I'll never forget how we battled from behind to win 5-3 on the worst pitch I've ever played on.

It was a wonderful experience being a professional footballer. We didn't play for the money, and certainly didn't play for ourselves. We played for Sheffield Wednesday and were proud of it. We felt like kings, and it was the height of luxury when we went to play in London, to stay in a big hotel and be taken to see a show at the Palladium on the night before the match. They were certainly the good old days!

The atmosphere in the dressing room was always special. My pal was Eddie Gannon, an Eire international who came to us from Notts County. Eddie and a Welshman called Doug Witcomb were our wing-halves. They were good footballers and great characters, too. Cyril Turton, the centre-half, was another character, on the field as well as off it. The crowd called Cyril "Mother" and it never ceased to amuse them the way he could run quicker backwards than he could forwards!

We always seemed to be laughing in those days, especially when Charlie Tomlinson and Dennis Woodhead were entertaining us. Alan Finney and Albert Quixall, who came into the team as teenagers, were another pair of comedians, forever up to some trick or other. When we were playing away, you could bet they'd get your room keys from the hotel reception and strip your bed while you were downstairs having a night-cap in the lounge!

A match in London I'll never forget was my FA Cup debut at Arsenal in January 1950, when I lasted barely half-an-hour because I was carried off after dislocating my right shoulder. I went up for this high ball with a Scottish winger called Ian McPherson and ended up in the back of the net with my arm gone. There were no substitutes then. We played with ten men for an hour, and Arsenal only beat us with a Reg Lewis goal two minutes from the end.

Of course, I only learned the details of the game when I met up with the lads on the railway station an hour or so after the game. In the meantime, I'd been at a hospital, where they put my arm back and strapped me up, and, thanks to the doctor who dealt with my case, the injury didn't prove as bad as everyone expected. In fact, I missed only two games.

The secret of my rapid recovery was a small solid ball the doctor gave me to take home. He told me to hold it in my right hand and squeeze it for two hours at a time, taking one-hour breaks in between. Keep doing that, he said, and you'll be back in light training inside a week and fit to play again in a fortnight.

I was a hard player in the sense that when I went for the ball I always intended to get it, but I was never dirty. You gave it everything you'd got, and so did your opponent. If you accidentally caught someone, they accepted it as part of the game, and you were always pals after the match. Johnny Kelly, of Barnsley, was one of the best wingers in the business, and we had some rare battles. But I never once heard him complain, and we were good friends when the final whistle went.

People often remember that I was sent off in a famous FA Cup replay with Sheffield United in January 1954 when Wednesday won at Bramall Lane for the first time in 33 years. I got my marching orders just past the hour following an incident involving Jimmy Hagan, but the truth is I never touched him. I'll tell you what, if I had done he wouldn't have played again!

Of course, you wouldn't expect a Sheffield derby match to be anything other than a tough battle, and this one was rather bad-tempered. At one stage

the referee, Jack Clough, called the captains together and gave them a lecture. He told them to calm their teams down – or else! He'd probably decided the next incident would demand strong action, and I happened to be the innocent victim.

Anyway, Jimmy went to get to a through ball, but when I went to tackle him, he turned away. There was no contact, and he didn't even fall. But Jimmy said something to the referee, and Clough sent me off. Internationals like Hagan, Raich Carter and Wilf Mannion were big stars in that period. They always seemed to think they deserved special protection, and were forever moaning to the referees.

I was disappointed not to see the finish of that match, because we won it 3-1 with late goals from George Davies and Jackie Sewell. It was a good match, and us coming back after going a goal down in the first half made it a great day for the Wednesday fans. We certainly felt justice was done, and being reduced to ten men brought the best out of our lads.

Naturally, I was sorry to leave Wednesday, but Tony Conwell and then Ron Staniforth came to partner Norman Curtis, so I accepted a move to Carlisle. The consolation was that I was able to continue to live in Sheffield and train at Hillsborough, so, in a sense, I was still at home and going regularly to the ground.

When I packed up full-time football, I became a salesman with Sunblest Bakeries and stayed with them for 30 years until I retired in 1989. I went to Wednesday matches regularly for years, and there was a time when the club used to send me a season ticket. Then, for some reason, they stopped it, but I've never stopped being a Wednesdayite.

Keith Bannister

Keith Bannister, who was a professional with Wednesday from 1945 to 1953, made 78 senior appearances and was captain of the team that won the Second Division title in 1951-52. He later had spells as a coach and scout, and was manager of the club's sports hall from 1983 to 1989.

My links with Wednesday as a player

extended from around 1937, when I was signed on schoolboy forms after being recommended by the legendary Ernest Blenkinsop, to June 1953, when I left to join Chesterfield on a free transfer. I made my Owls debut in a wartime game at Lincoln in February 1945, signing professional forms the same day when we stopped for a meal on the way home; and my first appearance in the Football League came against Bury on Christmas Day 1946.

However, the peak of my career at Hillsborough was in the 1951-52 season when I played 31 times at right-back and we won the Second Division championship – and I was captain. As a local lad, just playing for your home club gives you tremendous pride, but being skipper as well, especially when the club wins a title, makes it one of those unforgettable experiences you treasure for the rest of your life.

Ironically, I wasn't in the team when the season started, but, when it ended, I was proudly collecting the championship shield and making a speech from the directors' box to supporters who gathered in their thousands on the pitch after the end of our final match. I don't think I've ever witnessed such joyful scenes.

Fate is a curious thing, and it worked for me and against me all in the space of less than a year. One day I was on top of the world, then suddenly the outlook took a dramatic dip. Just before the start of the 1952-53 season, I tore my knee ligaments in a friendly at Scunthorpe, and, although I did play one more match in the first team, I couldn't regain a regular place and Wednesday ended up letting me go just a year after my greatest moment.

At least the fates had been really kind in 1951-52. Wednesday made a poor start to the season, winning only three of their first 11 games, and, for the match with Barnsley in early October, manager Eric Taylor decided on changes and brought in Derek Dooley and Albert Quixall. Nobody will ever forget what this meant for Derek, because it was his third chance and marked the start of a tremendous scoring run which made him perhaps the most famous centre-forward in the country.

My own recall came on that same October afternoon when we beat

Keith Bannister leading out Wednesday at Hillsborough in 1952.

Barnsley 2-1, but I was only brought in late on and given my first appearance of the season after Norman Curtis went down with a poisoned foot. "Mick" Kenny switched to left-back, and I seized the chance to make the No.2 shirt my own. When Curtis got back in the side at the turn of the year, it was Kenny's misfortune to lose out.

It was good to be in the team, but getting the captaincy was a bonus which, like my recall, was all down to an accident of fate. I hadn't done the job in the Reserves, and my appointment came about unexpectedly. Jack Sewell, who had only just taken over the duties from Doug Witcomb, missed the game at Swansea in late November through injury. I think Jack was out for about four matches, and when he was fit again, I remained skipper. It meant the next seven months were perhaps the happiest of my playing days.

It was, quite honestly, a joy being a professional footballer. I think I earned £14 a week, and £16 when we won, and

lived a wonderful life. We trained until mid-day, and, several times a week, a group of us would spend all afternoon playing golf. At other times some of us played snooker, and, fairly regularly, I would join Derek Dooley, Dennis Woodhead and Ivor Seemley on fishing expeditions.

It was so much better than work – what more could a man want!

Of course, it was a disappointment when the club decided they no longer wanted me, but I shall never forget that I was captain of a Wednesday team that achieved something – nobody can take that away from me.

When I left, I had a year at Chesterfield followed by four years at King's Lynn and two seasons with Macclesfield before, thanks to Dooley's recommendation, I returned to look after Wednesday's Hatchard League team on a part-time basis during Vic Buckingham's time at the club.

In the meantime, I worked as a rep for a local steel company, and, later,

became a partner in a brokerage firm for 14 years. Then, after a spell doing some match-analysis duties for Jack Charlton, I had the thrill of being brought back to Hillsborough on a full-time basis to became manager of Wednesday's sports hall for six years until my retirement in 1989.

Author's note: Keith remains as staunch an Owls' supporter as ever, although, like some other long-serving ex-employees, in 1997 he lost his complimentary season ticket and related privileges.

Frank Slynn

Frank Slynn arrived on trial in 1946 as a left-half. Circumstances prompted Wednesday to convert him into a winger even before they had signed him, and he made a big impression in that role until a broken leg at Christmas 1947 virtually ended his senior Hillsborough career, although he remained at the club until

Wednesday players relaxing during Cup training at Torquay in 1948. They are: Keith Bannister, Joe Cockroft, Redfern Froggatt, Charlie Tomlinson, Eddie Quigley, Dennis Woodhead, Frank Westlake, Dave McIntosh, Cyril Turton and Edgar Packard.

December 1950. He made 46 League and Cup appearances for the Owls, then played with Bury for three years and finished up at Walsall. He later spent nearly l4 years in the melting shop of Samuel Fox's Stocksbridge steelworks and retired in 1989.

I was recommended to Wednesday in the autumn of 1946 after being spotted playing for a works team in Birmingham, and came on a month's trial which led to the offer of a professional contract at £6 a week. That might not sound much, and I doubt if I ever earned more than twice that much in my four years at Hillsborough, but I would have played for 30 bob [£1.50] or even for nothing. I just loved playing football and it was wonderful being able to make a living as a footballer at a big club. I wouldn't swap my time in the professional game for the world, and treasure happy memories of my days with Wednesday.

I actually came as a left-half, but, while I was on a month's trial, the regular outside-left, Charlie Tomlinson, got injured in a Tuesday practice match. l was switched into his position and, after a run in the Reserves, Eric Taylor gave me my Football League debut in November 1946. From then on, I was considered a winger in my time at Wednesday.

It wasn't without irony that my debut came at Birmingham, because I'd been an amateur with them and had always hoped I might play with my home city club. I know I was rather pleased that, on my first Wednesday appearance, it was from my corner-kick that Tommy Ward headed us in front. Unfortunately, we ended up losing 3-1.

We were 21st in the Second Division and in a bit of trouble. It was a battle to beat the drop and was a close-run thing, but we did manage to avoid going into the Third Division North for what would have been the first time in the club's history. In truth, I didn't think we were a bad side. We lacked consistency, but on a number of occasions we showed we had the players capable of getting some good results.

One positive result I remember was the return game with Birmingham at Hillsborough in March, when we won 1-0. I had a hand in the goal, it being from my cross that Gil Merrick, the goalkeeper, got into a tangle and Fred Harris, the City half-back, ended up turning the ball into his own net.

However, the match which really stands out for me in that first season was my FA Cup debut in January. We beat Blackpool 4-1 in the third round at Hillsborough. At that time Blackpool had a very good side, and they were in the First Division. For some reason, that day our team just clicked, and we were always going to win. Redfern Froggatt scored twice, and George Hunt and Oscar Fox got the others.

I had a great afternoon, up against Eddie Shimwell, who had previously been with Sheffield United. It was one of those occasions when everything I tried came off. Eddie was one of the best backs in the game, but I gave him a bit of a run-around. The thing I remember is that he never resorted to rough tactics to try to stop me, even though I was causing him some embarrassment. He was a gentleman, and, at the end, put his arm round me and said I'd done well.

There was a much healthier look about the Wednesday team in 1947-48, although, for me, there was a disappointment in that I was switched to outside-right. Being a natural left-footer who only used his right foot to stand on, I preferred outside-left, but Dennis Woodhead, back from service in the RAF, claimed the No.11 shirt.

I played in the first 14 games, then in October took a knock which kept me out until the Christmas holiday. My second match back was the Boxing Day home game with West Ham, which, although I didn't know it then, was to be the one that more or less marked the end of my first-team days at Wednesday.

We beat West Ham 5-3 and Eddie Quigley scored four, including a first-half hat-trick. But I didn't see any of the goals. After only 11 minutes, I broke my right leg. It happened on the North Stand side of the ground, towards the Leppings Lane end. Quigley played this pass towards me, and when the ball fell short I had to turn back and stretch for it. I just got a touch before the defender came in and caught me. I have always said that, if I had been playing on the left instead of the right, and the same incident had occurred, I would have been able to avoid that challenge. But I was, so to speak, the wrong way round and didn't have the same dexterity.

Unfortunately, it was a very bad injury and there were complications. Apart from the break, my foot was in a terrible state, and, frankly, there were times in the next three years when I wondered whether I'd reached the end of the line. It was one long struggle to get fit, and very depressing. But people like Sam Powell, the trainer, and Joe Cockroft, our captain, were very good to me in the early months after the injury.

Joe Cockroft was an excellent player, a better and more knowledgeable wing-half than many might give him credit for. The other players appreciated him far more than supporters did. Of course, he was very experienced, but there was more to him than his footballing ability. He was wise, friendly and really a very kind and thoughtful chap – an ideal captain off as well as on the field. I missed him after he went to Sheffield United.

While I was out of the team, Oscar Fox came back into the side, and then, of course, Wednesday paid a record fee

for Eddie Kilshaw from Bury in 1948. Eddie made a big impact until he suffered a cruciate knee injury against Leicester which finished his playing days. I thought I had been unlucky, but Eddie was desperately unfortunate, and I never saw a man work or try harder to get fit again. He was another of football's gentlemen, and became a teacher in Huyton after leaving football.

Walter Rickett was another winger Wednesday signed, and there was a promising teenager called Alan Finney already on the fringe of the first team by the start of the 1950-51 season. So it was not only three years before I got back into the first team, but the competition on the wing had become such that, when I finally did get recalled for two games, they were both at left-half as Doug Witcomb's stand-in.

It was funny I should finally be chosen in the very position I had hoped to fill when I first went to the club, but there wasn't much hope of a long-term future in the role. We didn't win either game, Doug came back, and soon afterwards I went to Bury.

In fact, I enjoyed my time at Bury, but I never lost my affection for Wednesday. I had so many happy memories of the club, with some smashing pals such as Jimmy Dailey and Norman Jackson, with whom I was in digs in the early days. There was a lot of goodwill and banter in the Hillsborough dressing room, and I always remember when I first arrived being welcomed by goalkeeper Roy Smith and centre-half Edgar Packard, who were a sort of Laurel and Hardy humorous act. After all these years, I still chuckle at the memory of Edgar's very droll wit.

Jackie Marriott

Jackie Marriott was a winger who joined Wednesday for £2,000 from Scunthorpe United, then of the Midland League, in early 1947. Always a part-timer at Hillsborough, he made 159 League and Cup appearances for Wednesday and scored 19 goals before moving to Huddersfield Town in mid-1955. Now living in retirement in Scunthorpe, he reflects on some fond Owls' memories – and a couple of regrets.

My eight years with Wednesday were a great time in my life, and I often say

there are only two things I would change if I could turn back the clock. One is I should have become a full-time professional from the outset instead of waiting until after my Sheffield days were over, the other is I wish I had never asked for a transfer because leaving the Owls was the biggest mistake of my career.

Jackie Marriott.

I was 16 years old when I made my debut in the Midland League with my home-town club, Scunthorpe United, and it was about two years later that I joined Wednesday. The man who recommended me to Eric Taylor, the manager, was almost certainly Ted Catlin, who had a spell with us at the Old Show Ground from around 1946. Ted, of course, had been a pre-war favourite at Hillsborough, and it was flattering that a former England full-back should think so highly of my prospects.

I have heard talk about Mr Taylor making a 40-mile dash by taxi to sign me, but my memory of the transfer is of travelling to Sheffield to complete the deal. I still have a newspaper picture of myself standing outside the front door on that special day and pointing to the "Hillsborough" sign over the entrance. Perhaps Mr Taylor's dramatic taxi-ride had been to agree the fee with Scunthorpe, and I believe the cheque he signed when he bought me was subsequently placed in a frame in the boardroom at the Old Show Ground.

Anyway, at that time, I was working as an estimator draughtsman at Firth

Brown's in Scunthorpe, and, when my move to Sheffield was finalised, it was arranged for me to continue in the same job at the firm's sister company, Firth Vickers Stainless Steels, where I was employed at the foundry in Garter Street.

It was only some years later that I wished I had chosen then to become a full-time footballer, but the decision to play part-time seemed the right one at the time. It was not simply a question of equipping myself for a career after the end of my playing days. Staying in the steel industry in that early post-war phase meant I wouldn't be called up for National Service, and I felt I'd profit from not having my football interrupted by two years in the army.

In fact, my football suffered from not having the benefit of full-time training and coaching, and I'm sure I would have been a better player if I could have worked with the senior players and experienced staff on a regular basis. As a part-timer, I was training two nights a week, and, although Firth Vickers were always ready to let me have mornings or afternoons off if I was required for a practice match at Hillsborough, I missed out on many things which would have improved my knowledge and ability.

This was brought home to me when I went to Huddersfield in 1955, because I soon realised that my ball control was not as good as it might have been. It was partly my own fault, but largely down to the fact that Wednesday insisted on the ball being played into open space for the wingers to run on to. At Huddersfield they played the ball to feet, and I needed one touch too many. With the opportunity of more practice and instruction earlier in my career, I might have been better equipped to adjust to the different tactical approach.

At Hillsborough I was soon able to qualify for the £12 maximum weekly wage, but I remember that, when the maximum was raised to £14 and then £15, the Wednesday part-timers, who included Hugh Swift, one of the best backs in English football, remained on the old wage.

It is true that I was also getting around £5 or £6 as a draughtsman, but after tax I was not really as well off as a full-time pro – who also had the bonus of plenty of free afternoons!

I made my Wednesday debut at Burnley late February 1947, and it was sometime early in the following season that I moved into digs in Sheffield, living in the same place as Laurie Mackenzie. I had met my future wife, Eileen, many years earlier in Scunthorpe, and after our wedding in 1950, we took over the club house in Shenstone Road that had previously been occupied by Eddie Quigley and Clarrie Jordan.

Speaking of Quigley and Jordan, they were two of the best players in my time at Hillsborough. Quigley was my hero, and playing alongside him was both a thrill and a great education. Jordan was an excellent centre-forward who was always appreciated by his team-mates. Redfern Froggatt was also a very talented footballer, and the finest full-back I ever played with was certainly Hugh Swift. He was way above everyone else and ought to have had more honours.

Swift was always a tough opponent in practice matches, and I used to enjoy watching him in League games because then he was facing some of the best wingers in the game and he had this wonderful knack of timing his tackles so well that he always got the ball no matter how fast or tricky his opponent.

I especially remember one match when Hugh and I made the headlines together. It was early in that 1949-50 season which ended with Wednesday winning promotion on goal-average, and we went to White Hart Lane to face a Tottenham side already looking a good bet for the Second Division title. Although we ultimately lost to a Len Duquemin goal, I probably had the best game of my career.

I was playing at outside-left and gave Alf Ramsey, the England back, a real run-around. Meanwhile, Swifty had a great afternoon at left-back. I've still got the newspaper cutting which notes: "The England selectors went to the game to look at Eddie Quigley and ended up admiring the talents of Swift and Marriott."

I think about 35 of my 159 appearances for Wednesday were at outside-left, and, although I did occasionally excel in that position, I was never happy playing there. Being naturally right-footed, I considered myself essentially a right-winger, and all the more so as I

always seemed to be dropped after a few games on the left.

I do sometimes think I didn't really do badly on the left, and I have a memory of being played there on two or three occasions when we met Blackpool. The plan on those occasions was for me to follow Stanley Matthews and hamper him. Unfortunately, in one game I remember him putting the ball through my legs not once but three times – and there was nothing I could do about it!

Even so, I let him know that I was around, and, when he found me playing at outside-left when he came to Hillsborough for the Derek Dooley testimonial in 1955, he said: "Now then, Jack, I want you to bugger off tonight. Leave me alone and let's give the crowd a bit of a show." I was happy to let him do just as he pleased!

In truth, it was the frustration of being in and out of the Wednesday team, and often being used on the "wrong" wing when I did play, that prompted me to seek a move. I was fed up of being picked, staying in the side for two or three games, and then being dropped. It all came to a head early in 1954-55 when I was left out after feeling I had started the season well. I foolishly told Mr Taylor I wanted a transfer.

The irony was that I was happy at Hillsborough, and, as the season progressed, I was recalled and enjoyed one of my best runs – even though 12 of my final 13 games that year were on the left. I remember scoring in a 5-0 victory over West Brom on the last day of the season. We were relegated that year, but, even so, I was looking forward to continuing my Wednesday career.

Unfortunately, although I had forgotten my transfer request, the club hadn't. They were planning to strengthen the team for a big promotion push, and, as they believed I was unsettled, they used me in an exchange deal which took Roy Shiner and Ron Staniforth to Hillsborough. I joined Tony Conwell in moving to Huddersfield.

I honestly wish I had never asked for a transfer because I didn't really want to leave, and I will always contend that it was a mistake. I would have been wiser to have kept my mouth shut and accepted things as they were.

When I went to Huddersfield, I

finally became a full-time professional, but I have often wondered how different things might have been had I taken that step in 1947 or soon afterwards. One of the things I missed when I was feeling aggrieved at being in and out of the team was someone to talk to about the problem.

I think it just needed someone on the coaching staff to convince me that I was a better left-winger than I thought, and a bit of the sort of encouragement you get when you're among fellow professionals every day of the week might have changed my outlook. Success in football is all about confidence, and I always lacked faith in my own abilities whenever I wore that No.11 shirt.

But I shall always remember those Sheffield years as a high point. I had some marvellous colleagues at the club, some excellent friends at Firth Vickers, and some really good neighbours where we lived. It would have been nice to have stayed a lot longer than we did.

Norman Jackson

Norman Jackson, a full-back who joined Wednesday from Manningham Mills (Bradford) in October 1948 after impressing in trials with the "A" team, was limited to 31 League games owing to a knee problem which eventually led to him hanging up his boots. His senior Owls' debut, at Coventry in November 1949, lasted 63 minutes before the game was abandoned owing to fog.

I wouldn't have missed the time I had in football for the world but it was disappointing that injuries and a lack of the right treatment meant my career in the game didn't last as long as it could have done. If in my time there had been the medical standards and physiotherapy knowledge there is in football today, things might have been so different – but, then, a lot of my contemporaries would probably say the same.

I settled very well in Sheffield, and it was after moving here that I met my wife Doreen – at a dance at the City Hall. I think the only disappointment in the early days at Hillsborough was that my digs were a bit unsatisfactory. I was taken in by the mother of the secretary of the Supporters' Club, and she was so skimpy with the food that Joe Locherty and I felt we were being starved.

I took it on myself to find somewhere better, and found a home with a family called Rowley in Hawksley Avenue. The food there was excellent and they certainly knew how to put on a meal – so much so that, when Wednesday signed Jack Sewell from Notts County, the club asked me to introduce him to the Rowleys. I don't need to say they were delighted to have Jackie as a guest, but, as he was a big star and I was just an ordinary player, I did rather feel he got special treatment – and I lost my treasured exclusivity!

When I went to Wednesday, I was a wing-half, and actually made my debut in that position, but after Alan Brown came as coach, he switched me to fullback. I was quite good in the air and a strong tackler – the sort of player who liked to let the opposition know I was around. It took me a while to adjust to playing at right-back, but by the time Brown gave me a run of 21 games between March and late September 1951 I had settled into the role.

By then we had been up to the First Division and gone back down, and, unfortunately, early in the 1951-52 season when we won the Second Division title and Derek Dooley scored all those goals, I lost my place to Keith Bannister – and didn't get another first-team chance until we were back in the top grade.

Norman Jackson comes to the rescue of goalkeeper Dave McIntosh in a match against Fulham in 1951.

The 1952-53 season in the First Division promised to be a good one for me, then I ran into some knee trouble which meant I ended up being restricted to only nine games – and two matches against Portsmouth were probably turning points in my career.

In the first match I came up against a big raw-boned centre-forward called Duggie Reid, who kneed me in the thigh and left me with a "dead" leg. I rested it, but, on the following Friday, I had a try-out, and, while I felt I might be okay, I made the fatal mistake of telling Sam Powell, the trainer, that I might be in trouble should I get another knock on the thigh early in the next game.

At the time I was just starting to think I was a regular and my place fairly secure, so I agreed with Sam when he said that might be wiser to take another week to get the thigh 100 per cent fit. Only later did I realise I had really dropped myself. Mick Kenny replaced me in the team, and he didn't look back.

However, I did return for two or three games later in the season – just in time to face Portsmouth again. I was given such a roasting by Gordon Dale – at the time one of the best wingers in the old First Division – I was promptly dropped, and didn't play in the first team again.

Two things happened to hinder my chances of getting back. One was when Wednesday signed another right-back, Tony Conwell; the other was a continuing knee problem which eventually led to a cartilage operation. As captain of the Reserves, I was doing well and fancied my chances of getting back into the first-team until my knee failed to respond to treatment.

The trouble was, the club didn't have the equipment they have nowadays, and, although I was in no position to say a lot about it, I wasn't satisfied with the treatment I was getting. I really didn't have any faith in Sam Powell and Tommy Walker getting me fit. It wasn't their fault, for they were old players who weren't trained as physiotherapists, and they couldn't give me the expert attention which I obviously needed.

It got to a stage where my frustration was such that, without the club's knowledge, I started going to a chap in South Elmsall for treatment. My team-mates Clarrie Jordan and Cyril Turton said they'd often been to this man. "He's got nothing but an infra-red lamp and pretty good oil," said Cyril, "but he's quite good."

After training I used to travel with Clarrie and Cyril by train, and visited the clinic – it was a half-mile walk from the railway station – every day for about four weeks. The man put me on acupuncture treatment, and to a certain extent it worked. However, having paid for the treatment out of my own pocket, there was no dividend in the way of recovery.

Naturally, I was disappointed when Wednesday put me on the transfer list in 1954, but perhaps they gave up on me because they knew my knee was dodgy and unlikely to improve. I went first to Bristol City and then to Oldham, but things didn't really look up because the knee trouble got worse and you don't get much sympathy from managers when you're not fit to play.

As I say, it might have been a different story if only the attention had been available. I began a new career with a local firm, where I became a director, and when I look back I am always grateful that football brought me to Sheffield.

Eddie Kilshaw

Eddie Kilshaw became the costliest winger in English football when he joined Wednesday from Bury for £20,000 in December 1948, and it was his misfortune that he made only 19 League and Cup appearances before his playing days were ended by a serious knee injury. After leaving the game he turned to teaching, and enjoyed success in this role on Merseyside until his retirement in 1980, but, at the age of 78, he still retains fond memories of Hillsborough.

I was within three weeks of my 29th birthday when Wednesday signed me in late 1948, and, while the £20,000 fee, which was then a British record for a winger, seemed rather a lot of money, I was mature enough to ensure being such a costly buy never troubled me.

I could always smile when people raised the subject, and enjoyed the humour it sometimes provoked. I recall that one of my earliest games after moving to Sheffield took us to an away ground where the crowd was very close to the pitch, and, as I was placing the ball for a corner kick, this old lady leaned over and shouted: "Twenty thousand quid? I wouldn't give 20 Woodbines for you!"

Naturally, it was a great disappointment when the fates conspired to shatter my Wednesday career barely five months after I arrived, because I knew I could do a good job for Wednesday, and it was especially unfortunate that the accident which finished me occurred just when I was really starting to rediscover my best form.

I have to admit that I was as surprised as anyone when Wednesday came for me, because I was very happy at Bury and had no thought of moving. I had gone to Gigg Lane from my local club, Prescot Cables, and made my Football League debut at 17 in 1936. Of course, the war, during which I served in the RAF as a pilot, took six years out of my career, but, when I returned in 1946, things were soon pretty much as they had been before.

I remember two games against Wednesday in that first post-war season of 1946-47, and often think this might have been when Eric Taylor took note of my name. We put four goals past Wednesday at Gigg Lane on Christmas Day, with Eddie Quigley getting two; and, at Hillsborough on Boxing Day, we won 5-2, with Jack Lindsay, who had recently moved from Sheffield, scoring three, while I also got a goal.

Eddie Quigley, of course, was destined to join Wednesday before I did, and it will be of interest to recall that, although Eddie made his name as an inside or centre-forward, he started his career as a full-back. I know he probably played up front occasionally while serving in the navy during the war, but the switch wasn't permanent until one day in 1946-47 – and I remember how it all happened.

The two of us were enjoying a game of snooker in Bury's recreation room when we were joined by Norman Bullock, the manager. Norman asked us what we thought about the way the team was playing, and Eddie said we'd continue to struggle so long as we couldn't score goals. "Play me at centre-forward, and I'll show you how to put the ball in the net," he said.

Wednesday in 1948. Back row (left to right): Locherty, Westlake, Swift, Turton, Witcomb. Front row: Kilshaw, Quigley, Dailey, Froggatt, Woodhead.

The next match was against Millwall, and Quigley scored all our goals in a 5-2 win. I don't think he ever played at full-back again!

Eddie, you'll remember, was a well-built man who always looked slightly overweight and appeared rather lethargic on the field. He certainly didn't like to run about! But he knew how to use his head to save his legs – and he could score goals. He had a great positional sense and boasted a powerful shot.

Quigley was a man I liked playing with because he was also a very perceptive and accurate passer who kept his winger well supplied with long and precise balls, and I looked forward to renewing our partnership when the chance came for me to follow him to Sheffield.

The transfer certainly came out of the blue, although I had more than a hint that Bury were ready to sell me because, just previously, I had turned down the chance to move to Sunderland. On this particular day, I had travelled over from Prescot for a training session, and dropped off the bus near the end of Gigg Lane to find the club's

vice-chairman waiting. "Somebody's coming for you today, Eddie," he said, "and you have my permission to go, because it's a move which will suit you."

Soon afterwards, I was standing with a colleague, Reg Halton, when this car pulled up outside the players' entrance. Reg, who had asked for a transfer, said: "That's Eric Taylor, of Sheffield Wednesday. I'll bet he's come for me." I said: "No, Reg, it's me they want." And, of course, it was.

It is nearly 50 years since I went to Wednesday, but I can remember most of the matches I played for them. I know I didn't have a particularly good game on my debut at Luton, and I have not forgotten the only goal I scored for the club because it was direct from a corner in a game at Fulham – the referee, a chap called Major Green, gave it after his linesman said the ball had crossed the line at the front post.

It took some time for me to reach my best form largely because Wednesday's style was different from Bury's. At Bury they played the ball to my feet, while Wednesday had the policy of

putting passes into space. I was a player who needed to have plenty of the ball. I revelled in taking on defenders and loved to dribble.

The irony was that, in the game against Leicester which proved to be the last match of my career, it was evident that the team was exploiting my strengths, and I was getting so much of the ball I was like a dog with two tails. I was certainly enjoying myself, and felt it would only be a matter of time before I made a goal. Alas, circumstances prevented that happening, and I believe Leicester nicked a win with a goal from Jack Lee just before the final whistle.

The accident happened about 15 minutes from the end when we were kicking towards the Kop. This ball came inside and, as I went for it, the Leicester man, Tom McArthur, arrived a bit late with his challenge. He ended up with two legs wrapped round my left leg, which was so severely pushed back that my knee was dislocated. In fact, my cruciates were shattered, and the specialist who operated on me said I'd never kick another ball.

A Wednesday team group in 1957. Back row (left to right): Gibson, Staniforth, McIntosh, O'Donnell, Curtis, Tom McAnearney. Front row: Froggatt, Sewell, Shiner, Quixall, Broadbent.

The next 12 months were, to say the least, painful and frustrating. I did everything possible to try to save my career, and had some marvellous support and encouragement from the club, but, unfortunately, all the work proved in vain. After a year it was clear the situation was hopeless. Eric Taylor very generously offered me another contract, but I couldn't take the club's money or delay facing up to the truth.

I knew I had to accept that my professional football days were over, and my consolation was in having continued my studies and equipped myself to pursue a new career in teaching. My preparation ensured the switch was not as difficult as it might have been. Initially, I obtained an appointment back home in Prescot, but later I became a science teacher in Liverpool.

In Liverpool, I became associated with Huyton Boys, and had the good fortune to be manager of the team that won the English Schools Trophy in 1971. And it was while working with the boys – one of whom was Peter Reid, who later played for Everton – that I proved the Sheffield specialist wrong by kicking a ball again with my left leg.

Since I finished with Wednesday, I have had no contact with the profes-sional game, and never been to a match. I decided it was best to make a clean break and not dwell on the past, but, even so, I still have many good memories – not least of my time in Sheffield.

I met some fine people, and we were a happy band at Hillsborough. I particularly remember Eric Taylor as a hell of a good man. He was passionately devoted to Sheffield Wednesday. I recall once, when I asked him why he had paid so much for me, he said he would have bought an elephant if it could play football, attract the crowds, and bring success to the club!

Author's footnote: It is of interest to record that Kilshaw's only goal for the club, which earned a 1-1 draw at Fulham in March 1949, was scored direct from a corner and prompted almost as much controversy as had occurred in Wednes-day's home game against Fulham earlier in the same season.

At Hillsborough in October 1948, when Wednesday lost 2-1, Alf Rogers scored with a shot which went through a hole in the net. The goal was only given after much debate. Then, in the last minute, Doug Witcomb had what seemed a legitimate equaliser disallowed. He put the ball in the net from the penalty spot, but referee Green ordered a re-take because some Fulham players were still in the box and disputing his initial decision. When Witcomb finally took the penalty again, his effort was saved.

Major Green probably took some stick that day, and at Craven Cottage he certainly did not want to deny the Owls again!

Ralph O'Donnell

Ralph O'Donnell, who arrived from Upton Colliery in May 1949, was a highly-rated centre-half or wing-half who made 183 League and Cup appearances for the Owls between 1951 and 1962 and figured in the Second Division title triumphs of 1952 and 1956. Always known as "Rod", he spent only six of his 15 years with Wednesday as a full-time professional. Indeed, in 1958, he reverted to a part-time role to prepare for what proved to be a distinguished teaching career which lasted until 1994.

When I signed for Wednesday at the age of 17 in 1949, I was actually still at Hemsworth Grammar School, and the curious thing about the match in which Martin Heavey, a Wednesday scout, spotted me was that I had only gone along to watch and didn't expect to be playing. It wasn't my first game for Upton Colliery's Sheffield Association League team, but I had only a few senior matches to my name. I usually played with the second team in the Doncaster Senior League, and probably would not have travelled to Kilnhurst that evening if my Dad, who was on the club's committee, hadn't suggested I went with him. Dad was just leaving our house when I arrived home from school. He said: "Thee mum's not in, tha can come to Kilnhurst wi' me if tha likes."

When we reached the ground, it transpired Upton were a man short, and, although I was really a wing-half, I ended up volunteering to play at left-back. By a happy coincidence, I'd been playing rugby at school the same afternoon, so I still had my football gear, and especially my boots, with me!

Anyhow, Martin Heavey – his son played for Upton – invited me for a trial with Wednesday, and soon afterwards I got a postcard asking me to report to Owlerton Stadium to play for the "A" team in a Yorkshire League match against Selby Town.

I have to admit to being rather tongue-tied when I turned up and discovered John Logan was in charge of the "A" team. As a boy I had seen him play brilliantly at wing-half for Barnsley many times, and he was one of my heroes. I don't think I ever stopped being in awe of John, and, in the following years, always had a lot of time for him because he was invariably helpful and generous with his knowledge – and there was nothing John didn't know about the game.

John Logan was the essential football man who epitomised what people behind the scenes at a club were like in those days. He was typical of his generation of footballers. A Geordie brought up in a hard school, he wore his hair parted straight down the middle in the style of so many players of his time, and he loved his job. You always felt, with his playing days behind him, he was grateful to have a place in the game. He had known hard times, and there was a sense in which people in his role on the training staff were constantly looking over their shoulders, fearful of being put out of work.

He made his experience evident in so many little ways, and constantly seemed keen to keep busy and show his usefulness. For instance, to watch him knock some tops on to your studs (they were the old leather type then), doing both boots in about two minutes flat, was to marvel at his dexterity and speed. You knew he'd done it a million times.

Towards the end of my spell on trial, I played in the "B" team in the last match of the 1948-49 season at Penistone Church, and I recall that, when we met up to travel to the game, Charlie Morton spoke to me. Charlie, who used to dole out the expenses, asked me to sign an amateur form for the following season – and was taken aback when I declined.

The upshot was, when we returned to Hillsborough after the game, there was a message asking me to see Eric Taylor, the secretary-manager. "What's all this?" he asked. I said I was 17, still earning no money, and proving a drain on my parents. I felt I might be better trying to persuade Upton to pay me a couple of quid a time to play for them instead of continuing as an amateur.

Mr Taylor said: 'Leave it with me, and I'll write to you." The following week, I got a letter in which he explained he understood what I had told him. He said he felt I "had the right idea" – and offered me £3 a week in the "A" team and £2 in the "B" team. I agreed and became a part-time professional.

Signing for Wednesday prompted me to leave school sooner than I might have done, but it didn't happen straight away. It was really a case of one thing leading to another in the following autumn. As it was a rugby-playing school and I now decided I wouldn't play rugby because I was playing football for Wednesday, I had to make a decision before someone made it for me. I chose to quit school and, having done that, it made sense for me to get my National Service out of the way by applying for an early call-up.

I joined the RAF in February 1950, and, as I negotiated an arrangement whereby I used up my annual leave allocation in the form of 48-hour weekend passes throughout the football season, I was able to get away to play with Wednesday fairly regularly. It worked

pretty well, and, by the time I made my Football League debut, against Bury at Hillsborough in November 1951, I was within a few months of being demobbed.

I don't remember too much about my debut other than that we won 2-1 and Derek Dooley, who was already well on his way to claiming a club scoring record, got both goals. I do recall that, at the time, I had managed only a handful of reserve matches, but, with both senior centre-halves, Edgar Packard and Cyril Turton, injured, I was the next in line – and Mr Taylor called me home from RAF Henlow by telegram. Unfortunately, in only my third Second Division match, against Coventry at home, I broke my jaw when my team-mate Mick Kenny accidentally kicked me in the face. However, I was back within two weeks, although I must have looked quite a sight playing with two lovely black eyes when we met Doncaster Rovers!

I was often in the wars in my Wednesday career. I suffered a broken leg three times – the first being in a League match at Maine Road in December 1953 when Manchester City's German goalkeeper Bert Trautmann accidentally dropped on me after we'd both gone for the ball.

Incidentally, I remember a funny incident when I was recovering from that injury. In those days there was a bit of a pitch at the back of the old North Stand, and I had gone there to try to strengthen my leg with some kicking. I was intending to hit this ball against a fence, but, being as inaccurate as ever, I thumped it over the fence and straight through a window in the stand!

As if that wasn't bad enough, the window in question was in what had once been a dressing room but was now a storeroom-cum-stable. Vin Hardy, a local greengrocer, kept his horse in there – and the poor animal was frightened almost to death when it was suddenly showered with flying glass thanks to my miskick.

Reference to Vin Hardy reminds me how different the set-up at the ground was in those days. Can you imagine a stable at the modern Hillsborough? Life seemed so easy going then, and, on the football side, things were probably pretty much as they had been for the previous 50 years.

There were some aspects of the training routine, for instance, that seemed rather ad hoc. We used to play a bit of head tennis, run around the pitch and whatever, and then appear for the next match. In the light of the knowledge I picked up later – notably when Harry Catterick arrived and everything became much more focussed and professional – I sometimes look back to those early days and wonder how we won any matches at all!

I was at Hillsborough until 1964, but my days as a full-time professional extended only from February 1952, following my demob from the RAF, to 1958, when Eric Taylor allowed me to revert to a part-time arrangement so I could pursue my studies to become a teacher.

I recall those six years with a great deal of pleasure, although I always remember my full-time career kicking off with a setback, because, in the same month as I started my new phase, I lost my first-team place following a 5-4 defeat at Barnsley – and it was over a year before I got back.

Thankfully, I was more or less a regular for the next five seasons, and we had some ups and downs but plenty of good moments. It was good to be involved in two Second Division championship successes, and if I missed out on the run to the FA Cup semi-final in 1954 because of a broken leg, I enjoyed being part of the team that went straight back to the old First Division in 1956 – by which time I was playing at left-half following Don McEvoy's arrival.

The friends I recall best were Cyril Turton, who came from South Kirkby, and Clarrie "Canny" Jordan, from Doncaster, because the three of us used to travel to and from Sheffield together on the train. Later, we had the benefit of Norman Curtis's car, and, of course, ultimately, my wife and I had a club house.

When I say I enjoyed my full-time years, I mean the actual day-to-day contact and the camaraderie were especially enjoyable. I loved it. Yet, somehow, the life of a full-time professional never really appealed to me. There was a sense in which it seemed a pointless waste of time. I increasingly felt I wanted to do more with my life.

I loved playing, and, naturally, liked winning and always wanted us to succeed. But I could never get upset about losing. I accepted that if the other team beat us, it was invariably because they were better than us. I enjoyed the training and being with the other lads, but it seemed wasteful to me that, after a couple of hours of training in the morning, we'd pop over to Kitson's Cafe for fish and chips – and that was it, the day was over. It was some consolation that, unlike some of the others, I didn't have to hang about but could get off home.

I felt I wanted to do something more fulfilling, and, thankfully, Eric Taylor understood my frustration. I believe that, after I ceased being a full-timer, I managed only about 14 first-team games in the next four seasons, with none in my last two years at Wednesday. But it was the right decision. I never actually lost my enthusiasm, and I think Harry Catterick, for instance, appreciated the way I maintained my fitness and was able to step into the first team on one or two occasions when there was a bit of a crisis.

I know Harry was pleased when, around January 1961, I came in for five games which coincided with four wins in which we scored 17 goals – one of those games being a 6-1 victory at Fulham. I think I was on the losing side only twice in my last ten first-team appearances. I might well have played in the First Division after 1962, but a broken leg in a reserve match against Stoke sidelined me for a long time, and, frankly, I knew it was just about the end.

Anyhow, I went to college in Sheffield for two years, had a year at Carnegie College in Leeds, and, after qualifying, took up my first teaching appointment at Owler Lane School in Sheffield. I remained with Wednesday until 1964, when I left to join Norman Curtis, my old Hillsborough colleague, in non-League football at Buxton. By then, I must admit, I was just about finished, and I've often said my service to Buxton probably cost them about £1 a kick!

Unfortunately, ahead of that, I'd been sacked from my first teaching job because of a conflict between school and football which was not really of my making. I asked the local authority for permission to join Wednesday on a tour of Nigeria, and believed this had been given. However, two days before we were due to fly out, they said I couldn't go. I had to tell them I was sorry but I had no option but to fulfil my obligation to Wednesday.

I was living in a club house and, with one thing and another, was still dependent on the money I got from football because teaching wages then were peanuts. Anyway, as Peter Swan was away with England, Wednesday wanted me, and I couldn't back out at the last minute. When I returned from Nigeria, I found myself out of a job, dismissed for "taking leave without permission". The club took up my case without success. Anyhow, subsequently I obtained a position with the West Riding Authority at Wath-on-Dearne.

When I first looked for a career in teaching, I had no intention of seeking to graduate as a PE teacher, but I sort of drifted into the sports side when it was pointed out to me that perhaps I should make use of the knowledge and experience I had gained in professional football.

So it happened that in 1966, by which time my playing days were over, I became football coach to Stoke-on-Trent Schools, and, following local government reorganisation in 1973, I worked on a broader basis with Staffordshire Schools, with whom I was responsible for games in general, until my retirement in 1994. My schools football included three years as assistant manager of England Boys and five years as manager until I resigned from the role.

The combination of football and teaching in my career has ensured an eventful and rewarding life, and I certainly look back on my time with Sheffield Wednesday with a lot of pleasure. There was a time, by the way, when I used to take a job in the summer months to help make ends meet. Once, for instance, I worked in a petrol station. Another time, when I was employed by C&A, Eric Taylor commented that, if I wasn't careful, I'd be earning £1,000 a year! It just goes to show how times have changed, and reminds me how grateful I was to have the work.

Author's Footnote: It is worthy of note that Alan Finney, a former team-mate of O'Donnell's, commented: "Rod was one of the most underrated players at Hillsborough, very much admired by his colleagues because he was so quick. He

was probably not as good in the air as he would have liked, but, in terms of his ability on the ground, he was not dissimilar to Des Walker, and, if he had not preferred to play as a part-timer, he might have gone much further than he did."
(The nickname Rod followed Ralph from his schooldays because his initials were R.O.D.)

Alan Finney

Alan Finney was a winger who could play on either flank, although he was essentially an outside-right. He made over 500 appearances and scored 90 goals for Wednesday between February 1951 and January 1966. He was capped three times at Under-23 level and gained England "B" honours. In his Owls career he figured in three Second Division championship teams, played in the FA Cup semi-finals of 1954 and 1960, and was an ever-present in the side that finished runners-up in Division One in 1961.

I was born at Langwith, where my father worked in the local colliery, but it was not until after we moved to Armthorpe, when I was around seven or eight, that I got involved in football – and I graduated from street games typical of that wartime period to playing for my school and then Doncaster and Yorkshire Boys. At the time I was one of a group of lads who took great delight in watching Doncaster Rovers. Always happy to walk the four miles or so from our village to Belle Vue whenever Clarrie Jordan and our other favourites were playing, we didn't miss a home match for years.

It was a scout called Martin Heavey – I think he worked at a local pit – who said he would arrange for me to have a trial with Wednesday. He first mentioned it when I was about 14, and I finally got the call quite unexpectedly one day when my dad had taken me to watch the West Indians play in a Test match at Trent Bridge. Dad had a friend in Nottingham, and we'd gone to stay at this man's home. We got back from the cricket one evening to find a telegram had arrived from Wednesday asking me to attend the public practice match the following weekend. I played in a game for youngsters which was like a curtain raiser to the official traditional Whites versus Stripes match.

Alan Finney.

I signed as an amateur and started in the Hatchard League team at 15. Then I went into the "A" team, which played in the Yorkshire League, and this was when I first met up with Albert Quixall. Of course, Albert and I became great pals, and our names are still linked in the memories of many older supporters because we graduated through the Reserves and into the first-team together as partners on the right wing.

We were always very close then, and, later, when we got married, we each in turn acted as best man for the other. Naturally, we had a lot of fun when we were two teenagers travelling with a Wednesday team in which everyone else seemed a comparative veteran. We loved making apple-pie beds and buying gadgets with which we could trick or shock the other players, and, fortunately, everybody took it all in good part.

Albert and myself were both in the Reserves at 16, and we must have been doing well because, at 17, we were called up for our Football League debut on the same day in February 1951. The game was a home fixture with Chelsea, but I don't remember much about it except that, as the outside right, I was told to hug the touchline, which meant I often felt a bit remote from the main action. I've often said that, if I could have my time again, I wouldn't be a winger, because it was sometimes very frustrating not being able to really get involved in a game.

Anyway, I played in seven matches in that 1950-51 season, and, in the final game, at home to Everton, I got my first League goal. I think it made the score 4-0, and we finished up winning 6-0. Unfortunately, Chelsea beat Fulham the same afternoon, which meant that, despite our emphatic victory, we were relegated from the First Division – the final irony being we went down on goal-average.

By then I was a full-time professional, and, looking back, it was a step which took some coming to terms with. Like Albert, when I left school I'd taken up an apprenticeship. In Albert's case he went as a joiner, while I joined a firm connected with British Railways and was learning to be a coach and waggon repairer. But, as soon as we were old enough to accept professional terms, the club wanted us to give up our trades to concentrate totally on football.

People like Johnny Logan, who looked after the "A" team, and the senior coaches, Sam Powell and Tommy Walker, were very good to us at this time. Sam and Tommy were two grand old-timers, pre-war Wednesday favourites in whom we often confided. Sam, who unfortunately died of a heart attack while still a comparatively young man, was a particular favourite with me.

Someone else who took me under his wing in those early days was Clarrie Jordan, the centre-forward. When I watched Doncaster Rovers as a boy, Clarrie had been my great hero, and now he was my mentor and guide at Sheffield, introducing me to all the other players and warning me about those I ought to keep away from!

It was the start of a friendship which lasted right up to Clarrie's death in February 1992. What a man he was! I doubt if I've known anyone so courageous in the face of adversity. In the last years of his life, he had both legs amputated, but he refused to let his misfortune get him down. Everybody loved Clarrie because he never stopped being cheerful.

He used to keep a pub not far from where I live, and, although we didn't see each other regularly, we always enjoyed our get-togethers. I remember once bumping into him at a professional snooker match at a club in Doncaster. We both had so much to say to one another that we were still talking during the game, and, finally, the referee halted play to tell us he'd show us both a red card if we didn't shut up!

I visited him after he lost his first leg, and I'll never forget going to the Infirmary after they'd amputated his other leg. I walked down a corridor and, when I looked round the corner to see into the ward, I saw him from the back and I was quite literally overcome with emotion. I can't explain the sadness I felt. With tears running down my cheeks, I just turned and left. I couldn't let Clarrie see me in that state when he was still so chirpy despite being left so helpless by a fate he didn't deserve. I was glad I had played alongside Clarrie, for he was one of the best and most respected forwards of his time.

Of course, it is good to have known so many outstanding players and friends as I did in 15 years as a professional with Wednesday. Apart from Clarrie, who was a special case, it seems wrong to single out individuals because there were so many who did well for the club.

I was in three Second Division championship sides, in 1952, 1956 and 1959, and we reached the FA Cup semi-final in 1954 and 1960 when we lost both games at Maine Road. I don't think we could complain about the defeat in 1954 because we were well beaten by a Preston side in which a certain Tom Finney was the man who made them tick. It was a much bigger disappointment when we lost to Blackburn six years later because we'd beaten them 3-0 in the League a few months earlier, and we really thought we were in with a great chance of going to Wembley. But we knew our luck was out when we had what seemed a perfectly good goal disallowed.

Mind you, by 1960 we had a very good side which was starting to look capable of winning something. We'd been coming together from around 1958, and, after Harry Catterick arrived, he made the slight adjustments which saw us develop into a very formidable outfit. The team that finished second to Tottenham in the old First Division in 1960-61 was without question the best I ever played in.

It was in that season when we went to Manchester United and thrashed them 7-2 in an FA Cup replay with a performance that illustrated just how good we could be.

In the first match, at Hillsborough, I had a bit of a run-in with Maurice Setters, the United defender. I remember he warned me I'd better put some pads on the back of my legs when I went to Old Trafford.

Some people thought that we had thrown away our chance of winning in the first game, but that night in February 1961 we really sorted United out. Keith Ellis got a hat-trick, and Johnny Fantham and me each scored twice. I can tell you we celebrated in style afterwards, when one of the directors took us all out for a meal.

Harry Catterick's arrival in 1958 was good for me, and I think that under him, with Tommy Eggleston as coach, I enjoyed my best spell at Hillsborough. Harry was a great one with the psychological warfare which he used to get the best out of certain players. I've seen him drop lads from the first team in practice matches to make them think they were about to lose their place, and he'd even take the likely stand-in with us when we travelled to League games. Then the man who thought he was going to be left out would thank Harry for his reprieve by going out and playing a blinder!

Eggleston was a hell of a coach, but I think the best coach I ever had was Jack Mansell. Under Jack our players were probably physically fitter than at any time in my years with Wednesday. His training methods and routines were like something I had never experienced before.

It was all a far cry from the training in my early days at Hillsborough, when we used to arrive at about ten o clock, get out the old tracksuit bottoms and basketball shoes, then run round the perimeter of the pitch until half-past eleven. I remember Dennis Woodhead, always the wit in the team, had a habit of putting words to songs, and, as we jogged round and round, he'd sing "Two more laps and you'll get a ball – maybe!"

After all the running, we'd go behind the old North Stand, which we called the scratching shed, and round off training with a session on the tennis courts. Half of us would play head tennis while the rest staged a five-a-side match; then we'd switch games, and once that was over, it was the end of training for another day. Apart from a practice match once a week, that was our daily routine – all very basic when you think of how things were done later.

One variation was when we were taken out to Bakewell in Derbyshire, or somewhere similar. We'd go off in a bus, which would drop us eight or ten miles from our hotel, and, wearing walking boots, we'd be expected to be back at base in time for lunch – and those who didn't make the deadline went hungry!

But they were happy days, and I've so many good memories. I was always sorry my time with Wednesday ended on a negative note because that was the last thing I wanted to happen.

The worst spell for me came after Alan Brown returned and took over as manager in 1964. To be honest, I'd never got on very well with him when I was a young player and he was the coach in the early 1950s. When he said things, you were never quite sure what he meant sometimes, and I don't think anybody really understood him. Somehow you always felt he was never being absolutely straight with you.

When he came back, he didn't want to know anyone who was aged around the 30 mark, especially if they weren't prepared to look upon him as if he was God. He made it clear he wanted the older players out – and I think I was the last of the group to leave.

Late in Brown's first season, in March 1965, I got injured at Burnley, and I played only three more times for the first team. It was the beginning of the end, and I have always felt that the injury I suffered at Turf Moor knocked two or three years off my football career.

Andy Lochhead was the man who did it. Someone played a ball, and I was second favourite to get it. Having been in the game as long as I had, I should have had more sense. Lochhead came in over the top and down the outside of my right ankle, damaging my ligaments and my Achilles tendon. I'm often reminded of that day because, more than 30 years later, I still have trouble with the same ankle.

I knew my Wednesday years were

coming to an end, and, after being associated with the club for nearly 20 years, having played around 500 games, and not costing them a fee, I thought they might give me a free transfer – and with it the chance to do better for myself than happened.

Unfortunately, when I joined Doncaster Rovers in January 1966, Wednesday demanded £5,000, even though, in truth, I was one of the walking wounded and destined to spend more of my time at Belle Vue on the treatment bench than on the training pitch. The fee might sound like peanuts today, and it wasn't a huge sum in 1966, but it was enough to prevent me getting the kind of deal that might have been possible if I'd been given a "free".

The disappointment was compounded when it came to my testimonial. I had been promised a match, and there had been talk of an attractive fixture with Sheffield United being arranged at Hillsborough. But I had nothing in writing, and the club subsequently decided that, as Wednesday's ground was being used for World Cup matches that summer, they couldn't fit in a match for me. I said I was prepared to wait until well after the World Cup was over, but, instead, the game was played at Doncaster, with Wednesday providing the opposition.

Quite honestly, it was not how I'd imagined celebrating my long service to Wednesday. One last big occasion at Hillsborough would have been nice, but it wasn't to be. Yet, if it all ended with a sense of anticlimax, I have to admit that when I look back now I remember best the happy times we had – and they really were the good old days!

Albert Quixall

In the 1950s, Albert Quixall was often described as the Golden Boy of Hillsborough. The former Sheffield schoolboy international made 260 League and Cup appearances and scored 65 goals for Wednesday between February 1951 and September 1958, collecting five England caps. Then, with great reluctance, he became Britain's most expensive footballer with a £45,000 move to Manchester United. Although he has resided in Manchester for 40 years, he remains as big a Wednesdayite as when a kid at Meynell Road School.

Sheffield Wednesday were an obsession with me for many years before I ever dreamed of playing for them, and my feeling for the club hasn't really changed. I never wanted to play for anyone else and sometimes wish I had never left. I would have been happy to have stayed with them right to the end of my career.

My family lived on Parson Cross, just up the hill from the ground, and, as a boy, on match days I used to walk from our house in Doe Royd Crescent to watch the first team and the Reserves. When the first team was in action, I'd be standing in the queue outside the Spion Kop end on Penistone Road as early as 12 noon. I'd ask someone to save my place while I dashed round to the players entrance to collect autographs. My great Wednesday hero then was Jackie Robinson, and just to be able to stand near and touch people like him, Joe Cockroft, Dave Russell, Frank Westlake, Hugh Swift and others was fantastic.

When I went on to captain Meynell Road School and play for Sheffield and England Boys, naturally a lot of clubs began taking an interest in me, but when Jerry Bronks, who was secretary of the Sheffield Schools Football Federation, asked me which club I wanted to go to, I told him there was only one. So he took me to Hillsborough and introduced me to Eric Taylor.

As there were no apprentices in football then, when I left school I started work at Thos. W. Ward's, being in the office for six or seven months before getting a job in the joiner's shop. Later I worked for a construction firm called George Longden's, whose top man was a prominent Wednesday director. I was then training two nights a week at the ground and playing with the "A" and "B" teams, but, naturally, I was impatient to become a full-time professional. That happened around January or February 1951 when I was 17, and the thrill of training every day alongside people like Redfern Froggatt and others who had been my idols was an experience I savoured.

It was like a dream when, about the same time, I made my first-team debut. I actually made two senior appearances before I was given my Football League bow, and I imagine those initial two

Albert Quixall.

games will be of interest because they are not the sort of fixture that are common nowadays, and it serves to show how different things were in the early post-war period.

Wednesday had been put out of the FA Cup in the third round at Fulham, but, despite the fact that several regulars were injured and we were struggling at the foot of the table, the club wanted a fixture to fill the blank on the day of the fourth-round. So they arranged a friendly match at Leicester, and I was chosen at inside-right, with Jackie Marriott my wing partner.

A fortnight later, another blank caused by the FA Cup was filled with a Sheffield & Hallamshire County Cup semi-final against Sheffield United at Hillsborough. You can't imagine now what a big thing this competition was in those days, and, of course, with the local teams being in different divisions, Sheffield derby matches were a rare attraction. This game was particularly special for me because I had my first experience of a 40,000 crowd, another boyhood hero, Jimmy Hagan, was in the United team, and, to my delight, we won 2-0.

It was a week later that Alan Finney and me had our first taste of First Division football. Alan, my wing partner, was also 17, but about three months younger than me. We played together in two home games against

Chelsea and Manchester United in the space of three days. The first match was drawn, and we lost the second, but my consolation was marking my League debut with a goal. I don't think I did anything wrong, but I obviously wasn't seen as the immediate answer to Wednesday's quest for someone to help in the fight against relegation, because soon afterwards the club paid a record £35,000 to Notts County so that Jackie Sewell could fill the No.8 shirt.

I didn't play again in the League team until October of the following season, when, of course, we were back in the Second Division. My return coincided with Derek Dooley's recall and the start of that astonishing scoring run of his which helped us win promotion and the championship. Derek and I had progressed together from the "A" team to the first team, and it was terrific to see him finally making the grade.

I remember when we played at Brentford on Good Friday in that 1951-52 season, Derek came to my rescue in an amusing episode. Before the game, after I'd gone outside to pass a couple of complimentary tickets to someone, the steward on the players' entrance wouldn't let me back in!

"Who are you?" he asked. When I said: "I'm a player," he took one look at my boyish face, chuckled and said: "You're joking, son. You're not playing here!" Fortunately, just at that moment, Derek appeared, and, with a bit of persuasion, the steward eventually decided to let me in.

It was later, in January 1953, that I was called up for National Service, and my team-mate Alan Finney was soon to be a colleague in the Royal Signals at Catterick. Unfortunately, being in the army restricted my appearances for Wednesday, but I did get an early leave to play in what proved to be a fateful game at Preston in February 1953 when Derek Dooley broke his leg in the accident which ended his career.

Over the years, in the "A" team and the Reserves, I had played exactly the same kind of ball for Derek as I did that afternoon at Deepdale – I shoved it through and Derek set off in a typical chase down the middle. This time, Derek and the goalkeeper, George Thompson, reached the ball at the same moment and collided.

I always remember returning to

Wedding day... It's through the goalposts for newly-weds Albert and Jeanette Quixall after their marriage in 1956. The Owls players in the picture are Alan Finney, Walter Bingley, Dave McIntosh, Norman Curtis, Don McEvoy, Ralph O'Donnell and Tommy McAnearney.

Catterick camp that weekend thinking Derek would be out for the rest of the season. Then, a couple of days later at the camp, the colonel came to me and said: "Do you know your buddy Dooley is fighting for his life?" He explained about Derek having to have a leg amputated. I was devastated. I just broke down and wept. It was a terrible thing to happen to such a smashing lad. I felt for his wife, Sylvia, as well, because I could remember how she had stood on the touchline at "A" team games supporting him. Just when his career was at a peak, everything had collapsed, but Derek and Sylvia showed a lot of character and spirit in the following months.

Derek and I had some wonderful times together, and we could amuse ourselves in the simplest ways which might seem quaint to the modern generation. I still often think of the Fridays after training when we used to wander up into the city centre and spend some time in Marsden's Milk Bar in Pinstone Street. Derek used to be amused at the way me and Alan Finney liked to pop into Wilson Peck's music shop, get the female assistant to play us all the latest hit records, and then tell her we'd decided not to buy anything. I think she knew there was no chance of us spending a penny, but she always went along with our little game!

I've heard a lot of Wednesdayites say they feel the 1953-54 season was my best at Hillsborough. Certainly it was something of a milestone. I played for the Football League against the Irish League in Belfast and gained the first three of my five England caps. One of those games was at Wembley, and, when Wednesday went all the way to the FA Cup semi-final, I thought I might be playing there again. But Preston beat us at Maine Road on a day when me and Jackie Sewell learned that Tommy Docherty was the hardest player we would ever meet!

Incidentally, a bonus that year was finishing six points clear of relegation. Unfortunately, we didn't beat the drop the following season, but we promptly won the Second Division championship again in 1955-56 – a season made all the more memorable for me because, towards the end of it, in March, I married Jeanette, the dancing teacher I met at the City Hall. That was also the season when I had the novelty of scoring more goals [17] than I'd done in all the five previous seasons put together.

I think it surprised some supporters when I bettered that tally by going on to become the leading scorer in 1956-57 with 24, and my total over two seasons of 41 in 84 games compared very favourably with 11 in the previous 132 games. Yet I wasn't suddenly a different Quixall. I simply became more conscious of trying to score after being content for so long to try to make goals for others. No doubt somebody on the training staff gave me a nudge on the subject!

The great disappointment was that 1957-58 saw us relegated yet again, although I suppose in retrospect the thing most people remember about that season is that in February it saw the Manchester United air crash. I had known some of the lads who died in that terrible tragedy, and, although I didn't know it then, it was to set in motion events which influenced my career more than a little.

By coincidence, Manchester United's first match after Munich was an FA Cup fifth-round tie against Wednesday at Old Trafford. The atmosphere inside and outside the ground was like nothing we are ever likely to witness again. The scenes outside were remarkable. Honest, there must have been 20,000 people with no chance of getting in, and I remember seeing Brian London, the British heavyweight champion, among them.

I always recall that game as one of those occasions you never forget because it was absolutely unique. I captained Wednesday for the first time that night, and, in a strange way, it was an experience I was proud of even though I knew it was a match we couldn't possibly win.

I've heard it said that it was on that night that Jimmy Murphy, who was United's acting manager, identified me as one of the men he would persuade Matt Busby to take to Old Trafford. I don't know whether there is any truth in that, but eight months later, by which time Busby was out of hospital and back at the helm, he made me the first player he personally signed after Munich.

I was happy at Hillsborough and Wednesday were always my first love. I didn't have any thought of leaving, and, with Harry Catterick just having taken over as manager, I was only thinking of playing in another Wednesday promotion team. So it was a surprise to me when I picked up the local paper and saw a headline suggesting I was in line for a move. I had no idea what what happening.

I remember that Wednesday evening we played Sunderland and won 6-0. I think we were 2-0 up early on and I got a goal, then Red Froggatt got a hat-trick in the second half. I know I played well, and I heard that Busby was at the game. Nobody said anything to me, but the next morning the papers announced I was on my way to Old Trafford. It was news to me.

Even when Eric Taylor called me to the ground, I didn't think I was going to leave. I suppose it was a factor in what happened later that Wednesday were ready to sell me. I thought, well if it's what they want, I'll do it. I could hardly fail to be influenced either by the fact that, as I saw when I met him in Taylor's office, Busby was very keen to take me to United.

It took me some time to settle at Old Trafford. That £45,000 fee doesn't sound much now, but it was hell of a sum then, and yes I did worry about being the most expensive player in English football. When you think of

what a player would get in a similar situation nowadays, some people will think it's incredible that all I got was the modest signing-on fee which the rules and regulations permitted at that time. It was all I expected, and, anyway, Busby was not a man to bend the rules for anyone.

Busby told me to play my normal game, and, after about half-a-dozen matches, I started to find my feet. I suppose the highlight was playing in the FA Cup winning side of 1963, but while my six years at Old Trafford were happy before knee trouble started causing problems, I don't think I ever stopped thinking of my Wednesday days as the best time of my career.

The camaraderie at Hillsborough was fantastic, something really special. Everybody was your mate, and you were everybody's mate. I loved it. They were good times. I often remember those early days when Red Froggatt, Eddie Gannon and the other older lads used to say: "Don't worry, we'll look after you." And you knew they meant it.

We had some fun, and we made some memories I'll treasure for as long as I live.

Norman Curtis

Between November 1950 and February 1960, full-back Norman Curtis, a product of Dinnington who was signed from Gainsborough Trinity, made 324 League and Cup appearances. Older supporters will remember that 19 of his 21 senior goals came from penalties – and he also once saved a couple of spot-kicks as an emergency goalkeeper! Now retired and living near York, he was happy to reminisce about a Hillsborough career which did not end until he was nearly 36 years old.

I started my working life as a butcher's boy in Dinnington, and my football career didn't really begin to develop until after service in the Royal Navy air crew towards the end of the war. Following demob, I went back to butchering, but only briefly, because I soon persuaded my eldest brother to get me a trial with Gainsborough. And, soon after signing me, Trinity decided they wanted me to live in that area. I

said I'd move if they fixed me up with some digs. They agreed, and, as a result, I took a job in a local engineering works and played as a part-timer in the Midland League.

It was in January 1950, when I was 25, that I joined Wednesday. Les Bedford, the club's chief scout, had watched me in a few games. I don't think Les had ever been a professional footballer, and he was best-known as one of the most outstanding opening batsmen in Yorkshire Council cricket. But he was knowledgeable about football, and, more than that, he was a real gentleman. He said he was banking on me to prove one of his best signings, and I remember how delighted he was when, within a year, I made the first team.

Strange as it might seem, I didn't move back to my native South Yorkshire to live after becoming a full-time professional, but remained based in Gainsborough and travelled to Sheffield six days a week. It was no problem because I always looked forward to training and never wanted to miss a single session.

I remember my debut against Bolton in November 1950 as a game in which I felt very nervous and, in the end, it was a relief to get it over. The match I remember better was my second appearance a week later, because it just happened to pit me against the legendary Stanley Matthews at Blackpool. We lost 3-2 and Stan gave me a real roasting. I didn't know whether I was coming or going and ended up dizzy and crippled with cramp. It wasn't much consolation when, at the final whistle, Matthews came over, said: "Well done," and patted me on the head.

It was a nice gesture from the man they called "the wizard of the wing", but there were one or two later instances when I don't think he felt quite so generously disposed towards my performance. Indeed, there was one famous occasion when I so frustrated him he complained I'd get football done away with!

That was the day when Alan Brown, our coach, took me aside just before we went down the tunnel and said: "Norman, stick with Matthews this afternoon. Follow him wherever he goes. Don't leave him, even if he goes to

Norman Curtis (right) in the Owls' dressing room with Dave McIntosh and Keith Bannister.

the toilet!" To be honest, Alan's instructions were put in rather stronger terms than I've used.

Anyway, that was the hardest and most exhausting 90 minutes I ever experienced, concentrating totally on watching just one man. I was on his heels every moment of the match. He wandered everywhere to try to lose me. He got so upset at one stage that he ran across to Eddie Shimwell, the Blackpool back, to ask him to go up the wing in an attempt to lure me away. Eddie argued that he was too busy looking after our winger Dennis Woodhead – and I heard every word Eddie said because I was as close to Matthews as Stan was to him!

I think the most hilarious moment came when we were standing together in Blackpool's goalmouth while all the action was taking place at the opposite end of the pitch in our penalty-area! We were under terrific pressure, with everybody back except me. Some of our fans must have wondered why I didn't leave Matthews and go back to help. But I was simply following instructions.

It was when we were coming out for the second-half that Matthews said I'd get the game done away with. I replied: "There's one thing certain, tha'll not get a kick this half."

I was never a footballing full-back like Ron Staniforth, but, if I was hard and uncompromising, I was fair. I wasn't on the field to let the other side play, I was there to do my best for Sheffield

Wednesday. I was proud of the club, and used to feel that I wouldn't hesitate if there was anything I could do to help the cause.

That was probably why I was nominated as the emergency goalkeeper. Of course, there were no substitutes then, and I often went in goal in practice matches. It wasn't that I fancied myself as a goalkeeper, and I wasn't the biggest man in the team, but I knew if I got some regular practice I wouldn't be frightened of the task if I suddenly had to do it in a big match.

Alan Brown nominated me for the job, and I think the first time I had to don the green jersey was in a home match against Liverpool in August 1952 when Dave McIntosh broke his left forearm. I was in goal all through the second half and it was some comfort that the only shot that beat me was from Billy Liddell, who had one of the best shots in the game.

The second time I deputised for McIntosh is the match most people remember when recalling my goalkeeping exploits. This was at Preston in August 1953, when we lost 6-0. I stood between the posts for an hour, and I was beaten five times.

But I did save two penalties in that match, and they were from Tom Finney and Jimmy Baxter, two men who were masters at spot-kicks. Finney liked to place them just inside the post, but on this occasion he didn't hit his shot hard

enough and I dived the right way to stop it. Then, later, Baxter aimed for the opposite corner and I again happened to throw myself to the correct side. I'd have been a hero if we hadn't lost so heavily.

In my time with Wednesday, of course, my name was associated with scoring penalties rather than saving them, not so much because I took about 24 and succeeded with 19, but because of the technique I adopted. We devised a plan whereby someone would place the ball on the spot and I would run from my position in defence and belt it as hard as I could. My theory was that, as the goalkeeper couldn't move, if the shot was on target, the ball had to go in the net.

Some people said if one of my penalties hit the goalkeeper, it would take him into the net as well as the ball. But that notion was disproved at least once.

I remember being very disappointed during extra-time in an FA Cup replay at Notts County in 1955 when, with us trailing 1-0, somebody handled Jackie Marriott's centre in the box. I really hammered the penalty only to see the ball ricochet off goalkeeper Gordon Bradley's body. There was an almighty scramble when I went for the rebound, and I think I put it into the net. But the referee gave County a free-kick.

The penalty-taking was something we worked on in training, and my involvement came one day when we were discussing candidates for the job. I had never taken one in all my time at Gainsborough, and must have gone nearly 60 first-team matches with Wednesday before I was given the job. But I remember Alan Brown asking for volunteers, and I said I'd do it. I was known as a hard kicker of a ball and felt that if I couldn't score from the penalty spot I wasn't worth my place in the team.

A coincidence I remember is that, in all the first three games in which I was called upon to take a penalty, I didn't take one but two. The first occasion was against Derby in October 1952, and both penalties stemmed from fouls by Norman Neilsen on Derek Dooley. They were my first senior goals and we won 2-0.

I got another penalty double against Portsmouth a month later, but we lost 4-3, and then I missed the first of the

Wednesday in 1951-52. Back row (left to right): Sam Powell (trainer), Norman Curtis, Eddie Gannon, Vin Kenny, Cyril Turton, Dave McIntosh, George Davies, Ralph O'Donnell, Dennis Woodhead, Doug Witcomb, Tommy Walker (trainer). Front row: Alan Brown (coach), Redfern Froggatt, Albert Quixall, Derek Dooley, Keith Bannister, Jackie Sewell, Walter Rickett, Alan Finney, Eric Taylor (secretary).

two I took against Burnley in the following February. My shot hit a post, but the miss didn't make any difference because we lost 4-2.

I remember in the dressing room after that match, I was still feeling upset about the penalty I'd missed, but Alan Brown told me to stop worrying. Alan was a hard taskmaster, and he was not a man you could kid. But he was often very kind and sympathetic, sometimes when you didn't expect it.

There was a spell of about three years when people like Roy Shiner, Alan Finney and Albert Quixall took on the penalty job. Quixall, by the way, was pretty good at it. Anyway, it was in this period that I scored the only two goals I ever managed from open play – and both were against Everton at Hillsborough.

I resumed taking penalties in the Second Division championship run of 1958-59 and scored five times. My last spot-kick for Wednesday came in September of the following season

when I got one in a 2-0 win against Luton, and I think I played only eight more games for the first team after that. A young man called Don Megson had come along to claim my No.3 shirt.

In fact, my last League appearance for Wednesday was not in my normal position but as Peter Johnson's deputy at right-back, against Everton in February 1960. Ironically, there was a penalty that day, but there was no question of anyone placing the ball on the spot for me to take it. Tom McAnearney had been nominated for the job, and I was delighted when he scored.

Ron Capewell

Ron "Lofty" Capewell was a 6ft 4½in goalkeeper who joined Wednesday as an amateur in November 1949, stepped into the professional ranks in the following February, and went on to play in 30 League and Cup games before moving to Hull City in July 1954.

I was brought up on the Arbourthorne and started my working life as an apprentice bricklayer. After leaving school, I played with the local youth club and had trials for the Yorkshire Boys' Clubs representative team. There was a time, before I was called up for National Service, when someone was supposed to be taking me and a lad called Ellis Stafford (he later played for Peterborough) for a trial with Wednesday, but, for some reason, nothing happened.

Then, after coming home from the army in September 1949, I went roof tiling for a living and started playing with Midhill WMC. It wasn't long afterwards that I was invited down to Hillsborough and became a Wednesday amateur. I was now training at the ground two nights a week, and it was after one of those sessions that I happened to mention to someone on the coaching staff that Southampton and Blackpool had been making inquiries about me.

I don't know if I expected this to

Owls favourites and their ladies at a Supporters' Club dinner in 1952. Players include Norman Jackson, Dennis Woodhead, Ron Capewell, Keith Bannister, George Davies, Derek Dooley and Jackie Marriott.

prompt such a quick response, but the very next time I went down to Hillsborough I was told to be sure to see Eric Taylor before I left the ground – and two days later I was signed as a full-time professional!

The next four years were a really good time for me. Training for a couple of hours, then having the rest of the day your own to spend as you please – it's better than pulling out your guts working at some manual job, isn't it? I used to knock about with Eric Kirby. He was another Sheffield lad and I think he played only once in the first team before going on to York, but we both enjoyed being at Wednesday. After training, Eric and I would often wander about Sheffield city centre, calling in at Wilson Peck's and getting the assistant to play the latest "pop" records. Every now and then we might buy one.

I started in the Yorkshire League side under Johnny Logan and progressed to the Central League under Tommy Walker. Then in September 1952 I made my first-team debut and started a run of 26 consecutive appearances in a home First Division match against Charlton. I got my chance because Dave McIntosh, the regular goalkeeper, broke an arm against Liverpool.

I don't remember much about that Charlton match other than that we lost. It was the game when Derek Dooley

was left out of the team for the first time, and that day thousands went to watch him play for the Reserves across at Bramall Lane.

I stayed in the team until McIntosh returned in February, and the games I recall from that run are a 5-1 win at Newcastle, a 5-4 defeat against West Brom at Christmas when we conceded three own-goals, and the return match at West Brom the following day when we won 1-0 with a goal from Dooley. Our results were a bit up and down, but we had some good players, and it was good to be in the same side as lads like Doug Witcomb, Eddie Gannon, Jackie Sewell and Redfern Froggatt.

I made my only FA Cup appearance for Wednesday against Blackpool on a foggy day in early January 1953. We lost 2-1 and I have never forgotten a goal that Stan Matthews scored for Blackpool just before half-time. Kicking towards the Kop, they got a free-kick near the halfway line right in front of the old North Stand. Somebody hit the ball high into our penalty box, and I went out and punched it away. Unfortunately, the ball finished up at the feet of Matthews, and he lobbed it over me into the net. He went on to help Blackpool win the Cup that year in a famous Wembley Final, and I can always say I was involved when his run started at Hillsborough!

When I got back into the side early in the 1953-54 season, it was again because McIntosh had broken an arm. But this time I managed only four matches before I lost my place to Brian Ryalls, who stayed in the team until "Mac" returned in February.

I didn't know it then, but my days as a first-team player were over, and in 1955 I got the dreaded letter which told me it was time to get on my bike. When that happens, you just have to accept it.

I moved to Hull City, and, looking back, this was a mistake because it didn't work out and my full-time career lasted only one more year.

In my last season at Hillsborough, I had developed a cist on a kneecap and ended up having a cartilage operation which didn't solve the problem straightaway because I continued to get fluid on the knee. At Hull, the knee was puffing up every time I played, and it was probably no surprise that I was soon on my bike again.

In the following years I played with a number of clubs, including King's Lynn, Hyde and Stalybridge. Meanwhile I worked as a stonemason, and then spent 16½ years at Whitbreads Brewery working on the delivery waggons.

The brewery job was nearly as good as being down at Hillsborough. But, really, I suppose nothing compares with being young and earning a living as a professional footballer, and I'm glad I had that experience.

Funnily enough, towards the end of my full-time career, I did learn that, in those first weeks after I came out of the army, Sheffield United had been trying to find me. I sometimes think that, if they'd succeeded, I might have gone on to enjoy a longer run at the top.

Mind you, to be honest, I have no regrets, and I'm glad I played for Wednesday because they were always my favourite club.

Jackie Sewell

Wednesday were struggling against relegation from the old First Division in March 1951 when they made Jackie Sewell Britain's most expensive footballer by paying what then seemed a staggering £35,000 to take him to Hillsborough from Second Division Notts County. The Cumbrian-born inside-forward went on to score 92 goals in 175 games for the Owls, and all his six England caps were gained in this period. Now living in retirement in Nottingham, Sewell, who became a car salesman after hanging up his boots following his return from a long spell in Rhodesia, recalls his Sheffield days as among the happiest of a career that spanned four clubs, some 560 games – and 250 goals.

My move to Sheffield came right out of the blue on what I'll always remember as an incredible day in mid-March 1951. I had no thought of leaving. I was 24 years old, settled at Notts County after being there since Major Frank Buckley had taken me to Meadow Lane seven years or so earlier, and, with over 100 goals to my name in under 200 games since the end of the war, I was enjoying my football. Certainly I was loving playing alongside my mentor, the legendary England centre-forward Tommy Lawton.

After training, I was walking round the back of the stand and making my way out of the ground when Eric Houghton, the manager, spotted me. He shouted me over. "There's somebody I'd like to introduce you to," he said, pointing to Eric Taylor, the Wednesday secretary-manager. "Hello, Mr Taylor," I said, and turned to leave. But Houghton stopped me: "Hang on, Jack, Mr Taylor wants to talk to you." When I asked "What about?" he replied: "A transfer to Sheffield."

I told them I wasn't interested, and again turned to go, but they walked along with me, and, to cut a long story short, we ended up in the Victoria Hotel. It was there, at about eight o'clock in the evening, that I finally signed for Wednesday. I kept saying no, but, with the transfer deadline at hand, the Notts directors were urging me to sign. They insisted I'd be doing the club a favour, and, once Eric Houghton went off to watch a third-team game, I was left exposed and my resistance began to weaken.

"Okay," I said at last, "if you want me to go, I will." I looked at Mr Taylor and told him: "I hope you know what you're doing." Always the gentleman, Mr Taylor said he was sure he would have no cause to regret it – and promised neither would I.

All through the discussions, I was petrified because there was nobody to turn to for advice. I wanted to talk to Tommy Lawton, but we couldn't reach him. My mind was in turmoil, and it was only after I'd signed that I realised my girlfriend Barbara would be wondering where I was. I dashed straight off to see her and explain what had happened.

It was only when I picked up a news-

Jackie Sewell (right) seen scoring Wednesday's first goal in a 2-0 defeat of Burnley in February 1953, with Derek Dooley in attendance. This was, in fact, the last time Dooley played at Hillsborough. The following week, at Preston, he suffered the injury which ended his career.

Jackie Sewell (right) pictured with Norman Jackson at their Hillsborough digs.

paper the next morning that the full impact hit me. Nobody had mentioned the fee. I knew it was substantial, but, until that moment, had no idea it was £35,000 and a new British record. Honest, I was shattered. I was desperate to see Lawton because Tommy always had the right words for any situation.

Tommy and I had such a good understanding on the field, it wasn't true, and, off the pitch, he'd been like a father to me. I used to go up to his home on Friday nights, and we'd sit together listening to records. There was no television then, but in those days we didn't need much more than a warm fire and good company to be content – and talking football with Tommy for hours on end was marvellous entertainment. I often stayed overnight at Tommy's, and, after breakfast, we used to walk to the ground together. Now, I went down to Meadow Lane on my own, looking for Tommy. When I saw Tommy I almost burst into tears. As we walked round the pitch, I pointed to the newspaper and

blurted out: "I don't know what I've done. They didn't tell me the size of the fee! How can I justify that?"

He assured me I'd be okay. "Just play as you normally do, have faith in your abilities and keep doing your best, and everything will be fine," he said. He told me to put the £35,000 fee out of my mind, which was difficult.

Incidentally, I don't remember what my signing-on fee was, but it was no more than £20 – a far cry from what players get today with the help of agents and all that!

I don't remember much about my Wednesday debut, other than that it was at Liverpool on 17 March and I scored with a late header from a Dennis Woodhead cross. We lost 2-1, our seventh defeat in nine matches. There had been some doubt about my playing because, at the time, I had a lovely black eye as a result of a smack in the face in an earlier game which left me with a cracked eyebrow. But I wanted to get my first appearance over.

The Liverpool fans gave me some stick. Once, when I was retrieving the ball for a throw-in, some women at the front of the terrace shouted: "You're not worth 35 pennies!", which made me laugh and eased the tension.

The Wednesday supporters were always good to me, and I remember my five years at Hillsborough as a happy time. It was an eventful period and there were some good players at the club. I already knew Eddie Gannon, the Eire international, who had been at Meadow Lane. I was aware that Eddie and the other wing-half, Welsh international Doug Witcomb, were intelligent and perceptive players who would both suit my style.

We always seemed to have a forward line that was capable of playing football. Redfern Froggatt was already an experienced campaigner who knew the game; Dennis Woodhead was full of tricks off the field and made excellent use of a very good left foot on the park. Also, as I discovered, some of the youngsters were very talented. Alan Finney was a very good lad, eager to learn, and Albert Quixall, of course, was already the idol of the supporters.

Albert did very well with Wednesday and had a good career, but his failing was a tendency to take things for granted. I often felt that he might have achieved more if he had been a better listener and shown a greater willingness to learn and work at his game. We often had tactical talks in the snooker room at Hillsborough, but Albert was never one for analysis, and I think that's why he didn't win more caps. He was content to go out and play his own way, and never quite understood that you couldn't do that at top level.

Eric Taylor called that phase in the early 1950s the yo-yo years. In my time we went down twice, had at least one escape from the drop, and were on the way to our second promotion in five seasons when I left. We also reached the FA Cup semi-final in 1954, when we thought Tom Finney was Preston's only serious threat but found a hard man called Tommy Docherty was the major reason for our defeat. I still wince when I think of the pain he made me suffer that day! The injury I received in that match was at least partly responsible for ending my international career.

We were fighting relegation when I arrived, and, after the defeat at Liverpool on my debut, we won five and lost only two of the next nine games. It looked like being just enough to save us, but it wasn't and we went down despite winning our final game, against Everton, 6-0.

Chelsea escaped on goal-average because they beat Bolton 4-0 the same day, and, so I was told later by my England colleague Nat Lofthouse, their cause was helped by a lenient referee who allowed Chelsea's Bobby Smith to score at least one goal which all the Bolton team and the crowd felt should have been disallowed for illegal use of a forearm.

Our consolation was that we promptly won the Second Division championship in 1952. Derek Dooley came into the team in early October, and he and I claimed 69 goals between us. Derek was a grand lad, and if he was big and awkward, he got goals. It didn't matter how, he had the knack of scoring. Derek himself and the team prof-

ited from playing to his strengths. It was a terrible thing when his career ended the way it did in February 1953.

Of course, it also left us with problems filling Derek's No.9 shirt. There was a time when, following his accident, I was persuaded to switch to centre-forward. I remember having a run of six games in the position towards the end of the 1952-53 season.

To be honest, I wasn't keen and told Mr Taylor I would only take on the job if I could do it my way. I stressed the point that I was no Dooley. However, having watched Lawton at close hand, I felt I knew how I could create space and make scoring opportunities for myself. I scored six in six outings, and, although the only match we won in that spell was the last one of the season, against Sunderland, I got a hat-trick and a 4-0 victory left us safe after another battle against relegation.

My departure from Hillsborough was as sudden and unexpected as my arrival. One day in December 1955, Eric Taylor rang and asked me to go to the ground, and when I arrived he said someone had come to see me about a transfer. I think I'd missed only three of 19 games that season, and while Quixall and Froggatt were holding down the inside-forward positions at that moment, I wasn't thinking of wanting to leave. So I asked: "What's gone wrong?"

Mr Taylor said: "Nothing, and, as far as I'm concerned, I don't want you to go anywhere. But it's you they want. They aren't interested in taking Quixall or Froggatt." I suppose he meant Wednesday were ready to let one of us go, and, as I was the one they had received an offer for, there wasn't much choice. In any event, as Albert and Redfern were Sheffield lads, I couldn't imagine they would want to move.

"Anyway," Mr Taylor added, "the person who has come in is someone who knows you very well – Eric Houghton at Aston Villa." I suppose going to play for the man who had been my manager at Notts County clinched it. The situation was the exact reverse of that at Meadow Lane in 1951.

The transfer was completed quickly, and, ironically, I made my Villa debut at Bramall Lane. I think it pleased a few Wednesdayites that I scored in a 2-2 draw against Sheffield United. At the

end of that season, United went down while Wednesday went up. I got an FA Cup winners' medal with Villa in 1957, and must say I enjoyed my four years in Birmingham. Indeed, it was in my time there that Barbara and I were married. However, the Sheffield days will always prompt good memories, some of the best of my career.

The McAnearney Brothers – A Dialogue

Tom and Jim McAnearney are unique among the brothers who have played for Wednesday in that each also served the club as acting team-manager. They arrived from their native Dundee as teenagers in 1951. Wing-half Tom went on to make nearly 400 appearances and build a big reputation between 1952 and 1965, while circumstances limited inside-forward Jim to around 50 senior outings between 1954 and 1960. Another brother, Jack, also had a spell at the club. Tom recently returned to Sheffield, and here he and Jim, a long-time Wednesday shareholder, take time off to reminisce about Hillsborough days which were the highlight of careers in which they totted up over 770 Football League games.

JIM: Tom was 18 and I was 16 when we came to Sheffield in November 1951, and, at the outset we continued our apprenticeships as bricklayers, working at James Longden's. In fact, we didn't become full-time professionals until we'd completed our time and also done National Service in the RAF – Tom finally taking the step in 1956 and me in 1958. Tom became a semi-pro when he arrived, and I did the same when I was old enough, but we both felt the need to have a trade before concentrating on football.

TOM: We were sent to Wednesday by Tommy Riley, a scout who had previously found Jackie Mudie and Ewan Fenton, two players who gave outstanding service to Blackpool. In fact, I had replaced Fenton in the Dundee North End team. Jim was still with St Stephen's Under-18s at the time we left Scotland.

JIM: People used to say that, although two years younger than Tom, I was the one who did all the talking, but this was really because Tom kept his Scottish accent longer than me, and it became a

Jim McAnearney.

TOM: In those days when you were a youngster coming through the "A" team and reserves, the older players taught you such a lot. They always seemed glad to pass on their knowledge and experience because that is what had happened to them in earlier years. They didn't resent playing in the Reserves, and, unlike in modern times, older players didn't want to be on their way and ask for a move the minute they lost their first-team places and their careers seemed to be on the wane.

There were always several senior players in the Reserves, and youngsters benefited in a way that seldom happens now when second teams are often packed with kids. In fact, sometimes even older players in the opposition had a good word for a young player. I recall us winning a Central League match 7-0 – I think it was against Bury – and Eddie Quigley, the old Wednesday man, had been my direct opponent. As we came off, Eddie asked my name and said if I kept playing like that it wouldn't be long before I'd be a first-team regular.

JIM: I remember Tom and I made our first-team debut together in a County Cup semi-final with Sheffield United at Hillsborough in May 1952 when I was 17 and he was 19. We'd only been in Sheffield about six months, and it was a massive occasion for us. There was a big crowd, well over 20,000, and I'll always remember how the sound of the cheering spectators hit you as you ran down the tunnel on to the pitch. I don't recall much about the game except that Jimmy Hagan was in United's team, and I think he contributed to a United win.

TOM: The first season we were at the club, Wednesday won the Second Division championship, and I got my initial taste of senior football against Liverpool soon after promotion to Division One. To be honest, I've forgotten the details, and I always regarded my third senior outing, at Preston in February 1953, as my real first-team debut. On the other two occasions I'd been chosen because Eddie Gannon was injured, but this time everybody was fit and I was picked on merit. Unfortunately, that Preston game was the one in which Derek Dooley broke his leg.

I do remember how difficult it was playing at Hillsborough when I was

bit of a joke in the dressing room that I was his "translator"! Tom also had a problem understanding Sheffield talk, and once, when we were at Longden's, I remember him coming to me and saying "That bloke keeps calling me Sidney." It turned out what the chap was saying was not Sidney but that well-known local expression "sithee"!

TOM: In terms of football, we had no problems, and one team-mate who was especially good to me was Clarrie Jordan, the centre-forward. We first played with him in the Reserves when he was coming back from injury, and he boosted our confidence by saying he'd never had such good service. We helped him get some goals!

Clarrie was my idol, and a great example and inspiration. He was always

enthusiastic and positive. Although I didn't lack confidence on the field, I was never too sure of myself off it and always worried about getting another one-year contract. Clarrie told me: "Don't underestimate yourself, you'll have a great career."

JIM: I especially remember Duggie Witcomb, the Welsh international wing-half, as a tremendous influence. He was a real gentleman, the epitome of wisdom as he smoked his pipe in the dressing room. He used to say: "Jim, don't kick the ball, pass it." During a game, if I hit a hopeful ball and it rattled against somebody, he'd come up and say in his quiet but firm way: "Do that again and you'll get my boot up your rectum!" Duggie always got the best out of you.

replacing Eddie Gannon, because Eddie was the idol of the crowd. He used to run with the ball and go past two or three men. I had a different style, and, anyhow, I was just a youngster, while Eddie was an experienced Eire international.

JIM: Tom's reference to Dooley reminds me that, earlier in the season when Derek suffered the injury which finished his career, he played with me against Sheffield United reserves. If you remember, after Wednesday went up into Division One in 1952, Derek had a very thin time and went ages without scoring. He was taking a lot of stick and getting very frustrated, and I think Eric Taylor dropped Derek because he thought it would help him regain his confidence.

The irony was a crowd of about 9,000 turned up for the Central League game at Bramall Lane while the gate at Hillsborough for Wednesday's First Division match with Charlton was nearly 10,000 below the season's average. It must have hurt Eric Taylor to think dropping Dooley had inadvertently put money into Sheffield United's coffers!

I recall that at the Lane Derek barely had a kick until about five minutes from the end. We were 1-0 down at half-time, and when Brian Slater equalised we looked set for a draw. Then Len Edwards knocked two long balls through and Derek scored twice – his first goals of the season and typically the result of the kind of chase he revelled in.

Like Tom, I made my first-team debut against Liverpool, my initial taste of the First Division coming in February 1954 when I was 18. The only thing I remember is the thrill of being on the same pitch as the legendary Scottish winger Billy Liddell, who was playing for Liverpool.

I don't remember when Tom and I first played in the same Wednesday team in the Football League, but it must have been about two years before we were both in the side that lost 5-1 in an FA Cup second replay against Preston at Goodison Park in January 1957. I was just starting a short run as Redfern Froggatt's deputy, and have never forgotten that I was given a rather tough time by a certain Tommy Docherty. At least "the Doc" came to me at the end,

and, putting an arm round my shoulder, congratulated me. "You're doing all right, son," he said. Coming from him, that meant a lot.

In that game I witnessed one of the finest performances I ever saw. Tom Finney, normally a winger, was playing at centre-forward for Preston, and his all-round ability and the example he set were something very special. His individual talent inspired Preston's victory that day, yet he was always a team player.

TOM: When I think of Cup disappointments I always remember the semi-final defeat against Blackburn at Maine Road in 1960 when all the crucial refereeing decisions went against us. Another thing I recall about that game is, following a throw-in, Bryan Douglas sold me a dummy which I should never have bought. It led to one of Rovers' goals, and I still have nightmares thinking about that!

Of course, a happier memory came earlier in that same Cup run when I scored the winner from the penalty spot against Manchester United at Old Trafford. For years I've remembered it as a last-minute spot-kick, but I'm told the records show it as happening just past the hour. Anyway, I don't think there's any doubt that it was Maurice Setters who conceded the penalty for bringing down John Fantham – and I'm fairly sure United had almost scored just seconds earlier.

JIM: We both have more happy memories of Wednesday than unhappy ones, but a disappointment I'll never forget was just failing to get a medal when we won the Second Division title in 1959. You needed 14 games to qualify, and I managed 11. It knocked my duck in when Harry Catterick dropped me from a winning team, and I don't think I ever forgave him.

When Harry sold Albert Quixall to Manchester United in September 1958, I got back into the team, but, after we'd beaten Leyton 2-0 and won 4-1 at Scunthorpe, I lost my place. I did come back later for five games, but, although we won four of them, I somehow knew it was the end.

TOM: The season after promotion in 1959, Catterick signed Bobby Craig and sold our Jim to Plymouth, and I will always feel Jim was the victim of circumstances. Harry was still using a

squad he'd inherited from Eric Taylor, and he felt obliged to bring in at least one man of his own. So he bought Craig, who was the same type of player as Jim.

Craig was a good player, but he did not make the team tick in the way Harry tried to promote in the publicity he gave him. Bobby didn't appreciate that he might not have succeeded without all the very good players he had around him, and he resented the fact that some team-mates who were making a bigger contribution were earning more money.

Bobby couldn't recognise when you were trying to help him overcome weaknesses in his play. Once at Fulham he complained I wasn't giving him the ball. He tended to stand and wait for it to reach him, and I knew he'd get clattered from behind by Eddie Lowe. I said you've got to move, and then I'll give you the ball. But he kept moaning, so at last I gave him a pass. Lowe promptly whacked him. Bobby said I'd deliberately set him up. I hadn't. I was just confirming he didn't have the sense to run when the ball was played to him.

I'm biased, but I think Jim could have done as well as, and perhaps better than, Craig given the same opportunity and encouragement – and Jim wouldn't have caused as much trouble!

A lot of things in football are all about opinions, and I didn't always agree with Catterick. In Harry's second season, he took the captaincy off me because I wouldn't kick a Birmingham player called Johnny Gordon. It had got to half-time and Harry said: "I told you to kick him." I said: "Look, he's doing nothing, and, anyway, I know Gordon. If I kick him, he'll kick me back, and where does it end?"

At that moment, Tony Kay spoke: "Leave it with me, boss. I'll sort him out." Harry rewarded Tony with the captaincy, which didn't please me, but we didn't fall out. He was entitled to his opinion, and, after he'd taken Kay with him to Everton, I became the captain again.

Catterick was a good manager, but you could understand why Jim didn't like him because of the way he treated him. I had a similar problem in later years with Alan Brown, though the irony was that Brown used to hold me up to the younger players as an example

Tom McAnearney.

of a good professional – and I still don't know to this day why he turned against me.

Jim and I were both "thinking" footballers. We went to Lilleshall and got our coaching badges at an early age, and, while we played in an era when you didn't talk back to a manager, there were times when you tried to discuss ideas, especially if, as happened with Brown sometimes, his ideas seemed baffling. It was after one such discussion that he suddenly took a dislike to me.

Things were never the same after we exchanged words at half-time in a match against Aarhus in Denmark in September 1964. The Danes had given us a bit of a chasing in the first half, and I blamed our tactics. Brown didn't take kindly to the suggestion, and, for the second time in my Wednesday career, I lost the captaincy.

Brown had promised me a coaching job, but I didn't get that – and, despite having been at the club for 14½ years, I was denied a testimonial match. When I went to Peterborough in November 1965, I learned the deal had been on the cards for six months. It was just my luck

that Wednesday reached the FA Cup Final the same season I left.

I never spoke to Brown again after I left. He was a stubborn man. Once he had made his mind up about something, there was no changing his opinion – even if he knew he was wrong.

JIM: If we were disappointed at the circumstances which led to us leaving, we both had a tremendous affinity with Wednesday, and a great feeling for the club. We were both delighted to return to Hillsborough as coaches at different times, and, frankly, I still feel Wednesday made a mistake in not giving Tom the manager's job when Jack Marshall went in 1969, and they should have given it to me after Steve Burtenshaw's departure in 1975.

TOM: When I came back in 1968, I had managed Aldershot and thought the idea was for me to take over eventually from Jack Marshall, but, being one of those stubborn beggers who always says what he thinks, I didn't get the job. Perhaps I was too honest when all they wanted was someone to say "yes". I was in temporary charge when Jack resigned, and my mistake was in disagreeing with Eric Taylor about the way

the club should go. I only ever went to one board meeting, and obviously when I explained what needed to be done it was not what the directors wanted to hear.

When they brought in Danny Williams, I told him that unless certain things were done we were going to struggle, and I was right. We were relegated when we lost the last game of the season, against Manchester City. Everybody knows it was a match we should never have lost. In fact, it was one that was harder to lose than to win.

A few weeks later, just as I was preparing to go on holiday, Danny called me in and said: "The directors have sacked you." I was later with Bury and had another spell at Aldershot, and when I retired from football I became a postman.

JIM: I came back when Steve Burtenshaw invited me to return as reserve-team coach in 1973. Having been manager at Rotherham from 1968 and being in between jobs, naturally it was good to be at Hillsborough again. Steve was a good coach, as he had proved at QPR and Arsenal. He had some good ideas, but as a manager he wasn't very forceful. He was a nice bloke, which was probably one of his main problems, and I always think he would have been ideal working under someone else.

After Wednesday went down to the Third Division for the first time in 1975, and then made a poor start in the following season, Steve and Gerry Young, the first-team coach, were sacked, and I was put in temporary charge.

I have to admit I was disappointed when Len Ashurst got the job. I hadn't anything against Len, but I thought they would have brought in somebody who had done something as a manager. I felt I could have done the job as well as Len, but, when he was appointed, I was ready to give him all the support I could.

I did that, and, ironically, it was when he agreed that I deserved a pay rise and went to a board meeting to apparently press my case that the directors decided to sack me. He called me in the next morning and said: "I've got some bad news, Jim – I've got to let you go."

I always remember Ron Staniforth, the other coach, turned up at my house to inquire what had happened. I told him, and, the following day, Ron went to see Len to ask why I'd been dismissed. He was told: "I've got some bad news for you as well – you're also sacked!"

That was the time when they made Ken Knighton a player-coach. Bert McGee and the board were cutting back, and they obviously thought it cheaper to pay Ken some extra and save on two wages, but it left them thin on coaching staff, because Tony Toms, whom Len had brought with him, was just a fitness man.

I was sorry to go, but always remained a Wednesday man at heart, and, indeed, I am a shareholder and still see them regularly. After leaving Hillsborough, I stayed in football for some years, which included a spell at Leeds, but it now seems a long time since I gave up the game and turned to selling machine tools for a living.

I have a lot of good memories, and so has Tom, and, since he retired from his job with the post office at Aldershot and retired to Oughtibridge, we've had plenty of time to share a game of golf and reminisce about the good old days!

Brian Ryalls

Brian Ryalls is remembered as an Owls' goalkeeper who was unexpectedly thrust into the limelight in September 1953 when he made his Football League debut in a Sheffield derby match at Bramall Lane at the age of 21. He was subsequently limited to 45 senior appearances for Wednesday before being released in 1958, but they included a number of other notable games. Now living in retirement in South Yorkshire, he recalls those Hillsborough years as a golden phase in his football career.

I joined Wednesday in January 1953 as a part-time professional at £3 a week, a wage which was the same in both winter and summer. It all came about after they had spotted me playing with Grimethorpe Athletic in the old Sheffield Association League. I was offered a trial and played in a Yorkshire League match against Retford Town. I think it was also Peter Swan's first game. I know the backs were Terry Whitham, who later played four times in the first team, and Terry Hartley; and I believe either Jim or Tom McAnearney, or probably both, played that day.

At the time I was 20 years old and working underground at Grimethorpe Colliery, where I had been employed from leaving school. Incidentally, it wasn't until I first went to the pit that I started playing in goal. I got the role in a Sunday team with some of my workmates. Before that I'd been a left-back. Mind you, I fancy I must always have had a hankering to be a goalkeeper because my top boyhood hero was never anyone else but the England man, big Frank Swift. I once saw Frank play for Manchester City at Barnsley, and, in my book, nobody ever compared with him.

I did have a spell as an amateur with Wolves, but they released me when a bout of illness put me out of action. Anyhow, I was happy in the pit team until Wednesday came along and I found myself playing in the Hatchard League and the Yorkshire League. The fourth team was run by two famous pre-war full-backs, Ted Catlin and Joe Nibloe, while Johnny Logan was in charge of the Yorkshire League side.

My memories of the third and fourth teams in my years at Hillsborough include seeing people like Don

Megson and Tony Kay arrive and start to make progress. I recall Megson playing at centre-half, but he came as a left-winger and it was only after he had played just about everywhere in the team that he became a left-back. In fact, I don't think he settled into that position until after I had left the club.

When I made my Football League debut, I had only made half-a-dozen appearances in the Reserves. I always remember that, as I left the pit one Friday in September 1953, I was only thinking about the Central League derby with Sheffield United on the following afternoon. That in itself promised to be something of a challenge.

However, when I got home there was a telegram from Eric Taylor awaiting me. When I read the instructions – "Report to the Athol Hotel at lunchtime on Saturday" – I knew I was about to meet United, not in the Reserves at Hillsborough but in the First Division at Bramall Lane!

At the time, Dave McIntosh, Wednesday's regular goalkeeper, was out with a broken arm, and I came into the side after "Lofty" Capewell had worn the green jersey in four games.

I don't recall too much about that derby match other than that there was a crowd of over 45,000, we lost 2-0, and another of my boyhood heroes, Jimmy Hagan, was in the United team. I know Hagan had a great afternoon. He scored one goal and made the other for Derek Hawksworth.

I also remember once, just as I was about to go for a ball from a corner-kick, Alf Ringstead chose that very moment to stand on my foot. It meant I couldn't move, and Alf knew exactly what he was doing against an inexperienced goalkeeper. I probably reminded him about that incident some years later when he and I played together at Frickley, and by that time I had no doubt learned a few tricks myself! Anyway, Alf was such a nice chap, I have long since forgiven him for taking advantage of a young newcomer.

I must have settled into the Wednesday team fairly well, because I stayed in for 28 games. I was still in the side the following January when we went back to Bramall Lane and, in the rain, avenged that League defeat by beating United 3-1 in a famous FA Cup third-round replay. It was the first time

Wednesday had beaten United at the Lane since 1933, and the victory was all the sweeter because nobody believed we had a remote chance of succeeding.

We even did it despite having "Mick" Kenny sent off, and we also came from behind. In fact, I stopped a penalty, though, to be fair, Bill Toner shot the ball straight at me. The feature of the match for me was a cracking goal from 35 yards by George Davies. I think it was the only time I ever saw George kick the ball straight!

Ten days later, we beat United again, this time in the return League fixture at Hillsborough. Jack Shaw scored two and Jackie Sewell got the other in a 3-2 win.

It will be of interest to note that, in November 1953, I was in the first Wednesday team to play under floodlights in England when we went to play at the Baseball Ground, Derby.

Another highlight of that first season was a match at Bloomfield Road in October. Nobody expected us to

achieve much because Blackpool were the FA Cup holders and had an outstanding team with a forward line featuring Stanley Matthews, Stan Mortensen, Ernie Taylor, Allan Brown and Bill Perry.

I'll never forget a farmer talking to us in our hotel before the game and saying if we won he would give every Wednesday player a chicken for Christmas.

He was as good as his word, but I think we surprised him and a few other people. The score was 2-1 in our favour, and it was one of those days when everything came off for me. I got to the ball even on occasions when I was going the wrong way. We never looked back after Dennis Woodhead scored in the first minute, and Alan Finney had added a second before Mortensen managed to put one past me just after half-time.

Unfortunately, the fates weren't always so friendly. We went to Manchester United on Christmas Day and Tommy Taylor put three past me and we lost 5-2. But my luck really ran out in February, for, making a low save at West Brom, I clattered into a goalpost and damaged my shoulder. The injury didn't just end my run – it started a long phase in which I think I managed only four senior games over the next three and a half years.

By the time I was fit again, lads like Alan Hinchcliffe and Len Williams were pressing for a chance to become deputy to McIntosh, and I remember there was a period when I would be in the third team one week, play in the first team the next, and then drop back to the Yorkshire League.

Ironically, and strange as it might sound, my progress was also hampered by the decision to become a full-time professional. This was because, although I was now 22 or 23, giving up the job in the pit meant I was no longer exempt from National Service. I accepted full-time terms very conscious of the fact that I would soon get my call-up papers and have to join the army. It was the way things were in those days, and you took these things in your stride.

I served my time at Ripon and didn't get away very often to play for Wednesday. In fact, I don't recall playing much football while a National Service

Brian Ryalls.

soldier. But I did play a lot of basketball, and our lads were good enough to win the British Army championship!

It was September 1957 before I got back into the Wednesday first team for a short run. I came in for Charlie Pllu and had five games. Then I was recalled again in late January and played in ten matches, the most memorable of which was, of course, the delayed FA Cup fifth-round tie at Old Trafford in February 1958 when Manchester United played their first game after the Munich air disaster.

Naturally, it was a very emotional occasion, and I don't think anybody expected Wednesday to do more than play a supporting role that night. There certainly weren't many in the 60,000 crowd who wanted anything but a Manchester victory.

Unfortunately, it was just a month later that I made my final senior appearance for Wednesday. The match was at Birmingham. I remember it as a day of sleet and snow which made the ball like a lump of soap, and a lad called Bryan Orritt scored the only goal of the game. In the following week Wednesday went out and signed Ron Springett from QPR. The rest, as they say, is history.

I was only on a yearly contract, and it wasn't renewed at the end of the 1957-58 season. Of course, Wednesday were relegated that year, and this was when Eric Taylor finally gave up the manager's job and the club subsequently brought in Harry Catterick. It was the end of an era for Wednesday as well as me.

I wasn't expecting to be released, but soon got fixed up with Frickley Colliery, and the deal included a job at the pit top. Later I played with Scarborough and Retford, and I finished up alongside some of my old pals in the Grimethorpe Ex-Servicemen's team, playing on a permit. In the meantime, I had a spell working at Upton Colliery and spent a few months in insurance. Then I had jobs with the NCB right up to my enforced retirement in January 1990 when I was made redundant. At the end I was running the offices at South Elmsall.

I have only been back to Hillsborough once since I left, and that was as long ago as October 1962 when I saw the famous match with Santos. To be

honest, I support Barnsley these days, and we have a season ticket at Oakwell. But I always look for Wednesday's result, and, whenever I think of my time at Hillsborough, it evokes a million happy memories of five years which left me without a single regret.

Keith Ellis

Keith Ellis was a 6ft 2in centre-forward who scored 60 goals for Wednesday in 118 games. Although he made his League debut in March 1955 and remained with the Owls until March 1964, all but 16 of his goals came in a spell of 90 appearances between October 1959 and January 1962. In his last two years he was limited to a handful of senior outings when a dispute with manager Vic Buckingham soured what had been a happy time at Hillsborough.

When I was a boy growing up in Handsworth, I don't think I had any ambition to become a professional footballer. I was keen on all ball games, and enjoyed my football. But I did well at most sports, and, in fact, it was rugby and not soccer at which I represented the city while at school. I discovered the oval-ball game, which was then quite a novelty, after moving from Whitby Road to the Central Technical School. Yet at that stage no one sport dominated my life, and, by the end of my schooldays, I was into a wide range of other pastimes, including mountain climbing and cycling.

Football was just one of a variety of interests, and, although I did play with a number of amateur clubs in that period, it was never particularly serious. There were more important things to consider, not least that, having started work at Edgar Allen's, my priority was concentrating on studies that would one day see me qualify as an engineering draughtsman.

The link-up with Wednesday came up almost by accident. Although I didn't play for any of the works' teams, I did participate in the firm's interdepartmental football tournament, and that's when a scout saw me and invited me to Hillsborough for evening training and a trial. I ended up signing amateur forms and playing in the "B" and "A" teams.

I remember how, every Tuesday and Thursday, I used to finish work and cycle from Vulcan Road to Hillsborough, enjoy the training session, then cycle from the ground all the way home to Handsworth. I was a very fit young man then!

I eventually graduated into Wednesday's Central League side, and then, at the age of 19, was given a run of five games in the first team towards the end of the 1954-55 season in which the club was fighting against relegation.

When I made my senior debut, against Preston at Hillsborough in late March, I remember being given a hard time by the opposing centre-half, Joe Marston. He was a big, tough Australian, and there was one painful moment when he hit me so hard I was flattened and left in a daze. It was very much a case of "Welcome to the big time, young 'un!"

I think it was soon after that game when I signed part-time professional forms, mainly because the club was keen to secure me. My father said there was no way I was giving up my job at Edgar Allen's to be a full-time footballer until I had qualified as a draughtsman – and that didn't happen until I was 21.

Unfortunately, I had no sooner completed my apprenticeship at Edgar Allen's than I received my National Service papers, so, although I promptly became a full-time professional with Wednesday, I spent the next two years in the RAF. Not that I regretted it, really, for I played football at every level in the Forces, and the experience of playing with many promising lads from other big clubs did a lot to help my development.

The records show that, after those initial five games in the spring of 1955, I played only 19 times for Wednesday's first team in the next four seasons. Following relegation in 1955, Wednesday went out and signed Roy Shiner, a centre-forward from Huddersfield, and his success would have meant few chances for me even if I hadn't gone into the RAF.

Yet time was on my side and I soon felt I was making progress, especially when, between February and early December 1957, I scored 14 goals while deputising for Shiner in 16 matches. The highlight was my first senior hat-trick in the final game of 1956-57, when

Keith Ellis – the Wednesday striker in action against West Ham in 1961.

I was up against a top-class centre-half called Trevor Smith – and we beat Birmingham 3-0.

I finally got a long run in the team from around October 1959, which was early in the first year after we'd won the Second Division championship for the second time in four seasons. Harry Catterick had taken over and led us to promotion, and now we finished fifth in Division One and reached the FA Cup semi-final – and I justified Catterick's faith in me with 14 goals in 26 games.

The team that finished runners-up to Tottenham in the First Division and reached the FA Cup quarter-finals in 1960-61 was certainly the best one I ever played in. It had been taking shape since the days when Peter Swan and Tony Kay started coming through. With home-bred lads like John Fantham and Don Megson establishing themselves, others such as Ron Springett and Bobby Craig proving outstanding signings,

and Peter Johnson, Tom McAnearney, Derek Wilkinson and Alan Finney giving us quality and experience, we had a hell of a good side.

I got 19 goals in 37 matches that season. Fantham, Craig and me shared 54 goals between us, and I like to think that, as well as scoring, I took enough stick and laid off enough chances to help make a few of the goals that fell to John and Bobby.

I had a few battles that year, and none more so than one with Maurice Setters at Manchester United on that famous night in February 1961 when we stunned a 65,000 Old Trafford crowd by winning an FA Cup replay 7-2. I got a hat-trick, and I always remember Setters thumping me after my first goal. "That's what you're going to get from now on!" he said. In the end, it was worth the punishment, and I have to say that, despite his hostility then, in later years we always got on very well.

The hat-tricks I scored against Bir-

mingham and Manchester United were memorable for different reasons, but I suppose the goal I remember best was in a 3-1 home victory over Everton in January 1962. Earlier that season I scored in a marvellous 4-0 win at Goodison Park, but the goal in the home return was a bit special – all the more so as I was back in the side after missing seven games.

Someone played the ball through and, left with a one-on-one situation with Brian Labone, I took the Everton centre-half on, went round him and cracked it past goalkeeper Dunlop. I was never the most delicate footballer, but I was proud of the style I showed on that occasion!

Ironically, the beginning of the end of my Wednesday career can almost certainly be traced to a specific conversation I had with Vic Buckingham at around this time. Vic succeeded Catterick as manager in 1961, and the incident I am referring to probably occurred in 1962. It took place in a car when we were travelling to training at the Sheffield University ground, being used because of the bad weather.

Vic was always a bit theatrical, and, of course, having been coach to Pegasus, the combined universities side, he had mixed with the upper crust. Frankly, there were times when I thought him a bit of a prat, but I accepted him for what he was until, during this car journey, he pronounced that all professional footballers were thick.

I took exception to the remark, and, after telling him he must be joking, made the point that I couldn't have gained my HNC qualifications in mechanical engineering without being intelligent. I resented being called "thick" and told him straight. No doubt he resented a mere pro footballer having a crack at him!

From that day, Vic never gave me a chance. As someone has pointed out, between February 1962 and March 1964, when I accepted a move to Scunthorpe, I played only 11 times in the first team. In fact, in my last 23 months I made only four appearances. I always remember Vic saying he would rather use goalkeeper Ron Springett at centre-forward.

So it was suddenly all downhill, which was a pity because it brought a sour conclusion to a period in my life which had given me a lot of pride and pleasure until the manager spoiled it. It was probably ironic that Vic's attitude towards me prompted him to look for another centre-forward, and, of course, he had the good fortune to find David Layne. Even then, he denied me the chance to join Southampton and Chelsea, and I was very frustrated.

Yet, if my Wednesday years ended in disappointment, I shall always have mostly happy memories of Hillsborough. I am a Wednesday shareholder, and so are my sons, and, if living in Harrogate and working in corporate entertaining is a situation which limits my visits to the old ground in modern times, you can be sure I still follow the club's fortunes very closely.

Don McEvoy

Don McEvoy, captain of Wednesday's 1955-56 Second Division championship team, was a centre-half who arrived from Huddersfield Town for a £15,000 fee in December 1954 and made 112 League and Cup appearances for the Owls before moving to Lincoln in January 1959. He ended his playing days at Barrow, where he also embarked on a management career which was to take him to Grimsby and Southport and back to Barrow. After quitting football in 1972 Don and his wife Doreen ran the Crown Hotel at Brighouse for many years. Although now retired, he keeps in touch with football through regular coaching sessions and broadcasting with a local radio station.

Don McEvoy.

The story behind my move to Wednesday is quite funny, really, because it came about after the club doctor at Huddersfield decided my playing days were over when, in fact, I was destined to figure in at least another 200 games with three clubs over the next seven years.

I had made over 150 first-team appearances for Huddersfield since becoming a professional in 1947. Most of those games were in the old First Division, and I was captain for four years. We had a very good team, and, though relegated in 1952, we promptly won promotion the following year, and, in my last full season, we actually finished third in the top grade, six points behind Wolves, the League champions.

So I was happy, enjoying my football, and, at the start of the 1954-55 season, certainly didn't think my days at Leeds Road were numbered.

Ironically, the injury which changed the course of events occurred when I was playing against Wednesday at Hillsborough in early September. We lost 4-1 and I suffered a groin strain. It was something I'd not experienced before, but while it gave me a bit of trouble, to suggest I was finished was stupid. Of course, I didn't know this had been said until some years later when Andy Beattie, the manager, told me that was the reason they decided to consider offers.

I could have gone to Blackpool, Birmingham or either of the Sheffield clubs, but didn't hesitate to choose Wednesday – a decision I never had cause to regret because my four years at Hillsborough were among the most satisfying and significant of my playing career.

Because I'm a Huddersfield boy, people tend to think my best years were those I spent at my home-town club, but my most rewarding days were with Wednesday, largely because Eric Taylor, in giving me a lot more responsibility than many captains get, gave me an insight into aspects of football I had not previously been aware of.

It was also in Sheffield that I acquired

PLAYING FOR WEDNESDAY 1933-1998

Don McEvoy (right) and the Wednesday lads celebrate their Second Division championship triumph of 1956. Eric Taylor pours champagne, and others in the picture include Froggatt, Curtis, McIntosh, Quixall, Tom McAnearney and Finney. Journalists in the background are Monty Marston and Ross Jenkinson, both of the *Sheffield Telegraph*.

coaching qualifications at a time when this was not as fashionable as it later became, and, after Mr Taylor put me in touch with Ernest Kangley, secretary of the local FA, I found I had a profitable sideline which actually earned me more than the £20 a week I was getting at the end of my playing days. Even when I moved on to Lincoln, the coaching I did for the local education authority meant I had a much better standard of living than many footballers in that era of the maximum wage.

Wednesday were in deep trouble when I arrived at the club in December 1954. They were already firm favourites for relegation, and ended up 11 points adrift of the safety mark. I think they had conceded 26 goals in the seven games immediately before I came. We drew 2-2 against the First Division leaders Wolves on my debut, but it was another three months before I collected a win bonus, and we won only once in my first 15 games!

Our consolation was in winning the Second Division championship at the first attempt in the following season. However, while everything turned out well in the end, I remember that campaign had a frustrating start for me

because I missed the first nine games with a knee injury. I've never forgotten the incident that caused it because, over 40 years later, I'm still having problems with the same left knee – and it can all be traced to a clash with reserve centre-forward Keith Ellis.

We were having a practice match down at Owlerton Stadium a few days before the start of the season. To be honest, I never liked those games against your own players because there's always someone who thinks it clever to clatter an established first-teamer.

In this case it was Ellis. At the time the lad had only about five senior outings to his name, but the Press had dubbed him "the new Dooley", and now he was feeling peeved because Wednesday had gone out and signed Roy Shiner from my old club, Huddersfield, to spearhead the promotion campaign. Ellis felt he had something to prove to someone.

I'd said to him before the game, "Don't do anything daft, it's only a practice match," but we hadn't been playing more than three or four minutes when he whacked me from behind and flattened me. I knew straight away my knee had gone, and my mood was-

n't improved when I spotted the trainers, Sam Powell and Johnny Logan, smiling as I limped off.

I told Ellis: "You're a daft bugger. You've just put me out for the start of the season. If you ever do anything like that again, I'll be the first man to smack you on the nose!" Anyway, at least Ellis didn't get a look-in that season. My pal Shiner played every game and scored 33 goals.

It was the end of September before I played again, and, in the meantime, I found myself exercising my knee on a bike in a treatment room and staring at a large fixture list on the wall. One day, just to amuse myself, I started marking the list and forecasting the results I thought we'd get for the rest of the season. After I returned to the team, I forgot about it, but, soon after we'd clinched the Second Division title, Eric Taylor called me to his office. "Here," he said, "I've been studying your predictions, and you only got one wrong!"

I had a very good working relationship with the manager, and, virtually from the outset, he wanted me to look after dressing room morale and discipline, which was a role I enjoyed.

Taylor had never been a professional

footballer, and he was at a disadvantage in not being able to come into the dressing room at half-time and give the players a verbal lacing. Of course, he left most footballer matters to Jack Marshall, the coach, but Jack was also not the type to throw his weight about. Jack was a likeable, friendly guy who knew the game but could never play the hard man.

I remember telling Mr Taylor quite forcibly about the Ellis incident. He was not surprised. I had got into the habit of knocking on his door and walking into his office to insist we got a few things sorted out. He liked people to say what they meant.

When I arrived there was a lot of silly bickering in the dressing room. It wasn't good for team spirit, and I felt it my job to improve things. I even bought a couple of pairs of boxing gloves, and when certain players started falling out, I told them to put the gloves on and sort it out once and for all while I refereed. I also offered to put the gloves on myself and take on anyone who troubled the manager with dressing room matters which we could sort out among ourselves.

We started having a regular weekly social evening which was not intended as a drinking session but an opportunity for everyone to relax together and get things off their chest as well as discussing tactics. We had golf outings and visited local clubs and hospitals, and things like that. Everybody didn't always readily go along with these activities, but having those boxing gloves on hand did wonders for discipline and team-spirit. Things didn't always run smoothly, but the atmosphere improved.

The incident that prompted Taylor to make me responsible for all dressing room matters probably sounds humorous in retrospect, but it wasn't funny at the time. It stemmed from some criticism the whole team was getting from the manager during a midweek discussion, and I grew increasingly annoyed because the real culprits were the forwards. In my view they weren't doing their job, and the defenders were being unfairly punished.

I remember suddenly picking up Albert Quixall and smacking him one. "That's the problem!" I snapped. Eric Taylor looked at me as if he couldn't believe what I'd done, and he slipped out of the door rather quickly. He didn't know how to sort it out, but I did. Jack Marshall told me later: "I don't know how you got away with that, Don, but keep doing it because it's what's needed."

I didn't always agree with Taylor. He was the boss and his word was final, but he always listened, and I think he appreciated having someone around who didn't say yes when the easy thing to do was say no.

I recall once telling the manager I thought Albert Quixall ought to be playing inside-left or be sold because, at inside-right, he was ruining Alan Finney, his wing partner. Of course, Taylor didn't entirely agree, and said Finney and Quixall always played together. I argued that Finney was doing all the work for Quixall to the detriment of his own game.

I don't know how long after this conversation it was, but I always remember being up at Hillsborough Golf Club one day when I got a call to go and see Mr Taylor immediately. I had entirely forgotten what I said about Quixall being sold, and his name never crossed my mind when I parked the car at the ground.

There had been some talk about Manchester United being interested in me, but, at the time, I was out of the team, and, one way or another, I suppose a move to Old Trafford was in reality a remote possibility. However, now as I walked towards the players entrance, who should I see but Matt Busby! I thought: "Crickey, my big moment has arrived. Matt's come for me!" I was even more excited when, after being ushered into Eric Taylor's office, the manager said: "Don, you've got your wish."

Unfortunately, his next words shattered my dreams: "We've just sold Quixall to Manchester United!".

Later, I had an opportunity to exchange a few pleasantries with Matt Busby and witnessed an intriguing exchange between him and Eric Taylor which is worth noting for posterity. At that moment, as I understood it, the fee for Quixall was £42,500. But Busby said to Taylor: "Eric, if it had been me, I wouldn't have sold him for less than £45,000." Quick as a flash, Eric replied: "Okay, Matt, in that case you can add £2,500 to the fee." And he did!

My last senior game for Wednesday had actually been against Chelsea in the February before Albert left in the following September, and I was destined to depart myself in January 1959 when I joined Lincoln.

Of course, I had known my days as a first-teamer were numbered as the end of that 1957-58 season saw us slipping towards relegation, for there was no doubt that Peter Swan was going to establish himself in the side and keep me out. My biggest disappointment that season was missing the FA Cup-tie at Old Trafford, Manchester United's first match after the Munich disaster, because I thought it was a game in which my experience would have been invaluable.

It was before the start of the 1958-59 campaign that I knew for certain that it wouldn't be long before I was on my way. One morning I got up and was having breakfast with my wife and children when Doreen said: "According to the papers, there's going to be a new manager at Wednesday."

"Oh," I said, "and who's it going to be?" When she replied "Harry Catterick", I told her: "Then you'd better start packing!"

When I was with Eric Taylor later that day and we were discussing the appointment, he said: "You don't seem too pleased." I told him he was dead right, and asked him to start looking for a good Second Division club for me – preferably one not too far away. I knew Catterick wouldn't want me around longer than absolutely necessary. He was, of course, an old Everton centre-forward, and, over the years, we had had some bitter battles on the field. Let's just say we didn't like each other very much.

It was Catterick who halted a five-a-side match a few months later to tell me Eric Taylor wanted to see me. Actually, he didn't use Eric's name. He said "Your manager wants to see you", making it plain he didn't consider himself my manager.

I was sorry to go, but Bill Anderson, the Lincoln manager, offered me decent terms and I accepted.

I think I've only been invited back to Hillsborough for a match once since I left, but we enjoyed our time there, and we were especially happy living at Grenoside. In fact, when I finally quit football, Doreen and myself did seriously consider settling in Sheffield. In the end, however, we decided to go back to our West Riding roots.

Jack Martin

When Jack Martin, a right-back who made 66 League and Cup appearances for the Owls between February 1955 and August 1960, came to Sheffield from Dundee in early 1954, he was following in the footsteps of his grandfather Bob Petrie, a wing-half who was not only a Wednesday favourite in the Olive Grove era but had helped the club to a famous FA Cup triumph 60 years earlier.

As a boy growing up in Dundee, I used to listen to my maternal grandfather, Bob Petrie, regaling me with stories of his time at Sheffield Wednesday in the Olive Grove era. He played for the club from 1894 to 1897 and was in the team that brought the FA Cup back to Yorkshire for the first time in 1896 when they beat Wolves at the Crystal Palace. I was certainly familiar with such giants as the famous winger Fred Spiksley, the legendary Tommy Crawshaw, and the 1896 skipper, Jack Earp, for my grandfather was always mentioning them.

Grandfather also had a spell in the Southern League with Southampton, and played for them in the 1900 FA Cup Final when they lost 4-0 to Bury. But it was always Wednesday he talked about the most. I can't honestly suggest he inspired me to want to play for Wednesday, but, had he lived to see it happen, I'm sure he would have been delighted when I followed in his footsteps.

Of course, he never played at Hillsborough, but it is an intriguing coincidence that we both made around 60 senior appearances in the famous blue-and-white stripes.

I came to Sheffield in February 1954 after being recommended to Wednesday by a scout called Tommy Riley. The club's chief scout, Les Bedford, went up to watch me playing with Dundee North End, and the upshot was the offer of professional terms.

When I arrived, I soon felt at home after going into digs with Tom and Jim McAnearney, who had both moved from Dundee about four years earlier. I

had played against Jim as a schoolboy, and Tom had once been with Dundee North End.

I was still only 19 when I made my Football League debut in February 1955 at Blackpool. I don't remember a great deal about the game other than that Stanley Matthews was playing, but I do recall that, at the time, Wednesday were struggling against relegation. They had gone 16 games without a win, and lost 11 of them. For the match at Blackpool, Eric Taylor, the manager, made about six changes. I came in for Tony Conwell at right-back, Barry Butler was switched from centre-half to centre-forward, and Norman Curtis, Don McEvoy, George Davies and Alan Finney were all recalled. Unfortunately, we suffered another defeat.

I had only played three times in the first team when I got an unexpected boost by being called into the Sheffield team that met an International XI in Derek Dooley's testimonial match in March 1955. I got my chance when Norman Curtis cried off at the last-minute with an injury, and it was quite something to be lining up on the same pitch as Matthews, Tommy Lawton, Jimmy Hagan and John Charles.

It was also a thrill to be participating in an historic occasion, for that was the first match played under floodlights at Hillsborough, and it was my first experience of playing in front of a 55,000 crowd.

When Wednesday were relegated at the end of that season, they parted company with a couple of full-backs in Mick Kenny and Tony Conwell, but, unfortunately for me, they recruited Ron Staniforth, and with an England back in my position, I knew my chances were going to be limited. I only managed two games in 1955-56 when the Second Division championship was won.

But I had decent spells in making about 40 appearances between 1956 and 1959. My misfortune was that, when I looked to be doing well midway through the 1958-59 season when we were again going for the Second Division title, I suffered damaged tendons in an ankle in a match against Bristol City – and it was an injury from which I never really recovered.

It all happened so simply, and nobody else was involved. I just went over on the right ankle with which I'd

had a spot of trouble before. I spent the next five weeks in Sheffield Royal Infirmary and came home full of optimism, but, in fact, the ankle was never the same again.

We were back in the First Division in 1959-60, but Peter Johnson, who had arrived at Christmas 1957, established himself as the regular right-back, and that meant I was limited to appearances as his deputy in my last three seasons at Hillsborough.

One occasion when I remember Peter was out injured and I played was when we met Sheffield United in an FA Cup sixth-round tie at Bramall Lane in 1960. United had all the play and we had all the luck, and two goals from Derek Wilkinson saw us through to the semi-final.

It was in the following August that I made my last appearance in Wednesday's first team, but I remained at Hillsborough for another two' years before I left to have a brief spell at Rochdale.

When I packed up playing, my wife Jean and I came back to Sheffield, and, for the next 28 years until I took early retirement about five years ago, I worked for British Steel, first at Stocksbridge and then at Tinsley Park.

I haven't been to watch a match at Hillsborough for many years, but I still take an interest in how Wednesday are doing, and, of course, I have lots of happy memories of friends and colleagues from my time with a club which, as Grandfather Petrie used to say, will always be special.

Peter Johnson

Peter Johnson was a full-back who could also play at centre-forward, and he even figured as an emergency goalkeeper for the Owls when Ron Springett was injured at Tottenham in 1962. Wednesday signed him from Rotherham United at the second attempt on Christmas Eve 1957 in a cash and exchange deal that took Albert Broadbent to Millmoor. Johnson, known to his Hillsborough team-mates as "Charlie", went on to make 207 League and Cup appearances and played under four managers before, after a year kept in the wilderness following a bust-up with Alan Brown, he moved to Peterborough in July 1965.

WEDNESDAY EVERY DAY OF THE WEEK

Wednesday first tried to sign me in November 1954 when I had been playing in Rotherham's Second Division team for barely a year and boasted under 40 League appearances. If I had said "yes" then, the fee, which was £20,000, would have made me the most expensive full-back in English football. But I refused point blank to even think of leaving Millmoor. I was playing at left-back at the time, and doing well. In fact, the entire Rotherham team was doing very nicely, for that 1954-55 campaign turned out to be the season when, had we not missed promotion on goal-average, we would have passed Wednesday on their way down from the old First Division!

Anyway, in November 1954, I was one of four Rotherham lads playing for the Sheffield & Hallamshire FA in an inter-city game with Glasgow, and it was on the train journey back from Scotland that Andy Smailes, our manager, told me about Wednesday's offer. He said Rotherham needed to sell somebody and was rather taken aback when I replied that it wasn't going to be me because I'd rather hang up my boots than move!

My decision was based on loyalty. All I had ever wanted was to play for Rotherham, and I was happy to have fulfilled that ambition. As a kid, I'd played in many a makeshift kickabout with Danny Williams, a great Millmoor hero, and his collier pals. They used to stop and join us in a game of football on the grass verges of Herringthorpe, and the biggest thrill of my life was when I finally graduated into the same Rotherham team as Danny.

I'd started as a £3-a-week part-timer and been happy to give up a better-paid job as a baker-confectioner to turn full-time professional for an £11 wage, and, frankly, I didn't want to go anywhere. Three years later, when I did finally agree to leave, I changed my mind only because the decision was forced on me.

I remember it was Christmas Eve 1957, and, with a game at Leyton the next day, we were doing some light training on the Millmoor pitch. Then Albert Wilson, the trainer, shouted that I was wanted in the office. When Andy Smailes announced Wednesday were back in for me and it was clear he was keen on the deal, I told him he could take it. I'd go this time. Even so, he wasn't very complimentary when I insisted on popping home to Wellgate to talk to my wife, Jean, before going with him to Sheffield.

I recall that, after signing at Hillsborough, I was puzzled when Eric Taylor, Wednesday's secretary-manager, wanted to know how far I could kick the ball. "Can you kick it from the penalty box to the halfway line?" he asked. I said yes, and he replied: "Good, that's what I like."

It was the first hint that Wednesday's tactics did not include short passing or playing football in your own half of the field, but, if I didn't entirely approve of the system they used, the situation was to take a turn for the better after Harry Catterick's arrival at the start of the following season.

Anyway, Christmas Day 1957 brought my Wednesday debut at right-back in a home match with Preston which finished with a 4-4 scoreline, and I faced the legendary Tom Finney. I marked the occasion by accidentally catching Tom on the bridge of his nose with my boot – and it must have hurt! It happened when I was attempting to hook the ball away and Tom got his head there first. I tried to apologise, but he said: "Forget it, son, what matters to me is the ball finished in the net!"

We played the return at Preston on Boxing Day, and I think I learned more from facing Finney in those two matches than in all the rest of my time with Wednesday. Not that I didn't learn a lot from every experience in nearly eight years at the club, playing alongside some outstanding team-mates, under four managers with differing personalities and philosophies, and being involved in reaching an FA Cup semi-final one year then finishing runners-up in the old First Division the next.

I always felt we were beaten by Blackburn in the 1960 semi-final because a clear off-side decision wasn't given against their centre-forward, Derek Dougan; and, of course, the 58 points we finished with in 1960-61 would have been enough to win the championship in just about any other year. Unfortunately, Tottenham chose that season to get 66, which was then a new record.

I hadn't been with Wednesday long when I was asked to switch to centre-forward. Around 40 of my 157 games for Rotherham had been up front, and I'd scored 23 goals, so I was happy to step in for Roy Shiner. I might have had a longer run in Wednesday's attack but for ending up with my ankle in pot.

The first time I wore the No.9 shirt was in the famous FA Cup-tie against Manchester United in February 1958, when we lost 3-0; and the second was a few days later when we drew 2-2 in a First Division fixture at Blackpool, where I scored our goals, but, unfortunately, damaged my ankle in a clash with Roy Gratrix when going for my hat-trick. If I'd reached the ball first I would have scored, but Gratrix just beat me to it, and the follow through brought the injury which sidelined me for six weeks.

I played only two more first-team matches that season, and, in the summer, Harry Catterick took over. In the event, I was limited to seven games in the year we won the Second Division championship, but, in our first season back in the top-grade, I established myself as first choice at right-back.

I enjoyed my time under Catterick, and, indeed, later under Vic Buckingham. In Harry's three years he developed a very good team in which there was a tremendous spirit and a great understanding. Some of the younger lads were just starting to peak, and it was a pleasure to be part of a phase we were all sorry to see come to an end when Harry moved to Everton.

I can honestly say I had a wonderful career with Wednesday until Alan Brown arrived in 1964. Unfortunately, almost from the outset Brown and me didn't hit it off. I never played again in the First Division after he came. To put it politely, we "had a bit of a do" on a pre-season tour of Germany, and things were never the same after that.

I have always stood by what I believe, and never been afraid to defend what I feel is right. I can't help it. On this occasion I spoke out and told Alan Brown he was wrong. You weren't expected to disagree with him. He turned round and said he could never be wrong. What I said then was 100 per cent true – he wasn't God. And I didn't apologise for saying it, I couldn't.

When we came home, I told the wife what had happened and said I didn't expect ever to kick another ball in the first team, and I was right, though Brown did create some sort of record when he made me 12th man for 13 games on the trot – and, with no substitutes then, it meant watching every match from the bench with no chance of getting on.

We used to do shadow training then, which involved the team playing and practising moves without any physical opposition except a goalkeeper. Brown later introduced a single defender to face the team, and I was his choice for this task. It was a bit of a challenge facing all of them at once, but, as I could read a game pretty well and I was quick, nine times out of ten I got the crucial block or tackle in. I thought I did very well, but, for some reason, my success seemed to make the manager's face go redder than red. Perhaps I wasn't being punished in the way he had wanted!

I was sorry my time at Hillsborough ended the way it did, because I had a great feeling for the club, and, for all but the last year, never regretted having switched from Rotherham to Sheffield. It was just a pity that, at the finish, I had no choice but to move on. At least I took a lot of good memories with me.

Author's Footnote: Jack Mansell, Wednesday's coach from 1962 to 1964, described Johnson as "a brave little player, always a great worker, a man who never stopped running." He added: "Peter's bravery was illustrated in a match at Spurs when he was limping with an obvious injury, and, when he mentioned being in pain, Vic Buckingham told him he was just a softie, and insisted he should play on. We knew how bad the injury was by the following Monday, for Peter was whipped into hospital to have his cartilage out!"

Duggie McMillan

Duggie McMillan, who has been in business at Wincobank Post Office for over 25 years, has a place in Wednesday's records as the promising inside-forward whose career was shattered at the age of 19, when, on a freezing December night in 1960, his first trip with the Owls' Football League side ended in tragedy as the homeward-bound team-bus crashed on the A1 and the young Scot, trapped under the vehicle, lost his right leg.

A month before the accident, at the end of November 1960, I had made my senior debut for Wednesday in a 3-0 defeat of Doncaster Rovers in a County Cup semi-final at Hillsborough, and now, at Christmas, I got the best possible present when I was named as one of seven forwards in the squad for the match at Arsenal on Boxing Day.

I had been with Wednesday for about 18 months, having arrived on trial in the spring of 1959, and it looked as if I was finally starting to knock on the door. When I first came, I'd suffered from shin splints in the early months, which meant that, after about 20 minutes of a match, I couldn't run. But manipulation of the shins in hospital solved the problem, and I went from strength to strength, getting into the Reserves and feeling I was making progress.

I was brought up in a village called Torphichen, about seven miles from Falkirk, and it was Wilf Sharp, the man who was right-half in Wednesday's 1935 FA Cup Final team, who sent me to Hillsborough for a trial. He saw me playing with a local juvenile side, Wallhouse Rose.

Duggie McMillan in action.

Duggie McMillan seen here taking the field with Derek Dooley ahead of the young Scot's testimonial match.

I came to Sheffield, played in the Yorkshire League team against Frickley Colliery, and afterwards Harry Catterick, Wednesday's manager, promptly offered me professional terms. Like an idiot, I asked for time to think it over. I can't imagine why I did that, because trying to be cautious only meant I did myself out of a month's salary!

Obviously, being a professional footballer was preferable to working as an apprentice joiner, and I never went back to that trade. It was good fun living in digs at Oughtibridge with Gerry Young, Peter Baker and a winger just signed from Airdrie called Billy McLean. I played in the "A" team and, once I got over my initial fitness problems, it was a good period. Incidentally, the Yorkshire League side at that time was in the hands of Sam Powell, who had been the first-team trainer until Harry Catterick brought in Tommy Eggleston as senior coach.

Considering how outstanding the Wednesday team was in 1960-61, it was something just to be on the fringe, and making the trip to Arsenal knowing I had a chance of playing was a thrill in itself. To be honest, I was excited just about being there, and travelling down on Christmas Day and staying overnight in a big hotel was an experience to savour. The coach was a new one being used by the club for the first time, and it was rated the height of luxury, with all mod cons, including tables, a drinks cabinet, a modern radio, etc.

I'd never been to London before, and was delighted when, on the morning of the game, Colin Parsons, the coach driver, took me and some of the other lads on a guided tour of some of the sights. I wouldn't say I felt as if I had finally "arrived", but it seemed like the next-best thing; and the future certainly appeared to offer a lot of promise. I knew my progress would please my family back home.

In the event, when we got to Highbury for the match, the pitch was very heavy, which prompted Catterick to make changes which didn't include me. If I remember right, Bobby Craig wasn't picked either – and I knew the gaffer rated Bobby very highly. Anyway, I was happy to get the 12th man duties

which, although they kept me busy and at everyone's beck and call, at least didn't prevent me watching the game from the dug-out. We drew 1-1, our goal coming from Keith Ellis, who had been recalled along with Derek Wilkinson and Don Megson.

I remember several players missed the homeward coach journey. Ron Springett, of course, lived in London, while Peter Johnson and Alan Finney went off with general manager Eric Taylor to catch a train from King's Cross to Doncaster, and Derek Wilkinson made his way to another station to get to Manchester.

As I recall it, the ride up the A1 for the rest of us went very smoothly until we reached a place, the name of which, as you can imagine, I shall never forget – Alconbury Corner.

Some of the lads had a game of cards at tables at the back of the bus, but, being on only £17 a week and unable to afford the stakes they were playing for, I was content to watch rather than participate. Anyway, I was still, as you might say, on 12th man duty.

Tommy McAnearney's memory is that when he and Peter Swan decided to take a break from the card game, have a drink and listen to some music, Tommy went up the bus to put Radio Luxembourg on. He couldn't locate it, so I followed him to the front and told him to come out of the way while I had a go at getting it.

I had my right leg on the step in the door well as I reached for the dial on the radio, and I remember I had only been there a few minutes when I glanced out of the window into the darkness and called to the driver as we went round Alconbury Corner: "Colin, we're going off the road!"

The next thing I knew was waking in terrible pain with my leg trapped in the steps and the coach on its side in a ditch. It all happened so quickly. I recall the pain and John Quinn climbing under the coach to give me his rosary beads. People have since mentioned that John sang to me to keep my spirits up, but, while I have no memory of that, I do know he was a terrific source of strength at a time when I could barely take in the shock of realising that my leg was so badly cut it hung by a thread. When Dr Sear arrived from Huntingdon Hospital, he had to complete the amputation before I could be released.

The other main victims were Peter Swan, whose collar-bone was broken, and Tony Kay, who suffered concussion and lacerations to his head. Harry Catterick broke a couple of ribs. Incidentally, Tommy McAnearney remembers that, when he walked back down the bus just before the accident, he was going to resume his window seat, but Swannie said he'd move inside – and sitting where Peter had been probably saved Tommy from serious injury.

I was in hospital in Huntingdon for about five or six weeks, and the club arranged for Dave Morris, a young full-back who played with me in the "A" team, to keep me company. Then, when I returned to Sheffield, apart from facing another operation, there was the challenge of coming to terms with the reality that my football days were over and I had no choice but to look in another direction for a career.

Once I was fit enough to work again, I found a position in the club's offices

for a while. They said they were going to get me something better, but a time came when I began to think that if I didn't move I might get pushed anyway. So I talked to Eric Taylor, and the upshot was I took a job at Gunstone's Bakery, where Wednesday director "Dick" Gunstone was the boss. I was encouraged because I knew that when Derek Dooley had lost his leg in 1953, he had enjoyed a successful spell at Gunstone's.

I earned £10 a week and finished up in the garage office, but, unfortunately, after a while it became clear there was no scope for progress. I talked to Eric Taylor again, but he said they couldn't find me anything else, so I went off on my own. For about six months I worked in the offices at Firth Brown Tools, then I joined Ready Mixed Concrete, where I had a spell in the office and later became a sales representative.

There was a spell after that when I was out of work for about six months, but then I decided to go to the bank manager – and that led to me getting a sub-Post Office. We didn't get the first we tried for, but were successful when we went for this one at Wincobank in Sheffield's East End, and we took over in November 1972. We have been there ever since.

I've known my wife, Madge, since before the accident, but, though we met in my playing days (it was at a dance at the old Locarno Ballroom), we didn't really start going out together regularly until later. We had started courting seriously by the time of my testimonial in October 1961 because I remember an amusing incident on the eve of that match.

The day before the game, I was told I was to travel to London with Eric Taylor to appear in *This Is Your Life* on which Derek Dooley was to be the surprise guest. The same evening I was supposed to be seeing Madge, because we had arranged to go to the railway station to meet my mother and aunt, who were coming to Sheffield for my testimonial.

Madge must have been very puzzled when she got a telephone call at her workplace from Eric England, the assistant secretary at Hillsborough. Eric said I couldn't keep my date, and mysteriously added that if Madge watched television (black and white in those days!)

that evening she would discover the reason. She couldn't be told any more: everyone was sworn to secrecy because nobody wanted Derek Dooley to know Eammon Andrews was poised to pounce with his famous red book!

My testimonial, by the way, attracted a 25,000 crowd despite the fact that it rained all through the day of the match, and the income was a very welcome nest egg for when Madge and I were married in 1963, although, of course, it never meant I would be protected from having to work for a living.

For a time after my playing days ended, I got involved in football again, as a coach with Hallam FC, and later, when Jim McAnearney had me working with the juniors at Rotherham United. It was very satisfying, but, in the end, I had to choose to concentrate on the Post Office business and, anyway, doing two jobs meant I had been spending less time with my two sons, John and Lee, than I wanted.

I still have regular contact with some of my old Hillsborough colleagues, notably John Quinn and the McAnearney brothers, Tommy and Jim, and we often play a bit of golf together. But I don't see much football now, though.

Of course, I follow Wednesday's fortunes with interest. Naturally, I sometimes look back and wonder what might have been but for that accident in 1960. Yet, all things considered, I am grateful to be able to say I have made something of my life and been happy – and that's been thanks to my family, and to friends who are old enough to remember when I was a promising teenage footballer.

John Hickton

John Hickton enjoyed his most successful years as a player with Middlesbrough, for whom he scored 185 goals in 482 games spanning 11 years, but the Chesterfield product had an eventful start to his career at Hillsborough, where he was on the Owls' books from 1959 to 1966. He bagged 21 goals in 56 first-team outings for Wednesday after being converted into a centre-forward.

It's amusing now to reflect that when I joined Wednesday after leaving Brimington School in 1959, I was the club's

John Hickton, a full-back who became a striker.

I was too young to have seen Derek play (his career ended when I was eight years old) but everyone recognised him as a legend at the club. We were all familiar with his scoring feats, and, when he took charge of Wednesday's Northern Intermediate League side, he proved a popular "boss" because he always had time for every lad in the squad. He was, quite frankly, a marvellous man.

I had always been a full-back or centre-half, but Derek decided I was a centre-forward, and I remember how delighted he was when I proved him right by scoring nine for the juniors in a 16-0 defeat of Stamford Town in an FA Youth Cup match played on the Hillsborough pitch in 1961, and promptly followed up with five more against Rotherham in the next game.

If Derek had had his way, I would never have played in any other position at any level, but, curiously, when I wasn't on duty with the juniors, I invariably reverted to defence in the Yorkshire and Central League teams.

However, though I made my Football League debut at right-back against Aston Villa in March 1964 when I was 19, all my first-team games thereafter were at centre-forward. In November 1964, with the club having problems in attack, I was given the No.9 shirt – and I wouldn't be surprised if it wasn't Dooley who had put the idea into the manager Alan Brown's head.

In that first spell up front in the first team, I justified Derek's faith by scoring ten goals in 26 League games, then, in the following season, I filled the same role in 23 of the first 27 games, and claimed 11 goals. I especially remember scoring with two headers against Everton early in 1965-66 because I was up against Brian Labone, the England centre-half; and then in the home game with Arsenal there was a hat-trick (two headers and a shot) which was the perfect Christmas present!

Unfortunately, around the beginning of February, I suddenly went out of favour and found myself back playing at centre-half in the Reserves.

This, of course, was the season when Wednesday reached the FA Cup Final. I had played in the third round success at Reading, but was left in the cold when my No.10 shirt passed to my great pal David Ford, who was now playing alongside John Fantham and Jim

very last groundstaff boy. I just got in at the end of a system which had been traditional in professional football for many years. The next intake of youngsters were called apprentices, and the reason the memory amuses me in retrospect is that while I was getting £3 12s (£3 60p) a week, the kids with a new job description earned £5 – and it was quite a time before I was put on equal terms!

However, all that really mattered then was having taken the first step towards fulfilling my boyhood ambition of being a professional footballer. I went on to have 20 years in the game, and I don't regret a minute of it because it was a wonderful life. We didn't make as much money as modern players do, but I can't imagine they enjoy the game as much as we did in my time.

I used to think that if I didn't make the grade in football, I'd go for accountancy because I was good at arithmetic. Happily, at school I was a good enough player to progress via Chesterfield Boys and Derbyshire Boys to trials with England, and, if I didn't get a cap, at least I was wanted by a number of big clubs, including Arsenal and Manchester United.

I chose Wednesday not just because they were a big club with an impressive set-up, but, as they were local, it meant I didn't have to leave home. Moreover, my father, a football fanatic, could maintain his habit of supporting me at whatever level I played.

I never had cause to regret starting at Hillsborough, for I made fairly rapid progress and found plenty of good influences.

The first of these was Derek Dooley.

McCalliog (he wore my old No.9 shirt following his move from Chelsea) in a new 4-3-3 system.

I was doing okay at the heart of the Central League team's defence, even scoring a few goals when going upfield for corner-kicks. So, when Vic Mobley, the regular centre-half, was injured in the semi-final triumph over Chelsea at Villa Park, I wasn't the only one who considered myself the obvious choice as his replacement. To this day I have never changed my belief that I was the man for the job.

However, just as it was soon apparent that Vic would not be fit for the Final, so it quickly became clear that Alan Brown had earmarked Sam Ellis as his deputy. Sam, who was then 19, had made four senior appearances at the time of Vic's injury, and he played in the remaining six League games of that season before making his FA Cup debut at Wembley.

I can't deny I was gutted at being passed over. Every footballer wants to play in a Wembley Final, and my only consolation was that, at 22, I was still young enough to believe there was time for me to get another chance. In the event, it didn't happen, and I often think back to 1966 and wonder about what might have been. I didn't hold it against Alan Brown, but, if he was the boss and entitled to make his own choice, I'll never forget my disappointment.

Of course, I was in the party of players who travelled to London for the Final, and, naturally, I was as heartbroken as anyone that Wednesday lost 3-2 to Everton on that May afternoon after leading 2-0. I really felt for all the lads – not least Gerry Young, whose mistake led to Everton's third goal. The irony was that Gerry had had a fantastic season in which he had never put a foot wrong, and the pity is that all the good things he did in his Wednesday career are often forgotten while his Wembley slip is still remembered whenever anyone mentions 1966.

It was wonderful to witness the way the people of Sheffield responded to the players when we returned home the next day, and, even though I hadn't figured in the Final, I was very proud to be a Wednesday man when I viewed the massive turnout of people from the Town Hall balcony.

As it happened, my days at Hillsborough were numbered. I didn't seek a move, but, in early September 1966, Alan Brown called me into his office and said Norwich and Middlesbrough wanted me. I might not have agreed with Brown's decision not to use me in the Cup Final, but I have to say that when he suggested I should choose Teesside rather than East Anglia, he did me a great favour.

He probably wanted me to join Middlesbrough as a favour to manager Stan Anderson, his old captain at Roker Park, but, in fact, it was the right choice for me, and I never had cause to regret moving to Ayresome Park. I went there as a centre-half but, as at Hillsborough, ended up a front man and managed 185 goals in some 480 games over the next ten years.

The statistics, however, don't tell the whole story of how happy I was in the North East, just as I suppose the figures relating to my Wednesday years don't really reflect the sense of fulfilment I felt in my time at Hillsborough.

I was fortunate enough to play for two very good clubs alongside some great colleagues, and I remember my days with both Wednesday and 'Boro with pleasure. I shall certainly never forget the thrill of playing before a capacity crowd on many occasions at Hillsborough and savouring the fantastic atmosphere which was unique to the old Kop in the days when that huge bank was packed with standing supporters.

Author's note: An irony of Hickton's sale to Middlesbrough for £20,000 was that within three months Wednesday paid a record £70,000 to bring in a new centre-forward, John Ritchie, from Stoke. Hickton, incidentally, scored five times in games against the Owls, including one in a famous 8-0 scoreline at Ayresome Park in April 1974.

Tommy Craig

Tommy Craig cost a club record £100,000 when he arrived from Aberdeen in May 1969 at the age of 18, and the red-haired Scottish midfielder with the lethal left foot made 233 appearances and scored 40 goals for Wednesday before moving to Newcastle in December 1974. Unrealistically high expectations and the fact that he came at a time when the Owls' fortunes were on the wane meant a difficult baptism in English football at Hillsborough, but Craig, now living in Glasgow, recalls his Sheffield days with affection.

As recently as the summer of 1996, I was back in Sheffield to attend the European championship matches, and an incident which occurred before the Denmark-Croatia game reminded me that Wednesday fans from the early 1970s still retain the same fond memories of me as I do of them.

I happened to go to the wrong entrance, and the steward on the gate politely informed me I would have to walk all the way round the ground to reach the right door. Then he looked at me and said: "Wait a minute, you're Tommy, aren't you? You're Tommy!" He didn't call me Tommy Craig, just Tommy, and, when I nodded, he smiled and asked what I was doing at Hillsborough. It was if I was a personal friend he hadn't seen for a long time.

"Hey," he said, "We can't have you going the long way across to the other side. Come with me, I'll show you a short cut." That warm gesture, and the fact that so many Wednesdayites spoke to me as I found my way into the ground, brought back a lot of good memories of a phase in my life when things might not always have been as easy as I might have wished, but there were more positives than negatives.

I still get letters from Wednesday fans. One I received recently included a poem in honour of my left foot! I think the majority of people felt that circumstances were against me for much of my time in Sheffield. They saw in Tommy Craig, the footballer, something they liked, but knew there was more to come after I left.

I well remember the day towards the end of the 1968-69 season when Eddie Turnbull, my manager at Aberdeen, revealed the club had received £100,000 bids from Wednesday and Aston Villa, and said I had to make a choice. I spoke to Tommy Docherty at Villa and Eric Taylor at Hillsborough, and, in the end, chose Wednesday because they were in the First Division while Villa were in the Second. Ironically, 173 of my 214 League games for the Owls were to be in the lower grade!

With hindsight, I can say I moved to

England too early. For the first 18 months I didn't begin to produce the football I was capable of, or had been progressing towards at Aberdeen. The circumstances didn't help, for Wednesday were experiencing a decline which continued, and I found myself in a situation in which there was no real stability.

It's said Eddie Turnbull told the Press on the day I signed that I "was capable of walking into any team in England". I don't remember that, but haven't forgotten Eric Taylor being quoted as saying I was "Alan Ball, Billy Bremner and Tony Kay rolled into one" – which was lovely to read, but rather more difficult to live up to!

People seemed to overlook the fact that I was only 18, still very much potential, and nowhere near the finished article. I was still at an early stage of my apprenticeship, but, because of the huge fee and the hype, everyone assumed I was already the complete footballer.

I had made my senior debut with Aberdeen at 16 and played for Scotland three times as a schoolboy and eight times at youth level, but, while making 45 club appearances, I'd been in an environment in which I was allowed to develop gradually. Now, suddenly, I was in at the deep end, and, as a record buy, expected to be ready-made to play a prominent role in transforming Wednesday's fortunes overnight.

It might have been so different if the club had been enjoying better progress, and I could have gradually settled into a strong team full of confidence; but the 1966 Cup Final side, which people say had the makings of an outstanding team, had all but broken up when I arrived.

I thought I did okay on my debut against Spurs in the final game of 1968-69, but, even then, I quickly sensed an unsettled atmosphere within the club. At the time, Tom McAnearney was in temporary charge, and, though Danny Williams came in the summer, people like Jim McCalliog and John Ritchie left before the new season started – and Vic Mobley and Don Megson were among those who departed in the following few months.

Having gone to Sheffield with high expectations for myself and the club, it was a major blow to experience relegation in my first season; and, unfortunately, it became evident very early that I was not Danny Williams' type of player. I was very much someone who had to be on the ball to make things happen, but the qualities I possessed were not enough for Danny, who wanted me to be what I wasn't.

I was too naive to fully understand what was happening around me at the club, still trying to find my feet, and I didn't fit in with Danny's ideas of how he wanted football to be played. I'm not saying he was wrong, but his way wasn't my way. His basic belief was that you roll your sleeves up, get stuck in, and let everything take care of itself.

Derek Dooley, however, made an immediate and positive impression. Even when Danny was manager, Derek was on the scene, showing understanding and warmth – he was always on hand to give me advice and encouragement. He was sympathetic, and, because he appreciated that I was very young and impressionable, he went out of his way to make me feel wanted, constantly showing faith in my ability to succeed.

When Derek was manager, I thought things were definitely progressing, and there was tremendous respect for him in the dressing room. He was the kind of guy who made people want to play for him. Everyone was ready to bust a gut for Derek, and we were all sorry things didn't work as they should have done for him.

A particularly outstanding memory of my time in Sheffield relates to Derek's first full season as manager, for in February 1972 I had the thrill of playing against the legendary Pele in a match with Santos at Hillsborough – and I must tell the story of how I claimed Pele's shirt that afternoon.

Derek knew Pele was my hero, and, when he said the great Brazilian was set for his first visit to Sheffield in ten years, I could hardly contain myself. I knew, however, that everybody and their grandmother would be after Pele's shirt at the end of the game, and the challenge was beating them all to it.

A couple of days before Santos were due at our ground, they played at Aston Villa, and we all went down on the bus. Throughout the match, I never took my eyes off the great man, and, shortly

Tommy Craig in pursuit of the legendary Pele.

Tommy Craig pictured with Tom McAnearney and Eric Taylor on the day he signed and became the club's first £100,000 player.

before the end of the game, I noticed he ensured he was ideally placed to make a dash for the tunnel – apparently it's common practice for the big stars in exhibition games to arrange a quick exit from the field by being on the near touchline at the end.

The knowledge prompted me to make a decision about the Hillsborough game. I was going to be standing closest to Pele in the 90th minute! To assist my plan, I knocked on referee Gordon Hill's door as we were going out for the second half. "Ref," I said, "Can I ask you a very big favour? Could you let me know when you're going to blow the final whistle?" He was quite amused when I explained why.

Anyway, towards the end of the second half I saw the clock on the North Stand showing a quarter-to-five, and, as Jimmy Mullen, our left-back, was the nearest to Pele, I had no choice but to urge him to go on a forward run. Then I sidled towards my Brazilian hero.

Almost immediately, the referee turned and winked at me, and ten seconds later, blew for time. I promptly pounced on Pele with such enthusiasm I'm sure I scared him. But he smiled when he realised all I wanted was his shirt. Jimmy Mullen didn't smile, however, as it dawned on him why I had sent him up the wing!

One of my everlasting memories of that afternoon is of Pele sitting in the visitors' dressing room after the game. Stripped to the waist, wearing only a pair of trousers and neither shoes nor socks, he signed hundreds of photographs which had been sold before the game. Supporters formed a queue which stretched from the dressing room door all the way out of the ground and as far as Penistone Road. Pele didn't put the pen down until every single fan had been been satisfied.

Naturally, I would have liked to have achieved more with Wednesday, but I shall always have a special affinity with Hillsborough, and I had plenty of good memories. Right from the start, the people were warm and kind. Moreover, it was during that phase of my career that I married my wife, Madeline, and our children, Tracey, Lesley and Shaun were born.

Colin Prophett

Colin Prophett was a centre-half who arrived from Crewe in 1967 and made 129 League and Cup appearances for the Owls between 1969 and 1973. He later raised his career tally of games to over 450 with four other clubs, and now lives in Chesterfield, working as a sales director of woodworking tools manufacturers Leuco GB Ltd while maintaining his links with football as a scout with Swansea City.

I had played for two or three years as an amateur with Crewe, turning out for the Reserves and the Midweek Floodlit League side, when the chance came to have a trial with Wednesday. It arose because Ernie Tagg, the Crewe manager, couldn't afford to sign me and another youngster on pro terms, and "Tim" Coleman, the old Stoke and Crewe winger, recommended me to his old pal, Jack Marshall.

Marshall, who had just re-joined Wednesday as Alan Brown's assistant, organised an invitation to play in a pre-season game at Bishop Auckland. Lawrie McMenemy was in charge of the team that day, and he must have given me a good report because Alan Brown decided to sign me. However, he initially took me as an amateur, for he and my father agreed I should finish my time as an apprentice fitter and turner at Rolls Royce's motor division before becoming a professional.

I never regretted having been an industrial rather than a football apprentice because, in those days, joining a club straight from school was a hit-and-miss affair, and such a lot of talented lads who ought to have made the grade fell by the wayside. The system wasn't as organised as it is now, and I saw quite a few lads waste their chance. At least when I finally became a professional at the age of 21 in 1968, I had a trade to fall back on – and was mature enough to be very sure I was going to give total commitment to football because I didn't want to drift back into an industrial setting if I could help it!

After a year as an amateur travelling from Crewe every Friday, staying in the Hunter House Hotel, then playing for the Reserves on Saturdays, I joined the paid ranks. By then Marshall had become the manager, but, towards the end of my first season, he left, and it was Danny Williams who gave me my League debut early in 1969-70 – which, unfortunately, was the year Wednesday were relegated.

I have happy memories of my initial taste of First Division football as a substitute in the home match with Liverpool and of my first full game at Arsenal – though I was disappointed that, playing in the unusual role of a right-sided midfielder at Highbury, I clipped the bar with a 20-yard effort when I should have scored.

I did get on the scoresheet when we met Sunderland at home on Boxing Day, and we won 2-0 on an afternoon often remembered because Steve Downes, who was making his debut after signing from Rotherham, scored a brilliant individual goal. Sadly, Steve never fulfilled the promise he showed that day, and it summed up our plight that this victory was the only one we managed in 18 League matches between early October and late February.

Remarkably, we came to our final two matches that season still in with a chance of beating the drop and sending Crystal Palace down with Sunderland. We needed three points out of four, and, after coming from behind to draw 2-2 at Manchester United, went into our last game, at home to Joe Mercer's Manchester City, knowing nothing less than a win could save us. Alas, we lost 2-1 on a wet and miserable evening I shall always remember more vividly and with a greater sense of frustration than any of the Wednesday fans in the 45,000 crowd.

As anybody who was present will vouch, City didn't want to win that night. Mike Doyle missed an early penalty which my little daughter could have saved, and I can still recall seeing Neil Young beat Peter Rodrigues several times down the wing – but, instead of doing the easy thing and hitting the ball into the goalmouth, he kept hammering it in the direction of Tony Book, who was miles away deep on the other side of the field at right-back.

People often remind me that the turning point in that match came midway through the first-half when Mike Summerbee was injured and City sent on Ian Bowyer, because it was Bowyer who got the goals which won the game for City. Everyone seemed to think someone had forgotten to tell him the idea was that Wednesday should win, but perhaps the lad interpreted manager Mercer's touchline anger as a signal to go for victory.

Summerbee actually injured himself when he went over the top as I was about to tackle him. The referee gave us a free-kick, which I took, and it was only later that I learned Mercer's furious gesticulations from the City bench were because he blamed me for the injury which put Summerbee's place in the following week's Cup-winners' Cup Final against Gornick Zabrze in jeopardy.

You can imagine how low the spirits were in the home dressing room at the end of that match, and, after getting showered and changed, I was hardly in the mood to accept what Mercer said to me as I walked past the directors' room on my way to the players' lounge.

When he snapped: "It's your fault Wednesday have gone down!" I said "Just a minute, Mr Mercer, why is it my fault?" He mumbled something about my tackle costing them Summerbee for their Cup game in Vienna.

I asked him: "Can I put one point to you? Who got the free-kick? We did, which shows the referee saw it was your man who committed the foul!"

Mercer was suddenly very apologetic, but being sorry couldn't change Wednesday's fate, and, just to rub salt into the wounds, for years afterwards whenever we met Ian Bowyer, he always enjoyed reminding us he'd sent us down.

Bowyer scored soon after coming on, then got the second just before the final whistle, by which time we knew anyway that Tony Coleman's equaliser, notched just past the hour mark, wasn't going to be enough. Somehow, you felt we just weren't fated to win that game.

Coleman, by the way, was an amazing character. I never think of him without remembering the day he drove me, Kenny Burton and Mick Prendergast back from a training session at Thorncliffe in his Jaguar. We were just dropping down from Wadsley Bridge when Tony was stopped for speeding, but, when the policeman recognised us as Wednesday players, he didn't even issue a warning. Only later did we realise just how lucky Tony had been, when he revealed he didn't have a driving licence and the car wasn't taxed!

I was a first-team regular in the first two seasons in the Second Division, during which time Derek Dooley replaced Williams, but lost my place after Peter Swan's return just before the 1972-73 campaign began. I didn't start a game until February, and that summer I joined Norwich. A year later I rejoined Danny Williams at Swindon.

I recall three games for Swindon against Wednesday which will be of interest. In two – at the County Ground in September 1975 and at Hillsborough in August 1977 – I was an emergency goalkeeper, first when Jim Barron was injured, then when we lost Jimmy Allen. I'm proud to note that I kept a clean sheet both times. In the 1975 game when we came from behind to win 2-1, I thought I'd failed to save a terrific free-kick from Mick Prendergast – then discovered the ball had lodged between my legs!

Ironically, my first Swindon goal came at Hillsborough in February 1977, but Wednesday won 3-1. It's probably the only time I haven't cheered an Owls' victory, for though it's 25 years since I left, I still retain a special affection for the club.

Peter Rodrigues

Peter Rodrigues, the full-back who joined Wednesday from Leicester for £50,000 in October 1970, made 174 League and Cup appearances before being given a free transfer in 1975. He gained 17 of his 40 Welsh international caps while at Hillsborough. A year after leaving the Owls he captained Southampton in their famous 1976 FA Cup Final triumph.

Things did not go as well as any of us wanted during my time with Wednesday, but, apart from the lack of success on the field, I certainly enjoyed my years in Sheffield – so much so that, when I was released at the age of 31 in 1975, I seriously considered hanging up my boots and staying in the area because I liked the people and the place.

I know we were relegated at the end of my final season, but, frankly, I didn't feel I'd done too badly, and it came as a shock when Steve Burtenshaw said he was giving me a free. I think the mistake Steve made was bringing in youngsters before they were ready, and, in my case, I didn't believe Danny Cameron was a better player than me. With about 400 League games and 40 caps to my name, I felt I had the experience and ability to still do a fair job for another couple of years.

It's funny how things work out, and, in this instance, fate had a pleasant surprise in store – though, even now, I can't help thinking how easily the pattern of events could have been very different. I might have been playing Third

Division football or running a pub instead of being captain of an FA Cup-winning side!

As I say, I thought: "If Wednesday think I'm finished, I might as well pack up and find another career." And, as I was ready to stay in Sheffield, I approached, a local brewery about the chances of going into the licensing trade. I don't know what I expected, but, for some reason, the feedback wasn't as encouraging as I'd anticipated, and, in the long run, perhaps the brewery did me a favour.

If they had shown the slightest interest, I would almost certainly have never left Sheffield, but, just when everything was up in the air, I got this call from Lawrie McMenemy, the manager of Second Division Southampton, and I ended up going down there and signing.

Even then, the immediate prospects didn't look too promising. Lawrie made it plain he wanted me as temporary cover for a lad called Steve Mills, who was recovering from a serious injury. In the event, Mills never made it back,

Peter Rodrigues shooting for goal in a match against Carlisle in 1973.

and, in the following November, I was asked to take over as Southampton's skipper when Mick Channon gave up the job.

The rest, as they say, is history, and six months later I was collecting the FA Cup at Wembley after a famous victory over Manchester United. It was a wonderful climax to my career and certainly compensated for having been the losing captain when Leicester reached the Final in 1969.

I often look back to my time at Hillsborough and wonder why we didn't do better. Danny Williams didn't remain long after my arrival, but he, and later, Derek Dooley, brought in some good players who certainly didn't lack ability or experience. The idea seemed to be to build a team around Tommy Craig, and, on paper, we had the quality, but, for some reason, the team didn't gell.

McMenemy did exactly the same thing at The Dell and made it work, but neither Danny nor Derek was able to do the same. The problem, perhaps, was that they were both nice guys. A manager who is a nice guy has to have a son

of a bitch as his coach, but, unfortunately, though Ron Staniforth was an excellent coach, he was also too nice.

To be honest, I always felt making Derek Dooley the manager was a sentimental appointment, made perhaps because the board was under fire and they felt bringing in a man who was a local legend would give the club the boost it so badly needed. I think there were people who believed Derek was "used" to ease the pressure on the directors.

Derek did a fair job in the circumstances, and you could never doubt the depth of his feeling for the club or his commitment. When it really mattered, he had a terrible run of bad luck with the virus that swept through the club in the autumn of 1973, and he was left terribly exposed when the chairman and vice-chairman resigned.

It was soon after that when he was sacked, and the horrible thing was the board did it on Christmas Eve. You can't forgive people for that. The players were all shocked, dumbfounded. If the new chairman and his directors felt the time had come for change, they

might at least have had the humanity to wait until after Christmas.

The irony was that things went from bad to worse afterwards under Steve Burtenshaw, but, if the latter stages of my time in Sheffield were disappointing, whenever I look back I always remember the happier days and the good friends I knew at Wednesday, especially such lads as Brian Joicey, John Holsgrove and John Sissons.

I managed only a couple of seasons at The Dell before I finally retired from football, and, since hanging up my boots, I've been in the licensing trade. Since 1994 I've been steward of a Conservative club in Southampton.

Jimmy Mullen

Jimmy Mullen made 262 League and Cup appearances for Wednesday between 1970 and 1980, and if his time at Hillsborough coincided with a period of decline followed by a long struggle towards revival for the Owls, the lad from Jarrow became a fans' favourite whose talents as a central defender and captain

Peter Rodrigues and colleagues Mick Prendergast, Steve Downes, Peter Grummitt, Jimmy Mullen and John Sissons meet a 1971 version of Ozzie Owl.

also gained him the respect and admiration of his fellow professionals. He later enjoyed success as a manager with Blackpool and Burnley.

My links with Wednesday date back to 1969, when Alec Barker, the club's scout in the North East, sent me to Hillsborough for a trial. At the time I was working as an apprentice draughtsman and playing with Hedworth Celtic, and, at 17, it was a great thrill to get the chance to follow in the footsteps of so many Jarrow products who had made the grade in professional football over the years.

My first match in Wednesday's colours was for the Juniors at Scunthorpe, where, if I'm not mistaken, a certain Kevin Keegan was playing for the home side. I must have done fairly well in that game, and the next, because I was offered an apprenticeship and was soon settled in digs in Leppings Lane with another Jarrow lad, Dennis Lymer.

One early milestone which was a source of great pride came on the day I was named as captain of the Juniors, and what made it particularly memorable was, when the team sheets went up in the dressing room, they revealed that all three Wednesday teams would be skippered by Jarrow boys with Dennis Lymer leading the Reserves and Gerry Young the first team.

Gerry, of course, was my hero, and he became one of my early mentors – a terrific guy who was a great example for any youngster, both as a man and a player. On the field, nobody did a better job with greater consistency than Gerry Young, and I always view it as an undeserved misfortune that he is so often remembered for the mistake which led to Everton's winning goal in the 1966 FA Cup Final.

I watched that match on television when I was 13 years old, and, even at that age, recognised what a good job Gerry had done. People forget he had the additional task of nursing Sam Ellis, who was then just 19 and making his Cup debut in that Final. The burden of responsibility on Gerry's shoulders must have been enormous, and you could only have tremendous admiration for the man when you saw how well he coped.

Yet, if the fates were desperately cruel to him that afternoon, the thing I really admire about Gerry is the way he learned to live with the business of always being reminded of one of the few mistakes he made in a long and distinguished playing career. Some people would resent the subject being repeatedly brought up and tend to get bitter, but Gerry, typically, invariably shrugs it off with a grin.

Gerry became a coach at the end of his playing days, and continued to do an excellent job for the club. I was always grateful for his help and guidance, and it was one of the saddest moments in my time at Hillsborough when I just happened to be around the medical room area on the day Gerry was told he was being finished after 20 years' service with the Owls. These things happen in football, but he was the victim of circumstances and didn't deserve to pay for being associated with someone else's failures.

Jimmy Mullen.

Gerry was there to give me encouragement on Boxing Day 1970 when I made my Football League debut for Wednesday at Hull, but the thing I recall best about that occasion, nine weeks after my 18th birthday, was the support I got from my fellow centre-back Sam Ellis. Ironically, it proved to be one of Sam's last first-team games for the club.

Naturally, I was very nervous, and this must have been pretty obvious to everyone as we had our team-talk in the hotel after the pre-match meal. Sam put an arm round me and said: "Don't worry about what you've heard or been told, I'll take full responsibility for you. Just keep your eye on me and listen to what I say." I went through the whole 90 minutes following Sam's instructions and that debut is an experience which I enjoyed and shall never forget.

Unfortunately, it took the edge of things that, after leading 4-1 with seven minutes left, we ended up with a 4-4 draw. We were delighted to hear the final whistle because if the game had lasted another minute we would probably have lost!

Danny Williams, the manager, was so flabbergasted by our late collapse, he was lost for words in the dressing room afterwards. I think he eventually said something like:

"That's what kills my pig, conceding three goals in four minutes. I know it's Christmas, lads, but do we have to be so generous?" We didn't know it then, but Danny was destined to keep his job for only one more month before being replaced by Derek Dooley.

I smile now when I think what a physically skinny lad I was in the early days. Willie Henderson once said I was so skinny, he thought that from my eyes to my belly button I resembled a clarinet! Ron Staniforth, the coach, had me and Dave Sunley on a diet of sherry and eggs twice a day, and we had to drink a bottle of milk stout every evening. This and extra weight training eventually helped me develop a decent physique.

When I look back, I still think it remarkable how I went on to enjoy a longer career and make more Owls appearances than the other lads who were apprentices around the same time. There were some very good prospects – people like Eddie Prudham, Allan Thompson, Dave Sunley, Kevin Johnson and Ken Johnson – and all of them should have gone much further than they did. I always thought Dave Sunley was set to go right to the top, but it didn't happen even though there was a time when he was such a promising striker one club offered £100,000 for him when that was a lot of money.

The circumstances weren't always ideal for any of us, but I was lucky enough to keep progressing. In fact, I never looked back after getting into the Reserves at an early stage, and, though I had my ups and downs in an Owls career which saw me serve under five managers, I remember it all with great affection.

Once, during Steve Burtenshaw's spell in charge, Ron Saunders wanted to take me to Aston Villa, but Wednesday turned him down – and I was happy to stay even though we were then struggling. It was around this time that we went to Ayresome Park and got thrashed 8-0 by Middlesbrough, and I remember Steve telling me after the game that I was the only Wednesday player who could hold my head up. It wasn't much comfort considering the circumstances, but it did help to know the manager appreciated my talents!

When Len Ashurst came, I was in and out of the team for a while, but then I think Len recognised that, for all the problems we were having in terms of results, I was maturing and developing my game. I became a regular, and when, one day before a home game, Len pulled me into the boot room and said he wanted me to take over the captaincy, I knew I had finally made the grade!

I remained club captain until Ian Porterfield took me to Rotherham in 1980. My last season was one to remember because we finally started the climb back with promotion from the old Third Division, and, of course, it coincided with my testimonial year. It was a time when the fans – and the Sheffield public – showed me just how much I had been accepted, and, though I was mainly a substitute in the later stages of our promotion push, I had no idea my Wednesday career was so close to ending.

I didn't really want to leave, and when Jack Charlton told me of Rotherham's offer, he insisted I didn't have to go. Indeed, he said there would always be a job for me at Hillsborough so long as he was the manager. But he admitted that, with young Mark Smith coming through and Mick Pickering fit again, my first-team prospects would continue to be limited; so, reluctantly, I accepted it was time to move on. With hindsight I can say it was the right decision, for it set me on a course which

broadened my experience and eventually led me into coaching and management – something I have never regretted.

But leaving Hillsborough was very sad, and my parents, who had never missed any of my home games and had attended a lot of away matches, were disappointed. I think my Dad feared I was making a mistake, but, in retrospect, he recognised it had been the correct choice. Sometimes you have to walk away from a place which means everything to you because it is the moment when it has to be done for the benefit of your career.

However, you can be sure I took with me some terrific memories of an unforgettable phase in my life.

Brian Joicey

Centre-forward Brian Joicey scored 109 goals in 311 games in a career which started at Coventry in 1969 and ended at Barnsley ten years later, and the 53 he scored for Wednesday came in 164 matches between August 1971 and March 1976 – a period he remembers as the happiest of his playing days despite the frustration of the last years. Indeed, once he settled in Sheffield, the likeable Geordie decided he never wanted to leave the area.

I had pleasant memories of Hillsborough even before I joined Wednesday, because, just over two years earlier, in April 1969, I'd played there for an FA Amateur XI against the UAU and scored four goals in a 6-0 win. The game had been one of the highlights in a memorable 1968-69 season in which I got 45 goals for North Shields – including the winner in an FA Amateur Cup Final defeat of Sutton at Wembley.

I became a professional with First Division Coventry soon afterwards and had played 44 first-team games, scoring ten goals, when, out of the blue, the move to Sheffield cropped up. The night before I was told of Wednesday's interest, I felt I'd had a good game against Roy McFarland and scored in a 2-2 draw with Derby. However, at the time I was in and out of the side, and Coventry were desperate to raise money to buy a new striker, Chris Chilton, from Hull.

That is how the £110,000 double deal which took me and Irish international Dave Clements to Hillsborough came about. I travelled up with Dave and his wife, Ruth, and we stayed overnight at the Hallam Tower Hotel in between talks with general manager Eric Taylor and manager Derek Dooley.

I well remember sitting alone in the foyer at the ground for what seemed like half a lifetime but was about two-and-a-half hours while Dave was in Eric Taylor's office discussing personal terms. When he finally emerged and said he'd signed, I said "Thank God for that!" By contrast, my own negotiations were completed in about 20 minutes, for I jumped at a move I knew would be good for me.

It was, in truth, a turning point in my life, and I never regretted coming to Sheffield, for, of course, it was early in my time here that I met my wife Sue – that happening courtesy of my teammate John Holsgrove.

John got into insurance and was always trying to get the lads signed up, and when I promised to pop in to see him sometime, I didn't realise that in doing so I would meet Sue, who was working for him.

I arrived at his office one day just before five o'clock, and John asked Sue to make me a cup of tea. She plonked it down on the table, and then had to rush off to catch her bus home. I'd seen her for about two minutes, but met her again soon afterwards when I went to the Fiesta night club. I suppose you could say our romance started when I said: "You made me a drink when we last met, can I buy you one now?"

Anyway, back in August 1971, I was on £35 a week at Coventry, and Wednesday offered me £60, with £4 for a win and £2 for a draw. I thought: "That'll do me." I was single then, with absolutely no ties, and, apart from what was a good financial deal, with the prospect of regular first-team football, I didn't mind dropping down from the First to the Second Division.

Wednesday promised to put Dave and me in an hotel while we found permanent homes, and, initially, booked us into the Hunter House Hotel. But it wasn't the same after the Hallam Tower, and I'll never forget how Dave told Derek Dooley in no uncertain terms that we weren't having it – and we

PLAYING FOR WEDNESDAY 1933-1998

ended up back at the Hallam Tower, where we stayed for months!

My first two seasons with Wednesday, when I got 36 goals in 85 games, were a great time in my life, and I wouldn't change that for anything. The pity was the way things went sour afterwards, but this was down to boardroom changes and decisions over which the staff and players had no control.

The club had not made a very good start to 1971-72, and, when I scored on my home debut, against Portsmouth in early September, it earned a 1-1 draw and our first point of the season. That goal incidentally, would be considered a foul in the modern game, and I might even have been sent-off, for, as the goalkeeper came out and was poised to pick up the ball, I slid forward and went through him before getting up to score.

Anyway, I know Derek Dooley appreciated it, and my 16 goals in that first season, including a hat-trick against Orient, pleased me and the manager. After Pompey, I think we won six of our next nine home games, and lost only twice at Hillsborough all season. Unfortunately, our away form let us down.

But I felt we really started to buzz in 1972-73. Again it was our away results that prevented us finishing higher than tenth, but, when we beat First Division Crystal Palace in extra-time in an FA Cup fourth-round second replay at Villa Park in February (I got a hat-trick on a night I'll remember as one of the best of my career!), it suggested better things might be just round the corner if the club made one or two good signings.

Unfortunately, in the following season things suddenly started going wrong, especially between early October and early January when we won only one game in 16, but I don't think anyone on the outside really appreciated how serious the virus was that plagued the club and put so many key players on the sidelines.

The cruel thing was not so much that the situation cost Derek Dooley his job, but that the board took the astonishing decision to sack him on Christmas Eve. "Doc" Stephen had resigned and Matt Sheppard had just taken over as chairman, and perhaps he felt something had to be done quickly; but they could have left it until the season of goodwill was over.

The timing was terrible, and it took the players a long time to get over the shock. I don't think I'll forget it as long as I live. Derek was not just a good guy who didn't deserve such heartless treatment, he had always been so passionately devoted to Wednesday and we all had a lot of time for him.

The irony was, with respect to Steve Burtenshaw, he wasn't the right choice as Dooley's successor, and it was a pity Gerry Young, who was in temporary charge before Steve's appointment, was not the type to push himself. Gerry was as passionate as anyone about the game and the club, and, had he really wanted the job, the lads would have given him everything because they respected him. Gerry, however, was happy to be in the background.

I don't think what happened under Steve would have happened with Gerry in charge, or even if Derek had stayed. It was sad that in Steve's first full season, we had a terrible run and ended up in the Third Division for the first time in the club's history.

It was a miserable season for everybody. I had a spell between November and April when I was limited to only four games through injuries, and it summed up the team's struggle that, when I scored an injury-time equaliser in the game with Oxford in mid-April, it was Wednesday's first goal in nine games.

It was actually my 50th goal for the club, but it was Wednesday's first at Hillsborough since mid-December! Amusingly, there was apparently some mystery about who had scored, and someone told me later that Burtenshaw had suggested that me and Dave Sunley should claim half-a-goal apiece. I was in no doubt that, after Sunley got his head to Jimmy Mullen's cross, I nodded the ball over the line as I came in from behind.

The attendance that day, by the way, was under 7,500 and the club's lowest home gate since the war – which said everything about the depth of a decline which was to get worse before it got better.

Len Ashurst took over in my last season, and, as I didn't get much of a look-in, I wasn't surprised when he gave me a free transfer in May 1976. His theory was he didn't want people around who had been there for some time and had got used to losing.

Naturally, I was sorry things ended the way they did, but, having settled in Sheffield and liking the place and the people, I didn't want to leave the area.

Gerry Young, pushed out when Burtenshaw was sacked, had gone to Barnsley as a coach, and it was his presence that persuaded me to choose Oakwell in preference to several other offers. I played for Barnsley until 1978 when, following a stroke, I had to quit League football. However, I did later play with Frickley, Matlock and Hallam, then had a long spell playing in charity games with John Quinn's All Stars until I finally accepted I was getting too old.

In the meantime, I found a sales career with GT Cars in which I have been successful.

Rodger Wylde

Rodger Wylde, who joined Wednesday as an apprentice after leaving Frecheville School at 16 in 1970, made 193 League and Cup appearances and scored 66 goals between November 1972 and February 1980 before moving to Oldham. After a playing career in which he topped 400 games and claimed over 150 goals, he qualified as a chartered physiotherapist and has served Stockport County in this capacity since 1989. He also runs a private practice in Sheffield.

As a youngster I supported Sheffield United, but it was Wednesday who signed me on schoolboy forms at 14. Though I stayed on at school to take my GCSE exams, I was a regular in the Owls' Juniors under George McCabe for some time before starting as an apprentice. In fact, my apprenticeship only lasted a year, and there's an amusing story about how I stepped up to full professional ranks.

One day as I was leaving the training ground, I met a chap who claimed to be a Chelsea scout. Being a bit naive, I listened as he said he'd like me to go down to Stamford Bridge. I thought it all sounded a bit strange, so I mentioned the incident to my Dad, who said I'd better tell the manager. I duly spoke to Derek Dooley, and the upshot was I never heard anything more about Chelsea, but Wednesday promptly offered me a contract.

I suppose I was lucky, because a lot

Rodger Wylde.

more or less stayed in. We beat the drop into Division Four by winning our last match that season, against Southend, and in 1976-77, when we finished eighth, I really made a mark with 25 goals. The irony was, my success nearly prompted a move to West Ham – and, once again, Len wasn't too pleased when I showed I had a mind of my own.

It was around the time of the transfer deadline when Len sent for me and said: "West Ham want to sign you, but they've asked if you'll go down there tomorrow to play in a practice match before they make the final decision."

I thought: "What do they want me to play in a practice match for when I've scored all these goals?" I told Len if they really wanted me they shouldn't need to see me in practice, and I wasn't prepared to do as they asked. In truth, I didn't fancy going because London never attracted me.

I was content to stay, and leaving was the last thing on my mind, although, when I look back and recall how disappointed I sometimes felt about Wednesday's lack of ambition, I think now that perhaps I ought to have moved on a long time before I did.

Len, of course, got the sack early in the season after I'd scored 25 goals, and Jack Charlton, who had been lined up to replace him, made it pretty clear that none of the lads he inherited was likely to fit into his long-term plans. When, on the day he first took charge, he said he was going to bring in players who would be "his" men, we all knew that at some stage we were going to be out.

In the event, I was one of the last survivors and played for nearly three years under Big Jack. But the inevitable end came during the 1979-80 season when, ironically, I started well with six goals in my first nine games, but didn't remain quite long enough to share in the club's Third Division promotion triumph.

I broke my foot in a match against Grimsby in November, but, remarkably, the injury wasn't diagnosed for three weeks. The accident happened when Grimsby's centre-half, who had been kicking me up hill and down dale all through the game, caught the underside of my foot with a full-blooded kick as I went into a challenge in which, to be honest, I was trying to get some of my own back.

of promising fellow apprentices were never offered terms. In fact, many eventually drifted out of the game and I've lost touch with them, though I do see one old colleague, John McKenna, when my children watch television – he became an actor and now appears in a Channel 4 soap called *Hollyoaks*!

Dooley gave me my first-team debut against Middlesbrough in November 1972 when I was 18, and I played a few games in Steve Burtenshaw's time. However, it wasn't until Len Ashurst was manager that I got a regular place, and, curiously, that didn't happen until after I'd been shipped out to Burnley on loan and caused a stir by refusing to stay a second month at Turf Moor.

I had done well in Burnley Reserves, with two goals in three games, but when Dave Merrington asked me to extend my loan, which meant staying over Christmas, I said: "No, if you don't know whether you want to sign me after how I've played this month, I don't think you'll ever know."

Ashurst called me into the office when I reported back to Hillsborough the next morning. He said: "If I'd seen you last night, I'd have sacked you, but then I thought about it and decided anybody who can turn a First Division club down to stay with a Third Division club fighting relegation ought to be appreciated."

He put me in the first team, and I

I remember thinking: "Bloody hell, that hurt!" and, afterwards, my foot felt really sore. But I played in the next match a few days later, and although I missed training four days in the following week, the pain eased and I played again on the Saturday. What was annoying was that, according to Tony Toms, Big Jack thought I was kidding about my injury and was making it up because I didn't want to train. That, of course, was not the case at all, and, as I was in so much discomfort, I ended up taking myself to the out-patients' department at the Hallamshire Hospital. I came out with a pot on!

It was only in retrospect that I saw it was something the club ought to have sorted out at the beginning, but why they didn't send me for an X-ray to prove whether or not I'd been kidding remains a mystery to this day.

My recovery was pretty rapid, and, in early December, I was back for the match with Chester. I scored a beauty that day. I picked up the ball near the halfway line, whacked it out to Brian Hornsby on the wing, and ran into the penalty area to head Brian's return into the net. After the game, Bert McGee, the chairman, came into the dressing room and announced: "That's the best goal I've ever seen!"

I thought the accolade from the chairman would ensure I was set for a long run in the team, but, though I played in the next match, at Exeter, I was subsequently dropped. At the time, we were all looking forward to the big Sheffield derby with United on Boxing Day, and, when I was in the squad that spent Christmas Day night in a local hotel, I expected to play.

It was one of the biggest disappointments of my career when I discovered I wasn't involved. Honestly, I couldn't believe it. The match, which Wednesday won 4-0, went down in local football folklore as "the Boxing Day massacre", and, naturally, I was delighted for the lads. But being overlooked confirmed that the writing was on the wall, and I made my mind up to ask for a move.

There was some talk of Sheffield United coming for me, and, after hearing from several sources that a cross-city switch was imminent, after training one day I was telling the lads what I'd been told. Unfortunately, I didn't hear Big Jack come into the dressing room

and stand behind me. Then I turned and spotted him, and he snapped: "You can tell your mates at Bramall Lane that you're definitely not going there – you can go anywhere else!"

Soon afterwards I signed for Oldham.

Peter Fox

Goalkeeper Peter Fox earned a special place in Wednesday's records as the club's youngest Football League player when, at the age of 15 years 8 months, he made his debut in the home game with Orient in March 1973. It was his misfortune to be at Hillsborough in a period of decline, and, limited to 52 senior outings in five years, in March 1978 he joined Stoke, for whom he made some 480 appearances before ending his playing days at Exeter, where he began his management career in 1995.

I was, quite literally, mopping out the home dressing room at Hillsborough when Derek Dooley, the manager, walked through the door and told me "You're in!" – meaning I was making my Football League debut against Orient the following day.

At the time I was a first-year apprentice about 98 days short of my 16th birthday, and the situation was like something out of a piece of schoolboy fiction. With both senior goalkeepers, Peter Springett and Peter Grummitt, injured, I was solving a crisis and becoming the youngest player in Wednesday's history.

Happily, I kept a clean sheet and we won 2-0, but, if I didn't have much to do and was always well protected by colleagues like Peter Rodrigues, John Holsgrove and Tommy Craig, it still proved a painful and eventful afternoon.

I finished the game in agony because, early in the second-half at the Leppings Lane end, I had to dash from my goal and collided with Barrie Fairbrother, the Orient forward, when we both met the ball at the same moment. Fairbrother was carried off, but, after treatment, I played on in pain, and only later learned my toe was broken.

That injury kept me out of action for six weeks, but I was a happy young

man, boosted for a long time afterwards by the memory of my debut. I remember, on the following Saturday, Hillsborough was the venue for an FA Cup semi-final between Arsenal and Sunderland, and, as I stood at the Leppings Lane end and watched the game, I gazed at the pitch and kept thinking: "I was playing out there last week!"

Peter Fox.

The time I spent with Wednesday coincided for the most part with a lean period in the club's history, and we all had our share of disappointments. Someone has said we won only 11 and lost 29 of the 52 games I played in, yet I have only fond memories of my Hillsborough years. It was a fabulous club with some great people who set me a good example and pointed me in the right direction.

George McCabe, who was in charge of the kids, taught me lessons and principles which stood me in good stead over a playing career which spanned over 650 games and lasted until I was nearly 40 years old. George was very strict, but knew how to look after youngsters, and I was always impressed with his philosophy and his great pride in the club.

I arrived at Hillsborough after leaving school in Scunthorpe in July 1972, coming at the same time as Ian Nimmo and Ronnie Ferguson, two other lads spotted by the same Lincolnshire scout. It was also the summer when Dooley signed Willie Henderson, the old Scottish international, and brought Peter Swan and David Layne back to the club after their life-bans were lifted. Peter Eustace returned from West Ham as well.

There was a lot of humorous banter and laughter in the dressing room when Swan and Layne were around, and Henderson, of course, was a great character as well as a wonderful player who could still beat anybody in a race over five or ten yards.

Willie was very generous, always giving a good tip to the lad who looked after his boots. Mind you, the lad was always having to paint Willie's boots blue, and we all had the experience of tying the famous Scot's laces because he simply couldn't see well enough to tie them himself!

I didn't make my second appearance in the first team until December 1974. By then, with Dooley having gone the previous year (Derek's departure on Christmas Eve was cruel timing for someone who was such a gentleman) Steve Burtenshaw was in charge. Sadly, things were not going very well – and they were destined to go from bad to worse.

Ironically, under George McCabe, the youngsters had a good run in the FA Youth Cup in 1974, and around this time I got back into the senior side. Unfortunately, though I enjoyed a run of 20 games in the second half of 1974-75, we won only one, lost 16, and were relegated to the Third Division for the first time in Wednesday's history. I think we once went 14 games and scored in only one.

The following season, when I played in the first game and then lost my place, was the one in which Len Ashurst came after Burtenshaw was sacked. It was about then that people like George McCabe, Gerry Young and Ron Staniforth also left, and, whatever the reasons, I always felt Wednesday lost some good, genuine people who were victims of circumstances which weren't of their making.

Len Ashurst recalled me in December 1975, and I played in 26 of the remaining 27 games, but, again, we were struggling desperately. We lost more matches than we won, and ended up going into the final match, against Southend, needing to win to escape falling into the Fourth Division.

In the event, we won 2-1, but it was a very big pressure game, and I recall that, after Mick Prendergast and Eric Potts had put us 2-0 up, we were cruising along when Southend scrambled a goal and, suddenly, it all got very tense and nervy.

Unfortunately, though I remained with Wednesday for another two years, I only played in one more senior game after the Southend match. Chris Turner got into the team in 1976-77 and established himself. Then, of course, when Jack Charlton replaced Len Ashurst, he felt that both Chris and myself were too small, and, preferring a big goalkeeper, he gave Bob Bolder the job.

I had a couple of games on loan at Barnsley. I also had a spell at West Ham, where I didn't play in the first team but had the very enjoyable experience of being sent to play for Hawaii in the North American Soccer League – a four-months spell during which I faced such legends as Eusebio and Pele.

However, my situation at Hillsborough had become increasingly frustrating, and I was at a crossroads in my career when the chance came to join Stoke, who paid £15,000 for me, in March 1978. It took a year or so to get a regular place, but I got my head down and, once established, never looked back. I had waited a long time for that upturn!

I sometimes wonder if I suffered in Sheffield because I got my big chance too soon, but, really, it didn't help to be in a losing team. The circumstances were hardly conducive to progress. However, as I've said, I have only fond memories of Hillsborough, and I can only recall some of the people I knew in those days with affection because they were good friends.

I always remember Mick Prendergast with great respect and admiration. When he was fit, he was a very good player, but he was terribly unlucky with injuries. He'd fight so hard to get over one injury, then suffer another. He was a player who gave everything in training and in matches, and was just as big-hearted off the pitch – the sort of lad who was invariably helpful to the youngsters.

There were a number of young lads, notably Garry Hull and David Herbert, who might have gone further if the situation at the club had been better, but youngsters don't make the same progress when they come into a team which is not doing well. Yet there was always a good spirit among the youngsters, and big Dave Cusack was a terrific character, so mature and confident he always seemed ahead of his years.

Some of the people behind the scenes made a big impression, too. Ron Ward, the caretaker, was another great character, and the women in the laundry, like Betty Pearson, were always there with a smile and a joke. There was a wonderful atmosphere behind the scenes, even when things weren't going too well on the pitch, and, right from the start, I always felt at home. You couldn't help but feel the decline the club suffered was temporary, and it was always a fair bet they would get back to the top. I was sorry not to be still around when it happened.

Ken Knighton

Ken Knighton was a tough and determined wing-half who already boasted some 300 League and Cup games with five clubs before joining Wednesday in 1973. Unfortunately, his 84 appearances for the Owls, and a subsequent spell on the coaching staff, coincided with a gloomy phase in the club's history. However, Knighton, who now works for Cable & Wireless as a sales manager in the Bristol area, retains only happy memories of Hillsborough.

I have a framed photograph on the wall of my home in Somerset which provides a constant reminder of one of the happiest moments in my time with Wednesday. It was taken on the day in late April 1974 when I scored the only goal in a match with Bolton Wanderers at Hillsborough – and it sealed a 1-0 victory which saved us from dropping into the old Third Division.

I had joined Wednesday from Hull the previous August, and that goal, in the 86th minute of the season's final game, was only my second for the club. In fact, it was the last I ever scored in the Football League, and I shall never forget it. I just happened to be at the far post when the ball reached me from the left, and it was a simple task to slot it into the net with my "weaker" right foot.

The irony was that, in normal circumstances, I might not have played. I had suffered an injury at Oxford three weeks earlier and missed four games, but, even though I was still not 100 per cent fit, I was desperate to play. I was the captain, and, having sat in the stand and seen us hammered 8-0 at Middlesbrough the previous Saturday, I felt anything was better than being a spectator on such a vital occasion.

It was marvellous to experience the effect that goal had on our fans in Wednesday's biggest crowd of the season [23,264], and I shall always treasure the memory of being carried off in triumph at the final whistle – the *Morning Telegraph* photograph of me on the shoulders of delighted supporters has a special place in my collection of souvenirs.

By coincidence, weeks before we knew that the Bolton game would be so crucial, I'd accepted an invitation to attend a presentation at a Supporters' Club dinner on the same evening. Goodness knows what the atmosphere at the function might have been like if the results had gone against us earlier in the day. Happily, it was one of the most convivial occasions I ever remember: the fans made me feel as if I'd scored the winner in an FA Cup Final!

That was the last act in an eventful season which had started with Derek Dooley signing me from Hull in August. At the time I was considering an offer from Luton, and, having been to Kenilworth Road and met manager Harry Haslam and director Eric Morecambe, I was tempted to say yes. But, being a Barnsley lad who considered Wednesday his team, when I got back home and learned the Owls wanted me, I knew I could only make one choice.

It was a decision I never regretted, though, of course, it was always a source of dismay that my stay at Hillsborough coincided with such a torrid time for the club. We didn't do as well as we wanted, but I was always very proud of being a Wednesday man.

I always felt the club's decision to sack Dooley halfway through my first season was outrageous and ill-timed

not just because the deed was done on Christmas Eve but because we felt Derek was finally starting to turn things round after a virus which had laid low most of the players. I hadn't been affected by the virus, but its effect on some of the lads was devastating – far worse than anyone really appreciated at the time.

What Derek lacked was a stronger right-hand man, and I've often wondered if it wouldn't have made more sense to have brought Steve Burtenshaw in as Derek's coach instead of giving Steve his first taste of management at a time when circumstances would have tested even a very experienced manager.

Unfortunately, while we beat the drop at the end of 1973-74 with that victory over Bolton, we had such a bad time in Steve's first full season as manager that our relegation fate was sealed with five games still to play. We knew we were down when we lost at Nottingham Forest at the start of April, and, just to rub salt in the wounds, that was the night when I conceded the penalty from which George Lyall sent us to defeat.

I was a bit disappointed when, on the following night, the local paper used a picture of me trudging off the pitch with a caption which suggested I was responsible for sending Wednesday down. Our fate might have been decided in that game, but it was our results over the season which cost us our Second Division place – and there were 11 games in which I hadn't played.

I didn't play many times in my third and final season as a Wednesday player, and 1975-76, which saw Len Ashurst replace Steve, was the year when we avoided a fall into the old Fourth Division by beating Southend in our last match. In the meantime, I had my final first-team outing in December and soon afterwards, around the time that George McCabe, Jim McAnearney and Ron Staniforth left the club, I joined the coaching staff.

At the age of 32, I obviously didn't have too long left as a senior player anyway, and it was very satisfying to take charge of the youngsters and help develop the talented lads whom Charlie Wain and Eric Gyte had brought to the club. I was enjoying my job, but, unfortunately, Len Ashurst's departure in October 1977 marked the beginning of

the end of my Wednesday career – though, at the time, I didn't know it.

When Len left, I had one game as Wednesday's caretaker manager, and we beat Chesterfield 1-0. What I didn't know until later was that Jack Charlton had sat in the North Stand that afternoon, and I certainly wasn't aware that, at the end of the game, Jack had gone round to talk to the directors about taking the manager's job.

When Bert McGee, the chairman, had asked me to take charge, I told him: "I'll be delighted to help out, but I need to know – is it worth my while applying for the vacancy?" He told me to apply because the board had no preconceived ideas about a candidate.

When I left the ground that Saturday evening at about 6.30, nobody had told me what was going on, but I hadn't been home long when I got a call from a journalist who said: "You might be interested to know that Jack Charlton has just been appointed Wednesday's manager."

Not having heard anything from the club or being put in the picture was disappointing, and it left a slightly bitter taste. However, I was briefly first-team coach and worked with Tony Toms, but, when I subsequently got an offer from Sunderland, it seemed a timely opportunity. Dave Blakey, the chief scout, had left to join Jimmy Adamson at Roker, and Dave recommended me for the senior coaching job.

It's history now that the appointment eventually led to me getting my first managerial job at Roker, and it's relevant to mention that I recruited my old Hillsborough team-mate, Peter Eustace, as a coach.

Frankly, I was delighted that Jack Charlton eventually started Wednesday's climb, and, 20 years on, it gives me nothing but pleasure to see the Owls continuing to thrive. The club gave me some fantastic memories, and I still cherish having been a Wednesday man.

Sometimes when I look back, I wonder why we didn't do better in my time. We could and should have succeeded because, at the peak, we had some decent players and a good spirit. The irony was that, when we were in decline and dropped into the Third Division, one of the things that worked against us was the splendour of the Hillsborough Stadium. It seemed like Wembley to some of the lesser clubs, and it was often to our disadvantage that the most humble visiting team saw meeting Wednesday as like playing in a Cup Final – it invariably gave them an added incentive to play above themselves.

Mark Smith

Mark Smith, a central defender who made 352 League and Cup appearances between 1978 and 1987, helped Wednesday climb from the Third to the First Division. He was attached to the club from the age of nine, started as an apprentice in June 1976, and became a professional in 1978. He later played with Plymouth, Barnsley, Notts County and Lincoln, taking his tally of League games past 500, and was assistant manager at Meadow Lane when Notts stormed to the Third Division title in 1998.

When I was a boy, you could stand in the back garden of our house on Shirecliffe and see Wednesday's ground,

and I suppose there was never any doubt about who I wanted to play for. So it was a thrill when, as a member of the Sheffield Boys Under-11 team, I was invited by George McCabe to train at Hillsborough on Tuesday and Thursday evenings.

I enjoyed those sessions in the gymnasium under Ron Staniforth. However, as I got older, there was a spell when I wondered what it might be like across the city at Bramall Lane, for, at the time, Sheffield United were in the First Division while the Owls had slipped into Division Three. I wasn't tied to Wednesday then, and when United asked me to try a few training sessions with them, I accepted. In fact, I was a United ball boy once, but then decided I preferred life with Wednesday and got my Dad to ring George McCabe and arrange my return.

That little episode might explain why, according to George, he made sure I was going to be a Wednesday apprentice by getting the forms signed on my 16th birthday in March and keeping

them in the club's safe until I left school in the following summer. He says he didn't want anybody to "steal" me!

I don't remember that, but I do recall how one of my earliest tasks after joining Wednesday was using a shovel to help with some earth-shifting up at the training ground. It's not the sort of work you'd expect apprentices to get involved in nowadays, when kids aren't allowed anywhere near machinery, but it was quite normal then, even if it didn't make you a better player.

George McCabe had developed a very good youth policy over the previous five or six years, and, in that period, we had some very promising youngsters who all went on to play in the first team. Some of us were luckier than others, and a turning point for me came when Ken Knighton decided to switch me from midfield to central defence.

Ken had taken over responsibility for the kids, and, frankly, when he insisted I was too tall to be a midfielder and had all the makings of a centre-back, I wasn't impressed. Only later did I

Mark Smith wins a heading duel in Wednesday's 1984 FA Cup clash with Southampton.

appreciate the wisdom of his words. Like George, Ken didn't stay long enough to see me make the grade, but I have always been grateful to him for ensuring I made the best use of my abilities. In fact, Ken's example was what prompted me to want to go into coaching in later years.

Jack Charlton's arrival, of course, enhanced my progress. He not only gave me my debut at 18, but was soon pushing me for England Under-21 recognition, and he also gave me the captaincy for a time. But the big bonus was benefiting from his coaching. As a man and as a coach, Jack was different class. His man-management, too, was something special. You could have the most outspoken argument with Jack, but, as soon as it was over, it was forgotten.

When I was at school I didn't get to many Wednesday games because I was usually playing somewhere else on match-days, but the Owls were always my team, and, when I became a professional, it really meant something to be involved in helping the club get back into the old First Division. Just before I became an apprentice, Wednesday had narrowly escaped the drop into Division Four, but, under Jack, we always felt things were moving upwards.

The year we won promotion from the Third Division was an especially memorable one for me, not least because I think I created some sort of record by scoring 11 times from the penalty spot, including nine in the League. One, of course, was the fourth goal in what Owls' fans always recall as "the Boxing Day massacre" – the famous 4-0 defeat of Sheffield United in 1979.

United were top of the table at the time, while we had been struggling, and that game is still seen as a turning point, for we went on to win promotion while the Blades slipped out of the reckoning. In my view, our 2-0 win at Reading a few days earlier was the result which really marked the start of our revival, for though we lost our next home match after beating United, it was at Elm Park that we found the touch which had been lacking earlier in the season.

It was funny the way I started taking penalties that season, and it might not

Mark Smith.

have happened if Brian Hornsby hadn't missed one in a League Cup match at Manchester City in September. When the referee ordered a retake because the goalkeeper had moved, the ball was thrown to me. I can't recall who threw it, or how I came to be at that end of the field. But I scored from the spot, and my first senior goal gave us a 1-0 lead. Unfortunately, we lost 2-1 in extra-time after City had snatched a late equaliser.

I scored ten penalties on the trot before missing one, and kept the job until Terry Curran decided he wanted to take them. Thereafter, my ambition was to score a goal from open play, and I finally managed it in our first season back in Division Two when, against Bristol Rovers at home in December 1980, I went up for a corner and hooked the ball into the net from close range after the goalkeeper had blocked a Mel Sterland header. I promptly embarrassed myself with my celebrations!

After the 1980 promotion, I suppose the next highlight was reaching the FA Cup semi-final in 1983, though the big day at Highbury was something of an anticlimax. The afternoon started with an element of farce when Pat Heard and David Mills were left behind at the team hotel when the team bus left for the

match. Somehow, that set the tone, for we never really got going against Brighton. For some curious reason, it didn't seem like a semi-final, and, strange as it might sound, I have to admit it was only years after the event that I appreciated just how close we'd been to Wembley.

The fans weren't happy about our performance, and I can still remember how, on the way home, a supporters coach overtook our team bus, and the fans made their frustration very plain as they saw the lads playing cards when I suppose they expected everybody to have their heads down in disappointment.

The following season, 1983-84, was the one when Howard Wilkinson came and we finally won promotion to Division One after a 14-year absence. It was a great year for the club, and a thrill to be a part of it, but my joy was tempered by a sense of frustration because, for the first time in my career, I was plagued by injuries. A knee ligament injury in a pre-season game at Lincoln caused me to miss the first four matches, then I did the same knee again in March and played in only one of the last 12 games.

I had the same problem in 1986 when the delight of reaching the FA Cup semi-final was marred for me when I got a foot injury in the last ten seconds of the quarter-final defeat of West Ham. At the time, the knock seemed so trivial I didn't even mention it, but, when we resumed training two days later, I was in difficulties, and even a five-day rest and a couple of jabs in the heel couldn't help me recover in time to face Everton at Villa Park.

In fact, I didn't get back into the team until the following January, and, by then, I had more or less decided there wasn't a future for me at Hillsborough. With hindsight I know the decision was the wrong one, but, at the time, I didn't feel there was any other choice, and it's too easy now to tell myself I might have been wiser to have hung on.

It didn't help that I was carrying a knee injury which, ironically, stemmed from a trivial incident just before my testimonial game. I knelt down to pose for a picture with the mascots, and as I stood up I felt a twinge in my knee. The knee then kept locking when I bent it.

I sometimes think Howard Wilkinson thought I was faking it, but I'd never do that, and nobody was more upset than me when the knee locked during a training session at Middlewood Road – just when I was back in the squad, and only a few hours before we were due to travel to Wimbledon.

The date, 12 December 1986, sticks in my mind because it was the day the Queen came to Hillsborough to formally open the new covered Kop. Due to the royal visit, we couldn't get near the ground, and, with all the roads sealed off, public and private transport in the area was at a standstill for several hours.

When I reported my knee problem to Howard, he said I'd better not go to Wimbledon, and, aware of his impatience and lack of sympathy, I had the additional frustration of knowing the only way I could reach my home at Stannington was by walking. As I had been expecting to travel with the team, my wife had taken our car to work that morning, and there would be no buses or taxis running for some time yet.

It was a long walk, uphill most of the way, and, in all my years with Wednesday, I doubt if I had ever felt so low in spirit as I did when plodding home that day. I certainly had plenty of time to think, and my head was full of negative thoughts. The last thing I wanted was to leave, but I came to the conclusion it seemed inevitable.

In fact, I got back into the side early in the New Year, but, while my 22 games included six in an FA Cup run which took us to the quarter-finals, I think we won only five of the 16 League matches, and there was a mood of change in the air. My last match came in the season's final game, at home to Wimbledon, which we lost 2-0. When I was brought off just past the hour mark, I sensed the curtain had come down on a Wednesday link spanning 18 years.

I went out of contract in June, and, while I was offered a nominal increase under new terms, the die was as good as already cast – the pity being to leave on a downer after so many good years.

After Hillsborough, everywhere else could only be second best, but, if I had my regrets, at least I took with me some great memories – of some good times, lots of laughs and happy days, and so many great friends and good influences.

John Pearson

John Pearson, the lanky striker who is now business development manager at Sheffield Football Club, made 128 League and Cup appearances for Wednesday and scored 27 goals between 1980 and 1985, and figured in the promotion side of 1983-84. In a League career spanning eight clubs he chalked up over 420 games and scored 66 goals.

I was Wednesday mad from a very early age, and it was through following the team's fortunes so avidly in the local Saturday sports paper, the *Green 'Un*, that I learned to read even before I went to school. I was reading quite well at three years old, and, by the time I was attending Shooter's Grove Infants, I could also write well enough to pen a letter to the Owls' manager, Danny Williams, offering my services as a player!

It was under Danny that Wednesday went down from the First Division, and, though I didn't go to the ill-fated Manchester City match in April 1970, at six I was old enough to be devastated by a defeat that meant relegation – all the more so as everybody said it was a game the Owls should never have lost.

As kids do, I dreamed that I might help get my favourite football club back into the top grade, and I probably imagined discussing the subject with Tommy Craig when he lived a few doors away from our house in Rockley Road. Unfortunately, I was so in awe of Wednesday's first £100,000 player, I hadn't the courage to speak to him!

Fate is a funny thing, and, remark-

John Pearson is congratulated by skipper Mick Lyons after completing a double against Middlesbrough in August 1982.

ably, when Wednesday ended a 14-year wait to return to the old First Division in 1984, I was in the promotion side – and, although I didn't score the first goal in the Owls' initial match back in the top-grade, I did get the third in a 3-1 defeat of Nottingham Forest. To be honest, the ball hit me on the knee and went into the net, but, fortuitous or not, it ensured I had fulfilled my boyhood dream of playing for Wednesday in the First Division and scoring.

Mind you, playing for Wednesday seemed a distant dream in my time at Marcliffe Junior School, but things looked up a bit after I went to Wisewood Comprehensive, although, ironically, when I got into the Sheffield Boys team at 14 it was through the exertions of Joe Slater, the manager of my Sunday League side, Sheffield Rangers. Joe invited the schools people to come and watch me in action.

Because I was a big lad, Sheffield Boys used me as a centre-half, but, once I felt my place was secure, I asked if I could revert to my normal position in midfield, and this ultimately inspired a switch to centre-forward. Anyway, I did well enough to catch the eye of the Wednesday scouts, Charlie Wain and Eric Gyte, and I didn't need asking twice to sign schoolboy forms.

I was offered an apprenticeship when I left school in 1979, and I shall never forget the thrill of wearing an Owls shirt for the first time when I made my debut in the Juniors as a late substitute at Barnsley.

However, better things weren't far away, for, in September 1980, less than two weeks after my 17th birthday, Jack Charlton gave me my Football League debut in the home game with Bristol City. It all came about rather out of the blue because Terry Curran was suspended after being sent off at Oldham the previous week, and Andy McCulloch was out injured.

I celebrated with a headed goal in a 2-1 win, but an unfortunate twist to my big day was that my parents didn't know about it until afterwards. They just happened to be on holiday in Malta at the time, and Dad didn't discover the news until, on the Sunday morning, he walked two miles to get a newspaper. He told me later he was so excited when he read the details, he nearly had a heart attack running back to tell my mother!

That promotion success in 1984 was a bit special, and I remember how hard we all worked. Howard Wilkinson drove us pretty hard, so we were fitter than most our rivals and the manager's organisation and attention to detail were key factors. Towards the end of the season we were a bit mentally shattered, but the spirit was fantastic. I played in 27 games and always feel it was a privilege to be part of that team.

The final game was at Cardiff, and when we won 2-0 we thought we had won the Second Division championship. We went back out onto the field to applaud our fans believing that Chelsea had only drawn at Grimsby. Unfortunately, when we got onto the bus to come home, we learned Chelsea had won 1-0 to pip us to the title on goal-difference.

Naturally, I never wanted to leave Hillsborough, and was upset when the time came to move on in 1985, but at least I finished my Wednesday career on a high note – with a hat-trick for the Reserves. In fact, I had already signed for Charlton Athletic, but for some reason the forms had been post-dated, which allowed me one unexpected last fling in an Owls shirt.

I felt very emotional when we took the field against West Brom, and, as we bounced back from behind to win 4-2, my strike partner Carl Shutt scored one and I grabbed three. When the third one went in, I thought I couldn't have ended my Wednesday story in a better way.

I left with lots of good memories, not least of some of the escapades a few of us enjoyed as apprentices. Like the Friday when we locked the dressing room door after finishing our cleaning duties and drank two bottles of champagne intended for Jack Charlton. The bottles, a gift from Liverpool, had been packed in our skip following a match at Anfield the previous evening. No doubt Gavin Oliver, Trevor Matthewson, Paul Shirtliff, Simon Mills and me all felt that what Big Jack didn't know, he wouldn't miss – and we've kept the secret until now. Sorry, Jack!

There was also the day when, having helped the club groundsman fork the pitch, a group of us decided to have some fun with his moped. One of the lads bump started it, and, never having ridden a moped, I asked if I could have a go. Alas, I promptly drove it straight into a wall and smashed it!

Of course, we paid up and bought a new moped, but one of my pals – I think it was Trevor Matthewson – took the rap for crashing the bike. He did it because, as I was then on the brink of breaking into the first-team, I feared I might get dropped from the squad if it was known I was the culprit. Happy days!

I went back to Hillsborough with Leeds United in 1987, and it was a happy coincidence that my return should be in an FA Cup semi-final. In truth, it was an occasion I thoroughly enjoyed, because playing on that pitch really meant something to me. Sadly, we were beaten 3-2 by Coventry City – and, of course, they had defeated Wednesday in the previous round.

Gary Megson

Gary Megson, the red-haired midfielder who made 286 League and Cup appearances and scored 33 goals for Wednesday in two spells between 1981 and 1989, completed a family double at Hillsborough, following in the footsteps of his father, Don, the long-serving full-back who captained the Owls in the 1966 FA Cup Final. Between them the Megsons totted up 728 senior games for Wednesday. Gary became manager of Stockport County in July 1997.

My earliest memories of Hillsborough date back to when I was a very small boy being taken to the ground by my Dad, and I can still vividly recall the unique smell of the boot room and the old leather footballs, and I remember the old snooker table in what was then the player's lounge. There was something very exciting about the atmosphere, and, as the son of a Wednesday player, I loved being able to wander about behind the scenes.

I celebrated my seventh birthday in the month when Wednesday played Everton the FA Cup Final, but can't recall much about the match other than that I went down to London with my Dad's parents. I have clearer memories of the World Cup matches which were staged at Hillsborough in the same summer of 1966: the games involving West Germany were wonderfully colourful.

WEDNESDAY EVERY DAY OF THE WEEK

Don Megson, pictured here with his sons Neil and Gary when they were small boys. Their father is looking through his picture collection ahead of his testimonial game in the late 1960s.

It must have been soon afterwards when I found myself training with some schoolboys in what was then the new gymnasium behind the cantilever stand. Alan Brown, the manager, was in charge of those sessions, and, as most of the other boys were older than me, I think I was there because my old man was doing something elsewhere at the ground and, as I happened to be at a loose end, I was invited to join in. Anyway, it was fun to be involved in a bit of Dad's world!

Dad's final appearance for Wednesday was early in January 1970, and he joined Bristol Rovers soon afterwards, but, in the following April, I remember being in the crowd at Hillsborough when a defeat against Manchester City meant relegation. I

Sheffield Wednesday in 1982. Back row (left to right): Mick Lyons, John Pearson, Andy McCulloch, Peter Shirtliff, Mick Pickering. Middle row: Richard Beaumont, Mark Smith, Gavin Oliver, David Redfern, Bob Bolder, Mel Sterland, Ante Mirocevic, Trevor Matthewson. Front row: Gary Shelton, Kevin Taylor, Charlie Williamson, Gary Megson, Gary Bannister, Gordon Owen, Paul Shirtliff.

was as much a Wednesdayite as anyone in the ground that night, and have never forgotten the strange atmosphere and the sense of shock at realising what the result meant for the club.

It was a curious coincidence that, when Wednesday finally returned to the top-grade in 1984, I was in the team, and could appreciate better than many just what promotion after 14 years meant to the club.

Being the son of Don Megson, I suppose many people imagined I would want to start my own career with Wednesday, but, whenever we talked about it in my days at Malin Bridge School, Dad and I agreed it might be best for me to begin elsewhere. In any event, by the time I was old enough to join a club, we were living in Bristol, which explains why I went to Plymouth Argyle as an apprentice in 1977 – though there was an intriguing ex-Sheffield link in that, at the time, Alan Brown was Plymouth's coach.

It was after less than two years at Everton, who had signed me in late 1979, that I found myself a Wednesday player in August 1981. I didn't really want to leave Goodison Park, but, once

it was apparent I wasn't going to stay, I felt that if I had to step down from the top-grade there would be nowhere better to go than Hillsborough.

It was like coming home because, at the time, everything was just as I remembered it from when I was a boy – the ground, the dressing room area and all the familiar places were exactly the same as they had been a dozen years earlier. The same friendly faces were all around. Norma Lane was still the manager's secretary, Lily Shelton was still cleaning and making endless cups of tea, and Betty Pearson, who had washed my Dad's kit, was still in the laundry and would now be washing my kit.

Of course, it was a move I never regretted, and I always felt we would soon be back in the old First Division. We didn't get promotion as quickly as we hoped, but things were definitely on the up and we had a good team and a great spirit. Ironically, if the old two-points-for-a-win system had stayed in place one season longer than it did, we'd have been promoted in 1982.

The club's finances were healthy after some difficult times, and Jack Charlton invested in players who came

from higher-grade clubs. Under Jack, and later Howard Wilkinson, we had a lot of players who had under-achieved elsewhere but had the ability and desire to succeed.

My particular mates were Gary Bannister and Gary Shelton, because we arrived together; but the thing about the club at that time was all the players were great friends. We were close and knocked about together. We were similar types: our careers picked up at Hillsborough, joining Wednesday was good for us, and we enjoyed succeeding together.

We ought really to have reached Wembley in 1983, when we had some great results in our FA Cup run, including a marvellous 5-0 defeat of Burnley in a home quarter-final replay. However, in the semi-final against Brighton at Highbury, on the day we just didn't perform, and, looking back, I think our mistake was in treating it as just another game when, in reality, it was a massive occasion.

Jack left at the end of that season, but, within a year, we had clinched promotion under Howard, and work-rate and organisation were the keynotes –

Gary Megson (right) is welcomed to Hillsborough by John Harris in 1981, watched by his father and former Owls captain Don Megson.

there were no big-hitters in the team, but everyone played their part in a system designed to get us into the old First Division.

I can admit with the benefit of hindsight that, following promotion, I made the wrong decision when choosing not to accept a new contract with Wednesday. However, with the club's circumstances dramatically improved, they had left the hard times behind and were going for bigger names, and I believed I deserved better terms than were on offer.

Yet while I found I could earn a lot more by moving 40 miles down the road to Nottingham Forest, it proved a mistake, and, frankly, after a subsequent spell at Newcastle, I felt myself fortunate to get a second chance with Wednesday when Howard brought me back in late 1985.

I had a good second spell at Hillsborough, which lasted until I moved to Manchester City in January 1989, and, of course, one of the highlights was when we reached the FA Cup semi-final in 1986 and lost 2-1 to Everton in extra-time at Villa Park. Unfortunately, once again it wasn't our day. There wasn't much between the teams, but we didn't take our chances and Everton did.

It always meant something special to follow in my Dad's footsteps and play for Wednesday, and, naturally, it would have been great to have emulated the old man by playing for the club in an FA Cup Final. I think he would have loved to see me top his record by winning with the Owls at Wembley.

Yet, if it wasn't to be, we both still regard Wednesday as our club. We share a million memories of some great times and lots of very special people. Wednesday's result is still the one we look for first, and my only regret is I've yet to convert my eight-year-old son Simon into an Owls' fan. Perhaps he'll have a change of heart when he is older and can appreciate what Hillsborough meant to the Megsons!

Martin Hodge

Martin Hodge, who returned to Wednesday as a coach in July 1996 at the end of a playing career spanning over 600 League and Cup games with nine clubs, is remembered as a goalkeeper and captain

Martin Hodge, a great favourite with the fans, collects his Player of the Year Trophy from Supporter's Club chairman Bill Heap in 1986.

whose 249 outings for the Owls between 1983 and 1988 featured an Owls' record run of 214 consecutive appearances which started in the 1983-84 promotion campaign.

Four years after I left Wednesday as a player, I came back with Hartlepool for a Coca-Cola Cup-tie, and the reception the Hillsborough crowd gave me that evening in September 1992 was something I'll never forget. The warmth and emotion in the standing ovation I received was unbelievable, and it reminded me why I feel this club and this city are very special.

When I first arrived on loan from Everton in the summer of 1983, I'd spent three years struggling with injuries and my career was at a low ebb. But then things took a dramatic turn for the better, and the experience confirmed me as a Wednesdayite for life. More than that, I found I made so many friends in Sheffield, I knew I would never want to live anywhere else – and it's been my base ever since.

Having come as understudy to Iain Hesford, the irony was he never made the first team, while I went on to play in 214 games without a break and establish an all-time Wednesday record. I've heard it said I got my chance because Iain broke a finger, but, in fact, I was already in the team before that happened. Indeed, within days of my debut

in the opening match of the 1983-84 season, Howard Wilkinson wanted to make my move permanent. It was a compliment that with hindsight he saw the £50,000 fee as a bargain.

I was grateful for the opportunity, but, after the disappointments of the previous years, I took nothing for granted. I prepared myself mentally, and my determination to keep my place and not give Iain the chance to replace me was reflected in the way I worked so desperately hard and with such single-minded dedication. Goalkeepers are friends even if they're rivals, but the man in possession has to put himself first!

The effort brought reward, and, while I'm not really bothered about statistics, that appearance record is something I'm very proud of. Supporters still talk about it, and tell their sons, while people ask: "Did you really go all those years without missing a game?" with a respect I appreciate.

Nobody can ever take away from me the memory of that first year, when we won promotion. The bonding between a group of players who were regarded as no-hopers, free transfer men, and under-achievers created an atmosphere which was unique. I think the first thing we did when I came was go off on the longest run in the world! But those six, seven and eight-mile runs generated a great collective belief as we pulled each other through the physical ordeal.

It was like something you associate with the army, but there was nothing regimental about those training sessions. We enjoyed them because we always ended up laughing. Once, for instance, we went up to Bradfield in the middle of winter. It was icy, and, though we were knackered at the end of another long run, Howard Wilkinson had us rounding the afternoon off by sliding down this bank on our backsides. We ended up falling about with laughter as we watched each other performing like a gang of schoolboys. It was all part of the bonding!

In the five years I spent with Howard, I must admit there were times when I wondered why we were doing this or that exercise, but I have to say he was the most professional manager I ever worked under. There was a purpose in all that we did, and, if those runs were intended to give us a change of scene while improving fitness, they also boosted team-spirit. I think Howard once said he got the idea from one of his old managers, Alan Brown, and, by the same token, some of us took the Wilkinson philosophy on board. It's a massive compliment to Howard that so many of his old Wednesday lads responded to his lead and have followed him into coaching and management.

Perhaps the biggest disappointment we suffered in 1983-84 was when Chelsea pipped us to the Second Division championship on goal-difference after we'd had promotion sewn up for weeks. I'll never forget the range of emotions we experienced on the final day of the season when we played at Cardiff. We won the game, and, having been told we were champions when we came off, savoured the sheer joy of believing our hard work – all those long runs, all those months of sheer grit and determination – had been rewarded. Then to learn 20 minutes later that Chelsea had pipped us to the title was just about the most deflating experience you can have.

I have mostly happy memories from my time as a Wednesday player. I remember best what we achieved as a team and the pride of being captain. What a wonderful compliment it was to succeed Mick Lyons in the job, for Mick epitomised everything you would ever want from a captain. He was brave, a dedicated and determined player, a marvellous leader, and he did so well

for the younger lads. The fans loved him – and, incidentally, I shall always be in his debt because he was the man who persuaded Howard Wilkinson to bring me from Everton in the first place!

Happy personal memories include my penalty save from Gordon Strachan at Old Trafford in 1985 and, as an old Evertonian, especially the one from Jan Molby at Anfield in 1986. People still ask me: did you really save a penalty in front of the Liverpool Kop?

1986 was memorable in that we finished fifth in the old First Division and reached the FA Cup semi-final, but the end of the season brought one of my biggest disappointments as a professional and marked a personal turning point. I have heard people suggest I was never quite the same again after I missed out on joining the England squad for the World Cup in Mexico – and there is some truth in what they say.

What may have been forgotten is that, after being put on stand-by because Manchester United's Gary Bailey was injured, I got a message to say I was going to Mexico. I was not only packed and ready, but had the tickets for the flight and was just about to get into the car taking me to the airport when I was told I wasn't wanted. Bailey had apparently decided he was fit after all.

Even all these years later, I can't really describe the disappointment. It was soul-destroying, not just for me but my family. The knock on the chin was so big, I struggled to come to terms with it for a long, long time. I had grafted so hard for so long, and come so close to the ultimate goal. When I'd started out at Plymouth, there had been people who didn't think I'd make the grade, but I'd devoted every hour God sent to make myself a goalkeeper, and overcome a lot of setbacks along the way.

What really hurt about the circumstances of that summer was Bailey, in fact, never kicked another ball. You have to bounce back, and eventually I did, but for a while I lost faith in football and the system. There was something so unfair about it, and you didn't always get what you deserved. With that experience, I could understand how Kevin Pressman must have felt when he wasn't named in the 1998 World Cup squad.

By coincidence, it was Kevin, of course, who had ended my run of consecutive appearances when, in Sep-

tember 1987, he was given his Wednesday debut at Southampton. We had played Coventry the previous weekend, and I'd ended up going to hospital with suspected ankle ligament trouble. I was struggling to get fit, but, with the team having lost four of our first five games, I don't think I would have played at The Dell anyway.

I was back after missing two matches, but, in the following March, I lost my place again, and, when Howard said he wasn't proposing to use me at the start of the 1988-89 season, I told him I thought I ought to consider leaving. I was ready to stay and fight for my place, but, having got the feeling the situation wasn't as simple as that, I couldn't face the prospect of permanent demotion to the Reserves after five years in the first team. I didn't want a repeat of my Everton frustration.

With hindsight, I can admit now that it was the wrong decision. Leaving Wednesday was the worst thing I could have done. I soon saw I'd cut my nose off to spite my face, and, while I went to Leicester and never gave it less than my best shot, my heart was still at Hillsborough. The irony was that, in the following season, Kevin was injured and Chris Turner, who had been brought back to the club, came in. I couldn't help but wonder what might have happened if I had never left.

Happily, in the longer term, there was to be a return to Wednesday as a member of the backroom staff in 1996. I never thought I would get the chance, but, after working in a coaching role at Plymouth, a bolt came out of the blue in the form of a call from David Pleat. He had been my manager at Leicester, and, while, to be frank, we hadn't always seen eye to eye at Filbert Street, he was honest enough to say he felt I had the knowledge and experience to do a job at Hillsborough.

I don't think he needed telling there was no place I would rather work.

Kevin Pressman

Goalkeeper Kevin Pressman, who became a Wednesday apprentice in June 1984 after two and a half years on schoolboy forms and turned professional in November 1985, ended the 1997-98 campaign with 280 appearances to his name in a career which brought many trials before he made the No.1 jersey his own.

I always remember the day I got engaged to my wife Joanne coincided with a Wednesday juniors match against Leeds up at the training ground, and I didn't celebrate the occasion by having the best game in the world. My display prompted Mick Hennigan, the coach, to have a real go at me. He said: "I hope your future father and mother-in-law weren't here, because if they'd seen you perform like that, they wouldn't have anything more to do with you – they'd stop their daughter marrying you!"

Well, I survived, and 17 years after I first became associated with Wednesday on schoolboy forms, I can claim to be the club's longest-serving current professional. I became an apprentice at 16½ and a full-time pro at 18, and, if it hasn't exactly been plain sailing down the years, I have no regrets. As I often reminded myself in times when things weren't going well, I couldn't be in a better job. I enjoy what I do.

When I was about 14, attending the Henry Fanshawe School and playing for Chesterfield Boys, there was interest from Manchester United and Wednesday. I chose Hillsborough not so much because it was closer to home but in consequence of John Harris, the chief scout, inviting me to start training two nights a week at the ground until I was old enough to leave school and start my career.

No other club said anything beyond "sign for us on schoolboy forms". Wednesday at least had something mapped out, and I knew I could look beyond starting with Middlewood Rovers. Over the years, people like Albert Phelan and Frank Barlow were helpful at key stages. They kept me going and helped me become a better goalkeeper.

But John Harris was probably the first key influence. He had the wisdom and experience, was always helpful, and took time to talk to me about what it meant to become a professional, always stressing the need to work hard and show real dedication to succeed in the game.

I was 19 and had been a professional for less than two years when Howard Wilkinson gave me my League debut at Southampton in September 1987. He told me in the bath after training on the Friday morning, and there was just enough time before the team-bus left to make a few quick phone calls to warn the family and let them make plans for a long journey.

As for the match, it was fast and quick compared with what I'd known, but, if I was busy, I felt I had a good game, and my confidence got an early boost when I made a good save from a free-kick and then got up to block the rebound.

Kevin Pressman.

The pattern of my first-team appearance record shows I endured six seasons of frustration before enjoying five more consistently successful years, and the experience of spending so long in the wilderness (and missing out on the 1991 and 1993 Cup Finals into the bargain) has made me appreciate the subsequent upturn in my fortunes. When I was stuck in the Reserves, I always classed it as a prison sentence – and when I returned to the first team felt as if I'd done my "time" and been released for good behaviour!

I had earlier decided that when I got back into the first team, I was never going to return to the Reserves, and that desire and determination kept me going and ensured I kept my standards high. I always felt I had the ability and never doubted I could prove to anybody that I was capable of playing in the top flight.

The 1989-90 and 1990-91 seasons are remembered because Wednesday were relegated in the first and won promotion and the Rumbelows Cup in the second, but my own recollections are that both campaigns were particularly painful in bringing serious injuries just when I was enjoying good runs. On New Year's Day 1990, a clash with Manchester City's David Oldfield left me with damaged cruciate ligaments; then on Boxing Day 1990, after I had made 29 consecutive appearances, I tore my thigh muscle against Wolves.

My thigh injury meant Chris Turner got back again, and I didn't play in the first-team again until the last match of the season. In the meantime, Wednesday not only clinched promotion but progressed to the League Cup Final. And I missed out. Helping the Reserves win the Pontins League was no compensation! I have to admit in the later stages of the campaign I let my disappointment show. With hindsight, it's easy to see it was stupid to walk around looking miserable. But I was young and took it all very personally.

I haven't forgotten what Ron Atkinson told me in our hotel on the morning of the Wembley match with Manchester United. Confirming I wasn't playing, he said: "I hope it's going to be a lesson to you. I don't like your attitude. It hasn't been right. Take heed, and when you do get back in the side, make sure you stay there."

Unfortunately, come the start of 1991-92 and what had promised to be a straight fight for the goalkeeper's jersey between me and Chris Turner suddenly became something quite different when Trevor Francis, who had taken over after "Big Ron" moved to Aston Villa, went out and signed the then current England man Chris Woods. To say it was a shock is an understatement. Trevor denied it one minute, and the next I walked out of his office – and straight into Chris Woods!

I only managed about half-a-dozen outings in the next two seasons, and this was the period when I felt I was serving a prison sentence and sometimes believed I would need more than good behaviour to earn an early release! Once again I missed out on Wembley – all four games – but, around the back-end of 1993, things took a turn for the better. I came in again when Woods was

Kevin Pressman – an unhappy memory for the Owls goalkeeper as he is sent off at Blackburn in 1995.

injured, and didn't let him get back. In the end my patience and persistence got some reward. I went from strength to strength, and it was particularly satisfying when I was given the first of my "B" caps and started being talked of in terms of being third in line for a senior England place.

Of course, earlier in my career there were no such things as squad numbers, but they came in with the launch of the Premiership, and when, at the start of the 1996-97 season, I was given Wednesday's No.1 jersey for the first time, I looked at the opening day's match programme and said to myself: "Now I know I've finally made it!"

If I've had my disappointments over the years, there have been a lot of nice moments, and, while there are a few saves I remember with pleasure, I suppose one of the things a lot of supporters will recall is the night I scored the decisive goal in the penalty shoot-out when we beat Watford in an FA Cup replay at Hillsborough in January 1998.

I scored in a shoot-out at Wolves in 1995, but we ended up losing that night, and, anyway, there wasn't so much pressure on me. This time it really mattered because it sealed a 5-3 win – and after I had saved Watford's second penalty!

Earlier, the Gaffer had said who was to take the penalties, and told me I was having the fifth one. When the time came, I struck it as hard as I could, and it was a fantastic feeling to see it go in – and then realise what it meant. It's something I'll never forget, but, then, there are so many things that have happened over the years that I shall always remember – and most of them with pleasure.

Part Two – Cup Heroes
Boys of '66

Don Megson

Don Megson became a Wednesday amateur in 1952 at the age of 16, but did not sign as a full-time professional until he was 23 – by which time he had completed his apprenticeship as a joiner and then spent two years doing National Service in the army. Between 1959 and 1970 he made 442 League and Cup appearances for the Owls. The "Don of Hillsborough" will always be remembered as captain of the 1966 FA Cup Final team.

Sheffield people have never forgotten how we made a bit of history at Wembley in 1966 by becoming the first team to do a losers' lap of honour at the end of an FA Cup Final. I have to admit it would have been so much nicer to be remembered for winning that dramatic duel with Everton, but, sadly, it wasn't to be, and I don't need to remind any Wednesdayite of the circumstances in which we lost a two-goal lead.

I'm often asked why we decided to salute our fans instead of disappearing straight to the dressing rooms after the presentations, and I invariably recall that the idea came about a month earlier in the Villa Park dressing room where we were celebrating our famous semi-final triumph over Chelsea.

As we sat there amid all the noise and banter, and toasted our success in champagne while still wearing our muddy gear, I told Tony Hardisty (who was then covering our games for the Sheffield evening paper): "I'm so proud of the youngsters who have got us to the Final, I promise you this, whatever happens at Wembley, we'll do a lap of honour at the end of the game – so we can thank the fans and they can show how they feel about what the lads have done."

To be honest, I'd said it on the spur of the moment, but it stuck with me, although, after an hour of the game against Everton, when we were leading 2-0, we seemed more likely to be running round the Wembley track with the Cup than without it – not that I had time to even think about it while we were still playing.

When the final whistle blew, the disappointment we all felt was over-

The Boys of '66. Back row (left to right): McCalliog, Eustace, Springett, Young, Ellis, Smith Front: Pugh, Fantham, Megson, Ford, Quinn.

Don Megson.

whelming. To lose on such an occasion is a blow at any time, but losing when you've had one hand on the most coveted trophy in English football is a shattering experience. All the same, I was always one of those people who gave absolutely everything during a match but accepted there was nothing you could do about a defeat once a game was over – and that attitude stopped me getting too upset on many occasions.

Somewhere I have a photograph of me and Ron Springett gazing at our medals on the pitch at the end, and I recall that just after this was taken, a

Wembley steward came over to us and pointed towards the dressing rooms – as if to indicate he wanted us to leave the arena so the Cup winners could take their bow.

I thought: "We're not going to trudge off just like that. We're proud to have got here, we're proud of having been involved in a memorable Final – and I'm still as proud of these lads as I was after the semi-final."

So I started to go off on the promised lap of honour on my own, and the first team-mate I saw was Peter Eustace. He was down, his face etched with disappointment. I recall saying: "You dare let me run round this field on my own!" Peter followed – and soon all the lads were running with me.

Okay, we didn't win the Cup, but we achieved a lot that year, and our run to Wembley created a terrific bond in the dressing room. That side, a blend of youth and experience, had the basis of a very good team which should have gone on to better things than it did.

The great disappointment for me was the way, after 1966, the club parted with players of a much higher quality than the ones who were brought in to replace them. When Alan Brown went in 1968, the club allowed a situation to develop which could only lead to a decline that could have been avoided – and hadn't seemed possible when our trip to Wembley inspired such high hopes for the future.

For me, like a lot of the lads, the real highlight of the 1966 Cup run was the semi-final. Chelsea were a very powerful team, a footballing side against whom few gave us much chance; but we were filled with hope when the rain created heavy and difficult conditions that could only be to our advantage. We were a team prepared to work and battle in what nobody doubted would be a tough, physical duel in the mud.

We set the tone from the start. When Chelsea kicked off and the ball was knocked towards their left wing, Wilf Smith hammered Bobby Tambling; and, soon afterwards, I made my presence felt on the opposite flank with a strong challenge on Barry Bridges.

Later, of course, George Graham clattered our centre-half Vic Mobley, who was reduced to a passenger, and I'll always remember being so incensed when I heard Graham tell a colleague

This Wednesday "A" team from 1955 shows where the careers of Don Megson, Peter Swan and Gerry Young began. The full line-up reads: Back row (left to right): Mick Turley, Terry Whitham, Peter Swan, Alan Hinchcliffe, Peter Smith, Don Megson. Front row: Frank Elliott, Gerry Young. Derek Williams, unknown, Peter Howells.

"I've done him!" that I tried my damndest to get him back during the next hour!

The pleasure for me was seeing how well our young players performed in that match. Graham Pugh, just 18 and making his Cup debut, topped a great display by putting us in front soon after half-time when David Ford headed a ball from John Fantham back across the box; and I always remember the joyful forward roll with which Jim McCalliog celebrated scoring our second goal a minute from the end.

At that time, the dug-outs at Villa Park were on the far side of the pitch, and, when the teams were walking off after our 2-0 win, Tommy Docherty, the Chelsea manager, ran up and called me an effing butcher. I reminded him he'd been no slouch at putting himself about when he was a player – and, anyway, what about what he'd done to Jackie Sewell when Preston had beaten Wednesday in the 1954 semi-final?

It was cruel on big Vic Mobley to miss the Final with his injury, and I was always sorry that Colin Dobson, who had played in the first three rounds, never got a look-in afterwards. I think Tommy Walker, who was then on the training staff, had especial sympathy for Colin. Tommy recalled that, back in 1935, he had known the disappointment of being dropped by a Wednesday manager during a Cup run which led to Wembley

At the time of the 1966 Final, I was nearing my 30th birthday and had been

connected with Wednesday for almost half my life. I may have been a Manchester product, but the blue half of Sheffield was my spiritual home, and I was proud of my Hillsborough links.

It was a scout called Ted Schofield who brought me to Wednesday's attention when I was 15. I was already playing non-League football with my brother Cyril at Mossley, but it was after a game for Lancashire Boys that I was invited across the Pennines for a trial. My first game was against Penistone Church in the Hatchard League, and, strange as it might seem, I was asked to play at outside-right.

Joe Nibloe and Ted Catlin, who had been the Wednesday backs in the 1935 Cup Final, had charge of the Hatchard League side, and Catlin, noting how left-footed I was, agreed I was no right-winger! Happily, he invited me for a subsequent outing on the opposite flank, and I must have impressed in that role because they signed me as an amateur.

I have lots of happy memories of the next few years, during which I played in the Hatchard, Yorkshire and Central League teams and enjoyed helpful advice from a range of older players. Redfern Froggatt and Jack Shaw were two old first-team men who were especially good to me.

Froggatt was one of the best people I ever met in football – a real gentleman. I doubt if I played with him more than half-a-dozen times, but, at 16 or 17 I got into the Reserves as Redfern's wing partner. He was a great bloke for calming your nerves and giving you exactly the advice and encouragement you needed.

Shaw, who had enjoyed his best years as a forward with Rotherham before moving to Hillsborough in 1953, was one of the few first-team players to step down into the "A" team towards the end of his career, and he did a tremendous job with the youngsters, being a bigger influence on them than any of the coaching staff.

By the time I was 18 I had a lot of games under my belt and became a part-time professional, but I still had three years of my apprenticeship to finish, and, with National Service to follow, my progress wasn't as rapid as that of some of the other young players who started out alongside me. It said everything that Peter Swan was coming out of the army and about to start a push for a regular senior place just as I was joining the Royal Signals at Catterick.

When I could finally concentrate totally on my football following demob, Harry Catterick had taken over and led Wednesday back into Division One in his first season, and it was my good fortune that he not only offered me full-time terms but made the suggestion which changed the course of my career.

I had played in nearly every position in the Reserves, and looked to be settled at centre-half, but Harry pointed out how great the competition was in that position. There was a queue of players wanting the No.5 shirt. Harry said my best bet if I hoped for a first-team place was to try playing at left-back. With hindsight I could see he felt Norman Curtis was nearing the end of his long run as a regular and a vacancy was coming up.

I settled into the No.3 shirt so well in the Reserves in the following weeks that, in November 1959, I made my Football League debut and went on to miss only four of the next 128 games. Moreover, before the end of my first season in the team I had played in an FA Cup semi-final and helped Wednesday finish fifth in the table; and, the following year, we finished runners-up to Spurs in the race for the League championship.

I even had the thrill of making my television debut during the 1960 Cup run! After we'd beaten Manchester United in the fifth round, I was invited into the studios to join Albert Quixall for a "live" interview.

I was lucky to step into a very strong team, a very well balanced side which included a lot of experienced and excellent players. I couldn't have started in better circumstances, and I think we lost only one of the first 18 matches in which I played. My second home game, I remember, was the day we thrashed top-of-the-table West Ham 7-0 and Bobby Craig's arrival from Third Lanark completed a blend which promised great things for Wednesday.

We might easily have won the Cup in 1960, when bad refereeing decisions cost us the semi-final; and in 1961 we had a points tally which in any other year would have been enough to win the title. Unfortunately, the nearest we got to honours again in my time at Hillsborough was the day in 1966 when Everton snatched the Cup from our grasp.

Yet, if the prizes proved elusive, it was a good time to play for Wednesday. We had some great days, and it was a wonderful phase in my life. For me, only the tail-end of my stay was not as satisfying as I would have liked. This was when the first signs of decline at the club coincided with a spell when I was frustrated by a calf injury I couldn't shake off, and I ended up playing a lot of games in the last year when I wasn't fit and had to rely on experience to get me through.

Perhaps my biggest disappointment was when we lost at home to Scunthorpe United in the FA Cup in January 1970. I had the miserable experience of being subbed for the very first time when not injured, and it proved to be my last appearance. Soon afterwards I left for Bristol Rovers, but it was still a blow I felt personally when Wednesday were relegated at the end of that season because, when you've had an 18-year association with a club, you still care and so badly want to see them succeed.

My Hillsborough days may have ended on a low note, but there were so many high notes – a lot of good memories.

Ron Springett

Goalkeeper Ron Springett, who made 384 League and Cup appearances, remains Wednesday's most-capped England player with 33 games for his country in nearly ten years at Hillsborough from March 1958 to May 1967. He cost the Owls £9,000, and when he returned to QPR it was in a unique exchange deal which took his youngest brother, Peter, to Sheffield. Peter went on to raise the Springett brothers' joint tally of games for Wednesday to almost 600.

When Eric Taylor was trying to sign me from Queen's Park Rangers in early 1958, he said if I joined Wednesday he would guarantee I'd play for England within two years. When I gained my first cap 21 months after the transfer, there was a telegram awaiting me in the Wembley dressing room before my international debut against Northern Ireland. It was from Eric, and read: "What did I tell you?"

I went on to collect 33 caps over the next seven years to take the club's record from Ernest Blenkinsop, and, while Nigel Worthington, the Northern Ireland international, has since bettered my total, it gives me a lot of pleasure to think I'm still Wednesday's most-capped England man.

I had some great years with Wednesday, and, if I have a regret, it's probably that I didn't move up to Sheffield to live. It was a brilliant club, the people were wonderful, and, although I continued to live in London, I always felt comfortable and very much at home whenever I travelled up to Hillsborough.

However, at the time of my transfer, Barbara and I were about to get married, and we'd just bought a house. We were both essentially "home birds", and, as London was the only place we knew, we didn't really want to leave. When you're content where you are, it's natural to prefer to stay, but, sometimes when I look back, I wonder what might have happened if we'd taken the plunge and gone north.

Of course, in later years my brother Peter chose to settle in Sheffield when he succeeded me at Hillsborough, and I know he never regretted the decision. He became very much part of the local scene, not only in his playing days, but, subsequently, when he launched a successful new career as a policeman. The affection and respect people felt for Peter was never more evident than at the time of his tragically early death at the age of 51 in September 1997 following a long battle against a crippling illness.

WEDNESDAY EVERY DAY OF THE WEEK

Peter, born 11 years after me, was still at school when I joined Wednesday, and, at the time, I was in my third season in the QPR first team, boasting about 90 appearances. There had been some talk of several top clubs being interested in taking me from the Third Division South, but the first hint I had of being watched by scouts came in December 1957 when we were playing at Southern League Hereford in an FA Cup second-round tie.

Someone said Wednesday were one of the clubs represented at the match, but, unfortunately, within ten minutes of the kick-off, I got clattered and was carried off. There were no substitute goalkeepers then, and, with winger Pat Kerrins taking over in goal, we crashed to a sensational 6-1 defeat. I think Hereford equalled the biggest FA Cup win ever recorded by a non-League club against Football League opposition.

The Wednesday's scout's journey was not, however, wasted, for Hereford's reward for beating us was a home date with the Owls – and Wednesday must have won that game because I recall they went on to reach the fifth round that year before going out to Manchester United in that famous first match at Old Trafford after Munich.

I was familiar with Wednesday's progress in early 1958 because it coincided with a period when they were trying to sign me, and, after the move looked to have fallen through, I believe it was the Cup defeat at Manchester which prompted Eric Taylor to renew his efforts revive the transfer.

Around the turn of the year, after I recovered from the injury suffered against Hereford, our manager, Jack Taylor, asked me to go to the ground to talk to Eric Taylor and the Wednesday officials, and this might have been when Eric first talked about a move to Hillsborough putting me in line for an England place.

Anyway, the upshot of those initial talks was that Barbara and I took the train up to Sheffield, and, after Eric England, the assistant secretary, had met us at the station and delivered us to the ground, Eric Taylor took us on a guided tour of Sheffield. We were very impressed, and the surrounding countryside, covered in snow, made a really beautiful picture.

But we asked for time to think about it, and, on the train going home, Barbara and I felt the wisest thing to do was to defer a decision and wait to see whether a London or southern club came in for me. However, it did seem that Wednesday were the only club to make a firm offer, and, when Eric Taylor talked to me again, I told him I'd sign if I could live and train in London. He said that wasn't acceptable, so it seemed like the end of the business.

I can't remember exactly how long afterwards it was, but one day I got a phone call from Jack Taylor. He said: "Wednesday have agreed to your terms." I went straight up to Sheffield and signed, making my debut in a 1-0 defeat of Bolton, with Albert Quixall getting the goal. It was only Wednesday's second clean sheet in 16 League games.

The following week, before Wednesday played at Arsenal on the Saturday afternoon, Barbara and I were married at a morning ceremony at a packed St Andrew's Church in Chelsea. All my new team-mates were present, and, after a brief reception at a friend's house just round the corner, the team-bus picked me up and took me with the rest of the lads to Highbury. I pinned my wedding carnation to the net, but it didn't bring me much luck, for we lost to a David Herd goal which he scored from about six yards after Vic Groves had headed against a post.

I played in the last nine games of that 1957-58 season, and, though we won four, we were relegated. However, in the following season, when Harry Catterick took over, we won the Second Division championship and the next few years saw us establish ourselves as one of the leading clubs in the First Division.

I think the arrangement by which I lived in London and trained with QPR worked very well, and it never affected my ability or form. Of course, had I played in any other position but goalkeeper, it would not have been practicable, but I kept myself at peak fitness and did not miss many games except when injured.

I used to travel up on the *Master Cutler* train every Friday, and the journey proved an enjoyable part of my weekly routine. The railway staff got to know me, and so did the regular passengers – and, with half the people on the train being Wednesdayites and the other half Sheffield United supporters, there was plenty of banter.

My pal John Fantham would meet me at the station and he and I would almost always go out for a meal to a restaurant at Barlborough. The Fanthams, including John's mother at Pitsmoor, made me one of the family, and, if I had to stay in Sheffield for the weekend, John used to take me to his place out at Bakewell.

I had the same room at the Hunter House Hotel every Friday when we weren't playing away, and, after home matches on the Saturday, I invariably caught the 5.25pm train back to London from Sheffield Victoria.

The only hitch in the arrangement occurred during Harry Catterick's time as manager. I didn't know about it until later, but it seems Harry had put something in the papers suggesting he would drop me if I didn't move to live in Sheffield.

All I know is that one week I received a call instructing me to travel up to Sheffield on Thursday instead of Friday because of "a problem at the club". It was a bit of a mystery to me, and all the more so when I got to King's Cross to find lots of reporters and photographers – and then found even more newspaper people awaiting my arrival in Sheffield.

Eric England whisked me down to Hillsborough, where I was met by Eric Taylor. "We're having a board meeting, and I'd like you to attend," he said. We went into this room, where all the directors and Harry Catterick were sitting round a big table.

Mr Taylor stood up and said: "Mr Catterick, I'd like to inform you that when we signed Ron Springett we made an agreement with him that he could continue to live and train in London. We don't make agreements with players and then break them. So we'd like apologies to him now, and confirmation that he's not under any pressure to come and live in Sheffield."

Catterick came across and apologised. He said he understood the agreement, but hoped I understood his point of view. I said of course I did, but I didn't feel the arrangement was detrimental to the club.

When I went to Wednesday, such

CUP HEROES

Ron Springett – the England goalkeeper is seen here getting treatment from trainer Bob Lyttle.

Cup run with the most pleasure, and especially the semi-final when we beat Chelsea in the mud at Villa Park. Some time after the event, Peter Bonetti told me Chelsea were so convinced we had no chance that day, they even had their Wembley souvenirs made in advance.

The story goes that Chelsea's plan was to shake up Vic Mobley early on, because they felt he was the key to our defensive strength. The irony was that, when George Graham collided with Mobley, initially it was the Chelsea man who went off. However, Mobley's injury proved the more serious. He was a passenger for an hour, though he still managed to create enough havoc to help us to a marvellous victory.

It was a pity we lost against Everton in the Final, especially after leading 2-0, but it was a day when the fates turned against us, and, despite the defeat, I shall always remember that afternoon with a lot of pride and pleasure. We were the first losing Finalists to do a lap of honour at Wembley, and the reception we got from the people of Sheffield when we went home on the following day is something I shall never forget.

When I left Wednesday in May 1967, it all happened very suddenly, and I didn't know a thing until, as asked, I turned up at the QPR ground one Sunday morning. The first surprise was finding brother Peter there, then Alec Stock, the QPR manager, explained he wanted to take me back to Loftus Road in a swop deal which would send Peter to Sheffield.

The terms Alec offered me proved acceptable, but Peter admitted he didn't know what to do. Like me nearly ten years earlier, he had never lived anywhere but London, and, naturally, he felt very hesitant. As the youngest in a family of seven, he was still at home with mum, and he was comfortable and doing well at QPR, where they had just won the League Cup and promotion.

I told him about Wednesday and the people in Sheffield, and said he would have no problem on either count. I knew if he wanted to progress, he couldn't choose a better move, and I don't think he was ever sorry about agreeing to move north.

He knew he would be under added scrutiny because he was my brother, but I was sure he would do well, and, looking back, I feel he showed great charac-

older players as Ron Staniforth, Don Gibson, Norman Curtis and Redfern Froggatt were still in the team, and I saw younger lads like Fantham, Megson and others join such as Peter Swan and Tony Kay as we created a side which was one of the best the club ever had. For some years, I don't think we finished out of the top six, and our record in 1960-61 was good enough to have won the championship in any other season.

It was a pity we found the trophies elusive in that period, but it was a good time for the club and for most of the players. Peter Swan got his first cap in my third international, and I think we played together 18 times for England.

I was delighted when John Fantham joined me and Peter in the team against Luxembourg at Highbury in 1961. John was playing only his third Football League game for Wednesday the day I made my debut, and he developed into one of the best players at the club. I have to admit I was disappointed when he didn't get picked again for England, because he deserved a chance to establish himself.

Tony Kay, incidentally, also played with me for England, but he'd left for Everton before that happened.

I suppose I remember the 1966 FA

83

ter in facing up to the challenge and making a success of it. I was proud of the way he did something I'd never done by settling in Sheffield and being determined to adjust to a new way of life.

It wasn't easy. I remember him telling me about one early game in which he made a brilliant save, tipping the ball over the bar when it had looked certain to go in the top corner. When he went to retrieve the ball from behind the goal, a wag in the crowd shouted: "Your Ron would have caught that!"

Peter was probably unfortunate in that his time with Wednesday coincided with a phase when things did not go well for the club, but there was never any doubt that he proved himself on merit.

The two of us together made over 1,100 League and Cup appearances in our careers, and the fact that more than half were with Wednesday serves to stress that it was a special club for both of the goalkeeping Springetts. It was certainly special for me from the outset, when I learned I was to get £2 more than I'd earned at QPR and was to receive all of £17 a week!

Wilf Smith

Wilf Smith, who was 19 at the time of the 1966 FA Cup Final, is now a successful Midlands-based businessman in the retail trade. The former Sheffield and Yorkshire Boys wing-half joined the Owls as an apprentice in late 1962, became a full professional in September 1963, and made 233 League and Cup appearances before becoming the game's costliest fullback when he joined Coventry for £100,000 in August 1970. He gained England Youth and Under-23 honours while at Hillsborough.

Both Sheffield clubs were showing interest in me when I was at school, and, ironically, United were the first to make an approach. However, in those days boys always preferred to sign for their favourite club, and, although Wednesday didn't make a move until after I'd left Pipworth Road in 1961, they were always going to be my first choice.

That was an era, of course, when people used to say lads should learn a trade before committing themselves to

Wilf Smith (second from left, front row) with some of his colleagues in the Wednesday junior team bound for a foreign tourney in 1963. Others in the picture include Peter Eustace, Vic Mobley, David Ford, Howard Wilkinson and Andy Burgin.

football, and, in fact, by the time Wednesday came in I had "signed up" as an apprentice electrician at the English Steel Corporation. I recall the first year of my working life as a time of biking down to the River Don Works every weekday morning, and, having signed for Wednesday as an amateur, training two evenings a week at Hillsborough.

The reason I subsequently accepted Wednesday's offer of an apprenticeship in November 1962 was not so much that I got fed up of working in industry, rather that, though I was a big 1ad and strong for a 16-year-old, I had begun to fear I might get left behind a bit without the benefit of full-time training.

I was still only 18 when I made my Football League debut against Blackpool on an icy Hillsborough pitch in December 1964. That came about partly because Gerry Young suffered a serious thigh injury at Tottenham [he was out for four months and it cost him a second England cap] and partly through manager Alan Brown's readiness to give youth a fling.

Brown, who later encouraged the development of teenagers like David Ford, Graham Pugh and Sam Ellis, was in his first season back with Wednesday when he gave me that initial 19-match run at left-half. Then, plainly recognising my strengths, he created an opening at right-back, where I replaced Brian Hill.

It was my good fortune that the season in which I established myself at right-back was the 1965-66 campaign in which Wednesday reached their first FA Cup Final for 31 years. Our League record didn't suggest we might go all the way to Wembley, but that Cup run somehow saw us exploit our strengths. We weren't the best team in the world, but we were physically strong, had a lot of discipline and character, and boasted the right blend of youth and experience.

There was a terrific mutual respect and spirit in the side. There wasn't anybody who gave less than 100 per cent. Some individuals had more ability, some worked harder, but we functioned as a unit. We were, in fact, a very happy group of footballers – all pals who would take it in turn to throw a party for the others when we got home from a Cup game.

If there was a bit of a loner in the team, it was Jimmy McCalliog – and I'm sure he'll not mind me mentioning it because we were good friends, and, when he came to us from Chelsea earlier that season, he stayed with me and my parents at our house in Chelsea Road for some time before his family moved up from London. Jimmy was a bit reserved, but it didn't prevent him from fitting in.

I don't think any of us really

Wilf Smith, seen here in action at Tottenham, where he is heading the ball clear with Peter Springett in trouble and Alan Gilzean challenging.

expected to reach the Final, but every step nearer made us believe just a little bit more that the fates were conspiring to make going to Wembley our destiny. The trickiest game of the entire run was in the third round at Reading, where we won 3-2 but might easily have been beaten. After that, though we had a few anxious moments in later rounds, somehow we never looked like losing – even though every match was an away fixture.

I remember when we went to Newcastle in the fourth round, most people didn't fancy us because we'd been thrashed on the same pitch in a First Division match just a week earlier. Remarkably, it was an entirely different story in the Cup game, which only went ahead after a major snow-clearing operation.

Even in the semi-final at Villa Park, where everybody from outside Sheffield expected Chelsea to coast to victory, we

had that winning look. On a heavy pitch, the likes of Pugh, McCalliog and Ford seemed to dance across the mud, and, considering Vic Mobley spent an hour as a hobbling passenger after damaging his ankle ligaments, it was probably our best performance of the season.

Of course, it was a great shame that we didn't succeed against Everton at Wembley. At 2-0 we should have closed it up, instead of which we let Everton hit us twice out of the blue. Perhaps it was a lack of sufficient all-round experience, perhaps it was simply fate. Anyway, whatever the result, we had good reason to be proud.

I know Alan Brown was a proud manager that day. For me, Brown was great. He could be a strange man sometimes, but I would never say a word against him, and it's doubtful whether anybody in that 1966 team had anything but respect and admiration for

the man. He didn't always do what you hoped, but what he did was invariably for your benefit.

I remember there was a dispute about the Wembley ticket allocation for the players, and it all came to a head on the day we were playing a League match at Blackburn about two weeks before the Cup Final. The FA rules permitted each player six tickets, but we knew it was customary for teams to be given more, and none of the lads was very happy when Brown insisted we could only have the six to which we were due. We considered this ridiculous, because most of us had more than six people in our families – and, as things stood, we couldn't even buy a few extra tickets.

It all got a bit heated, and, though I don't think anybody was serious, some of the lads were muttering about not playing, which, of course, prompted Brown to threaten to tell the Press! In the end, we backed down, but, in fact, we did get a few more tickets than six. In a sense, after making his point, Brown ensured we were looked after.

Brown was the sort of man who, once he made his mind up about something, he could seldom be moved. If what he decided hurt or affected some individual, it wasn't anything personal. A classic example was his decision to give Sam Ellis his Cup debut in the Final as deputy for the injured Mobley.

There were some reporters, I know, who wondered what Brown was playing at, and there were probably a few people at the club who felt the same way. Sam had actually deputised for Mobley in a few games before the semi-final, and had looked a bit awkward; but, once he settled himself down, he adjusted very well, became a consistent and effective defender, and certainly he never let anyone down.

That 1966 Wembley team did seem to boast the basis of a very good side. There seemed to be so much potential, and it was a terrific misfortune that the promise of great things just around the corner never became a reality. I often think the reason Alan Brown went less than two years later was down to frustration at not having the resources made available to enable him to really develop the genuine potential.

Things were never quite the same after he went, and, in my view, they took a sharp turn for the worse when Danny Williams came. Danny was a nice guy, but he got off on the wrong foot when he went on television and said Wednesday only had three good players. It did sometimes seem that Danny's brain wasn't in control of his mouth, and he didn't realise he was saying things which had the opposite effect to what he thought he intended.

Around that time, too, Eric Taylor made some comment about the team for the next match being "Tommy Craig and ten others". It may have been quoted out of context, but it was hardly good psychology because it seemed to suggest Craig, a new £100,000 signing, was the only player we had – and, anyway, the way they were talking put enormous pressure on a lad who was only 18 years old and a long way from being the finished article.

Somehow, it was all part of a climate which did not seem to me to offer much prospect of progress, and that rather than money was the reason I decided I had to leave. I had a major period in which I badly wanted to get away, and the longer it went on the more it affected my football. Unfortunately, in the meantime we were relegated when we lost our last match of the 1969-70 season.

I was nursing an injury when we met Manchester City. Nobody forced me to play, and doing so was a mistake. Some people thought I'd feigned the injury when I came off, but the truth is I shouldn't have played. Even so, with or without me, there was no way we should have lost that match, as anyone who was there will agree.

I was always sorry things ended the way they did because there was a sense in which the situation got out of hand, and, because the club wouldn't agree to let me go and there was talk of me going on strike to emphasise how determined I was to leave, I was the one who got a bad Press.

Whether or not, with hindsight, leaving Wednesday was the right thing, who knows? The way things went for the club in the following few years probably vindicated my view that they were not going the right way. However, as a local lad and a Wednesdayite, obviously I would have wished for things to have been different. Now, when I look back, it's the good times I remember – and we had a lot of those.

Sam Ellis

Sam Ellis, a centre-half who gained three England Under-23 caps, made 179 appearances for the Owls between 1966 and 1972 and went on to tot up over 450 League and Cup games as a player with four clubs before turning to a coaching and management career which has seen him serve Watford, Blackpool, Bury (twice), Burnley and Manchester City. In Wednesday's records his name will always be synonymous with the 1966 Wembley Final in which he made his FA Cup debut at the age of 19 – when, incidentally, he was earning £12 a week.

People have often suggested I gave up a career in banking to come into professional football, but that is rather stretching a point, for, while I was, in fact, working in a bank at the time I joined Wednesday, I had not long left school and was waiting to see whether my ten "0" Level and three "A" Level GCEs might be enough to get me to university.

In the event, Wednesday gave me an opportunity I never expected to come into football, and crossing the Pennines to take up that offer was a step I never regretted. Curiously, it might not have happened if David Elsworth, an old Owls fan living in Manchester, hadn't written to Alan Brown and said he would pay for me to have a week's trial at Hillsborough.

I always remember travelling over and being met at the railway station by the manager. The funny thing was that "Brownie" also greeted another lad who had not only been on the same train, but in the same compartment as me. It was Graham Pugh, and, in later years, we often laughed when we recalled how we'd sat through the journey like a pair of dummies and never spoken a word – little knowing that within two years we would be playing in a Cup Final together!

I arrived on the Monday morning, played against Huddersfield in a Northern Intermediate League match at Owlerton Stadium the following evening, and by the weekend I was a £10-a-week professional. I signed on my 18th birthday, Saturday, 12 September 1964, after my father and I had watched Wednesday beat Liverpool 1-0 with a goal from Johnny Quinn.

It is, perhaps, inevitable that people will always remember me as the lad who made his FA Cup debut in a Final, but, when I look back on my eight years at Hillsborough, the first thing I recall is the people – especially the unique atmosphere which made it an ideal place for a youngster to acquire the right principles. Over 35 years I've known some good dressing rooms, but none better than Wednesday's in the mid-1960s.

You couldn't have two better mentors than Don Megson and Gerry Young. "Meggie" was always looking after me, off and on the field, and Gerry was, without doubt, the best professional I ever played with. As for the manager – Alan Brown was the sort of man who, if he believed in you, would move heaven and earth to help you –

Sam Ellis – it really capped a memorable year for Sam Ellis when he was given his FA Cup debut in the Wembley Final.

and, from the outset, the unbending faith he showed in me boosted my self-belief.

I often joked that only "Brownie" and my dad would have played me at Wembley, but, seriously, the reality was his judgement was never based on sentiment, and, in my case, none of my fellow-professionals ever even hinted they were unhappy with his decision.

He gave me my League debut as Vic Mobley's deputy in a home game with Blackpool in early April 1966. I rated my performance as half-decent. We won 3-0 and it's always good to start with a clean sheet. However, just in case I was feeling too self-satisfied, I was brought down to earth by a comment from Alan Finney, our veteran winger. "By heck, Sam, you can play better than that, lad," he said – and I still wonder if "Brownie" hadn't set him up to say it just to deflate me!

I stayed in for three more games, then Vic came back, and, of course, it's history now that, two weeks later, Vic suffered damaged ankle ligaments in the FA Cup semi-final and I returned for a seven-match run which led all the way to Wembley. In the meantime, "Brownie" boosted my confidence with a daily ritual in which he would ask "Who's the best centre-half, Sam, you or me?" And then insist I replied: "Me, boss."

He never stopped giving me the benefit of his long experience as a defender, but all the while he made it plain he would give Vic every chance of recovering in time for the Final.

It was on the Monday before the Wembley date with Everton, after our League match with Burnley, when "Brownie" confirmed he was going to play me in the Final. He said I hadn't to tell anyone. Meanwhile, he told the Press no decision on Mobley would be made until the last minute – Alan wanted to do the right thing by Vic, though he already knew his chances of being fit were virtually nil.

As for the big day, I honestly don't remember a thing, but, of course, the facts of the match have been well documented, and, if there wasn't a fairy-tale end to the story, I shall always feel privileged to have been part of that team – and, indeed, to have been at Sheffield Wednesday in that period in their history.

Gerry Young

Gerry Young made 345 League and Cup appearances between 1957 and 1971. He served the club for 20 years, and is remembered as one of the most respected, loyal and dependable players the Owls ever had. The fates were not always kind

to the Geordie from Jarrow, but he remained the ultimate professional. A man with abundant cause to recall his career with pride, he now runs a trophy business within old colleague Johnny Quinn's sports shop a corner kick from Hillsborough.

I always remember when I married my wife Beryl in March 1963, the wedding, down at the old Ebenezer Chapel on Broughton Lane, was on the morning of a First Division match at Birmingham. Vic Buckingham, the manager, had said: "Don't bother about playing, Gerry, take the day off." But I told him there was no way I was going to miss the game.

Gerry Young with his bride Beryl after their wedding and before the Owls wing-half dashed off to play at Birmingham.

The thing was, two weeks earlier I'd got into the team at left-half, and, with Tony Kay having gone to Everton, saw the opportunity to make the position my own after six years in which I had managed only about 40 appearances and always been somebody's temporary deputy in just about every shirt in the forward line. I didn't fancy dropping out and risking someone else staking a claim for that number six shirt!

In the event, I went on to enjoy a run of 76 consecutive games, and, by the time I had to stand down after rupturing a thigh muscle at Tottenham in December 1964, I'd not only established myself in the side but won an England cap against Wales at Wembley Unfortunately, the injury, which kept me out for five months, cost me the chance of a second cap – and the selectors never looked at me again.

My wedding day, incidentally, went well, although I haven't forgotten that Vic Buckingham kept looking at his watch and was sweating on us getting to the Midland Station in time to catch the Birmingham train! We managed it okay, drew the game 1-1 with a Johnny Fantham goal, and I recall I got back to

the Brown Bayley's sports club that evening to find the reception was just about finished.

I know I was a bit concerned when I discovered Vic Mobley had already left the reception and gone home to Oxford, because he had the key to the club house which Beryl and me were moving into that night! Vic, who had been playing in the Reserves in the afternoon, was in the same digs as me, and, before starting out that morning for the wedding, I'd asked him to give the key to Beryl. Typical Vic, he'd for-

gotten. Luckily, we managed to reach Keith Ellis, who had been the previous tenant, and he still had a key.

You only have to hear me talk to know I'm from the North East. I've never lost my accent, but Sheffield has been my home since I joined Wednesday as a part-timer in May 1955, and I wouldn't want to live anywhere else. I had a few ups and downs in 20 years at Hillsborough, but the days when I was a player were the best of times because it was a great club with some smashing people – from the directors right down to the cleaners.

It's the people who make a place special. I often recall the way, when we went to play in London, we always went to the theatre on the Friday night, and directors like Harold Jessop or "Dick" Gunstone would buy the lads a box of chocolates each. As for the lads, well, with mates like Johnny Quinn, Don Megson, Peter Eustace and Vic Mobley, life was never dull.

A couple of little incidents that come to mind are of foreign trips. Once, for instance, we got knocked out of a tournament in Mexico, and Eric Taylor took us to New York. A gang of us walked down Broadway one night and called in at a restaurant where they were staging a big "do" – and I suddenly spotted the guest of honour, the legendary Jack Dempsey, at a nearby table. Another time, we flew into Hong Kong to be greeted by this little Chinaman who kept shouting: "I know your Queen!". It was only later we discovered he was really saying: "I know your Quinn!" – John having been there a year earlier with a British Army team.

There were so many good times, and, if I have a regret, it can only be that, having spent all my playing career at the club, most of the good things I did are forgotten, and I always seem to be remembered for the slip that led to Everton's winning goal in the 1966 FA Cup Final. It niggles me a bit, although these days I don't get upset when the subject crops up in conversation.

I can even laugh about it. Like the other day, when someone came into the shop and, with the 1998 Final coming up, we got talking about Wembley. Inevitably, the talk turned to 1966. This chap joked: "I blame Springett. He should have known it was a back-pass, but he was slow coming off his line!" I

Gerry Young.

CUP HEROES

said: "Aye, I thought that, and anyway he should have saved Temple's shot!"

Seriously, I know what happened, but you come to accept that it can't be changed. I still say it was fate when that ball slipped under my foot, but I always blamed myself. I was disappointed, not because we lost but the way we lost. That's football. Yet I would go through it all again because, overall, it was still a very special day. I played my only international at Wembley, but going there in a Cup Final is an experience every player treasures no matter what the outcome.

I have to say, incidentally, that the Press lads were kinder in 1966 than they seem to be today. I think if I'd made that mistake in modern times the media would have crucified me because there is so much more exposure and people are far more brutally critical now.

The great thing for me is that I had a good career in the game when some better players I knew as a kid didn't make it. You need the skill, but it takes something extra to get there, and I'm grateful I had the heart and the patience to persist when, frankly, it would have been easy to give up the struggle. Like my pal Johnny Quinn, I suffered at times because I was too versatile. Even when Harry Catterick decided left-half was my best position and I filled that role when we won the Central League championship, it wasn't the end of my long wait for recognition.

In fact, even after that, I found myself playing in the first-team as Keith Ellis's deputy at centre-forward, and, when I got hat-tricks against Manchester United and Roma in 1961, I knew it wouldn't be enough to get me the job on a permanent basis. Is there any wonder that, once Tony Kay left, I didn't want even my wedding to affect the chance I had waited for so long? Happily, Beryl understood!

If the team in the early 1960s was Wednesday's best in my time, the spirit at the club in the period when we reached the Cup Final was something special, and the thing that hurt was the way it all went wrong afterwards.

When we were relegated in 1970, on a personal level my disappointment was all the greater because my testimonial match came just a few days after we'd gone down, but what really saddened me was how the decline at the club had been allowed to happen.

Unfortunately, it got worse, and, when you knew what the club had been only a few years earlier, to see Wednesday in the Third Division and looking like no-hopers was painful beyond words. When you're a player or a coach, you have no control over the decisions which bring a situation like that about, but, of course, you still pay the price. It was a sad moment when, in October 1975, I was told my services were no longer required – after half a lifetime and on my 39th birthday!

I must admit I've never enjoyed football since I stopped playing. I don't get to matches and don't regret being out of it, but I was pleased when Wednesday's fortunes started taking a turn for the better again. Football has changed and I suppose a lot of people aren't too interested in the past, but I still remember the way it was in my era with a lot of pride and affection. I'm glad I had that time!

Peter Eustace

Peter Eustace was a cultured midfielder who made 280 League and Cup appearances for the Owls in two spells between 1962 and 1975. In 1983 he returned to Hillsborough as assistant to Howard Wilkinson, whom he succeeded as manager in late 1988. He later managed Leyton Orient, and in recent years he and his wife Mandy have run the Cheshire Cheese pub at Hope.

You can never talk about the FA Cup run of 1966 without the conversation being dominated by references to the influence of Alan Brown, the manager. He deserved the credit for getting us to Wembley, for we did it on the back of his knowledge of football and psychology.

I doubt if there's ever been a younger FA Cup Final side, for six of us were aged 21 or under, and, while on the day we paid for a lack of experience and lost

Peter Eustace, seen here when he returned to Wednesday and was signed by Derek Dooley after a spell at West Ham.

WEDNESDAY EVERY DAY OF THE WEEK

3-2 after leading 2-0, it was a good and talented team that functioned as a unit in which everybody worked very hard for each other. Don't forget we were drawn away in every round, but the spirit was such we felt we could go anywhere and give anybody a game.

We all know that what you achieve on the field is down to individual skills, but while certain players made crucial contributions at different stages along the way, the secret was really the way "Brownie" had us organised – plus his ability to inspire each of us raise our game. Ordinary players became good ones and good players very good under Alan, who had the knack of boosting your self-belief and at times making you feel wonderful. Mind you, there were days when he could also make you feel exactly the opposite!

In my early career I had the fortune to benefit from the influence of some very good people, but "Brownie" more than anyone else shaped me for the rest of my life because he set very high standards. You couldn't always live up to them, but his principles encouraged you to set your own sights higher.

"Brownie" was also a super tactician, years ahead of his time. When people nowadays mention "total football", I remember this was what Alan Brown talked about over 30 years ago. His theory was you should be good enough to start at right-back and maybe finish as a left-winger in the same game – he wanted a squad of men who could play it off the cuff and make the right decisions in whatever position they found themselves on the field at any given moment. He used to say a good player produced 35 good performances in every 42-match season, and if you couldn't achieve that you fell below what he expected.

Yet, if he was a hard taskmaster, everybody was devastated when he left to rejoin Sunderland in 1968. It was a bitter blow, and people will never know how much it affected the club and the players. One day he was there telling us how to play, how to live, and everything else – the next day he was gone. We all suffered to varying degrees. Some missed his influence more than others, but the club lost the opportunity of seeing that 1966 team, with adjustments, achieve what once seemed within its reach.

Graham Pugh was probably a classic example. He had shown what a good player and excellent prospect he was when getting into the side as a teenager in 1966, but, without Alan Brown to sustain and guide him, Graham lost out and never fulfilled his true potential. People say it was down to injuries, but I think "Brownie" would have helped him overcome that problem.

In fact, "Brownie" was superb when you were injured, in the sense that he always gave you heart by coming to see you – sometimes when you wished he wouldn't! If you were in hospital, he'd sit at your bedside for an hour or more and never say a word. You had to make the conversation and do all the talking, which was more tiring than playing in a match! Yet his concern was a boost to your morale when you needed it most.

To go back to the start of my career, the first major influence was an old Wednesday winger called Frank Slynn. When Frank finished playing, he went to work at Stocksbridge Works, and, as that was the area in which I grew up, it was where I got my first job after leaving school shortly before my 15th birthday.

Even at that age, I progressed into the works' first team very quickly, and Frank arranged for me to have a trial with Wednesday. The upshot was I started playing with the Owls Juniors and soon had to make an important career decision because of a conflict between my duties as an apprentice mechanical engineer and my football. My job involved working on Saturday mornings – which wasn't possible on those weeks when Wednesday's Northern Intermediate League side travelled away on Friday nights. In the end, my gaffer said I had a choice to make.

Deciding to become a Wednesday apprentice was not difficult, for I was already enjoying the encouragement of the two old Hillsborough heroes then in charge of youngsters, Derek Dooley and Hugh Swift. Derek, of course, was a legend at the club, and Hugh, a former England "B" full-back, was equally good with the kids. Like Derek, Hugh had seen his playing days prematurely ended by injury, but he was a quietly-spoken man who compensated for his own disappointment by doing everything he could to help the next generation of Wednesday players – and he did it with kindness and consideration.

Again, when I became a pro, I was lucky because the senior players in the dressing room were a great help. Tom McAnearney and Peter Swan were especially influential, but there were also people like Redfern Froggatt, Alan Finney and Don Megson who made a contribution.

McAnearney was the first man to make me understand that football is more about brain than brawn and encouraged me to think about the game. He taught me it's not just a case of running round the field as fast as you can – he showed me that it's about going into positions where there's space, making time for yourself, looking for ways of helping your team-mates out of trouble by being available, etc.

"Swannie" was England's centre-half then, but always had time for the kids. He took a liking to me, and, as well as always being ready with a few tips, with one small gesture of friendship when I was an apprentice he showed what a great bloke he was.

One day heavy snow had made getting to work very difficult, and, as I wondered how I was going to get home after training with no buses running to Stocksbridge, Peter drew up in his car and said: "Jump in – I'm taking you." It meant him going 12 miles out of his way, and he could easily have made an excuse about having to get home to his family.

I've mentioned Alan Brown, but two of his predecessors also made a big impression on me – and don't forget, in those days, as an apprentice you felt so insignificant while the managers seemed so powerful, and when they noticed you it made your day.

Harry Catterick never really spoke to me, but I recall that, after Derek Dooley had asked him to take a look at me in the juniors and he'd watched us play for about ten minutes, he always gave me a sweet whenever he passed in the corridor. He didn't say a word, but just put his hand in his pocket and offered me a sweet – and, as I took it to mean he must be pleased with me, it was a gesture which made me feel good!

Vic Buckingham was a completely different type from Catterick. He was an extrovert who would talk to anybody, and, though I didn't always fully understand what he was saying to me,

Peter Eustace returned for a third time in 1983 when he joined new manager Howard Wilkinson (centre) and physiotherapist Alan Smith to assist in the promotion push which took the Owls back to the top flight after a 14-year wait.

his words stuck and made a lot of sense as time passed. He would talk about football being a mental game, and describe a good team as a meeting of minds – he would say it's no good if the players don't connect and aren't on the same wave-length.

Overall, I spent something like 18 years playing and working for Wednesday, and, naturally, I have a lot of fond memories of every phase – not least of coming back in 1983 to work alongside Howard Wilkinson and, in our first season together, being involved in seeing the club finally get back to the old First Division after 14 years in the wilderness.

I was with Sunderland when Howard invited me back, and, being a Wednesdayite, I jumped at the chance. It was a period when percentage football was coming into the game, and, when Howard explained how we were going to play, although it was something I hadn't been involved in before, I saw that it worked and suited the players we had at that time.

That it was successful is evident when you consider we won promotion, played in about a dozen Cup quarter-finals (including replays), and, as well as reaching the FA Cup semi-final in 1986, would have qualified for Europe but for the ban which followed the Heysel Stadium disaster.

People tend to forget what Howard Wilkinson did at Wednesday. The progress we made in three or four years was brilliant, and the pity was the resources which would have enabled Howard to push the club another step forward were not made available sooner. It was ironic that the change in the club's philosophy came too late for Howard, though, like me, I'm sure Howard is pleased that Wednesday did ultimately take that vital step.

Howard took the club as far as he could in the circumstances that existed in his time, and we can only speculate on what might have happened if he had been given the backing most of his successors have enjoyed.

When I reflect on that period, I sometimes wonder whether I should have gone to Leeds with Howard, but, being a Sheffield lad who had always dreamed of managing Wednesday, I chose to stay, and maybe it was a mistake to believe I would get the financial support that Howard had been unable to persuade the people then running the club to give him.

I told them what we needed was an influx of quality players and a change in the system we played. Howard had been saying the same thing for a long time, and, as things were, with a lack of resources highlighted when injuries forced us to play Mel Sterland as a centre-forward, there was nothing more certain than that relegation would soon become a reality if we didn't improve the situation dramatically – and quickly.

I thought I'd get a little more back-ing than I did, and, frankly, I felt let down and believe I took the blame for a situation which wasn't of my making. I was disappointed when it ended for me the way it did, but never felt sorry for myself. Worse things have happened to others in football, and, strange as it may seem, I can look at the pattern of events and recognise that the departure of Howard and then myself created the climate which, following the appointment of a high-profile manager like Ron Atkinson and changes on the board, prompted the introduction of policies at the club which had been long overdue.

Even then, they had to go down before the real revival began, but there has been nobody happier than me to see Wednesday thrive. In my book they will always be special, for Hillsborough holds a million great memories of good times and people who helped me enjoy a rewarding career in the game.

Jim McCalliog

Jim McCalliog was British football's most expensive teenager when Wednesday paid Chelsea £37,500 for him in October 1965. He made 174 League and Cup appearances and scored 23 goals, figured in the 1966 FA Cup Final, and in 1967 became the first Owls' man for 47 years to play for Scotland. His playing career spanned over 500 games and six clubs.

Joining Wednesday was a brilliant move for me, because though there was a lot of hype and publicity about a record fee being paid for a teenager with only 12 senior games to his name, I felt at home from the minute I arrived in Sheffield. Certainly I never had any trouble fitting in. Then, at the age of 19, to play in an FA Cup Final within eight months of signing was a wonderful bonus.

Alan Brown, the manager, was probably the best man I ever met in my life. He was an incredible guy, a tough disciplinarian with very rigid principles, yet remarkably considerate and kind. He wasn't the type to tell players they could have a night out, and there was no way he'd ever buy you a drink. But he would often do unexpected things which made you realise he was a lot more human than some might think.

Brown had been watching me for a long time before he persuaded Chelsea to sell me. I remember the day he came to see me at our house in London because, when we went for a walk to talk things over, he invited my brothers and sisters to tag along. My Dad and Mum knew nothing about football, and transfer talk was totally new territory to them. There were no such things as agents then, and nobody to protect and advise us. But my parents instinctively felt they they could trust Alan Brown, and they were right.

As we walked, he said: "You don't worry about the fee, son. What I see in you is the potential to play at a high level. Everybody tells me you obviously enjoy your football, and that's what I want you to do with us." He was as good as his word, because, in all the time he and I were together at Hillsborough, he never once took me into his office and told me how to play. He just let me go out and do what was natural to me.

To be honest, I sometimes wish he had been tougher with me. In a sense, things happened too quickly for me, and while I appreciated the freedom he allowed me, I think I ultimately needed someone to pull me back. I was a capable lad and, as the eldest in a family of five children, was used to responsibility; but I needed help from someone who knew football and understood what I was going through in that spell when my career was taking off.

When I first arrived in Sheffield, I stayed in the Grosvenor House Hotel, and, later, the club found us a large family house at Nether Edge where me and my three brothers and a sister were very comfortable and content. My brother Freddie, who had been an apprentice at Chelsea, moved up to Hillsborough soon after me.

Incidentally, during that spell at the Grosvenor, I remember being very flattered when Arthur Askey, the comedian, came to my table at breakfast one morning and wished me well – a lovely gesture from such a famous man. The whole Cup run of 1966 stands out in my memory because, for whatever reason, things just happened for us. We played away in every round, and even in the semi-final and the Final we were the "second" team on the billing. At Wembley we were put in the visitors' dressing room, but any hint that we

CUP HEROES

Jim McCalliog, seen here, ironically, putting the ball past his old Wednesday colleague Ron Springett when the Owls beat QPR at Hillsborough in December 1968. At Wembley in 1966, the Scot scored Wednesday's first goal.

were always the outsiders never bothered us.

We never looked inferior to any of the teams we met, and you have to credit Brown for getting the blend and the self-belief just right. In my view, the only thing the manager got wrong was not playing John Hickton at Wembley when Vic Mobley wasn't fit.

I know Chelsea blamed their semi-final defeat on conditions which didn't suit their kind of football, but we beat them fair and square. In the Final we played Everton off the field for 65 minutes. They never got a kick, and, even now, I can't understand how we came to lose that match after leading 2-0.

Years later on a trip to America, I was introduced to Jimmy Gabriel, who had played for Everton. I told him: "It's nice to finally meet you, because I didn't see much of you at Wembley in 1966!" The only thing Gabriel did was take the mickey when wasting time with keep-ball at a corner flag seconds from the end of the match. From a personal point of view, when I look back now

more than 30 years later, I feel that something died in me at the end of that Cup Final. I remember walking into the Wembley tunnel and, turning towards the pitch, saying to myself: "I've got to come back here." Any disappointment I felt on the day was tempered by a determination to enjoy some more big days in my career.

In fact, I did return to Wembley within the year when I gained the first of my five full Scottish caps and scored in a famous defeat of England – and, of course, in 1976, I played in another FA Cup Final and emerged a winner with Southampton.

But what disappointed me in the wake of 1966 and ultimately prompted me to seek a move was the way the club failed to take things forward. The money they made from that Cup run should have enabled them to invest in getting some players who might have turned a good team into a better one. We could have gone from strength to strength.

We had some outstanding young

players who had only just got established in the team, and three good signings would have made a significant difference, equipping us for when some of the older players were ready to step down. But the board wouldn't spend, and it was soon obvious their misguided policies would condemn Wednesday to being permanent also-rans.

The season after the Cup Final was, in fact, a good one for the club and for me. We reached the quarter-finals, and, though Chelsea beat us with a late goal, we played well. I can't have done too badly because Scotland officials at the game awarded me my first senior cap soon afterwards, to add to the two Under-23 caps I collected at Wrexham in November and at Newcastle in March.

It was towards the end of the 1966-67 campaign that I asked for a move. I was unsettled partly by Wednesday's lack of ambition, but must admit mixing with other internationals raised my awareness of what it might be like at a club with genuine potential for long-term success. One Scotland colleague actually told me his club were poised to come for me. I waited and waited for developments, but, unfortunately, they never happened.

Subsequently, I did accept new terms at Sheffield after celebrating my 21st birthday with a performance I really enjoyed in a 2-0 win at Sunderland in September 1967. That night, I remember, all the lads came up to my house and we had a great party. We brought in outside caterers, and the champagne flowed. Mind you, at the time I didn't drink alcohol, so I had to get merry on orange juice!

It was only a few months later when Alan Brown walked out and went back to Sunderland. That was a major turning point in Wednesday's history, because something went out of the club the day he left, and things fell into a decline which it took many years to halt.

Jack Marshall took over, and while he was a nice bloke, he didn't have the strength or authority that was needed. I don't think anybody was surprised when he only stayed in the job for less than a year.

Everything came to a head for me with a trivial incident which somehow summed up the lack of imagination and the reluctance to change attitudes which was the club's undoing. It occurred one day after training during a pre-season trip to Ireland in 1968.

"Jolly" Jack said we could dress casually for the evening meal, but, as I was going down the stairs just before dinner, I saw that Eric Taylor, the general manager, was stopping the lads and sending them back to get changed.

Taylor told me: "You'll have to go and put a collar and tie on." I replied: "You're not my boss. It's nothing to do with you. If Jack Marshall says I've got to do that, fair enough." So I entered the dining room in casual dress. Jack, looking very serious, came over and said:

"You'll have to go and get changed." I asked him: "Is that you telling me, or him?" In the end, I had my meal in the hotel kitchen with the chef.

I thought the whole thing was pretty pathetic, really, and, everything else considered, it didn't encourage me to want to stay. I didn't think the situation was likely to improve when Danny Williams took over because I soon saw I

had nothing in common with him. We couldn't talk football.

Yet, when I left to join Wolves in August 1969, I took with me some terrific memories of some good days and great pals. We all got on well together, though I especially remember Peter Eustace and Wilf Smith as close friends; and Dave Smith, who was Brown's coach in my first two years, was a brilliant help to me.

Yes, when I look back on my career and ask where were the really happy times, I have to include Wednesday.

I'm now licensee of the George & Dragon in Wetherby, and a few months ago I was reminded that many Owls' supporters haven't forgotten me. One Saturday night I went upstairs to our private quarters and was returning to the bar when I heard the sound of singing – the place was packed and a gang of lads were belting out *Yellow Submarine* with words which included my name. I thought someone was taking the mickey.

When I walked into the room, everyone cheered. Then I was mobbed – they were slapping me on the back and shouting: "Good old Jim!". They were Wednesday fans on their way back from an away match, and their enthusiasm made me blush. But it was nice to be remembered.

John Fantham

John Fantham scored 167 goals in 435 League and Cup matches for Wednesday between February 1958 and October 1969 and still holds the club aggregate League scoring record (147). Although capped only once by England, he is remembered as one of the outstanding strikers of his era. Now a successful businessman in the machine tools industry, he seldom gets to Hillsborough and sees little football, but retains abundant happy memories of his years with the Owls.

When I was at Burngreave Secondary Modern School in the early 1950s, I always hoped to follow in my father's footsteps and become a professional footballer. I played with Sheffield and Yorkshire Boys, and, from the earliest days, had a knack of scoring goals. It seemed to come so instinctively that a

career in the game was perhaps inevitable.

All the same, my father never pushed me. He may have played with Wolves, Rotherham and Stockport in the 1930s, but he was happy to let me progress in my own way. He used to say nobody can teach you to play football: people can put you on the right lines, but they can't give you natural ability if you haven't got it.

In fact, my father would have preferred me to become a cricketer rather than a footballer, and, as I was better at cricket and gained city and county honours at school, he might have got his wish but for the problem that it took longer to develop a career in cricket – and I didn't fancy waiting when progress in football was much quicker.

When I left school, I started work in the offices at Firth Vickers, later having a spell at Laycock's, and, meanwhile, I played with the YMCA. At one stage there was a possibility of joining Wath Wanderers, the Wolves nursery side in South Yorkshire, but, as I'd already started training down at Hillsborough on Tuesday and Thursday evenings, Wednesday quickly decided to sign me as an amateur, and, as soon as I was 17½, offered me professional terms.

Although I made my Football League debut against Tottenham a few days before my 19th birthday in February 1958, it was the following October before I got the chance to establish myself in the side. This happened because, in September 1958, Wednesday sold Albert Quixall to Manchester United for a record £45,000, and, after Jim McAnearney had replaced him in two games, I was called up for the derby match with Sheffield United at Hillsborough.

It was only my tenth senior game, but it proved a milestone and I didn't look back. Unfortunately, my memories of the afternoon have always been tinged with sadness because my personal success coincided with a family tragedy when my father collapsed and died as he left the ground after watching me play.

We always parked on a street off Leppings Lane, and our arrangement was for him to go back to the car at the end of the match and wait until I joined him for the drive to Greenhill. On this day, I arrived to find no sign of my

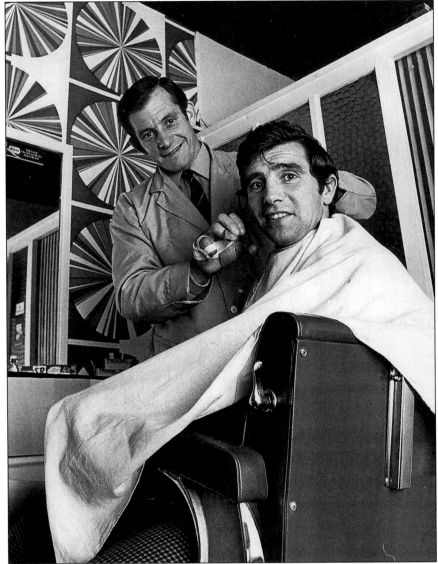

John Fantham, the man who claimed Wednesday's post-war scoring record, launched his business career with a successful venture into hairdressing, and here he ensures that Cup Final team-mate Johnny Quinn looks smart after a snipping session at Fantham's Division Street shop. Quinn, one of the most versatile players at the club, has run an All-Stars charity football team for over 25 years.

struck twice to level the scores, was an unknown who never did anything else in his career. Nobody ever heard of him again, and it was as if he had to have his moment of fame that afternoon before disappearing back into obscurity.

Another thing – I've watched Everton's winning goal on film many times, and, for me, it was an incident which had "fate" written all over it because everything fell into place for Everton in a way you couldn't have planned. Talk about our name not being on the trophy!

It wasn't just that a hopeful long ball from Colin Harvey would normally have been cut out by Gerry Young. Gerry was one of the safest players in our team, but, even when the ball unexpectedly slipped under his boot, it went only a couple of yards behind him, and, in most instances, he would have had time to recover. Also, you have to say that usually, in situations like that, a forward hesitates or stops when he sees a defender is set to cut out a pass. But that day Derek Temple, who was running on Young's blind side, kept going, more in hope than expectation – and when the ball dropped right into his path, he was away.

Of course, a one-on-one with the goalkeeper still takes some succeeding with, and, with Ron Springett getting his angles just right, you have to say Temple's finish was excellent. Yet, having studied the film so many times, I feel the ball sat up nicely for him just at exactly the right moment, and he was able to hit it so sweetly into the only place where Springett could have been beaten.

We always hoped we might compensate for that defeat and make an early return to Wembley. At 27, I knew it would have to happen sooner rather than later for me, and, in the event, we didn't go back. Indeed, much sooner than we could have imagined, the club's fortunes were on the wane and the 1966 team began to break up following Alan Brown's departure in early 1968. After that, Wednesday somehow lost their way under Jack Marshall and Danny Williams.

At least before I left in 1969, I had the consolation of claiming Wednesday's post-war aggregate scoring record. In January 1968 I equalled Redfern Froggatt's tally when I scored my 140th

father, and wasn't aware what had happened until I'd made my way home alone. I was always sorry my father never saw me get any of my 167 Wednesday goals. The first time I scored was the week after his death.

In my first season as a regular, we won the Second Division championship, and our initial two seasons back in the First Division were memorable for the club. In 1960 we reached the FA Cup semi-final and lost to Blackburn; then in 1961 we finished runners-up to League champions Tottenham.

The irony of our run to Wembley in 1966 was that the 1960 team was probably the better side, more experienced and looking much more capable of progressing beyond the semi-final. In 1960 we didn't have the luck, but the fates

were kinder to us six years later when few people really expected us to go as far as we did.

For me, the most memorable moment in the 1966 Cup run was when we beat Chelsea at Villa Park. Nobody thought we stood a chance, but, somehow, everything went for us – even the weather conspired to lend a hand! There was a lot of rain ahead of the match, and the pitch was very heavy and muddy. It certainly wasn't a day for fancy football, but, if the conditions swung the balance in our favour, it was a tremendous performance in which we had to battle to succeed.

Yet, if we seemed destined to get to Wembley that year, I always felt we weren't fated to win the Final, even after leading 2-0. The chap Trebilcock, who

League goal against Sheffield United, and it was probably appropriate that I made the record my own when we met Tottenham – the club against whom I'd made my debut almost ten years earlier.

People often ask which of my goals I remember best, and think I'm kidding when I say I struggle to recall them. They were all good goals at the time I got them, but, apart from the fact that I know some came from six yards and some from 25, and some were headers while others were tap-ins, the details have disappeared from my memory.

I was lucky enough to play with such good players as Alan Finney, Derek Wilkinson and others, who fed so many quality balls across the penalty area that I always had a lot of chances; and, playing alongside the likes of Keith Ellis, David Layne and John Ritchie, I was always getting knock-downs and benefiting from their presence. I suppose my strength was being in the right position by keeping on the move in the box and anticipating the chances. That instinct never left me.

In all my days with Wednesday I never wanted to play for anyone else, and now, when I look back, I have so many happy memories of some outstanding players, some great friends, and lots of laughs.

At different times I was linked with Blackpool, Leeds and Tottenham, and it was said that when Harry Catterick came back to sign Tony Kay in 1962 he also wanted to take me to Everton but was refused. I was happy to stay and was sorry when Danny Williams decided to let me go to Rotherham because I felt I still had something to offer.

I think I can say I have enjoyed my work in the 25 years since I retired from football, but I shall always recall my days with Wednesday as a special time – I wouldn't have had it any different!

David Ford

David Ford, an England Under-23 striker who made 135 League and Cup appearances and scored 37 goals for the Owls between 1965 and 1969, is remembered as one of the outstanding youngsters "blooded" by Alan Brown in the 1965-66 campaign which coincided with a run to Wembley. He moved to Newcastle in late 1969 and when Sheffield United brought *him "home" in 1971 he joined the select band of men who have played with both city clubs. Now a successful businessman, he is an Owls' shareholder and season-ticket holder and remains a Hillsborough regular.*

When I reflect on my career in football, I tend to feel I didn't do as well in the game as I was capable of doing, largely due to injury problems; but, all the same, I recall those days with great pleasure. To play for the club I supported as a boy was a tremendous source of pride. It meant something very special, and playing for Wednesday in an FA Cup Final and scoring at Wembley is a memory I'll always treasure.

David Ford – scored at Wembley.

I was about seven years old when my Dad first took me to Hillsborough I remember Blackpool were the visitors, the legendary Stanley Matthews played, and Dennis Woodhead scored for us. Later, I was one of a group of 10 or 12 lads from Wybourn who used to stand at the Leppings Lane end one week and on Bramall Lane Kop the next, but Wednesday were always my team.

My Dad, Tom Ford, was always a Wednesday man – and still is at 88. He worked at Nunnery Colliery for 35 years, played in the pit team, and, though only 5ft 4ins tall, he was hard as nails and built like a whippet, and loved his football. I inherited his passion for Wednesday. I also followed his example in being a pretty useful sprinter as a kid, and, when the PE teacher at school encouraged me to concentrate on athletics rather than cricket in the summer, it strengthened my legs for football.

As a schoolboy, when I watched people like Redfern Froggatt, Keith Ellis, Tony Kay, Bobby Craig and Peter Swan, I never imagined I might one day share the same dressing room as them. I have never forgotten seeing Ellis score three in a famous 7-2 FA Cup win at Manchester United in 1961, and, in the same season, an abiding memory from the quarter-final replay defeat at Turf Moor is of Kay dashing 30 yards to tackle Jimmy McIlroy when the Burnley man was taking the mickey and time-wasting near the corner-flag towards the end of the game. Tony got the man, the flag, the lot!

At school I played for Sheffield Boys Under-11s in the same side as Tony Parkes (who made his name as a player, coach and manager at Blackburn), but, after I'd become the first lad from Wybourn for years to pass the 11-plus and gain a place at the City Grammar School, my hopes of more games with Sheffield Boys were dashed by a headmaster who refused to let me even train with the city team and insisted I could only play for the school.

My consolation was to get picked a couple of times for Yorkshire Grammar Schools, and, in the light of later events, it's amusing to reflect that my call-up on both occasions came when Howard Wilkinson, later a Wednesday colleague, wasn't available because he was playing for England Grammar Schools. Howard, by the way, once helped Abbeydale GS beat my school team 13-2, and always seemed destined for a career in professional football.

In my case, having been "banned" from Sheffield Boys, I left school at 16 without being spotted by a club and spent the first three months of my working life in the Estates department at the Town Hall. You could say it was my mother who rescued my football ambitions when she wrote to Wednesday and asked them to give me a trial.

I was invited to play in about four five-a-side matches in the old small gym at Hillsborough, and then Derek Dooley, who was in charge of the juniors, gave me a "proper" trial against Scunthorpe. I scored in a 2-1 win, and, on the following Tuesday, after scoring

David Ford's winning goal in the quarter-final at Blackburn is saluted by Fantham (8).

again when I played in a FA Youth Cup match in which we beat Rotherham 6-0, I was offered an apprenticeship at £10 a week – the same as I'd been getting at the Town Hall.

Being only 16 and playing in an Under-18 league was tough, but I developed quickly and loved my time with the juniors. Dooley, who worked in the Development Fund office, was a great bloke. As his "agent" selling lottery tickets to my fellow apprentices, I had a good excuse to spend hours talking football with him in his office. He created a good spirit among the kids, and away trips were always fun, with sing-songs on the team-bus inspiring him to dub me "Carl Denver" when he wasn't calling me "Rocky"!

Talking of singing, Mick Hennigan, a fellow apprentice who later worked under Howard Wilkinson as a coach for Wednesday and Leeds, used to amuse us in the dressing room every Friday when he'd stand on a table and perform the Frankie Vaughan hit *Tower of Strength*. It didn't exactly qualify as entertainment, for Mick was tone deaf! However, he lacked nothing in enthusiasm, and we were all sorry when he wasn't offered professional terms.

I was one of the lucky ones and had graduated to the Reserves by the time I was 17. In fact, the later step from the second team to the first team wasn't nearly as hard as the initial jump from the juniors, but I managed to adjust,

and, when Alan Brown arrived as manager in 1964, one of his first acts was to include me in the senior squad for a pre-season trip to Germany.

Unfortunately, a couple of minutes from the end of my debut against Werder Bremen, I not only got cramp in both legs but suffered ligament damage to my left knee when this big German back tackled me. It halted my progress for 18 months, but, happily, when I got fit again there was the wonderful compensation of a first-team run which saw me play in the FA Cup Final within a few months.

Amusingly, I recently attended a quiz at which someone asked the name of the first Wednesday man to appear in a League match as a substitute. I didn't know the answer, and had to be reminded the player was me! It's the only thing I'd forgotten about my debut in October 1965.

I had been picked to play with the Reserves at Blackpool, and, having travelled up on the Friday, on the Saturday morning I joined some of the other lads on the promenade and was looking for somewhere to buy some rock when Sam Ellis, my team-mate, jumped out of a taxi and dashed up to announce: "You're wanted back at Hillsborough, you're playing against Sunderland this afternoon."

As Sam had brought my boots along, he pushed me in the taxi and I was driven at top speed to Sheffield. I think we

reached Hillsborough barely half-an-hour before the kick-off, and, having got myself in quite a state on the journey, it was a relief to find I'd actually been named as substitute. This was the first season subs had been permitted, and so far Wednesday hadn't used one. However, the match had only been in progress about five minutes when I was called on – I think it was Don Megson who came off injured.

Everybody seemed to think I'd had a good game, but, although I made my first start the following week, it was February and the FA Cup-tie at Newcastle before I gained a regular place and embarked on that short but unforgettable spell which saw me end the season playing in the Wembley Final.

I got my first Cup goal in the 2-1 win at Huddersfield, scored twice when we beat Blackburn at Ewood Park, and savoured the most fantastic feeling of all when I pounced on a rebound from a John Fantham shot to put us 2-0 up after 56 minutes against Everton. What a comedown it was to see the Cup plucked from our grasp as Everton hit back to win 3-2.

That 1966 Final was my only appearance at Wembley, but, at the time, being 21 and anticipating a long career, I was convinced I'd go back not once but twice or more. In fact, we all felt sure we were going to the Final again the following season when we reached the sixth-round – only to lose at Chelsea to a last-gasp goal from Tommy Baldwin.

We'd beaten Chelsea in the 1966 semi-final, and, in December of the same year, crushed them 6-1 with a memorable performance at Hillsborough in a First Division match; and, in that quarter-final of 1967, with the minutes ticking away, the last thing the Chelsea lads wanted was to have to replay at our ground. To lose the way we did was cruel – and I missed seeing Baldwin's goal because, five minutes from the end, I was taken off with concussion after being clattered by "Chopper" Harris!

The following season, 1967-68, was the one during which Alan Brown left, and, for me, it marked the start of a frustrating period which, ironically, began in unfortunate circumstances just a couple of days after I scored one of my best-ever goals for Wednesday –

and at a moment when, as a team, we felt we were really taking off.

We went to Tottenham having won five of our first six games, and, though we lost 2-1 at White Hart Lane, on the way home we all felt the scoreline didn't reflect how well we'd played. Naturally, I was feeling quite pleased – in beating three men and putting the ball across Pat Jennings and into the net off a post with my weaker right foot, I'd scored a very satisfying goal.

Then, two days later, I was involved in a car accident, and a very difficult time followed. In terms of my football, I suffered an injury to my right knee from which I recovered much quicker than might have been expected, but, just when I was ready to return, I damaged the ligaments in my left knee after being clattered by Don Megson in training.

So, between September and the end of March, I made only one start, and, afterwards, always felt the problems with my left knee prevented me from being able to perform on a long-term basis – a point emphasised when you note that, from September 1967 to December 1969 when I left Wednesday, I started only about half of around 100 games.

I have to admit I often wonder whether things might have been different if Alan Brown hadn't resigned in February 1968. I lost having someone to drive me when he went. Yet, for all the frustrations, Wednesday were my team, I desperately wanted to do well for them, and, to be honest, couldn't believe it when Danny Williams chose to sell me to Newcastle.

At the time I was nursing a shocking bout of 'flu and confined to our house at Park Hill, but Tommy McAnearney arrived to take me to the ground, and when we got there Joe Harvey, the Newcastle manager, was waiting to see me. They offered me twice the money I was getting at Hillsborough, but, even so, I didn't want to leave. I spent an hour in another room alone trying to decide what to do, and, in the end, moved on because it seemed I was surplus to Wednesday's requirements.

As I said earlier, I didn't achieve as much as I felt I was capable of in football, and it was a source of regret that, after such a bright beginning, my career ended in anticlimax. At least I have

compensated by enjoying more consistent and lasting success since finishing playing, and, for the last 25 years or so, I have been doing again what I did as a kid – supporting Wednesday as a fan.

David Smith

David Smith, who played with Burnley, Brighton and Bristol City, returned from Libya to spend three years as Wednesday's trainer-coach, and he was on duty at the 1966 FA Cup Final. In 1967 Alan Brown axed Smith, plus the long serving Tommy Walker and Johnny Logan. Smith later managed Mansfield, Southend, Plymouth, Dundee and Torquay. Now in semi-retirement in Devon, he still does some coaching at "grass roots" with boys aged from five to eight.

Alan Brown had a lot of time for me – first because he had given me my Football League debut at Burnley in 1954 and I was one of his protégés, and second because he had been impressed with my ability to fight back from a succession of serious injuries. So, when I learned he had become Wednesday's manager and applied for a job, he appointed me to the coaching staff. I arrived in Sheffield following a spell in Libya.

At the outset I was just another member of the backroom staff and shared senior duties on a rota with Johnny Logan. My main brief was to help develop the more promising kids at the club, and Alan Brown did the first team coaching as such. Johnny and me packed skips, cleaned boots and did a variety of other jobs.

In fact, "Brownie" was one of those people who liked to do all the important work himself. Take the day Vic Mobley got hurt in the 1966 semi-final – a game, by the way, which I watched from a seat among the supporters in the stand. We had a part-time physio in Bob Lyttle, but it was Alan who strapped up Vic's ankle and decided he should play on when doing so cost the lad the chance of playing in the Final. Vic's ankle was like the Malvern Hills on the Sunday morning!

It was my good fortune that while Logan [he had been at the club since 1946] dropped for sponge-man duty at

the semi-final, I was on the bench when we went to Wembley. I think only got on the field twice, but it made my day!

Contrary to what you might think, when the lads went to Lilleshall for special training in the week before the Final, Alan Brown took the players there on his own. He didn't even take a physio. Johnny Logan and myself were left behind to pack all the new Cup Final kit into a skip at Hillsborough, and we joined up with the players on the day before the big game.

In the Final, we would certainly have won if we could have kept the score at 2-0 a few minutes longer than we did. After the game, I remember trying to console Sam Ellis and Graham Pugh as they wept buckets of tears in the dressing room. My abiding memory of the weekend is the fantastic reception we got when we returned to Sheffield on the day after the match. It was a very humbling experience.

I suppose when people recall that 1966 Final they tend to reflect on how the ball skidded under Gerry Young's foot and Temple pounced to score the winning goal. I imagine it's something Gerry learned to live with a long time ago, but I have to say that when I think of Gerry Young it is as the best professional I ever worked with.

Gerry was a very special man. In my early days at Hillsborough, he gained his only England cap, and was set to get another when he suffered a ruptured thigh muscle. I have never known a man work so hard to get fit.

In those days, when a player was about ready to come back from injury, we used to give him "the Spion Kop test". This involved running from the end of the players' tunnel, jumping over a wall, running up and down two Kop gangways (a lot of steps!), and back to the tunnel – all in a specified time. Gerry did this, and then played in the Reserves the next day. He was fit, but not match-fit, and by half-time he was literally on his knees. I wanted him to come off, but he insisted on playing the full 90 minutes. It wasn't just his determination, but that he refused to think of taking the easy option, which proved his dedication.

There were some great people in that 1966 team, but for me Young was the outstanding professional – and Johnny Quinn was only just behind him.

Welcome Home (1) Brown and his Owls' 1966 team get a great reception from crowds on The Moor.

Welcome Home (2) The Wednesday lads take a bow from the balcony of the Town Hall.

Alan W. Brown Remembered

Alan Brown's name will always be synonymous with Wednesday's 1966 FA Cup run to Wembley. He was the Owls' team manager from the summer of 1964 to February 1968, having previously served as chief coach from January 1951 to August 1954 prior to embarking on a management career

Alan Brown, a remarkable manager who inspired so many of his men and prompted some of them to take up coaching.

with Burnley and Sunderland. Brown's sudden departure in 1968 signalled the start of a dramatic decline at Hillsborough. That Brown was one of the most intriguing managers in Wednesday's history is confirmed by this selection of memories spanning both his spells at the club. He died in March 1996 at the age of 81.

Howard Wilkinson, the former Owls' manager who is now the Football Association's Technical Director, remembers Alan Brown's influence in the shaping of his long-term career in the game.

In many respects, it was Alan Brown who gave me the bug to go into coaching and management. He came to Sheffield in 1964 and confirmed the teachings of Jack Mansell, who had been a coach at the club when I was just starting out as a professional footballer. Jack was the first man to make me feel there was more to it all than I had imagined possible, and Brown picked up on the same theme. Jack and Alan were very different types, but both played from the same hymn sheet.

Brown made me understand very early on that developing players was as much about education as coaching – how they developed as players was linked with how they developed as people. Brown had standards on and off the field, and for him there was no dividing line – the player and the person were the same.

People have often called Brown intimidating, but in the chats I had with him that was not the case. I don't think he enjoyed being a public person, and so created an image which kept people at arm's length. Many of those who responded to his so-called reputation, or "image", never got to know him.

I found him a man with a great deal of warmth and humour. The thing I liked was he had a great deal of professional humility. He didn't profess to know everything, and what he didn't know he was prepared to admit. He knew it was not possible to know everything, even about a game in which he'd spent a lifetime, and he always insisted that to keep pace with developments you had to keep learning.

My chats with Brown got me interested in reading about coaching theories, and, when I left Wednesday and went to Brighton in 1966, the notion of coaching as a friend was firmly implanted in my mind. So, when I was offered the chance of taking a coaching course, I jumped at it. The rest, as they say, is history, and it all really started with Alan Brown.

When I decided to leave Wednesday as a player, it was because I decided I wasn't going to make the grade at that level. Now, when I look back, I recog-

nise that Brown, who said it was entirely up to me whether I stayed or left, was prepared to show more patience over my progress than I was myself.

Sam Ellis, remembered as the teenager who made his FA Cup debut in the 1966 Wembley Final, is another player who was inspired by Brown's example to pursue an interest in coaching which ultimately led him into management.

I think it's fair to say the reason Wednesday went into decline after Alan Brown left in 1968 was because nobody among his immediate successors had the strength of character to maintain the harmony he had brought to the club. He was a tough disciplinarian, but had the ability to bond everybody together in a way which created a very strong team-spirit.

On the day I was starting out on my first foreign trip with the club, a small incident occurred on Sheffield Midland Station which told me everything about the respect and discipline of the period. When "Brownie" put his case and club bag down on the platform, within minutes every player had done exactly the same – and suddenly there was this long and immaculate line of luggage, with not a single piece out of place.

He was someone who always led by example, and if he had this public image as a cold man, he didn't lack a sense of humour which he sometimes expressed in a subtle way that showed how well he understood footballers.

For some reason, I often thought he was always picking on me, but, in a sense, it was probably an indication that he approved of me when he had a bit of fun at my expense.

Once when we were training at Lilleshall, he took us on a cross-country run and, as usual, he was leading from the front. On this particular occasion he got so far ahead that he lost us, and, on the way back, when we got to the end of the long road leading to Lilleshall, four of us hitched a lift in a greengrocer's van. Who should we pass halfway down the road but "Brownie". You can be sure we kept our heads down and hoped he hadn't spotted us!

Later, as we went into lunch, he said to me: "You beat me back." I insisted I hadn't, but he replied: "Yes, you did – but you can't run faster than me, so you must have had a lift." I said: "No, not me, boss."

He paused and then said: "I'll tell you what, after lunch, you and me will go back to the gates and have a race, and, if I beat you, I'll know you had a lift back today."

To cut a long story short, I was in such a state, I couldn't even think of eating anything. I was hungry as hell, but too fearful of the race and the implications of defeat to do more than look at the food. Then, when I went outside to await "Brownie", he suddenly appeared and said: "Sam, I've got things to do, we'll not bother with the race."

He knew I hadn't eaten and was starving. He also knew I'd already inflicted punishment on myself for having hitched an "illegal" lift!

David Smith, who played under Brown at Burnley and was Wednesday's trainer-coach for three years in the mid-1960s, comments:

When you were a player under Alan Brown, you always felt that if he had faith in you there was no way you were going to fail. He did wonders for your self-belief. He had proved this with me in his time as Burnley's manager, because he pulled me out of the Reserves and gave me my chance when others might not have done.

He could see things in players that others didn't recognise, and a classic example of this was Sam Ellis. The first time I saw Sam in training, I thought: "It's going to take a lot of hard work to turn him into a good player." But Brown had faith in Sam, and never had any doubt that Sam had made enough progress to justify being called into the team to make his FA Cup debut in the 1966 Final.

Brown showed the same faith in Graham Pugh. He could be very tough on kids who let him down, and young "Pughie" felt the full force of Brown's wrath on several occasions. There was the time, for instance, when "Pughie" and Brian Woodall held a party at their digs one weekend when their landlady had gone away. After the party, the place was a mess, with cigarette burns in a lounge carpet just one of the complaints. Brown sent the pair home to Chester for a few weeks, but it didn't stop him playing "Pughie" in the semi-final – the lad's Cup debut.

Graham Pugh, the teenager who made his Cup debut in the semi-final at Villa Park – and scored.

Colin Dobson, you may remember, was one of the players who figured in the early matches in the 1966 Cup run and then fell out of favour. I remember Colin getting the wrong side of "Brownie" during a match in Denmark. Colin was a very skilful player, but a bit soft at times, and in this game he had a stinker in the first 45 minutes. "Brownie" grabbed him as he came off, and took him into the toilet for a verbal going over. Colin was white as a sheet when he returned to the dressing room.

I always remember Colin saying to me: "Thank goodness I'm on the wing which is furthest from the dug-out in the second half. At least I'll be able to avoid Brown." Unfortunately, "Brownie" decided to watch the rest of the match from the stand on the opposite side of the ground, and he spent the whole of the second half berating Colin – much to the amusement of the Danish fans, who thought "Brownie" must be some mad supporter from Sheffield!

Don Megson recalls the day Alan Brown made him captain – and remembers, too, that the manager had a quick temper.

It was in September 1964 when we were playing Aarhus GF in Denmark that "Brownie" threw the ball to me and told me to lead the team out for the second half. It came at the end of a rather

heated exchange between him and Tommy McAnearney during the half-time break. Tommy had endured a bit of a chasing in the opening 45 minutes, and he said his piece when "Brownie" blamed him for the situation.

I always remember that "Brownie" was having a real go and in full flow when this little chap, one of the local team's officials, walked into the dressing room carrying a tray of sliced oranges. "Brownie" suddenly stopped talking, took hold of the tray, and promptly followed this old guy out through the door – and threw the tray and sliced oranges along the corridor!

He was a hell of a calm man who could be ice-cool, but once he lost his temper there was no holding him. Once, at Chelsea, he was giving us a pre-match talk when the radio or club intercom suddenly blared out a message. He walked up to the offending piece of equipment, ripped it off the wall, and flung it into the bath!

Colin Dobson, who lost his place during the 1966 FA Cup run, made the mistake of talking to one of the club's directors about wanting a transfer. You didn't discuss such things behind this manager's back, and, when he learned what had happened, "Brownie" stormed into the dressing room, grabbed hold of Dobson, and tried to hang him from a peg on the wall.

David Ford belonged to that generation of young players who thrived under Brown's management and felt his loss when he suddenly walked out on Wednesday in 1968.

Certain people have a knack of getting something extra out of certain people – and Alan Brown had a big impact on a lot of the youngsters after he took over in 1964.

I was 18 and had no first-team experience when he took me on a pre-season tour to Germany in 1964. He gave me my debut against Werder Bremen when, unfortunately, I suffered a knee injury in the last couple of minutes of the match. At the time, we didn't know how serious it was, and I spent a week in bed in Germany before coming home to have hospital treatment.

It was typical of Brown that he carried me up the steps of the plane before we flew home, carried me down them when we got to England, and personally drove me home to Park Hill when we reached Sheffield. He could easily have got someone else to do this, and it meant something to youngsters when a manager did these things for you himself. When I was involved in a car accident and suffered another knee injury in 1967, he was just as considerate, fetching me to and from home at regular intervals to spend some time in the dressing room with the lads because he wanted me to be involved and knew it was a difficult time for me.

Yet he could be strange sometimes. Once when I was still in the Reserves but supposed to be going to Holland with the first-team, I played in a Central League match, didn't think I'd done too badly because I'd hit the woodwork twice, but got back to the dressing room to stand accused by Brown of not having pulled my weight. He said I wouldn't be going to Holland after all – and I stayed behind. I wondered afterwards if he was just winding me up, using a bit of psychology to make me try even harder than I was doing.

When he left, we were devastated. For many of us it was like losing your dad, and I missed the way he had of driving me to reach for higher goals. I often think my career might not have taken a downward turn if he had stayed at Hillsborough, and there's no doubt a lot of the players who did not achieve their full potential would have done so with him behind them. He was a genius.

Jackie Sewell, who cost a British record £35,000 when he joined Wednesday in 1951, recalls:
I played with Alan Brown for a few months at Notts County in 1948. He came to us from Burnley in October of that year, but he didn't stay long. He was an experienced centre-half with a big reputation, but I think he barely played a dozen games. The problem was that he and Tommy Lawton didn't get on. They couldn't stand the sight of one another. In that situation, there could only be one winner – and it wasn't going to be Brown.

Within three months, Brown was asking to be released, and I believe he packed up football, went back to Lancashire, and ended up running a cafe until Wednesday recruited him as a coach.

He was a strange man who had the knack of frightening the life out of you, and in my time under him at Sheffield I always tried to keep my nose clean because, quite honestly, he'd belt anybody who stepped out of place, no bother.

I remember he once arranged for a bus to take us out into the countryside for special training. We were taken about ten miles out and, after being dropped off, went away on this long run through all these rough tracks and bracken. A couple of hours later, we were heading back, still running, in the direction of the bus when we realised that several of the lads had got left behind. We suggested to Sam Powell and Tommy Walker, the trainers, that perhaps we ought to slow down to let the others catch up.

"No way," said Brown. "If they can't keep up, it's too bad. Once we're on the bus, we're going. Those who aren't here will have to walk back to Hillsborough."

There was one famous occasion when I was the captain and Brown introduced a new tactical plan. The lads didn't like it, and they liked it even less after we lost about three games on the trot. Before the next match, we had a players' meeting in the snooker room and the lads decided they were going to revert to the old system whether Brown liked it or not.

Of course, it was a difficult situation for me. Did I tell the lads they couldn't do it or I would report them to Brown, or what? Did they expect me to face Brown alone as their spokesman and explain why they didn't agree with his plan? You had to be a very brave man to dispute Brown's judgement!

The game in question was away, and, when we got to our hotel, we had another meeting. The lads only wanted to know if I was going to do the same as them and revert to the old system. I said I didn't have much choice because I couldn't play according to one plan while they were playing another. They suggested that I would only have to act as their spokesman if we lost.

Well, reverting to the old system paid off quite handsomely. We won 2-1 or 3-1, and I remember that when we got back to the dressing room afterwards Eric Taylor and one or two of the directors came in to congratulate us on our victory. We felt rather pleased with ourselves. Then Brown appeared.

He immediately exploded, but reserved his real anger until the first training session after the match. He gave us the biggest rollicking I can ever remember from a coach. It didn't matter that we'd won. The point was that we had defied him. As you can imagine, as captain I came in for some additional criticism from Brown. Let's just say I gave him a reasonable explanation of my position. Alas, I don't think he was impressed.

Whether we played to the new system or the old one immediately after that, I don't remember. But I do know that in the following summer Brown went to Burnley to become their manager, and I've often wondered if that was just a coincidence

Redfern Froggatt, one of Wednesday's most popular early post-war players, remembers a day when Brown made him and his team-mates really shiver:
Brown wasn't exactly popular on the winter's day when he caught up with a group of the lads as we were strolling back to the dressing room after training on the practice pitch behind the North Stand. There had been a heavy snowfall, and Harry Liversidge and his staff had cleared the snow off the running track round the main pitch and piled it at the end of the tunnel. Brown suddenly instructed us to remove our track suit tops and said: "When I say dive, throw yourselves into that pile of snow!"

We thought he was either kidding or barmy, and we would dearly have loved to have refused. But you only argued with Alan Brown if you wanted trouble!

Keith Bannister, who was captain of the Owls' 1951-52 Second Division championship side, comments:
If you did what Brown asked and gave him everything, he would do anything for you; but if you crossed him, you were in big trouble. The problem was that you could sometimes cross him in quite an innocent way – like once when we were staying in Bakewell and, having bought a new jumper in a local shop, I decided to wear it at dinner. Brown accused me of being improperly dressed and tore me off a strip in front of everybody. The fact that I was captain didn't save me from a public tongue-lashing.

He hated individuals who stepped

out of line, but often made us all pay for the sins of one or two. Once when we went for a long run through Beeley Woods, four of the lads decided to deliberately get lost, and they ended up nipping across the River Don and returning to the ground hours ahead of the rest of us. Brown was easily able to identify them the next morning. They were the only players without blisters on their feet!

However, instead of punishing them, after training Brown ordered everyone to run round the pitch, and he just kept us running for what seemed an eternity. We were only allowed to stop when we were virtually collapsing from exhaustion. Poor Dave McIntosh could barely crawl back to the dressing room – and he hadn't been one of the guilty players!

Jim McAnearney remembers when he sat alongside Owls coach Brown in the dugout:
The first time I ever travelled away with the first-team squad was in April 1954 when we went up to the North East to play Sunderland and stayed over at the Seaburn Hotel ahead of a visit to Newcastle a few days later. I didn't play at Roker, but got into the team at St James's Park.

I was sitting on the bench at Roker, and, as there were no substitutes in those days, I could relax and enjoy the match. Or so I thought. During the game, Len Shackleton, the Sunderland and England inside-forward, produced a typical piece of brilliance when he flicked a ball over George Davies with the back of his heel and ran round the Wednesday man to collect his own pass.

The crowd, of course, went mad with delight, and I was so thrilled by such skill that I instinctively clapped Shackleton. Suddenly I got this whack across my face – and I was staggered when I realised Alan Brown had smacked me. He just glared and said: "Don't applaud the opposition – they never do anything good!" I never forgot that.

It was on that same stay at the Seaburn that somebody messed up Brown's bed. It was probably Alan Finney and Albert Quixall. Unfortunately, it was the kind of joke Brown couldn't stomach. The next morning he got all the players out on the beach. He pulled me out of the line and excused me, but then said to the others: "I want to know who messed my bed up last night." When nobody spoke, he threatened to fight every player in turn until the culprit owned up. In the end he forced everybody to run into the sea fully dressed!

Ron Ward, the former Owls' caretaker, remembers:
Alan Brown was probably the most difficult of all the managers I worked with. If Alan said black was white, then black was white – no argument! Yet, if he was a funny beggar at times, I must give him his due and say that if he promised to do something for you, he would move Heaven and Earth to do it.

Kenny Johnson, one of the apprentices who joined Wednesday in Alan Brown's time, comments:
It was a shock when Alan Brown suddenly left and went back to Sunderland in 1968. I felt it because I had been at the club less than a year, and, with hindsight, it always seems to me that something important was lost with his departure.

He was the old sergeant-major type, and on the training ground Brown always led from the front, but you never felt he asked anyone to do what he couldn't do himself. He might not have been the easiest of people, but he got the best out of players. When I arrived as a 15-year-old in 1967, Brown was at the helm, and with a backroom team comprising Jack Marshall, Lawrie McMenemy and Ian McFarlane, there was a sense of being part of a big happy family in which everything had to be done properly but there was a sense of order and respect.

There seemed to be an easing of discipline after Brown went, and the club went into a big decline. Somehow things went from bad to worse. You couldn't believe how it all changed, and, frankly, I got a bit disillusioned at the way it was all going. It was a brilliant club when I joined, and those early days were the best of my life.

I always thought Don Megson and Gerry Young should have become more involved than they did instead of being shoved out. I remember when I was an apprentice, Meggie took charge of us for a Northern Intermediate League match one afternoon, and, honest, he

was brilliant. I thought I had seen a future Wednesday manager, but, of course, that never happened.

The thing was, Meggie could have inspired the same kind of respect Brown had. I don't think Jack Marshall or Danny Williams, great guys though they were, had the qualities which made Brown different. Derek Dooley was a popular figure, but, in my view, he, too, was the wrong choice because he had been out of the game such a long time.

It was a pity Wednesday did not recover sooner from Brown's departure, because a lot of the young players who failed to make the grade did so as a result of being affected by a climate of decline.

Benny Hill, who was on the sports staff of the Sheffield Telegraph *in Brown's time, recalls:*
Alan had a reputation as a difficult man, and, when you knew you had to deal with him for the first time, you were inclined to be a bit frightened – scared of his likely reaction. I was a bit apprehensive when, on getting confirmation of his appointment late one evening in 1964, I got the job of doing a hurried interview with him by telephone just ahead of our deadline.

It was a relief to find him friendly and helpful, and he gave me a good piece with some excellent quotes. Indeed, I got a second telephone interview which also went very well the next day. Then came the acid test – a visit to meet him in Sunderland!

Having told him what time I was due to arrive, it was a blow when the train was delayed and I had to call from York to say I'd be two hours late. Having feared a rebuff, I was surprised when he said: "Oh, don't worry, just call me when you get into Sunderland."

When I announced I'd arrived at the local station, and asked for details of how to reach him, he said: "Stay where you are, I'll come and fetch you." Considering what people had said about him, I found his concern for my welfare remarkable. Even more surprisingly, I discovered he was already entertaining my rival from the Sheffield evening paper, Tony Hardisty. Tony, who had travelled up earlier by car, was enjoying a royal reception.

At his home, Brown took time to show us his aviary then invited us to

Wednesdayites don't need reminding that it was a double from a guy called Trebilcock which hauled Everton level in the 1966 Final. Ellis, Eustace, Quinn and Smith see the Cornishman's shot beat Ron Springett.

stay for a meal. With his wife, two daughters and an elderly lady who I assumed to be his mother, there were already five sitting at the table. "What we have cooked for five, we shall now divide between seven," he said with a smile.

After he had settled in Sheffield, I did see many examples of why some people called him an enigma and others felt he was difficult. On one trip to London with the team, we all went to a West End theatre on the Friday evening as usual, but Tony Hardisty and myself made the mistake of taking two minutes too long to get our coats from the cloakroom afterwards. We dashed out into the street to find the bus taking the team back to the hotel had left without us – Brown wouldn't wait once all the players were on board, and we had no choice but to make our own way to the team's headquarters.

He never apologised. He wouldn't consider it necessary.

Peter Pollitt, a long-time supporter, remembers:

Brown was a tough man who could strike fear into people, but he had a soft side, too.

When he was in the Huddersfield Police in his early days, he used to come with their team to play against the Sheffield Police at the Niagara Ground. When the match was over, he wouldn't join his colleagues in taking a shower before relaxing in the bar. He'd whip his football boots off, sling them round his neck, put some pumps on his feet, and immediately set off to run all the way back to Huddersfield!

Someone once said he insisted on carrying a full pack on his back while he ran, although I don't know if that's true. But certainly he was a fitness fanatic, and a great one for self discipline. Alan never did anything by halves, and there was a spell when he developed a passion for Moral Rearmament and lived by a set of very rigid principles which his family were also expected to follow.

I remember an incident at Newcastle during Wednesday's 1966 FA Cup run. I was standing talking to Alan's wife, Connie, in the tea-room after the game.

She was enjoying a sherry, but, the moment Alan appeared through the door, she suddenly thrust the glass into my hands. I don't know what Alan thought when he saw me holding a pint of beer and a glass of sherry. No doubt he felt I was in the grip of the devil! But at least Connie escaped the wrath she knew she would face if he'd caught her drinking.

Many people were unaware that Alan had a big aviary at the foot of his garden at his Bents Road home in Sheffield. It was where he "switched off". He used to spend hours at a time talking to his budgies and canaries. He called them all by their names, and to see him speaking to them so softly and with such affection, you couldn't imagine this was the "iron man" of Hillsborough!

Boys of '91 and '93

The Boys of '91. Back row (left to right): Shirtliff, Turner, Palmer, Pressman, Madden. Middle row: Spry (staff), Barker (assistant manager), Sheridan, Bennett, King, McCall, Worthington, Hirst, Smith (physiotherapist). Front row: Nilsson, Wood, Williams, Ron Atkinson (manager), Pearson, Wilson, Francis.

Nigel Pearson

Nigel Pearson, who cost Wednesday £250,000 from Shrewsbury Town in October 1987 and made 224 League and Cup appearances for the Owls before joining Middlesbrough in July 1994, is remembered as one of the club's most popular and respected players – a defender assured of a lasting place in the Owls' Hall of Fame as captain of the promotion and League Cup "double" team of 1990-91. He topped a memorable season by being voted Man of the Match at Wembley.

The day after we'd been unexpectedly relegated from the old First Division in 1990, the players all went off to Spain for a short break which had been arranged well ahead of the late slip which shattered what had seemed to have been a successful push towards safety.

In the circumstances, we were hardly in a holiday mood, but, if we felt a bit sorry for ourselves for a couple of days, we perked up after Ron Atkinson held a meeting at which he said: "Look, we've been relegated and have to face up to it. But you're here now, so enjoy yourselves, and then, when we get home, let's make sure we get back to the job of winning promotion in the right frame of mind."

I think the players had already decided that, as it was us who had taken the club down, we had a collective responsibility to put it right. Several lads, such as Roland Nilsson, John Sheridan and Carlton Palmer, had clauses in their contracts which would have allowed them to leave following relegation, but nobody wanted to walk away from the challenge.

The great thing was not just that we did what we set out to do by winning promotion at the first attempt, and enjoyed a marvellous bonus with the Rumbelows Cup success – but we did it by playing football which reflected the commitment and team spirit which created a very special atmosphere. There were so many different and sometimes contrasting characters in the dressing room, but, to a man, we all got on – and that doesn't happen very often.

If you talk to the lads themselves, and to supporters who have followed the club for a long time, they will say that in 1990-91 under Ron and in perhaps the first 18 months under Trevor

Francis, some of our football was the best they've ever seen from a Wednesday team.

That promotion season inspired so many wonderful memories, and for me one of the happiest was that a great year coincided with the birth of our first child, Hannah – ironically, on a February day when we were playing a League match at Swindon. When news of Hannah's impending arrival reached me at the team's hotel at about five o'clock that morning, I woke Ron Atkinson up and said I was dashing home to be with my wife Nicky for the birth.

Ron asked: "Are you coming back to play tonight?" I said, all being well, I would – and, borrowing Danny Wilson's car, I drove from Wiltshire to Sheffield, arrived in time to welcome my daughter into the world, and then sped back to play against Swindon. Even a 2-1 defeat couldn't spoil an otherwise perfect if exhausting day.

The moment I especially remember from that 1991 Cup run is not the relief and overwhelming emotion of those first seconds after the final whistle at Wembley, or the honour of being the first Wednesday captain for 56 years to walk up those famous steps and collect a major trophy.

No, for me the high point was the second leg of the semi-final against Chelsea, and especially the realisation that victory meant we were bound for Wembley. For most of us, it was the first time, and our joy was beyond words. The atmosphere in the ground was fantastic, and the delight of the supporters, young and old, was something I'll never forget.

There was one incident which might seem trivial but was special for me. As the players did a lap of honour at the end and the fans gave us scarves and hats, one young girl thrust a little cut glass owl into my hand. It remains one of my most treasured souvenirs of a wonderful night, and means as much to me as the Man of the Match trophy I went on to win at Wembley.

Perhaps the only down-side to my season was the way it ended in the disappointment of missing out on the four matches in which we finally clinched promotion. I suffered concussion early in the first game after the Final, a home match with Leicester, and what infuri-

Nigel Pearson, a great captain.

ated me was how it happened. I don't mind being injured in accidents, but that blow to my head wasn't an accident. You can be sure Steve Walsh, the Leicester captain, knew I was going to mention it the next time I saw him. However, I don't hold grudges and prefer to dwell on the positive memories of that year.

Of course, when we reflect on the past, we always tend to see it through rose-coloured spectacles. Now all I readily recall from my time at Hillsborough are happy memories. But, in truth, life isn't like that, and, if I'm honest, when I look back, there were many disappointments, some sticky times, and not a few difficult spells as well as a lot of good days.

Take 1993, for instance. That was the year when a broken leg suffered in the Coca-Cola Cup semi-final at Blackburn ended my season in February and meant I watched from the sidelines as we reached the Finals of both major domestic Cup competitions and made a unique four trips to Wembley.

As the birth of our daughter had coincided with our progress towards double glory in 1991, when our son, James, was born during our push for

another double success in 1993, it seemed a happy omen. We were playing at Ipswich in the Coca-Cola Cup on the January day when James arrived, and I undertook another long drive to and from Sheffield on the day of the match. I was back in East Anglia in time to help us draw that night. Then we won the replay, but, barely three weeks later, my season quite literally collapsed at Ewood Park.

That, as they say, is life. It was a blow, but, if it was unfortunate, at least I could sympathise with my pal Peter Shirtliff, whose misfortune was just as great. He also missed both Finals – the first with a broken arm, the second with a calf strain – and the cruellest irony was a guy who had served Wednesday so long would have had the honour of captaining the team at Wembley.

To be honest, my personal disappointment was accentuated by a sense of feeling I had gone past my sell-by date at Wednesday. I'd been there too long, I'd involved myself in things which were none of my business, and I'd become too emotionally attached to the club. I've always been somebody who wears his heart on his sleeve and says what he thinks, and it made for a difficult time which, unfortunately, ended in tears.

In fact, I remained at Hillsborough another year, and didn't really want to leave, but, if it wasn't a choice of my making, circumstances dictated that it should be the case. In the event, joining Middlesbrough turned out to be the best thing that's happened to me, in that I enjoyed a new lease of life and played some of the best football of my career on Teesside. Moreover, I did play in two Cup Finals in the same year in 1997, and 'Boro returned to Wembley in the Coca-Cola Cup Final in 1998.

I suppose it's an intriguing coincidence that, with the League Cup having featured in so many milestones in my career, this was the competition in which I came to Wednesday's notice in 1987. In six years at Shrewsbury, I had made nearly 200 appearances, and, frankly, it seemed the time had come to try to better myself. Happily, when we met Wednesday over two legs in the second round of the League Cup, Howard Wilkinson spotted me.

One afternoon I got a call out of the blue saying Wednesday wanted to speak to me, and while, to be honest, the move was not financially rewarding, I was attracted by an opportunity which proved to be a very good career step for me.

Initially, things didn't go quite as well as I had hoped, for I dislocated an ankle at Manchester United in March, and, when this meant I missed the Mercantile Credit Centenary Final, I wondered if I was going to be one of those players who would never play at Wembley.

Later in 1988, of course, Howard Wilkinson left. I think he felt he'd done as much as he could with the resources then available. It was only after Ron Atkinson came that Wednesday made a conscious decision to change direction and invest more heavily in seeking success.

Between Howard and Ron, Peter Eustace had a spell as manager, and the one thing Peter did which was good for me was making me captain in December 1988. I have to admit it was a difficult time for me personally, because I replaced Mel Sterland, who was a local hero. Some supporters were not pleased by my appointment at Mel's expense, and I got a bit of hate mail over it – but it was an opportunity I wasn't going to turn down, and, ultimately, I think it worked out to everybody's satisfaction.

When Ron came he was like a breath of fresh air to the club. He gave the players an opportunity to express themselves and enjoy their football. He is very good at taking the pressure off players and making them feel they can go out and play to their strengths. It was a philosophy that paid off when we won promotion and the Rumbelows Cup – and I was proud to be captain of that side.

Chris Turner

Goalkeeper Chris Turner made 205 League and Cup appearances for Wednesday in two spells between 1976 and 1991, and the highlight of a successful career which spanned some 600 games with four clubs was helping the Owls win their first major trophy for 56 years in the famous League Cup and promotion "double" campaign of 1990-91.

There is nothing better than to play for the club you've supported all your life,

Chris Turner, who enjoyed two spells with the Owls. Having been a Wednesdayite all his life, to help them win the Rumbelows Cup was a major highlight.

and to help them win a Cup Final at Wembley is a dream which only comes true for a fortunate few. I was one of the lucky ones!

My parents, Dennis and Margaret Turner, have always been Wednesdayites. Dad first took me to Hillsborough when I was four years old, but my earliest memory of the Owls is the 1966 FA Cup run, when I was seven – and especially a wet day at Villa Park when we beat Chelsea in the semi-final.

Unfortunately, Dad couldn't get tickets for the Final. When we played Huddersfield in the fifth round, he managed to buy some through Don Megson, the captain. But he wasn't so lucky when the Owls went to Wembley. We had to settle for watching the game on a black-and-white television, and I couldn't have imagined then that I'd be in the team the next time Wednesday reached a major domestic Cup Final.

It can only have been about four years later, when I was 11, that George McCabe invited me down to Hillsborough for training. Mind you, if it was the first step on the road to a career with Wednesday, I have to admit there were times I actually hated those

schoolboy sessions in the gymnasium. I always seemed to go home with sore fingers and an aching head after being pummelled with a hard ball which hurt if you saved it and, in rebounding off a brick wall, walloped the back of your head if you didn't!

However, I started to enjoy training once I became an apprentice after leaving school in March 1975, though some memories of the period have little to do with football, or even with the traditional boot-cleaning duties.

For instance, I recall long summer days when all we did was help Derek Blunkett, the groundsman, by riddling tons of soil. It was back-breaking stuff. Just as frustrating was the week before a Hillsborough semi-final: football training for apprentices was abandoned, and instead we cleaned doors, shelves and areas where nobody ever went but which had to be spotless for the big occasion!

It was Len Ashurst who gave me my senior debut at 17 in the pre-season Ship Cup tournament of 1976, and I made my League debut soon afterwards on a sunny August afternoon at Hillsborough, where we drew 0-0 with Walsall. An abiding memory is of tipping the ball over the bar from a header early in the match and experiencing for the first time the thrill of hearing my name chanted by fans on the same Kop where I had stood until two years earlier.

I settled in very well, and played in all but one of the next 82 League and Cup games. However, it's the match I missed which sticks in my memory. After a run of 18 outings, and just when I thought I was established, Ashurst dropped me for the home game with Rotherham. It seemed so like the end of the world, I wept all the way home! Anyhow, we lost that game and I was promptly recalled.

The next disappointment came after Jack Charlton took charge. He preferred a bigger goalkeeper and started picking Bob Bolder, and, eventually, when my contract expired in 1979, I seemed to have little choice but to move on to Sunderland. My career really took off after I went to Wearside, but I never really wanted to leave, and, while the next nine years, during which I played over 300 times for Sunderland and Manchester United, were good to me, I was delighted to be able to return to Hillsborough in September 1988.

I might never have gone to Roker Park but for the fact that Ken Knighton, my old Wednesday youth coach, was the manager, and, of course, Peter Eustace was up there, too. Peter, indeed, was involved in the negotiations which brought me back to Wednesday, and I didn't meet Howard Wilkinson, the manager, until the day of my medical at Claremont. I always remember Howard standing outside the nursing home and showing me a slip of paper on which the details of my contract were written. It didn't take me long to say "yes".

Howard talked about me coming back, taking my coaching badge, and graduating on to the staff as part of a plan to ensure some continuity, loyalty and "true blue" input at the club. Remarkably, within four weeks, he'd moved on to Leeds, and my hopes of a long-term career at Hillsborough beyond my playing days suddenly didn't look so promising!

In fact, things weren't going too well for Wednesday at the time I arrived. We pulled ourselves out of relegation trouble when Ron Atkinson first came, but the following season, when everybody expected things to take off, we went down. I always remember us drawing 1-1 at Wimbledon (where John Fashanu equalised for them with a dodgy penalty) to reach the magical 40 points, and, after the game, we went straight off to spend three or four days in the Isle of Wight happily convinced we had ensured our First Division survival.

For three-quarters of that 1989-90 season we played some super football and didn't deserve to get relegated, but we lost a lot of games by a single goal and too often our performances weren't reflected in the results. In the last match, against Forest, we were too open and they hit us on the break. That defeat was one of the worst moments ever.

I have never forgotten how, when we reported for pre-season training ahead of the 1990-91 campaign, "Big Ron" told us: "The priority is promotion for the first team, but I also want the Reserves and the youth team to win their leagues." Well, we got promotion, the second team won the Pontin's League, and the kids reached the FA Youth Cup Final – and the Rumbelows Cup made it a fantastic season.

One of the ironies was that me and Kevin Pressman shared the first-team goalkeeping job yet both qualified for a Pontin's League championship medal. However, having been first choice at the end of the previous season, I wasn't very happy when Kevin was chosen ahead of me in the early months of 1990-91. At 32, I didn't want to be in the Reserves.

I didn't regain my place until late December, but, happily, I stayed in the side and shared in an unforgettable second half of the season. Wembley, naturally, was the high point, all the more so as we beat my old club, Manchester United. It was a marvellous day, and we produced an excellent team display typified by an outstanding performance from Nigel Pearson, our captain.

In fact, United only had one real opportunity – and I shall always remember my save from Brian McClair as one of the best I ever made. It came just eight minutes from the end.

After Wembley, I played in five of the last six League games and, at the time, I couldn't have imagined that the night we clinched promotion with a win against Bristol City would signal the end of something for me – my last League appearance for Wednesday.

Although Ron Atkinson left and went to Aston Villa that summer and Trevor Francis took over, the situation seemed to be simply one in which

Kevin Pressman and myself would again be competing for the goalkeeper's jersey in 1991-92. At the start of pre-season training, Trevor said he didn't know which one of us would get his vote because, in his words, "you're equal in ability".

Following a trip to America, we began a run of four or five pre-season friendlies, and Trevor said whoever was in goal for the last of these, at Portsmouth, would keep the job for the first League match, against Villa. However, come the Portsmouth game, he was still so undecided he gave us half a match each – and we tossed a coin to see which of us would start the game.

With the new season only days away, the situation remained unresolved, or so we thought. In midweek, there was an unexpected twist which shocked both me and Kevin – Trevor had paid Glasgow Rangers £1.2 million for Chris Woods.

I found it all the harder to take in because, a week or so earlier, Trevor and I had been in the dressing room when the news broke that Rangers were ready to sell Woods but wanted over £1 million. I said: "Who's going to pay that much for him?" Trevor replied: "Yes, it's too much money." Then he'd gone out and paid it!

I think Kevin went straight down to bang on Trevor's door and ask the score, but, while I recognised it meant

Chris Turner (right) and Liverpool's Alan Hansen prepare to lay wreaths at the Leppings Lane end in November 1989 when the Merseysiders made their first visit to Hillsborough after the semi-final tragedy.

I'd have to think about finding another club, I still had two years left on my contract and didn't see the need for panic and hasty decisions.

In the event, however, I left as early as the following October, when I teamed up again with Peter Eustace at Leyton Orient. As had been the case 12 years earlier, I didn't want to leave, but, once more, it seemed the only solution – although I must admit I look back now and wonder whether it might have been better to have stayed.

If I had decided to hold on, perhaps Kevin would have been the one to move, and, what with five men on the bench (including a goalkeeper) coming into Premiership football, who can say what might have happened?

My consolation is at least I did have some great times with Wednesday, and I've so many good memories made all the more special because they relate to the club I supported as a boy. Also, Hillsborough gave me the kind of start in professional football which taught me habits that still stand me in good stead as I try to pass them on to the next generation of players.

Footnote: Chris Turner is now youth coach at Wolves.

John Sheridan

John Sheridan, the Republic of Ireland midfielder whose goal sealed victory in Wednesday's 1991 Rumbelows Cup Final triumph, made 242 League and Cup appearances and scored 33 times for the Owls between November 1989 and September 1996, with 29 of his 34 caps coming during his seven years at Hillsborough.

It was typical of the spirit in the Wednesday dressing room that we were all desperately disappointed when Carlton Palmer missed the 1991 League Cup Final after being sent off in a Second Division match two weeks before we were due to meet Manchester United at Wembley; and, as Carlton was my particular pal, before the big game I promised to run straight to him if I scored that day. I suppose it was my way of saying he was part of the team even if he was suspended.

That's why now, seven years later, Carlton always comes into my thoughts

John Sheridan – he will always be remembered as the man whose goal sealed Wednesday's first major trophy in 56 years.

whenever I recall the 38th-minute goal that gave us victory. I remember how Gary Pallister tried to head clear from Nigel Worthington's free-kick, and the ball dropped just nicely for me. My first-time shot was one of those which can either go into the crowd or find the back of the net. But I knew I'd struck it well, and, though the goalkeeper got a touch, luckily the ball went in off the post. As I saw it reach the net, I turned straight to the bench and started running towards Carlton. I doubt if I've ever moved so fast in my life. Nobody could catch me, and Carlton was heading in my direction just as fast – it was a marvellous moment I'll never forget.

Manchester United were the firm favourites, but they knew they had a game on their hands that afternoon, and nobody could deny we were worthy winners. We'd gone into the match full of confidence, and really believed we could do it. What a thrill it was for a Stretford lad like me to have helped beat United at Wembley!

Some people suggested United might exploit the fact that Roland Nilsson had not been long back after an injury lay-off, but Lee Sharpe, who was one of the best young players in the

game at the time, never gave Roland the anticipated run-around. I don't think I've played with a better full-back than Roland. He was world-class, and we never had any doubts about him coping that day. Anyway, he had John Harkes backing him up as part of our game-plan.

In fact, we had a good team full of quality and boasting a terrific atmosphere in the dressing room. Every time you walked through that door, it was just one big mickey-take, with so many great characters ensuring we always had plenty of laughs.

All the same, we were deadly serious about getting promotion. The Cup was a wonderful bonus, but bouncing back to the old First Division at the first attempt was the priority, and we all felt we simply had to achieve that to compensate for the terrible disappointment of being relegated the previous season.

I had arrived in November 1989 after just a few months at Nottingham Forest following a summer move from Leeds. The only game I played for Forest was in the League Cup, and I wasn't too thrilled about not getting a look-in with the first-team. But I was playing well and ready to fight for my place, and when Wednesday came in, I wasn't keen to move. Frankly, I was wary of joining a club at the bottom of the table.

However, Brian Clough more or less said I hadn't a future at Forest, so I agreed to switch to Sheffield, and it turned out to be the right decision because my Wednesday days proved the most successful phase of my career. I played my best football there, without doubt, and, while the initial incentive was simply a first-team place, there was so much more to savour in my time at Hillsborough.

It was unfortunate that, after pulling things round with some good results in my first season, we should go and get relegated by losing to, of all clubs, Forest on the last day of the campaign. A lot of us could have used a get-out clause in our contracts and left, but, like the others, I was happy to stay and felt that was the right thing to do considering Ron had given me a chance at a time when my career had been at a low ebb.

Although we finished third in the table in 1990-91, we were the best team in the Second Division by far. Of course, believing ourselves to be a First

Division side didn't mean we'd automatically get promotion, because many good clubs had gone down and struggled for a few years before achieving that goal.

We knew we had to prove our abilities with the right results. Happily we got off to a very good start and never looked back. In the end, we regained our First Division place with style, and the only thing that spoiled it was when Ron Atkinson decided to leave and go to Aston Villa. I was away on international duty at the time the news broke, and didn't even get the chance to say goodbye.

In my view, if Ron had stayed at Wednesday another three or four years, we would definitely have won more major honours. There was no messing about with Ron, he knew how to treat players and get the best out of them. Of course, we did well under Trevor in the next two seasons, but Ron had that extra something which I'm sure would have taken us that little bit further.

Unfortunately for me, I had a bit of injury trouble in 1991-92, and had to have a knee operation in the following summer. I didn't make my first appearance in 1992-93 until late October, and, though I was able to play a part in the runs which took us to both major Cup Finals that season, the truth is I rushed back too quickly.

We had signed Chris Waddle that year, and I think I hurried my return because I wanted to play with him. I was okay in the matches themselves, but the reaction afterwards was not what it should have been. The trouble, of course, is when the team's winning, you want to be part of it, and you tend to try to make light of aches and pains. The way we performed in some of those Cup games in 1993 was very satisfying, and it suggested further progress was just round the corner.

However, after we lost the two Finals that year, I think we got rid of too many players too soon. Several lads went who shouldn't have gone. The addition of one or two players to supplement those we had would have enabled us to profit from a blend of new blood and experience, but some experienced men were allowed to leave when, really, I doubt if any of them really wanted to go.

I know when my time came to go, I also left with a certain reluctance. Of course, I was disappointed about not being in the side, and, in truth, the promise of first-team football elsewhere was the crucial issue, but I knew I was leaving a place where I had had some wonderful times and a club which meant a lot to me.

What did hurt was the way it all happened. When I moved to Bolton in late 1996, I just walked out of the door as if I was going home like on any other day in the previous seven years. But I knew I wasn't coming back tomorrow, and somehow it was as if that didn't matter to anybody. Nobody said thank you, and, well, I just felt so disappointed.

David Barber, Wednesday's head groundsman, relates an amusing footnote about the day John Sheridan took an unexpected soaking during a light training session when the Republic of Ireland midfielder was recovering from a knee operation.

I remember it was a beautiful day, and I was sitting in the garage looking out through the door, which was slightly ajar, when I was sure I saw John pass by. Then he suddenly reappeared and I could see he was absolutely drenched.

What had happened was that, after doing a few laps of the running track, John had gone on to the pitch to finish off with a few stretching exercises. Unfortunately, he positioned himself near the automatic sprinklers, and, as they were pre-set, they suddenly switched on and were jetting 200 gallons a minute on to the pitch.

John was not amused to find himself getting the full force of an unscheduled shower. He ran round to seek out me and my lads, and, naturally wasn't too impressed when we reacted to the sight of this soaking footballer by laughing.

We tried to explain that, contrary to what he suspected, none of us had deliberately turned on a tap. John was in no mood to believe the sprinklers were on a timer, and he made sure I knew how he felt by filling a bucket full of cold water and throwing it all over me!

Later, of course, he could see the funny side. But he made a point of being extra careful whenever he exercised on the pitch after that!

Peter Shirtliff

Peter Shirtliff was one of only two members of the triumphant 1991 team who had played with Wednesday in the Third Division. He joined the Owls from school at 16 in 1977, made his debut at 17 in 1978, and, although limited to three appearances in the 1979-80 promotion run, was a regular in the team that reached Division One in 1984. He made 359 League and Cup appearances in two spells, but injuries cost him the chance to captain Wednesday at Wembley in 1993.

As a schoolboy, I used to go to as many of Wednesday's home games as possible, and, naturally, jumped at the chance to sign for my favourite club. A number of other clubs had watched me playing for Barnsley Boys and made approaches, but, when George McCabe, the Youth Officer, invited me and my Dad to look round the ground and offered to put me on schoolboy forms, I didn't hesitate.

I don't remember the first Wednesday game I ever saw, but have never forgotten seeing the famous 5-4 defeat of Manchester United in 1968. I was only seven then but no doubt already dreamed of playing at Hillsborough myself one day. Incidentally, another early game which sticks in my memory was an afternoon in the early 1970s when I saw a young teenager called Trevor Francis score for Birmingham against the Owls – little thinking I would eventually play alongside him or that he would become Wednesday's manager.

I spent 13 years of my career with Wednesday, and they were good times. In the first period, from 1977 to 1986, I grew up alongside some good lads with whom I played a lot of football at different levels, and, there being so many local products, in 1984 we could really appreciate what it meant to see Wednesday get back to Division One after such a long wait. Then, when I came "home" following a spell at Charlton, I played in an outstanding team which in 1991 won promotion and the club's first major trophy for 56 years, the Rumbelows Cup.

By the time I became an apprentice in 1977, George McCabe had gone, but John Harris, who had been appointed chief scout, was always there with

Peter Shirtliff – a memory dating back nearly ten years before the Rumbelows Cup Final, to 1981 when "The Duke" scored the winner against Oldham at Hillsborough.

advice and I appreciated the help of someone who had such a great knowledge of the game. Later, I also benefited from playing in the Reserves under Frank Blunstone. Frank was a big influence. He didn't want defenders just to kick the ball up the pitch, but had us playing a passing game and encouraged me to think about my football.

I hadn't been long with the club when Len Ashurst left and Jack Charlton came, and, being a centre-back, it was a terrific bonus to get tips from a man who had played in my position in England's 1966 World Cup team. Jack was very good for the young players, his impact at the club was fantastic, and some of his coaching sessions were superb.

I was still three months away from becoming a full pro when Jack gave me my first-team debut in August 1978. Ironically, he asked me to play in an unaccustomed role at right-back, and, later in the same season, I had a long run in that position after Ray Blackhall suffered a serious injury. It took me some time to claim a regular place at centre-back, but the great thing was I was always learning.

Things took a turn for the better in the first two seasons after promotion to the Second Division, for I made some 60 appearances and it proved a notable phase for the Shirtliff family because

my brother Paul also got into the side. I especially remember a couple of games when Paul and I played together in February 1982. On his full debut at Norwich, we won 3-2, and three days later we shared a 3-3 draw with top-of-the-table Luton in a home match we should have won.

The season when we finally won promotion back to the top-grade was particularly memorable, and all the more so as we also reached the quarter-finals of both the League Cup and FA Cup. I played in 47 of our 53 games, and I think what made it special was knowing the club was again enjoying some of the big occasions like those I remembered as a young supporter.

Unfortunately, by the end of the 1985-86 season, when we finished fifth in Division One and reached the FA Cup semi-final for the second time in four seasons, I didn't feel there was a future for me at Hillsborough. It wasn't a case of wanting to leave, but knowing I had a painful choice to make.

In the event, I think the move to Charlton and the three years I spent with them made me a better player. The experience of captaincy certainly brought my game on no end, and, by the time I was fancying a move back north, it proved a happy coincidence that Ron Atkinson should want to take me "home" to Hillsborough.

It's history now that my initial season back with Wednesday coincided with my first taste of relegation, but the consolation was the way we not only won promotion at the first attempt but went on to win the League Cup. It was probably one of the best seasons the club has ever had.

Some of the football we played that year was fantastic, and we were encouraged to play with style by Ron.

It was so enjoyable. I recall a day when we beat Plymouth 3-0 and they never got a kick. We were too good for the Second Division, and I'm sure if you asked Ron he'd say that was one of the best sides he's ever managed.

The only disappointment for me was missing the last four games of the season because I had to have a back operation which sidelined me until October. Now, when I look back, I'm grateful that at least I played in the Rumbelows Cup Final because, in 1993 when Wednesday went four times to Wembley, I missed out on them all.

The irony of the 1992-93 season was that things suddenly went wrong for me just when I was enjoying being captain in a spell in which we won seven and drew two of nine games and shot from 15th to fourth in the table. Then I broke my arm in a game against Liverpool at the end of February and was out for eight weeks. I missed the second leg of the League Cup semi-final, the all-Sheffield FA Cup semi-final and the Coca-Cola Cup Final against Arsenal.

I returned for the League match with Middlesbrough in early May and played with a protection on my arm, but I ended up trying to do too much, strained a calf muscle, and suffered the devastating blow of realising I had no chance of making the FA Cup Final.

That summer we signed Des Walker, who returned to English football from Italy, and, putting my disappointment behind me, I found myself looking forward to enjoying the experience of playing alongside Des. Unfortunately, when we started pre-season training, Trevor Francis broke the news that he'd accepted an offer for me from Wolves.

I was probably more sorry to leave the second time because the atmosphere at the club since my return had been special, and, in the last season, the social life among the over-30s had been so good. I knew it was something which would never be recaptured, and I treasure the memory.

Author's note. After two years at Wolves, Peter returned to his native South Yorkshire and joined Barnsley, where he later found a place on the coaching staff under Danny Wilson. He is now assistant manager at Oakwell.

Roland Nilsson

Roland Nilsson, the classy defender who cost Wednesday £375,000 from FK Gothenburg in December 1989, made 185 League and Cup appearances for the Owls before returning to Sweden for domestic reasons in May 1994. He collected 31 of his caps while at Hillsborough, and was one of the most popular players in the club's history. In 1997 he resumed his career in English football with Coventry.

I still treasure the memory of my time with Wednesday, and shall never forget the day in May 1994 when I left to go back home because the send-off the supporters gave me after the match with Manchester City was one of the most emotional experiences of my career. I knew I was liked by the fans from things people had said over the years, but the way they showed their feelings that afternoon was something very special. For me it was the icing on the cake after having found so much to enjoy while in Sheffield.

I always remember that when I was playing for Gothenburg, there were rumours of Manchester United wanting to sign me. In 1989-90, it was suggested they were hoping to take me to Old Trafford on loan until the end of the season, but, because of my family, I wasn't keen on an arrangement which could have ended with me staying only a few months.

When Sheffield Wednesday got in touch, it was clear that Ron Atkinson was ready to bring me to England on a permanent basis, and, of course, I never regretted accepting his offer. We had some good times and there were so many good things to recall from those years – not least promotion and five matches at Wembley.

The best of days, without doubt, was when we won the League Cup by beating Manchester United in 1991. I had a long period out of action with a cruciate ligament injury that season, and the big problem was that though I managed to recover in time to play at Wembley, I was not really match fit. I was injured in October at Millwall, and did not play again in the first team until two weeks before the Cup Final.

My comeback match was at Portsmouth, and, apart from recalling that I managed to get through the game okay, my memory of the day is when Carlton Palmer got himself sent off – which meant him missing the Cup Final. It was silly, really, because when Carlton was shown a yellow card for a bad challenge, he argued with the referee and was then shown a second yellow card – and a red one.

I think I got through the Wembley Final pretty well, really, but I was grateful to John Harkes. He was my partner, my back-up. My fear was whether I

Roland Nilsson – the classy Swedish defender is seen here with manager Ron Atkinson following his arrival from Gothenburg in the 1989-90 season.

could survive the full 90 minutes, and, in view of the threat of Lee Sharpe, Harkesy and I worked together all the previous week preparing for all possibilities. We talked a great deal and our preparations were worthwhile.

Of course, there was a big celebration at our hotel after the match. I was as thrilled by our result as anyone, but I was a bit knocked out and felt the pain of a rib injury, so I only stayed for the meal and then went off to bed for a good sleep.

The happiness we felt in 1991 was in contrast to the disappointment in 1993 when we lost to Arsenal in both Cup Finals. When we drew in the FA Cup Final, it meant I had to play in two important games in two days – first for Sweden in a World Cup qualifying match in Stockholm, then for Wednesday in the Final replay. Wednesday arranged a charter flight to get me back to London after the international, and I think it was about one o'clock in the morning when I reached our hotel.

But I played at Wembley the next evening, and lasted until four minutes from the end of extra-time. The scores were still level as I walked off, but, right at the finish, Arsenal got the winner.

My physical exertions rather than disappointment at our defeat left me pretty sick for the next four or five days. Even if we had won that game, I think I would have been poorly for at least a couple of days.

Alan Smith, who was Wednesday physio when Nilsson was with the Owls, adds a footnote to Roland's story:
Roland Nilsson was always a fantastic athlete and a great professional. When he was injured during the season in which we won promotion and the Rumbelows Cup, he made a record-breaking recovery. He was back in training within five months, played in the Reserves at Rotherham a week later, and was playing for the first team three weeks after that. He went on to play in the Cup Final and all the games in the promotion run-in.

I remember him being taken off on a stretcher at Millwall in October, and it was quickly evident he had suffered a major knee injury. When we got home to Sheffield, I took him to Tom Smith, the specialist, and after we'd put his leg

in a splint and got him on crutches, he went off to Sweden, where Jan Esktrand, a brilliant surgeon, operated on his knee.

Thereafter Roland had regular treatment at Hillsborough, from where I kept in touch with Jan Esktrand and reported on his progress, and Roland used to go over to Sweden about once every four to six weeks. To say Roland was a great lad to work with would be an understatement. He was so professional and dedicated.

I always remember the time in 1993 when he played for Sweden one night and flew home to play for Wednesday in the FA Cup Final replay the following night. He played for all but the last three or four minutes of extra-time at Wembley, and the physical achievement of playing two such major games in 24 hours could only have been done by an exceptional athlete. If anyone deserved a winner's medal that day, he did.

But Roland was not just a great athlete and an outstanding footballer – he was a very special man.

Nigel Worthington

Nigel Worthington joined Wednesday from Notts County for £125,000 in February 1984 and made 417 League and Cup appearances before moving to Leeds in June 1994. As 50 of his 66 games for Northern Ireland came in his time at Hillsborough, he earned a special niche in Owls' history as the club's most-capped player. The one-time Ballymena defender figured in the promotion teams of 1984 and 1991, helped Wednesday win the Rumbelows Cup in 1991, and was in the 1993 FA Cup Final side.

I spent 10½ years at Hillsborough and remember most of that time as being just one big party – in the sense that it was a happy place where there was a unique spirit and everybody throughout the club generated mutual goodwill and respect. There were no divisions: the players, the office staff, the washroom ladies, the groundstaff – somehow we were all as one, with everyone pulling in the same direction.

It was my good fortune to arrive just when Wednesday were on the brink of returning to the top-grade after a 14-

year absence, and, though we subsequently had a few setbacks and disappointments, I treasure the memory of so many highlights – not least promotion in 1984 and 1991, and the unforgettable bonus of our 1991 League Cup success.

A double triumph made 1991 extra-special, and all the more so because it compensated for the blow of being relegated in 1990 just when we had thought we were safe. Everybody was so devastated when we lost that final match of 1989-90 against Nottingham Forest and the full implications of the defeat dawned upon us.

The hurt to our pride was still nagging us when we reported for pre-season training more than two months later. The players not only knew they had let themselves and the supporters down, but desperately wanted to put things right – and we were determined to give it everything we'd got to try to ensure a prompt return to the top-grade.

We knew there was no way we could guarantee results, but the will to succeed was there. We went out and really tried, and, in the event, reached our goal in style – producing lots of good football along the way to give our supporters something to savour as well as making them happy.

It was because we started so well in the League that Ron Atkinson told us to relax and enjoy the Cup games. What influence that philosophy had on us winning the Rumbelows Cup, I don't know, but the pressure was invariably off in those matches. We just went out and played with freedom and confidence – and the results kept going our way!

There were so many magical moments on that run to Wembley. For instance, that marvellous strike by John Harkes at Derby. He collected a cross-field pass from me, went forward, and hit a 30-yard beauty past Peter Shilton. What a way to score your first goal in English football!

Then there was that free-kick routine involving me and John Sheridan which led to a vital goal from Peter Shirtliff at Chelsea in the first leg of the semi-final. We used that routine three times in the game before Chelsea decided to put someone into the hole I was running into to collect Sheridan's

Nigel Worthington, seen here introducing his son David to a character called Ozzie Owl.

Of course, I knew Howard from when he'd been at Meadow Lane. He had always taken a lot of time with me following my arrival from Ballymena, and I had nothing but admiration for him. He certainly didn't have to "sell" himself, and, as for Wednesday, they were having a marvellous run just then, and, frankly, I couldn't wait to be a part of all the good things that were happening.

Howard was an outstanding manager. His keynotes were commitment, professionalism and organisation. He made us work very hard, but, if you look at the length of the careers of the lads who played under him, you'll see that his approach and example were tremendously beneficial.

To play in the last 14 games of that promotion season was wonderful. Because of my injury, my debut was delayed for two weeks, but then I started with a win against Brighton, and, before the end of the season, I even managed my first goal. This came at Huddersfield, and I recall it as a left-foot effort from the deep which wormed its way through a crowded goalmouth. Never mind that it might have taken a deflection on the way in, it was still a great goal!

We were sorry when Howard left, and, by the same token, there was a sense of disappointment when Ron Atkinson departed after that memorable 1990-91 campaign. Everything had gone so well. Then it was: is "Big Ron" staying or going? Yes, he is, no he isn't! Alas, after he'd said he was staying, he went. When Ron did finally go, everyone at the club had a shrewd idea who would take over, and, of course, they were right in tipping Trevor Francis for the job.

Trevor's first two seasons were memorable. We kept the ball rolling, there was very little change in personnel, the spirit was good, and, as well as qualifying for Europe, we reached both major domestic Cup Finals in one year. Unfortunately, from then on, for some reason things changed dramatically.

Even though we lost to Arsenal in both the Coca-Cola and FA Cup Finals, 1992-93 was a tremendous season. I shall always remember the thing that seemed to make a major difference was Trevor's decision to stick Paul Warhurst up front. It was a switch that could eas-

disguised free-kick – and by then we were in control!

We won the Rumbelows Cup with a magnificent team performance against Manchester United at Wembley We went there as underdogs, but every single Wednesday man worked his socks off and I don't think anyone could deny we were worthy winners. John Sheridan's match-winning strike was, of course, a moment to treasure, and it was pleasing to think it stemmed from a free-kick of mine which Pallister had headed out under pressure from Nigel Pearson's challenge.

One of the ironies of being in that 1991 Wembley team was that, in early March, I had a cartilage operation, but, such are the wonders of modern medicine, I was back in the side within a month.

To return to the beginning of my Wednesday story, my move to Sheffield came out of the blue, ironically just as I was nursing damaged knee ligaments suffered in Notts County's match at Arsenal in late January 1984. Mind you, I jumped off the treatment table at Meadow Lane pretty quickly when Jimmy Sirrel, our manager, revealed that County had accepted an offer from Sheffield Wednesday – and, within what seemed minutes, I was dashing up the M1 to meet Howard Wilkinson.

A Wembley triumph – Nigel Worthington, John Sheridan and John Harkes celebrate after Wednesday's famous FA Cup semi-final defeat of Sheffield United.

ily have been a miss, but it proved a big hit – a wonderful stroke which paid spectacular dividends. The majority of Paul's goals came in Cup games, and he was magnificent in the League Cup semi-final first leg at Blackburn.

I don't suppose any of us will ever forget the famous all-Sheffield FA Cup semi-final at Wembley. It was an occasion worthy of the Final. The atmosphere, the colour and the game itself. What a day! Although we had to wait until extra-time to seal victory, we won in style. The scoreline could have been much more emphatic than 2-1. The only disappointment was I got myself booked for a challenge on Franz Carr in that match, which meant missing the Coca-Cola Cup Final.

But I was back for the FA Cup Final, which, as you know, went to two games. Frankly, I thought we had our best chance in the first meeting. Chances fell to Mark Bright which on another day would have gone in for him. The way we lost the replay was, of course, very

unfortunate. It was always going to be a long slog, but to lose in the last seconds of extra-time was a terribly cruel blow – more than a few of us will always be haunted by the memory of the ball going through Chris Woods' hands after Linighan got his head to that last-gasp corner.

Nigel Pearson, unfortunately, missed the four games we played at Wembley in 1993, and one of my abiding memories of that season is not about how well we played at times, but the night at Ewood Park in the Coca-Cola Cup semi-final when Nigel broke his leg. It was typical of the man that, despite the seriousness of his injury, he tried to get up and carry on.

Pearson will be remembered by Wednesdayites as a great character and captain. In terms of the way he played, you might say he wore his heart on his sleeve, because there were no half-measures with Nigel when he went for the ball, and he epitomised the spirit within the team. Only Nigel could feel he was

letting his team-mates down when he's just suffered a broken leg!

I played under three outstanding captains at Hillsborough. The others were Mick Lyons and Martin Hodge. The one thing they all had was a tremendous pride in being chosen to lead the team, and they gave the job everything – off as well as on the field.

In my time, so many lads were genuinely proud to play for Wednesday, and a story which illustrates the point concerns Mick Lyons and John Pearson. Mick had a pre-match dressing room ritual in which someone would stand in front of him while someone else would throw a high ball, and Mick would smash it back with his head.

On this occasion, he rose above John Pearson, headed the ball, but, as he came down, he caught John in the face with his arm. Blood suddenly gushed from John's face, and we could see his eyebrow was split right open. With just minutes before we were due to take the field, the lad had the painful experience of having five or six stitches put in his head. But it didn't stop John going out and playing a full 90 minutes – nothing was going to prevent him from doing his bit.

Yes, we had some good days, and, naturally, I was sorry when my time at Hillsborough came to an end in 1994. I have to say nobody would have been happier to have stayed than me, but, frankly, Trevor didn't bust a gut to try to keep me, and it did seem as if circumstances were pointing me in another direction. It was a period when there was a big break-up of influential players who had a lot of feeling for the club, and, perhaps it was a pity. But these things happen in football.

At least when I left I took with me some great memories which will always stay with me.

Phil King

Phil King, who arrived from Swindon in November 1989, made 159 League and Cup appearances for the Owls before moving to Aston Villa in August 1994 He played in the team that achieved a promotion and Rumbelows Cup double in 1991, and was in the Coca-Cola Cup Final side of 1993. Supporters voted him Player of the Year in 1991-92, and he gained England "B" honours while at Hillsborough.

I so enjoyed my five years with Wednesday and felt so passionate about the club that, even now, if you cut me I'd probably bleed blue blood. My great regret is it all ended too soon, and it really hurt to leave Sheffield. My time at Hillsborough produced a million happy memories, with lots of laughter and only a few tears.

Mostly I remember the atmosphere, not just in the dressing room, but on the pitch and in every aspect of the club. The spirit among the lads was terrific, and it showed in the way we played as a team. There were no bigheads, nobody considered himself better than anyone else, and, professionally and socially we always stuck together.

As for the fans, they made me feel so at home I delighted in being among them at presentations several times a week, and, making many friends in the area, it gave me a great kick to get

Phil King knew some good moments in his time at Hillsborough, not least the satisfaction of ending a long goal-famine with a strike against Southampton in 1993.

involved in coaching a team of young teenagers called Clowne Comets.

The move to Sheffield came out of the blue, and the irony was that, on the day Ossie Ardiles told me Swindon had agreed a fee with Wednesday, I was nursing a twisted ankle suffered in a match at Brighton on the previous night. After I'd met Ron Atkinson at a Cirencester hotel and agreed to sign, I went up to Hillsborough the next day, and, when Alan Smith, the physio, looked at my black-and-blue ankle, he said I wasn't fit enough to make my debut at Nottingham Forest.

But I told Ron I'd give it a go, and, with John Sheridan also making his Owls' bow the same afternoon, we won 1-0. It was only Wednesday's second win in 12 games, and Ron was so

pleased that, on the way home when I sat in the back of his Mercedes with my foot up to ease the pain, he used his portable phone to ring my wife and tell her how well I'd played!

Unfortunately, we were relegated at the end of that season. We'd made a great recovery and looked safe, but four points from our last seven games was too little to prevent us going down on goal-difference – and I was already familiar enough with the local scene to know the agony was compounded for Wednesdayites because Sheffield United sealed promotion on the day we were doomed by a home defeat against Forest.

But what a season we had in 1990-91, with a prompt return to the top grade and a Rumbelows Cup triumph!

The great thing was we did it in style. Some of the football we played that year was tremendous, and I could go on at great length about memorable matches and unforgettable goals.

The team had exactly the right blend. Nigel Pearson was a good captain. Him and Peter Shirtliff, the old boys, were a great centre-back combination; Carlton Palmer's tackling and workrate and John Sheridan's skill and distribution gave us a perfect balance in midfield; and Paul Williams and David Hirst were a prolific strike partnership. With Roland Nilsson and Danny Wilson on the right flank, and me and Nigel Worthington on the left, plus goalkeepers Kevin Pressman and Chris Turner, we had a quality side.

I think we won eight and drew four of our first 12 League, games, and I always remember our first defeat was at Millwall. We were on a roll-over bonus which went up £100 every time we won, and, when we led 2-0 at half-time, I was thinking about how I was going to spend the money. Then Nilsson did his knee ligaments and Pearson injured his back, and, with Millwall scoring twice in the last few minutes, we lost 4-2. Defeat was bad enough, but it also meant the bonus system went back to square one!

Of course, the real bonus, the one that no money could buy, was our League Cup success. Getting to the Final was a wonderful experience. Just to be at Wembley and to walk out in front of your family and your own fans is the dream of every footballer, but to win as well was sheer magic. When we came home, and, later, when we paraded the Cup through the streets and stood on the Town Hall balcony, it was a fantastic feeling.

The celebrations at our London hotel that Sunday night were something special. Paul Carrack, you'll remember, had brought out this song about Atkinson's Barmy Army. As my daughter had never stopped playing the record, I knew the words backwards, and Paul, who was doing the entertainment that evening, asked me to lead the lads in singing it on the stage. Our performance, with several encores, was as well received as the one that had beaten Manchester United!

Naturally, I was disappointed when Ron left, all the more so as he'd

promised me a new deal and his departure meant I didn't get it. The hang up over my contract clouded things, though the situation didn't go flat until much later – and, in the meantime, we had a tremendous first season under Trevor Francis, and, as well as finishing third and qualifying for Europe, the supporters named me Player of the Year.

Ron had laid the foundations, and, initially, Trevor improved things. We played some brilliant football in 1991-92 and, though in the end we finished seven points adrift of Leeds, there was a time when the championship looked tantalisingly close. On the season's penultimate Saturday, we went to Crystal Palace and were winning 1-0 thanks to a great Paul Williams goal set up by John Sheridan's superb skill – then our faint title dreams were shattered when Mark Bright equalised for Palace in the last minute.

In 1992-93, of course, we reached both major Cup Finals and played in the UEFA Cup, but, on a personal level, it was hardly a vintage season. Looking back, perhaps I was a bit pig-headed when Trevor didn't offer me the contract I expected, and maybe I sulked a bit when he didn't come round to thinking I deserved a better deal. But my woes were compounded when I did my cruciate ligaments in training and was sidelined from late August until the end of February.

Ironically, I was no sooner fit than I was playing in another Wembley Final, against Arsenal in the Coca-Cola Cup, replacing Nigel Worthington. I always remember watching from the bench when Wednesday beat United at Wembley in the famous all-Sheffield FA Cup semi-final, and, having seen Nigel get booked, I knew it meant him missing the Arsenal game. My initial reaction was to sympathise with Nigel, and only later did I realise I was the only other left-back available.

However, I was a stone overweight, didn't do myself justice, and don't have happy memories of that Coca-Cola Final. I had the satisfaction of making the cross from which John Harkes scored, but Arsenal came back to inflict what proved to be the first of two Wembley defeats we suffered at their hands that season.

Early in 1993-94, when I reverted to

a midfield role, I recall finishing a game against Aston Villa in August with my head bandaged after being cut in a heading duel with Paul McGrath. I got the man-of-the-match award for my pains, and felt things were looking up, but, sadly, it was a season when, in fact, my situation went from bad to worse. Another fall-out with Trevor, and the arrival of Andy Sinton, marked the beginning of the end.

When I left shortly before the start of the 1994-95 season, it was not without regret, and I still often recall the good times we had in what for all of us in that phase was a marvellous period in our lives.

David Hirst

David Hirst, who joined Wednesday from Barnsley in August 1986 for an initial £200,000 plus an extra £50,000 after gaining the first of his three England caps in 1991, scored 128 goals in 358 games for the Owls before making a £2m move to Southampton in October 1997. He figured in all Wednesday's "famous five" Wembley appearances between 1991 and 1993, and hit a century of League goals for the club.

I was 18 when I joined Wednesday and was two months short of 30 when I left, and, while I might jest of having arrived as a young kid and departed an old man, the years in between were very special. I'll always remember them with pride and affection. It was a good time which I was sorry to see come to an end.

It's funny, really, that Hillsborough became such an important part of my life because, only three days before I signed, I had told a good pal of mine – a big Owls' fan – I wouldn't sign for Wednesday for a gold pig. At the time I said it, I meant it. After all, I was a Barnsley lad, the Owls were our big rivals, and, anyway, Howard Wilkinson's tough training routines, said to involve a lot of running, didn't appeal to me and I didn't know I would come to have cause to be grateful to Howard for giving me a chance to step into the top-grade.

In fact, as a schoolboy I'd been to Hillsborough for a two-day trial, but had ended up walking away at the end of the first morning session at the training ground. I played in a 20-minute game, and was walking off the pitch when one of the chaps in charge asked my name. When I told him, he said: "Oh, we've been looking for you – we didn't think you'd turned up." So my Dad said: "If they don't know you're here, it's not worth staying!" – and we went home.

I could have gone to Huddersfield, but as Barnsley was just down the road from our home in Cudworth and I'd played for their juniors as a schoolboy, I accepted the offer of a two-year apprenticeship. I'd made my Football League debut at 17 and had scored nine goals in 28 games when, one morning in August 1986, I arrived at Oakwell for training as usual and was met by coach Eric Winstanley.

When he said the gaffer, Allan Clarke, wanted to see me, my first reaction was to wonder what I'd done wrong to prompt such an early call to the manager's office. Allan explained he'd sold me, and, though he wouldn't reveal the fee, he said the club was Wednesday. I had to phone my Dad, go home and get changed, then travel with them to Sheffield.

Four hours later, I was back home having signed for a club I'd said I would never join, but it was a step I didn't regret. When I scored with only my second touch on my home debut as a substitute in a 2-2 draw with Everton, I little realised that ten years later I would still be there to claim my 100th League goal for Wednesday against the same opponents – and, in the meantime, serve under five managers and become so synonymous with Hillsborough I almost felt part of the fixtures and fittings!

When I started with a goal, I think the fans thought: "We've got a bargain here." But I didn't score again for another seven months, and although that was a memorable strike which sealed a victory over Manchester United, I was in and out of the team for a long time, and my Wednesday career didn't really take off until Ron Atkinson came.

Ron boosted my confidence because he told me to go out and do what I did best, whereas before I'd been asked to do things that weren't in my locker. Ron insisted that if I worked on my strengths and wasn't expected to do

what I couldn't do, the goals would come. He persisted with me even when I was having lean spells, so must have felt his patience was rewarded when I claimed over 50 goals under his management.

Of course, the peak season was when we won promotion and the Rumbelows Cup in 1990-91, with my tally of 32 the best by a Wednesday man since before I was born – and it put the top on a memorable year when I won my first England caps in the summer.

That was a wonderful time for me at the club, but I couldn't have done it if I hadn't been in an outstanding team. We had some great players, lots of flair and a terrific spirit. Even now, when people talk about my goals that year, I especially mention Paul Williams. He was the ideal strike partner, probably the best I've ever had. Paul was so unselfish, doing all the running while I got the benefit – although I like to think I made a few goals for him, too!

The key to the team's success was having a lot of experienced players who didn't just have ability, but knew what was needed to create the right atmosphere in the dressing room. We were like a family, tight-knit, sticking together off as well as on the field. We had a great captain in Nigel Pearson and lots of characters. There was so much laughter and happiness around then, but, if we might still be joking at ten-to-three, we could be deadly serious when the real business started at three o'clock.

Nigel had a great sense of humour and was quite a comic, but he was a natural leader. If someone was down or having problems, he was a tremendous source of strength. If we had two or three bad results, or if there had been a hint of a fall-out in the camp, Nigel would organise a night out for the players and their wives and girlfriends, and the theme would be "let's get together and sort this out".

After a meal and a few glasses of wine, people tend to be honest about what they really think, and those social occasions had exactly the right effect because we invariably returned to work with the problems solved and an already good spirit made stronger.

I think one reason Wednesday's progress continued long enough after Ron left to enable us to reach two Cup

Finals in 1993 was that it was still pretty much his team, with key characters still in the side. The pity was that backbone of experience was prematurely removed when too many influential players were sold before they should have been.

I always felt I was lucky to play with experienced professionals who, right from the time I started out as a teenager, took me under their wing. In the early days it was people like Mel Sterland, Gary Megson, Gary Shelton, and Lee Chapman who guided me, and, later, Danny Wilson, Peter Shirtliff, Viv Anderson and Nigel Pearson.

It goes without saying that the big disappointment for me was the injuries which plagued the later years of my time at Hillsborough. If I got over one injury, I soon seemed to get another, and the frustration was very depressing at times. People often point to the day in August 1992, when I broke an ankle as Steve Bould tackled me at Arsenal, as the start of my long run of misfortune, but it was typical of my luck that, in March of the same season, I suffered a torn thigh muscle at Ipswich when there was nobody near me and I was through on goal. At least I had another goal to my credit before returning to the treatment room!

I was also grateful to be fit enough to play as a substitute in both the all-Sheffield FA Cup semi-final and the Coca-Cola Cup Final that season, and, even though we lost twice to Arsenal at Wembley, it was some compensation for me that my injury hoodoo didn't prevent me from figuring in the FA Cup Final and scoring. Later in 1993, of course, I started with the Achilles tendon trouble which virtually wrote off the next 18 months.

Now when I look back and remember the endless hours I spent working under physio Alan Smith's supervision to get fit, I often think that without his dedication and discipline my career might have come to a premature end.

Alan was always very strict, and, while I didn't always appreciate that this was in my best interests when he was belting me round the gymnasium and driving me on, I learned to understand why he has gone right to the top in his job. It's because he isn't just technically good at his job – he's also organised, enthusiastic and knows what makes players tick.

Ironically, as a player the working day is much longer when you're injured than when you're fit, and, being full of your own moans, you tend to forget that Alan worked those long days all the time. He'd be running players to hospital appointments in between daytime treatment and fitness sessions, then be back for more in the evening. I remember many a time when, because it wasn't convenient anywhere else, he's had me training under the lights of the Kop or the car park long after everybody else had gone home.

It's when you're out of the side with an injury that you really appreciate the dressing room banter, and, when Nigel Pearson and I happened to be sidelined at the same time, we had some good fun at the expense of the other lads. There was one time when we warned Graham Hyde that if he wore the same tracksuit for four days on the spin, we'd make sure he didn't wear it again. We cut out the legs, Sellotaped them back on, and then had a good laugh when his tracksuit bottoms fell apart when he put them on.

Nigel's sense of fun knew no bounds. He once brought a goldfish from his pond at home, put it in the canister of drinking water in the dressing room, then waited to see the reaction of the players when, returning from training gasping for a drink, they discovered the fish floating before their eyes.

A few weeks later, Nigel produced a replica fish carved out of a carrot. It must have taken him hours to make, but he obviously felt the effort worthwhile when it provoked so much hilarity among the lads.

So, if there were disappointments, they were always outweighed by the good times which have left me with a lot of happy memories, and, as I've said, I didn't want to leave. Unfortunately, a situation arose where I didn't think I was figuring too much in the manager's plans, and, when that happens, you have to make a decision.

I remember very well the day David Pleat called me in and said: "Southampton want to speak to you, do you want to go?" By that time there had been a few possibilities in the pipeline, and I'd made my mind up to leave if the right opportunity came up. It seemed to be the right choice because perhaps a

little bit of spice had gone out of my career and I wasn't going to get it back in the circumstances that existed at that time.

The pity was, I didn't really get a chance to say goodbye. For the bulk of my time with Wednesday, there had been a great family atmosphere, and I had grown up working alongside people like Norma Lane, the manager's secretary, Dot Swann and Betty Pearson in the laundry, Dave Barber the groundsman, and many others who were an essential part of the club. They knew what the time at Hillsborough meant to me, but I would have welcomed the chance to also tell the fans who had supported me for so long that I would never forget the good times we had shared.

John Harkes

John Harkes, a USA international midfielder who raised his tally of caps to the half-century mark during his three years with Wednesday, will always have a place in English football history as the first American to play in a Wembley Final when he helped the Owls defeat Manchester United to win the Rumbelows Cup in 1991. His 118 appearances for the club included two more Cup Finals. Now back in the United States, he has fond memories of his Sheffield days.

The time I spent in England, and especially the years at Sheffield Wednesday, were so eventful, and such a terrific experience, I could write a book. The first season was unforgettable. Everything happened so quickly, it was like a dream, and people have said if it had been written in a novel it would have seemed too far-fetched to be true to life.

Of course, it did happen, and, within six months of making my senior debut in English football, I was playing in a winning team in a Wembley Cup Final. Yes, it was wonderful, but, before it all started working out for me, things were very hard – and, more than once, I would have gone back to New Jersey if anyone at home had given me the slightest encouragement.

I come from a place called Kearney, which is about a 20-minute ride from New York City; and, as my parents were from Scotland and many of our neigh-

bours also had British or European origins, I grew up very familiar with football (or soccer as we call it back home). Having made good progress in the game in my days as a student in the United States and gone as far as was possible within the system over there, I wanted to have a spell in England because I felt it would improve my knowledge and ability.

It was in January 1990, following contact with Ian St John, the old

John Harkes – the American knew the joy of being on the winning side at Wembley in 1991, but, although he is seen here celebrating his goal against Arsenal in the League Cup Final of 1993, it all ended in tears.

Liverpool and Scotland player, that I arrived with Tony Meola, a goalkeeper, for a two-weeks trial at Wednesday, and I remember playing for the Reserves at Mansfield and Walsall. Ron Atkinson said he was satisfied with what he saw, and asked me to stay on, but, with our national team preparing for the World Cup at that time, I felt it was best for me to return home until after the tournament. Anyway, I didn't really want to commit myself to a club until I'd had a good look round.

When I came back to England at the end of the following summer, I initially went to Blackburn Rovers for ten days, and the story of my season might have been very different had they not offered me a contract which, frankly, was crap. As it happened, Billy McNeil at Celtic invited me up to Scotland, but that opportunity didn't work out either because, at the end of the week, a director got fired and Celtic said they didn't want to pay money for me.

So I found myself in Sheffield again, and, when I look back, it always seemed I was destined to join Wednesday – although, on my return, Ron Atkinson made me work hard for a contract because I don't think I had exactly pleased him during my earlier stay when I had said I wanted to see other clubs before making a choice!

But I have to say Ron was brilliant for me, and when he took me on at Hillsborough it changed my life. For weeks I had been very homesick and despondent, with lots of phone calls to Kearney saying: "I want to come home, I can't take it". But the folks there always replied: "Stick it out, you'll be all right – the beginning is always the worst."

I shall always recall my time in England as a period which taught me to grow up and face life – and I had to learn very quickly. At university back home, I thought I was mature and enjoyed a kind of independence, but it was really a life without any responsibilities. Once I got to England, I found living on my own and trying to establish myself in professional football very hard. Even the trivial things seemed to add to the difficulties.

People said the way I really felt didn't show, because I always seemed to be full of zany fun, but that was just a front. Many times I wished my girlfriend Cindi (we were eventually married in 1992) could be with me to settle me down and share my problems. We had known each other six or seven years then, but, while she might have liked to have come over with me, we had agreed she would stay in the US and complete her education.

Yet I was comfortable and at home in Sheffield, and the way things turned out helped my confidence grow. I did okay in the Reserves (six goals in five games) and Wednesday signed me until the end of the season with an option to buy me from the US Soccer Federation – which they subsequently did for a £75,000 fee. In the meantime, there was a development which gave me an unexpected chance in the first team.

In October 1990, the manager said he wanted me to try playing at right-back and promised if I did well he would use me in the Rumbelows Cup match with Swindon. I had never figured in that position before, and the opportunity arose because Roland Nilsson had damaged his knee ligaments and was expected to be out for at least six months.

After that everything happened so fast. We drew the home game with Swindon, but won the replay. Then, after another draw at home against Derby in the next round, we again succeeded in a replay; and I didn't just have the thrill of scoring for the first time in English football in our 2-1 win at the Baseball Ground in December – I hit what the television people made "the goal of the season".

There were reporters at that match who didn't even know I was an American, and most of them had never heard of me; but now, after I'd beaten the England goalkeeper, Peter Shilton, with a shot from over 30-yards, they all wanted to talk to me! Apart from scoring, I thought I'd done well, because I helped make our second goal for Paul Williams. I think it was Wednesday's first win at Derby for over 50 years.

One of the things I enjoyed telling my family about when I phoned home in those early months was the thrill of playing alongside Trevor Francis. They knew how, as a boy, I had watched Trevor play for Detroit Express – and I'd even had my photo taken with him during a two-day trip from New York. It seemed such an unbelievable twist that we should now be in the same team.

When we played in the Rumbelows Cup Final, I was making only my 30th appearance in Wednesday's first team. With Roland back, I had a midfield role which included giving him some support. The day went very well. To face Manchester United, finish a winner,

and make history as the first American to figure in a Wembley Final was something I knew would be very difficult to top. Of course, in 1993 I played in two more Finals, scored in the Coca-Cola Cup Final, and went to Wembley four times – but it could never compare with 1991, and I don't say that because we didn't win a trophy.

People warned me that the season after our Cup and promotion double would be tougher, and certainly on a personal level it proved frustrating. I tore my ankle ligaments twice, made only 24 appearances (13 as substitute) after being carried off at Wimbledon in early October, and returned to face a big fight for my place. At least in late September I'd had the thrill of not only playing at Anfield but scoring a goal which, for different reasons, was just as satisfying as the one I got at Derby the previous year.

There were also a lot of things to remember with pleasure in 1992-93 – getting the chance to play with Chris Waddle; heading the first of the four goals we scored in 16 minutes at Blackburn in the Coca-Cola Cup semi-final; and scoring at Wembley in April. Sadly, Arsenal beat us twice – and the FA Cup Final replay in May, when we lost in the last seconds of extra-time, was my last game for Wednesday.

Trevor sold me to Derby, and I was sorry to leave. My consolation is I still look back on my time in Sheffield as an experience I'll always treasure – and I know I left a lot of friends there.

Ron Atkinson

Ron Atkinson's first spell as Wednesday's manager, from February 1989 to June 1991, coincided with a remarkable phase in the club's history. The peak was the promotion and Rumbelows Cup double of 1991, a year after a shock fall from the top-grade, and the period will always be synonymous with quality football and a dramatic change in boardroom policy. "Big Ron" upset a lot of fans when he walked out to join Aston Villa, but he was the man to whom the Owls turned to boost their bid to steer clear of relegation after David Pleat was axed in November 1997.

Peter Shirtliff, the defender whom Atkinson brought back to Hillsborough in 1989, remembers how "Big Ron" took the Wednesday players on a night out ahead of the 1991 Final.

When we played Manchester United at Wembley on that unforgettable Sunday in April 1991, on the Friday evening before the big match Ron decided the best way to ensure we relaxed was by taking us out to a restaurant for a meal and a few drinks. It was a social occasion to which wives and girlfriends were invited, and it coincided with Trevor Francis's birthday.

In fact, a few drinks turned into quite a few drinks, and I think there were rather a lot of sore heads on the Saturday morning! I remember we kept asking ourselves: should we really be doing this two days before a Cup Final? But it was Ron's way of relaxing us and ensuring we didn't start getting all uptight. We certainly enjoyed ourselves, and, when the day of the Final dawned, we still felt a warm glow of enjoyment. In fact, we continued to enjoy ourselves for the 90 minutes on the field, and it ended up being a great result which was a prelude to a great night at our hotel.

As preparation for a Final, it might not have been straight out of the text book, but it worked.

Ron is a great character. He is positive about life and positive about his football – and it's infectious. If you asked me what is his strength, I'd say it's the knack of inspiring a positive response. His drive, his will to win, the courage to play real football. He wants to play winning football, but wants you to play with style, and players respond to that.

The way we played in 1990-91 was the perfect reflection of Ron's philosophy, and I'm pretty sure the fans loved it.

David Hirst, the striker who profited from Ron's encouragement to play to his strengths, comments:
Ahead of going to an Italian restaurant on the Friday before the Rumbelows Cup Final, we had a few drinks in a private room at the Royal Lancaster, and I remember thinking how crafty Ron was to bring Martin Edwards, the Manchester United chairman, into the room just when we were all getting into the party spirit.

There we all were – laughing, joking

Ron Atkinson pictured on the day in 1989 when he first arrived at Hillsborough. He stayed until 1991, when he walked out. After spells with Aston Villa and Coventry, he returned in 1997, just managed to save the Owls from relegation ...and then Dave Richards and the Owls' board stunned him with the sack in 1998 when his successor was eventually Danny Wilson.

and drinking. I don't know what Martin Edwards really thought, but I can imagine him being tempted to think: "If we're playing this lot on Sunday and they're partying now, we haven't got a problem."

Of course, we weren't going over the top, we were just enjoying ourselves, and there was no way we would have done anything to impair our performance in the Final. Ron knew what we were doing was part of the preparation, but I wonder if there wasn't a bit of psychology in it, too?

Roland Nilsson, the Swedish international full-back who was one of Atkinson's earliest signings, comments:
Ron Atkinson is a very special manager because he is a man who gets players to perform at their best and encourages them to have faith in their abilities. You have to admire his knowledge of the game and the way he handles people, and it was a very enjoyable experience to work with him.

In that 1990-91 season, when we won promotion and the League Cup, I was out with a serious knee injury for six months; but Ron insisted he wanted me to continue to travel with the team and be a part of what was happening.

He has a lovely sense of humour, and is always full of banter. When I was still

on crutches and struggling to get on the team-bus one day, he asked: "When are you going to be fit? You're not much good to anybody in that state." But he said it in such a way that I could only laugh. He always makes you realise by his actions that he is really such a warm and human person.

Danny Wilson, Wednesday's new boss, whom Atkinson identified as a key signing ahead of the 1990-91 promotion campaign, remembers his old boss:
I think it may have been Richie Barker – he had been our coach at Kenilworth Road – who suggested to Ron that I might be the sort of player who could do a decent job, and I remember the subject was touched upon when we bumped into each other while on holiday in Marbella just after Luton (where I was the captain) had escaped relegation at Wednesday's expense.

The season when we won the Rumbelows Cup and promotion and brought a major trophy to Sheffield for the first time in many years was really fantastic, and the group of lads we had at the club that year was one of the best I've ever played with. There wasn't just a great camaraderie – they were very good players as well. On the pitch we looked after each other, and off the pitch everybody got on famously.

It's never easy being a manager, but it was easier for Ron because of the blend of players he had at the time – and, of course, he had created that blend. He knew what he wanted, knew how to get Wednesday out of the Second Division, and made it work.

Ron is like Brian Clough – a one-off. Nobody can try to emulate him. In my time under him, he did things which quite a few other managers have copied since. Like the way he had comedian Stan Boardman with us on the team-bus going to the 1991 League Cup Final. He knew that having someone to make us laugh and keep our minds off the big match would ensure we arrived at Wembley relaxed and in good spirits.

Author's Footnote: Atkinson succeeded in steering Wednesday clear of the drop in 1998 – just! But the club chose not to extend his contract when it expired at the end of the season. The "Big Ron" who returned was not quite the same man as the one who had inspired the Owls seven years earlier. Ironically, while Trevor Francis had learned his fate on FA Cup Final day 1995, Atkinson's departure was announced on the day after the 1998 Final.

Trevor Francis

Trevor Francis, once British football's first £1 million footballer and capped 52 times by England, joined Wednesday in the twilight of his playing days when he arrived from QPR on a free transfer in January 1990. He made 89 appearances, and scored nine goals over the next three and a half years, and, in the meantime, succeeded Ron Atkinson as manager. In 1992 he led the Owls into Europe for the first time in nearly 30 years and in 1993 took them into the Final of both domestic Cup competitions. Ironically, he was sacked on FA Cup Final day in 1995 – the announcement, which followed weeks of speculation during which Francis maintained a dignified silence, being timed to ensure minimum media exposure. Here Trevor recalls memories of some of his own and some of the goals he helped to make and saw scored in his time at Hillsborough.

A goal I remember with particular affection was far from being one of the best of the 200 or more I scored in English football, but it sticks in the memory because it was important and came on the night in May 1991 when we beat Bristol City 3-1 at home to clinch promotion back to the top-grade.

I think it was from my pass that David Hirst gave us the lead in that match, and my goal, our second, removed any lingering traces of tension. It was hardly spectacular, being a tumbling header which the goalkeeper was unable to prevent from going over the line, but the joy it created among supporters was something to savour. It virtually ensured that we had fulfilled our dream of gaining promotion at the first attempt to atone for the disappointment of the previous year's dramatic relegation experience.

Trevor Francis, seen here scoring his first goal for Wednesday, against Bristol Rovers in October 1990.

That Bristol game, incidentally, was a night when I played from the start – a point worth making because I think 47 of my 76 League games for Wednesday were as a substitute, and, after I became player-manager in 1991, all but one of my 28 appearances were from the bench.

However, I have some happy memories of coming off the bench to make a useful contribution – not least the Nottingham Forest match at Hillsborough in September 1991 when I put myself on after 72 minutes and managed to score the winner just two minutes from the end. I have an added reason to treasure the memory because it was the last goal I scored in League football – and how ironic it should come against the club who had once made me the first £1 million player!

By coincidence, we had beaten another of my former clubs, QPR, the previous week on that memorable afternoon when Carlton Palmer claimed the first hat-trick of his career.

Of course, I have had as much satisfaction from goals I have helped to make, and I remember several instances from that marvellous 1991-92 season in which we finished third in the table and Wednesday qualified for Europe for the first time in 29 years. I shall never forget how we went into our penultimate fixture, against Crystal Palace, still harbouring a slim hope of snatching the League championship, but, if we had the disappointment of not seeing the dream become reality, at least we can say we had a lot of golden moments to savour during that phase in Wednesday's history.

It was particularly satisfying to play a part in our first victory of 1991-92, against Everton, when I delivered a cross from the left with my right foot and, after David Hirst's effort had been blocked, Viv Anderson managed to stick the rebound in for a late winner. I was happy to resume my place on the bench ahead of the final whistle – content that my first win as the Owls' manager was virtually assured!

There was another occasion when we were trailing 2-1 to Luton in a home game in February 1992, and I went on as sub to make my first appearance in four months – and, to my delight, succeeded in setting up an equaliser for Paul Williams and then had a hand in a John Harkes goal which sealed a 3-2 win.

A few weeks later I frustrated Neil Warnock and his Notts County side with a similar late arrival on the scene which eventually resulted in a cross from which Hirsty got a typical match-winner. I always felt with David Hirst that, if you got the ball into the goal-mouth for him, he would invariably reward you with a goal, and one perfect illustration of this was an occasion when he came back from injury to play against Crystal Palace, and promptly celebrated with a double.

I could go on at length to mention other great goals from Hirsty, and some special ones from Chris Waddle, Paul Warhurst and others, but I think my abiding memory of my time at Hillsborough is of some of the lovely football we played on so many occasions. Qualifying for Europe, reaching two major domestic Cup Finals, and win-

Trevor Francis in pensive mood in his role as the Owls manager. Many felt his dismissal in 1995 was handled badly by Dave Richards and the Owls' board.

ning the famous all-Sheffield FA Cup semi-final of 1993 – it all added up to some good memories.

I have to admit to being disappointed at the way things ended for me at Sheffield Wednesday, but I never regretted taking up Ron Atkinson's offer to join him at Hillsborough. I always remember him being the first person to phone me after I finished at QPR in late 1989. He made it plain he wasn't ringing to offer condolences, and said: "There's no point in dwelling on it. Get yourself up here and play for me." I said "yes", and it was a good move for me.

I even recall my last match as Wednesday's manager in 1995 as a memorable game, in that we beat Ipswich 4-1 and won with a flourish. In fact we murdered them!

Of course, at the time it was one of the worst-kept secrets in football that I was probably going to go, and we went into that final match knowing there was a possibility that we could still go down. In the event, what happened at Hillsborough that afternoon didn't influence the relegation issue, but, at the outset, we needed a point to be sure of being safe.

My coaches said a 0-0 draw would be

enough, but I wanted to be positive and go for a win. I was pleased with the way we prepared for that game, and delighted with how we played. Guy Whittingham scored twice, Mark Bright got one, and I believe Michael Williams notched his first Premiership goal. Looking back, I suppose I can say I went out with a bang!

When, a week later, I parted company with the club, it was not without irony that it happened on FA Cup Final day – exactly two years after I had led Wednesday out at Wembley!'

Mark Bright

Mark Bright, the striker whom Francis brought from Crystal Palace at a cost of around £350,000 in the exchange deal which took Paul Williams back to London, comments on his first Wednesday manager:

I know Trevor Francis came in for some criticism towards the end of his time with Wednesday, but he achieved a great deal at Hillsborough and his record is there for everybody to see. He led the club into Europe by taking them to third place in the table in 1992; then we reached both major domestic Cup Finals in 1993 (playing at Wembley four times!) and we finished seventh and reached the Coca-Cola Cup semi-final in 1994.

Wednesday were desperately unlucky in the UEFA Cup game in Kaiserslautern in October 1992 when David Hirst was sent off because an opponent conned the referee with a blatant dive; and it was really heartbreaking the way we lost the 1993 FA Cup Final replay in the last minute of extra-time.

Trevor inherited a good team, and, true, perhaps he let some people go sooner than he should, but he also brought in some quality players.

Even managers who had achieved only half of what Trevor did in such a short time wouldn't have got the sack as he did, and, in my view, Trevor has nothing to be embarrassed or ashamed about.

Chris Waddle

Chris Waddle, who cost £1 million from Olympigue Marseille in the summer of 1992, made 145 appearances and scored

A Wednesday squad pictured in the summer of 1993. Back row (left to right): Warhurst, Pressman, Palmer, Pearce, Woods, Watts. Middle row: Barker (assistant manager), Jemson, Watson, Nilsson, Bart-Williams, Worthington, Hyde, Waddle, Smith (physiotherapist). Front row: Sheridan, Walker, Pearson, Trevor Francis (manager), Hirst, King, Bright.

14 goals for Wednesday before concluding his playing days with spells at Falkirk, Bradford City and Sunderland prior to becoming player-manager at Burnley in 1997. The man who boasted 62 England caps in a career which included over 400 games (106 goals) for Newcastle and Tottenham, certainly gave Hillsborough regulars something to cheer. Here's a memory of Waddle in the words of Trevor Francis, the manager who brought him to Sheffield.

Chris Waddle was an inspired signing, although I don't think the Wednesday directors were entirely convinced when I wanted to bring him to Sheffield. They pointed out that he was 31, as if they felt he was too old and, at that age, unlikely to be good value at £1 million. But Chris was magnificent, and he gave the supporters some wonderful moments they will treasure for a lifetime.

In his first season, of course, Chris made such an impact that he was named as the 1992-93 Footballer of the Year by the Football Writers' Associ-

ation. He did enough to show that his exile from the England team was, to say the least, premature; and, of course, he helped us reach the Coca-Cola and FA Cup Finals. Our misfortune was having to meet Arsenal in both Wembley games, and losing to them in the FA Cup Final replay in the last seconds of extra-time was a traumatic experience we all still find rather painful to recall.

I don't imagine anybody who saw the all-Sheffield FA Cup semi-final at Wembley in April 1993 will ever forget the goal Chris scored against Sheffield United. What a start it gave us when he cracked that 28-yard free-kick past Alan Kelly less than 65 seconds after the kick-off!

That semi-final was such a wonderful occasion, and, when you look back, I suppose it is fair to say it was really our Final. A match which started with Waddle's wonder strike and ended with Mark Bright's extra-time headed winner from a John Harkes corner-kick was certainly very special – and so difficult to top.

I often recall the FA Cup quarter-final game at Derby, when we drew 3-3, as one of the most dramatic of that run, and it was another match in which Waddle's superb skill and vision was crucial even though he didn't get on the scoresheet himself.

We led 1-0 when John Sheridan scored from the penalty spot, but subsequently trailed 3-2. Then, for the second time in the match, five minutes from the end Waddle was involved in making a goal for Paul Warhurst, doing so with the kind of pass to Nigel Jemson which I doubt if any other player would have had the perception to see as being "on".

Naturally, the match many supporters will always recall as being synonymous with Waddle was the 5-0 defeat of West Ham at Hillsborough in December 1993. Chris was absolutely outstanding that afternoon, making three of the goals and then topping a great performance by scoring himself.

I also remember a superb Waddle strike when we went to West Ham in

Chris Waddle and the bandaged Viv Anderson knew the despair of defeat in the Coca-Cola Cup Final of 1993.

Chris Waddle – few players gave Wednesday fans more pleasure in the 1990s.

Paul Warhurst scoring in the 3-3 draw at Derby in the FA Cup quarter-final of 1993.

January 1995 and won 2-0 – Chris curled the ball into the net with his left foot from the right edge of the penalty area. A few weeks later, when we won 1-0 at Leeds, it was Waddle who sealed the points with another goal to treasure.

There were other memorable moments, too. No wonder the fans used to sing about "walking in a Waddle Wonderland"!

Paul Warhurst

Trevor Francis recalls the success of Paul Warhurst's conversion from defender to striker in a season when the Owls' triumphant march to both major Cup Finals included a dazzling display at Blackburn in the 1993 Coca-Cola Cup semi-final first leg.

I think most people would agree that Paul Warhurst, who cost us £750,000 from Oldham, was one of my best signings. Certainly, the decision to switch Paul up front paid off, for he scored 18 goals in that 1992-93 season – and, as 12 were in knock-out matches, you can see how he did as much as anyone to get us to Wembley in both the FA Cup and Coca-Cola Cup.

Paul's pace was his strength, and many times when he was playing at the back you would see him surge out of defence and create problems with a perceptive forward pass. One example which comes to mind was in one of his early games, at Leeds in 1991, when he broke upfield and fed David Hirst, who went on to complete an excellent move with a fine goal.

In the autumn of 1992, when we were having injury problems up front, I thought it might be worth playing Warhurst in attack, but, when I put the idea to him, he thought I was joking. But I was very serious, and was convinced he had the ability to become one of the best ten strikers in the country – which he did. Within weeks he was enjoying such success in his new role, he didn't want to revert to his old one even when an injury crisis in defence made it necessary!

There were a lot of memorable games in that season, but there was a spell in the Coca-Cola Cup-tie at Ewood Park in February 1993 when we touched a peak in terms of team performance which was absolutely fabulous, and two goals from Warhurst completed a sensational turnabout as we went from 1-0 down to lead 4-1 with four strikes in 16 minutes.

We knew it was going to be tough at Blackburn, and when Rovers took an early lead things didn't look promising. However, John Harkes headed a quick equaliser from a Chris Bart-Williams cross, John Sheridan flicked in a second goal after a one-two with Warhurst, and then Paul himself struck twice in four minutes with bursts which typified his speed and confidence.

We won that first-leg 4-2, and the only major blight on the night was when Nigel Pearson suffered a broken leg which caused him to miss all four Wembley matches.

The return leg with Blackburn saw us win 2-1 to complete a 6-3 aggregate, but an abiding memory of the game at Hillsborough was when Roland Nilsson mis-hit a pass across the face of our goal – and the ball hit the inside of the far post! Rovers had just reduced the aggregate score to 4-3, and, for a moment, our dreams of making it to the League Cup Final went on the blink. Fortunately, David Hirst came on as a substitute and eased our nerves with a superb goal from a Chris Waddle cross, and Mark Bright got the second.

Warhurst, of course, left to join Blackburn early in the season after the "double" Cup runs.

Mark Bright

Mark Bright, who arrived from Crystal Palace for £350,000 in the £1 million exchange deal involving Paul Williams in September 1992, went on to score 66 goals in 166 games for the Owls and raise his career tally to around 190 before leaving Hillsborough in January 1997. After an abortive spell with Sion (Switzerland), he joined Charlton.

When people look at my career, they will see I made my name at Crystal Palace, where my partnership with Ian Wright will always be remembered. But my time with Sheffield Wednesday was a significant phase which I recall with pleasure and pride. I have to admit to being a bit sceptical when I made the switch up north, but it was a move I never regretted.

It's true the tail-end of my Wednesday spell, under David Pleat, was frustrating, but, overall, my only disappointment was we didn't have a single trophy to show for all our hard work in the years under Trevor Francis when we deserved at least one major prize.

I think I scored 20 goals in my first season and 23 in my second, and those were probably the best times. The 1992-93 campaign was especially packed with great memories as we went to Wembley four times – the famous all-Sheffield semi-final being a fantastic highlight.

When I reflect on that season, the match which stands out as a turning point is the fourth-round FA Cup-tie with Sunderland. This was the day when I suddenly had the feeling we were going to go all the way to Wembley. It's strange how you have those moments when something happens to make you really believe it's going to be your year.

We looked like being forced into a replay, for Sunderland were defending very well and making life hard for us. Then, just when an unwanted trip to Roker Park seemed a certainty, in the last minute of the game Nigel Worthington swung over a cross from the left. It wasn't particularly threatening, but Tony Norman, the goalkeeper, dropped the ball, and it bounced just nicely for me to head in the net!

Of course, it was like a dream come true when not only did the semi-final draw pair us with Sheffield United but, happily, the Football Association finally agreed to stage it at Wembley. I think the match, and the way the supporters responded, did the city proud – though there was one sad and regrettable incident with the tragic death of a fan in unfortunate circumstances.

It may have been a semi-final, but circumstances and the fantastic atmosphere generated by 75,000 fans made it seem like a Cup Final. I shall always remember the colour and the balloons, and the unique spirit of that afternoon. It was certainly no ordinary semi-final, but, though it was an occasion to be savoured and enjoyed, at the end of the day it was not a game you wanted to lose whether you were a player or a supporter – nobody wanted to go home and face the inevitable taunts from fans of the winners!

Fortunately, we won, and it was my goal that settled it. I had scored in a semi-final before, with Crystal Palace, but getting the winner, and at Wembley, was an unforgettable experience. My reaction was one of relief, really, because, although we had dominated the game and scored as early as the first minute, Sheffield United had pulled level and forced us into extra-time. When we kept failing to turn our supe-

Mark Bright heading the goal that sealed a famous Wembley triumph over Sheffield United.

riority to advantage there must have been people who thought United might go and nick a shock victory.

That was the day when, in the dressing room before the game, Trevor Francis said he had a feeling I was going to score the winner. He was so emphatic about it, but I never really thought it would happen – until it did!

I don't need to say that losing in both Cup Finals to Arsenal was not a pleasant experience. There are certain things you tend to blank from your memory, and those games are a good example in my case! It was disappointing for the fans, and all the more so as it must have been hard on their pockets making four trips to Wembley. It would have been nice to have given them at least one trophy, but, sadly, it wasn't to be.

I certainly have more positive memories than negative ones from my years in Sheffield, and we had some great characters in the dressing room. You always knew that Danny Wilson would graduate into management, and you respected the knowledge of people like Viv Anderson, Nigel Pearson and Peter "The Duke" Shirtliff. To play with such as Chris Waddle, John Sheridan, Roland Nilsson, David Hirst and others was a tremendous experience. Quality was very much the name of the game.

I was sorry that it went a bit sour at the finish. These things happen in football but it hadn't happened to me before to be out of the team for so long. It was a strange situation and something of a character test for me. I felt really down, but kept working hard in training and no one could criticise my effort.

Supporters tend to go on about the money players get, and remark on the cars they drive and the big houses they live in, but, to a footballer, what really matters is playing. To play is everything, and, when you're not playing and feel you're being mistreated, no amount of money can make you happy. I was in Sheffield to play football, which was my job, but I wasn't playing.

The irony was that it happened after I'd been given a new contract – and after I turned my back on the chance to join West Ham. When I went out of contract, I spoke to Harry Redknapp and Peter Storey at West Ham, but David Pleat, who had just arrived at Hillsborough, said: "Whatever you do, don't sign – I'll get you what you want at Wednesday."

I always thought I would go back to London one day, because I had a house there, but I knew I would only return for the right reasons – and they involved joining the "right" club. I was almost persuaded to join West Ham, because Harry Redknapp sold me on the idea and said he knew I could do a job for them, and, frankly, my gut feeling was to say yes and go home to London.

But I thought Wednesday were the bigger club. Moreover, David Pleat had a good reputation as a manager and I was curious to work with him. I have often said my great regret is that Ron Atkinson left Wednesday before I went there and returned after I had moved on, because he was one of the managers I really would have liked to have worked with. Brian Clough and Kevin Keegan were others in that category, and, at the time, the prospect of working with Pleat, who was known as a good footballing talker, was intriguing.

Against my better judgement, I accepted a new deal with Wednesday, and, sadly, after Pleat had talked me into staying, things just went wrong. I never said anything about it publicly, and just got on with my job, hoping the situation would change. I hoped either something would happen to get me playing again, or I'd get moved on. I think there was the opportunity to move me on, but, whatever the reasons, I didn't feel David Pleat was doing his best for me and we didn't see eye to eye.

It was a sad end to a very enjoyable phase in my career, and, now that it is all behind me, I can honestly say it has not coloured my memories of my time in Sheffield. It's all history now, and we've all moved on, but those years we spent at Hillsborough were certainly very special. I'm glad we had that time together.

Part Three – Tales from the Boot Room

Harry Catterick.

Talking about Harry Catterick

Harry Catterick had served his managerial apprenticeship at Crewe and Rochdale before joining Wednesday in 1958. He led the Owls to the Second Division title in his first season, to fifth place and the FA Cup semi-final in his second term, and then saw them finish runners-up to Tottenham in the race for the Football League championship in 1960-61, towards the end of which campaign he ended his three-year stay at Hillsborough and walked out to join Everton.

Ralph O'Donnell, who played for the Owls from 1949 to 1964, recalls:
Harry Catterick was a man who made a tremendous difference to Wednesday, and he was very good to me personally. He came just around the period when I had gone part-time, so I didn't have a lot of contact with him in the early stages. However, it was quickly obvious that there was a significant change of emphasis after he came. Somehow, everyone suddenly seemed more focussed, and there was a more professional outlook.

I never remember seeing Harry on the training ground much. He'd put a track suit on and kick a few balls about if a photographer came, but he left the training to Tommy Eggleston, and Tommy was excellent on that side of things.

Harry was a hard man in many ways, but he knew how to handle people and get the best out of them. As I've said, I had gone part-time, but there was a spell when I was brought into the team following a run of injuries which had created problems for the manager. I think I did all right.

Around this time, I remember, I was due a benefit, and, because I had gone part-time, there was some talk of my payment being scaled down. I believe some people felt I was not entitled to the full £750.

Anyway, we were playing in London, and, after we arrived at the hotel where we were staying overnight, I happened to get into the lift – and almost at the same moment, Harry walked in. I was very much in awe of him, and didn't speak. But he said: "Oh, I was wanting to have a word with you. You're due a benefit, and you can take it from me that there'll be no scaling down – you'll get the full sum."

I did, too, and I'm sure it was entirely down to Harry Catterick.

Jim McAnearney, the former Wednesday inside-forward whom Catterick sold to Plymouth in 1960, comments:
I have to admit I didn't like Harry

Catterick because I always felt he treated me badly, and I was bitterly disappointed when he dropped me from a winning team in 1958-59. With three more games, I would have qualified for a Second Division championship medal, and I didn't think he was fair. But that doesn't stop me saying he was a good manager, one of the best Wednesday ever had.

It was Catterick's misfortune that he and Eric Taylor didn't get on. If Taylor said black, Catterick said white, and a situation developed whereby Catterick tried to get Taylor out – which was a mistake because at that time nobody could shift Eric Taylor.

I inadvertently got caught up in their feud. I had an arrangement with Taylor about my contract, and, when I wanted it changed and went to see Catterick, I made the mistake of explaining how the arrangement had worked before he came. Catterick was not exactly polite in declining to change my contract. In fact, he was the first manager who had sworn at me in telling me to leave his office!

My brother, Tom, of course, tells a story about how Catterick took the captaincy off him because he refused to kick an opponent. Tony Kay, who volunteered to sort the other player out, got the job!

Keith Ellis, the centre-forward who enjoyed his best years following Catterick's arrival, comments:
Harry Catterick was good news for me. It was under him that I finally came to the fore. Although he was hard, he was always fair. He had his pets, and I wasn't one of them, but I had no complaints.

His secret, apart from his football knowledge, was his man-management. He knew who to needle and who not to needle. He could identify those who responded to a fatherly arm round the shoulder. He used to needle me to death, but he knew that was how to get the best out of me.

Peter Johnson, who established himself at right-back in Catterick's second season and was an ever-present in that 1960-61 campaign when Wednesday's 58 points were not enough to win the championship, comments:
Harry Catterick was a man's man. He always got straight to the point, and there was no beating about the bush

with him. He knew the game and could not only assess the strengths and weaknesses of individuals and teams – he could communicate that knowledge to his own players. He understood footballers and knew how to handle players to get the best out of them. In my case, he'd never tell me off when I made a mistake, never say what I'd done wrong. He'd say: "You ought to have known better," aware that I knew very well what I'd done wrong and was ready to hold my hands up.

Catterick always believed that the priority in any team was a good defence. Before away games he would say: "We've got a point already, and we haven't kicked a ball yet." Our bonus was £2 for a win and £1 for a draw, and, in the dressing room before an away match, he'd say: "You've got a £1 already." But he'd make the point before a home game that the opposition were starting with a £1.

He would often say to me: "I saw your wife and kids last week, and I noticed the kids are ready for a new pair of shoes, don't you agree?" He was saying, in effect, roll your sleeves up and earn the bonus that will buy those shoes!

It was a sad day for Wednesday when he left, and I've often said that if I could turn back the years and go back into football, Harry Catterick is the man I would choose to be my manager. I can't speak more highly of him than that.

George McCabe, a Sheffield-based FIFA referee who served on the Football League from 1951 to 1969, recalls how he used to train at Hillsborough until Harry Catterick arrived in 1958.
I have to stress that Harry and I became good friends in later years, but, when he was manager at Rochdale and I refereed one of their matches, we had a bit of a barney over a ball. I can't remember the details, but the argument got very heated.

I was working as a representative with Heeley Tools, and, having a good relationship with Wednesday, used to train at Hillsborough a couple of times every week. When I went to the ground one day soon after Harry had been appointed manager, he spotted me working out and asked what I thought I was doing.

I explained I had Eric Taylor's per-

mission to use the facilities, but Catterick snapped: "Well I'm the gaffer now and you haven't got my permission." The upshot was another sharp exchange, I walked away and after that I did my training at Bramall Lane.

Vic Buckingham Remembered

Many a tale was told in the Hillsborough Boot Room about the remarkable Vic Buckingham, Wednesday's team-boss from June 1961 to April 1964. A former Tottenham full-back who had gained wide managerial experience at home with Pegasus, Bradford (PA) and West Brom, he broadened his outlook with success in two years at Ajax (Amsterdam) before moving to Sheffield. The Owls finished sixth in the old First Division in each of his three seasons. Vic, who died at the age of 79 in 1995, is remembered as "a character" whose dress and sophisticated manner smacked of show business – typified by Howard Wilkinson's recollection of how, on the day the Owls boss arrived at the youngster's Hoyle Street home to talk about signing the lad, he arrived in his "posh overcoat, silk scarf and Rex Harrison hat" and proceeded to drink most of the family sherry before departing!

Jack Mansell, who returned from Holland to become Buckingham's coach at Hillsborough in 1962, recalls:
Vic was a good manager who never shirked responsibility, never passed the buck. He knew the game and understood players, and if, for the most part, he was easy going, he commanded respect. When he was ready he would give players a right rollicking, and they never answered back because he frightened them. He and I would often have a ding-dong in his office, then go out and have a friendly lunch together with the argument completely forgotten.

He tended to stay out of it, and I always felt he might have done more in the dressing room. He'd come in before a match and at half-time, and afterwards, if we hadn't won, he'd spend one minute rollicking the players, but leave them alone if they'd got a result.

You would call him a character. In his time at West Brom he was involved in a car crash, and this might explain

Vic Buckingham, Wednesday's manager from 1961 to 1964, seen here with Sheffield-born Mark Pearson after his move to the Owls in 1963.

why he was moody. He'd be happy-go-lucky one day, and like Churchill's black dog the next. Some days he was dreadful. On a black day he'd give everybody a rollicking, then he'd go home and return the next morning as good as gold.

He was very laid back. We used to train up at the Atlas & Norfolk ground at Shirecliffe, but, except for one period of about five days, I never remember him taking training. He invariably left that to me, just showing up when it suited him and seldom getting involved.

We'd be out on the pitch working, and Vic would turn up in his car. Sometimes you'd see him get out, remove his trilby, scarf and overcoat and put them on the back seat, and then get a golf club from the boot. He'd walk on to a corner of the field, hit a few balls, then suddenly bugger off without having spoken a word to anybody – not even "hello"!

Tom McAnearney, Wednesday's long-serving wing-half and captain, recalls:
I remember when Vic Buckingham arrived, he came up to me in training and, putting a hand on my shoulder, said: "The Danny Blanchflower of

Sheffield Wednesday." Then he turned to Tony Kay and said: "The Dave Mackay of Sheffield Wednesday." I suppose he was paying us a compliment and boosting our confidence.

Vic knew the game, but, unfortunately, his planning sometimes left something to be desired – like on the day at Leicester City when I spent all the first-half playing 4-2-4 on my own!

What happened was that Vic called me into his office and said henceforth I wasn't to undertake any defending duties. They would be done by Tony Kay, and all he expected from me was to use the ball as a creative player.

I assumed he had called the others in and told them individually what was happening, but we hadn't been playing long when it was obvious that I was playing a different game from my teammates! Kay, in particular, was giving me some real verbal "stick", and Gibson, the Leicester inside man, was having a right picnic.

We were two-down at half-time, and, naturally, when we got to the dressing room, the lads wanted to know what I was doing. I told them what Vic had said, and they looked puzzled: "What 4-2-4? It's news to us!" Of course, Vic wasn't there to defend me.

Anyway, I decided to go back to my "normal" game, and we played really well in the second half. In fact, I'm pretty sure we pulled back and ended up with a draw.

Jack Mansell

Jack Mansell, Wednesday's coach in an eventful spell between 1962 and 1964 when Vic Buckingham was manager, remembers life at Hillsborough and recalls an amusing story of an incident which occurred on a 1957 trip to Sheffield as a Portsmouth player.

My earliest memory of Hillsborough concerns a match in which I didn't play but endured the curious experience of listening to a radio commentary in which I was repeatedly reported to be having a nightmare game against a Wednesday winger called Derek Wilkinson. It might have been funny but for the fact I was in hospital with suspected appendicitis at the time!

It happened towards the end of a playing career which saw me make about 270 League appearances with Brighton, Cardiff and Portsmouth. On this day in April 1957, I was scheduled to be at left-back when Pompey visited Wednesday, but on the train journey north. I suffered some stomach trouble, so, instead of going with the rest of the lads to Hillsborough, I ended up in a Sheffield hospital.

In fact, an injection removed the pain and the doctor said I could go home after an overnight stay under observation, so I settled down to listen to the game on hospital radio. I knew Bill Albury was wearing my No.3 shirt, but, unfortunately, someone had forgotten to amend the commentator's match programme. Derek Wilkinson, it seems, was giving Bill a right chasing, and the commentator seemed to delight in insisting it was me getting the runaround – which didn't help my blood pressure, I can tell you!

I had played in a 4-4 draw and a 3-1 win for Pompey at Hillsborough, but on this occasion, with Albury "ghosting" for me, we lost 3-1, and, so I'm told, Wilkinson scored one and Roy Shiner got two.

In the event, the spot of trouble which put me in hospital did eventually

Jack Mansell.

lead to an operation. However, it was probably a couple of years before that happened. In the meantime, I kept having stomach problems, and it was partly because it took so long to diagnose exactly what was wrong that I left Portsmouth and embarked on a coaching career which, ironically, eventually brought me back to Sheffield.

To cut a long story short, it was after a spell as manager of Eastbourne United (where I took over from Ron Greenwood) that I went to Holland and enjoyed a run of success at Blau Wit which prompted Vic Buckingham to offer me a coaching job at Hillsborough. Vic, of course, had been with the other Amsterdam club, Ajax, and knew I'd led Blau Wit, then newly-promoted, to third place in the top division in my first season when everyone was tipping them for relegation.

I always remember I spent my first three months with Wednesday living at the old Grand Hotel, which has long since been demolished. Vic called me into his office one day and asked why I was still in the hotel not realising he'd forgotten to set in motion arrangements for me to have a club house. That was typical of Vic – he knew his football, but in some things he was not always so on the ball!

I enjoyed my time with Wednesday. I

learned a lot from Buckingham and from people like Eric Taylor, who was a clever little guy, very bright. The club also had some very good players, many of them genuine characters, and it was an experience working with such as Tony Kay, Alan Finney, Tom McAnearney and the rest. Derek Wilkinson, by the way, was still there – and amused to learn how I once faced him while sitting up in a hospital bed!

The Wednesday lads kept you on your toes and you had to earn their respect, but it was rewarding when you got a response to your efforts, and I don't think I ever had any trouble with any of them.

One player I especially remember working with and getting pleasure at seeing him enjoy some success after I left was Vic Mobley. Vic, you'll remember, was built like Garth, a great hunk of a man. When he first came to Sheffield from Oxford City, he couldn't jump, but we talked and worked together for hours on end, and I literally taught him how to jump and master his timing to win high balls. Nobody was more delighted than me when he got England Under-23 recognition, and but for an inopportune injury he would have been capped at senior level.

The only disappointment of my time with Wednesday was not doing better than we did. Finishing in the top six wasn't good enough, and, as you know, when Vic Buckingham's contract expired in 1964 it wasn't renewed.

Vic was a good manager, but, at the time he left, I fancied the job, and, without being boastful, honestly felt I could do better than him, or at least move things on a stage further. There were things Vic didn't do as a manager that I would have done, and, in my opinion, the situation would have improved. I might well have failed, but I would have liked to have had a try, and, with the talent available, we would more than likely have succeeded.

Unfortunately, when I applied for the job, Eric Taylor said they wanted someone bigger than me. Eric said what a good letter I'd written and what a lot they thought of me as a coach, but explained that as Wednesday were a big club they needed a big name.

They brought in Alan Brown, and, as I didn't want to work under him, I left and went back to Holland. About a year

later, of course, I returned to South Yorkshire as manager of Rotherham United, and I suppose one of the most satisfying nights in my time at Millmoor came when we travelled to Hillsborough and beat Wednesday in the League Cup in September 1966. Wednesday had played in the FA Cup Final in the previous May.

To be honest, I don't remember much about that match under the Hillsborough floodlights other than Frank Casper scored the only goal. I'm told it was Wednesday's first-ever tie in the League Cup, because in previous years they had declined to enter the competition.

However, the only thing I recall about the entire evening is that, on the way to the ground, we stopped and picked up a couple of Rotherham supporters. I know we decided to travel from Millmoor via the back lanes to avoid the traffic, and, suddenly coming upon these two lads in red and white mufflers, we invited them on to the team-bus.

It made their night, and the result certainly made mine. I had won there before as a visiting player in 1955, but it was much more fulfilling to do it as a manager. I just hope the man covering the game for hospital radio got the names of my players right!

Kenny Johnson

Kenny Johnson arrived at Hillsborough as an apprentice in 1967 and became a professional in 1969, but left Wednesday in November 1971 for Newcastle without getting beyond being a second-team regular. However, after playing at Limerick, Darlington and South Shields, the Chester-le-Street product chose to settle in Sheffield, where he is a self-employed builder and manages Hallam FC.

Every Monday we used to have a little ceremony called The Dragon Awards, and Johnny Fantham, wearing a pair of crocodile skin shoes I always envied, was the judge, being assisted by a jury which comprised such first-team lads as Gerry Young, Don Megson and Brian Usher.

The venue was always the first-team dressing room, where "Judge" Fantham would use the trainer's bench as a desk, and the apprentices would be brought in to watch the proceedings of the "court". The idea was that someone would be nominated for a Dragon Award if they had been seen out with a "dodgy" bird the previous weekend – "dodgy" meaning a girl who was not regarded as good looking.

Naturally, those brought before the meeting were single lads – often second-teamers, but sometimes first-team players. Witnesses gave evidence, and those facing the "charge" could present a defence – all very formal, but also hilarious. It was just good fun, really, and there was some terrific humour when people like Ian McFarlane, the coach, was around.

I think Sam Ellis won the award more times than enough, but, on one famous occasion, Peter Eustace was nominated and declared guilty. Peter, of course, was a very good-looking lad, and nine times out of ten at any social function he would end up with the most attractive young lady. He was widely known as either "The Count" or "The Squire of Stocksbridge", because he always dressed with style in the latest fashion.

One night, however, he took a girl home who wasn't up to his usual standard – and poor old Peter did not take too kindly to collecting a Dragon Award!

Author's Footnote: Kenny had a three-months stint back at Hillsborough a few years ago when, in his capacity as a builder working as a sub-contractor to Gleesons, he was involved in installing new turnstiles and building a new boundary wall at the Leppings Lane end in the wake of the FA Cup semi-final disaster of 1989. "It was as if time had stood still, because, 18 years on, people like Ron Ward, Lily Shelton and Norma Lane were still around – and meeting them again evoked memories of what I still recall as probably the best period in my life."

Recalling Danny Williams

Danny Williams, who made more than 620 appearances for Rotherham and later managed the Millmoor club, was Wednesday's team-boss from the summer of 1969 to January 1971, arriving at Hillsborough soon after piloting

Danny Williams (left) pictured with Sammy Todd, the Burnley player he signed when he was unable to get Brian O'Neill.

Swindon to a famous League Cup triumph.

Peter Rodrigues, the Welsh international back whom Williams signed from Leicester in 1970, comments:
Danny was a great character, always full of fun. On away trips, he kept us entertained with a continuous stream of jokes and tales about his experiences in football. I remember once, when we were having a lean spell in which we went several games without winning, he told a director who had missed the previous match: "Aye, the highlight was when we won a corner – the lads were so thrilled, they did a lap of honour!"

Kenny Johnson, a young professional with the Owls in the time when Williams' was manager, also remembers Danny's humour:
One of the famous stories told about Danny was the day when the team played in an FA Cup-tie at Tottenham and lost heavily. Danny commented: "Aye, one day we'll get t'Cup off the King at Wembley."

A director hastened to correct him. "Don't you mean the Queen, Danny?"

"No, it'll be the King by the time this lot reach the Final!"

Jackie Sinclair, the Scottish international winger signed by Williams from Newcastle in 1970, recalls:
I played under some good managers in my time, including Jock Stein, Joe Harvey and Matt Gillies – and Danny was one of the bosses I really liked and

respected. He enjoyed a laugh and a joke, but he was a man who worked with his sleeves rolled up to his elbows, and that summed up his approach to life and football. He gave you everything. He preferred players with flair, and his teams always played positively with wingers, but he wanted lads who were like him and had lots of heart to top up their skill.

I know it was a terrible blow to Danny when we were relegated in 1970, because we shouldn't have let it happen. We threw it away, really, and ought never to have lost that final game at home to Manchester City. We were beaten by nerves, and the irony was that, a few days earlier, we had produced a performance of real character at Old Trafford and put ourselves in a position which gave us a real chance of escaping.

We'd gone to Manchester United knowing that if we didn't get something, we'd be down; and, when George Best and Bobby Charlton put United 2-0 up after only eight minutes, it looked like curtains. But Tony Coleman pulled a goal back just before half-time, and then Jack Whitham got an equaliser on the hour. A 2-2 scoreline was a great result and just reward for sheer spirit.

We came home convinced we were going to escape relegation, which, in truth, was a remarkable situation considering we had lost nine and won only five of 16 games since just before Christmas – and for ages had looked favourites for the drop. Of course, we knew nothing less than a win in our final game would be good enough, but we didn't feel a victory was beyond us.

Sadly, it all went wrong when we met Manchester City in front of a 45,000 Hillsborough crowd. Frankly, I don't think City, who had a Cup-winners' Cup Final date the following week, were too bothered, and when Mike Doyle missed an early penalty I just felt we were fated to get the right result.

But, as I remember, in the first half-hour, there were two incidents which proved more significant than the penalty miss. We lost Wilf Smith, who limped off to be replaced by young Steve Downes, and City lost Mike Summerbee, who was injured in a clash with Colin Prophett. City's substitute, Ian Bowyer, had barely had time to settle when he scored.

It was a wet and miserable night, but our spirits were lifted when Coleman equalised just past the hour-mark. Unfortunately, we couldn't get a second goal, and, of course, our fate was sealed when Bowyer headed City in front a minute from the end.

I think Joe Mercer, the City manager, was upset by Summerbee's injury, but, as I recall, it was Summerbee who conceded the free-kick in the incident which saw him carried off – though I believe Mercer didn't appreciate this until after the game. To be honest, the despair in our dressing room was such that we weren't too concerned with what the City manager thought. We were down and Danny knew we faced a long battle to get back.

Jack Whitham, for whom the Manchester City game in April 1970 was his final League outing for the Owls before he was transferred to Liverpool, reflects on his year under Danny Williams:
When you add it all up, you don't go down because you lose your last match. It's what you've done over the season. At the end of the day the club paid for a lot of things which weren't right over a long period. Yet we should never have lost against Manchester City, and the sickening thing was they didn't come to play that night.

When we looked at the last two fixtures of the season, the match at Manchester United was the big game because we were expected to lose there – and we knew defeat meant relegation. In the event, we got a point, and to then lose at home to City in the way we did was unbelievable.

Frankly, the difference in discipline at the club between what it had been under Alan Brown and what it became under Danny Williams was embarrassing. Brown's management technique might not have worked in these days when players have so much power, but in the 1960s his style, while it was based on fear to some degree, gave us a sense of purpose and somehow generated a tremendous team-spirit. Danny's manner was just the opposite, and, sadly, he never won the respect of most of the players.

An example of what upset everybody was the way Danny dealt with one incident involving Tony Coleman, a winger who had come from Manchester City.

Tony was in digs with me at the time, and one morning at about three o'clock we were roused from our sleep by the telephone. Tony answered it, spoke to someone, then got up, dressed and left the house. When he didn't turn up for training a few hours later, nobody made any comment.

That was Tuesday. On the Wednesday, when Tony still didn't appear at training, Danny asked me: "Where's Tony?" And I could only say I hadn't a clue where he'd gone after leaving the digs at 3am the previous day. On the Thursday, Danny called me into his office and again asked if I knew where Tony was. I still didn't.

Come Friday and Danny sent for me again. He said: "Look, I really need to know where Tony is because I've got to pick a team." I said I was as wise to Tony's whereabouts as he was, and, in fact, told Danny I was surprised he was even thinking of putting him in the team.

I should mention that, in Coleman's absence, Willie Lawson, the winger who had been brought down from Scotland, was working his socks off in training, boosted to think he had a chance of playing at the weekend.

On Saturday, an hour before the kick-off, the team sheet appears, and, at No.11, it says: "Coleman or Lawson." We couldn't believe it, and, anyway, there was still no sign of Tony.

Then, at ten minutes past two, Tony suddenly walks into the dressing room. He told Danny he'd had one or two "personal problems", and asked: "Am I playing?" Danny said: "Yes – get your kit on."

How many managers would have done that? In Alan Brown's time, not even a player 20 times better than Coleman would have got away with disappearing without a word for five days. To be honest, I think he would have drowned Tony in the Don! But Danny wasn't "Brownie".

No Christmas Cheer for Dooley

The sacking of Derek Dooley on Christmas Eve 1973 has passed into Hillsborough folklore as one of the most ill-timed and heartless acts in the club's history. Almost three years earlier, in January 1971, Dooley had been persuaded by under-fire chairman Sir Andrew Stephen and general manager Eric Taylor to give up his job as Development Fund organiser and succeed Danny Williams as Wednesday's manager. His departure, which ended a 26-year association with the Owls, stunned everyone at the club.

Jimmy Mullen, who played 43 of his first 45 League games for Wednesday under Dooley, remembers:

It was traditional on the last day before Christmas for the players to gather in the dressing room after training for a pleasant little ritual. A tray of drinks, port and sherry, would be brought in, and the custom was for the club chairman to make a toast, then we would raise our glasses and wish each other a merry Christmas.

On that Christmas Eve in 1973, I remember being called out of the shower sooner than expected, and I stood in a corner of the dressing room with just a towel around me while Matt Sheppard, who had recently become chairman, spoke. On this occasion, however, there were no smiles and he didn't propose a toast, but said he had to give us the sad news that Derek Dooley had been sacked.

We were all absolutely gobsmacked. I shall never forget the sense of shock, not just because Derek had been sacked but because, at 21, it was the first time I'd had the experience of being told such stunning news by the chairman. You normally read of managerial sackings, even at your own club, in the papers.

Derek was a lovely man, and we couldn't believe he was being sacked on the day before Christmas. Nobody was in the mood for seasonal greetings, and, anyway, I don't think a tray of drinks was passed round that day.

Ken Knighton, who was signed by Dooley before the start of the 1973-74 season, recalls:

I had played 18 League games for Wednesday when Derek Dooley was sacked. The decision was outrageous, the timing unbelievable, and I have never forgotten how I heard the news.

At the time I was still living in Hull, but staying in Sheffield during the week and going home after games. On the Saturday, which was three days before

Christmas, we had drawn at Crystal Palace. It was a result which pleased Derek, who felt we had finally turned the corner and were starting to get over the effects of the virus which had caused so many problems. He told me that, because it was Christmas, it wouldn't be necessary for me to go over to Sheffield for training on the Monday.

In fact, I did a light workout at Hull, and when I got home there was a telephone call from Gerry Young. I thought he'd rung to offer seasonal greetings, and, when he said Derek had been sacked, I couldn't believe it.

I always regarded Derek as an outstanding individual, someone you respected and would never give less than your best for. I knew as much as anyone what he had achieved as a player, and always felt he had a presence. He was very charismatic, but he was very decent, thoughtful and had the knack of being exactly the same with everyone.

As a manager, I think he might have been better with a stronger personality as his right-hand man, but, at that particular time, he had been so unlucky in losing so many players because of a virus which had swept through the club, and, if he'd been given a few more weeks, the whole situation might have improved dramatically.

But what was unforgivable was to sack him on Christmas Eve. Nobody deserved that, and Derek was the last man it should have happened to. I know Derek has said since that he never considered himself immune from the sack if he didn't get the results, but what hurt was the timing.

George McCabe, the former FIFA referee who was Wednesday's Youth Development Officer from 1970 to 1976, remembers:

There were a few tears at Hillsborough on the day Derek was sacked. I'll never forget the moment when Derek came back from a meeting with Matt Sheppard, the chairman, and announced he'd just been sacked. We couldn't believe it. A few moments earlier we'd been happily discussing how we were going to spend Christmas Day, but the seasonal spirit evaporated in an instant.

Later, Sheppard sent for me. He said: "I've just had a terrible task to perform

– I've dismissed Derek." Then he offered me the job of caretaker manager, but there was no way I could accept. Derek was a pal, and he'd been a great guy to work for. The last thing he deserved was what had happened to him that morning.

Dave Cusack

Dave Cusack was a 6ft 2in centre-back who joined the Owls as an apprentice in October 1971 and made 109 League and Cup appearances between 1975 and 1978. He also played for Southend, Millwall, Doncaster Rovers and Rotherham. Now business manager of a leisure company in Southend, he still turns out occasionally with Basildon United in the Essex Senior League. Here he recalls some incidents from his Hillsborough career.

It was the custom to invite an apprentice into the boot room to tell him whether he was being taken on as a professional, and one day in 1974 I was called through from the dressing room to find Steve Burtenshaw, the manager, sitting there with coaches Gerry Young, Ron Staniforth and Jim McAnearney.

"I'm sorry, son, but we're not going to sign you. These three think, yes we should take you, but I don't agree," said Steve, who was a great coach and a decent guy but he had a touch of arrogance which could be disconcerting to a youngster.

Looking back, I sometimes wonder whether Steve was just winding me up to test my reaction, but, having set my heart on becoming a professional with the club I'd supported as a boy, and knowing I'd worked hard to achieve that goal, I wasn't amused and didn't exactly appreciate the manager's approach.

I showed that I, too, could be arrogant when provoked, and said: "I'm not effing bothered anyway, because if you don't want me, somebody else will." Then I turned and walked out of the room with all the affronted dignity I could muster.

I don't know what was said after I left, but the next day they offered me professional terms, and, about a year later, ironically a couple of months before he was sacked, Steve gave me my first taste of senior football in a pre-season friendly against Kilmarnock. I only came on as a sub late in the match, but they were the biggest 20 minutes of my life.

I know Steve was pleased I went on to enjoy a career in which I played around 500 League matches with five clubs, but it was Jim McAnearney, having been one of my staunchest supporters in the Reserves, who gave me my League debut for the Owls in a 4-1 win against Millwall at Hillsborough in October 1975. At the time Jim was acting team-boss, and, though Len Ashurst arrived soon afterwards, I kept my place and played about 40 games that season.

I always remember, in the dressing room before the Millwall game, John Haselden, the physio, told me: "When you get out there, for the first 20 minutes you'll not know whether you're on your head or your arse. You'll be so hyped up and pump so much adrenalin, you'll feel knackered and disorientated. But if you keep everything you do simple, you'll soon find your feet and start to enjoy it."

I did enjoy it, and for three seasons I was a regular. I might not have left when I did but for the fact that, towards the end of Jack Charlton's first season, he was using Jimmy Mullen and Hugh Dowd as his centre-backs, and, as my contract was due to expire, I felt it might be time to accept an offer from Dave Smith at Southend.

With hindsight, I might have been wiser to have stayed, but I was a bit stubborn and pig-headed in those days, and, with Jack away in Argentina on television duty at the World Cup, I'd more or less decided my own fate before he came home.

Reference to Jack reminds me of a tale about my Irish mate Hugh Dowd when all the Wednesday players went up to the Charlton farm in North Yorkshire for a spell of special training.

Of course, Hugh was always the reluctant marathon man, but one morning when Jack told us to run to the local village and back, he seemed quite keen – until, a few yards beyond the farmyard gate, he suddenly disappeared. At the time, I thought I'd simply lost sight of him and he was somewhere near the back of the pack. It did cross my mind that he might have pulled a muscle or something.

When, at last, we were nearing the end of the run, and the farm reappeared in view, Hugh emerged from behind a wall and rejoined us – trying desperately to make it look as if he'd been with us all the time. Only Hugh could turn a five-mile run into a 400-yard jog and get away with it!

Len Ashurst – and a Winter's Tale!

Len Ashurst, who had served his managerial apprenticeship at Hartlepool and Gillingham, was Wednesday's team-boss from October 1975 to October 1977 and is generally credited with having laid the foundations upon which his successor was able to create a long-awaited

Len Ashurst on the bench with John Haselden, Ron Staniforth and Tony Toms.

"I've been roughing it on these moors for years and I'm STILL no good at football!"

Ralph Whitworth, a cartoonist on *The Star* and *Morning Telegraph*, was a great Wednesdayite who often featured the Owls in his work. This famous "Sheep on the Moors" cartoon captured the humour of the night Len Ashurst's players endured the winter chill of the country-side. It serves as a tribute to Whitworth, who died in mid-1998.

Hillsborough revival. He is also remembered for shocking the players with a wintry "overnight" in the open!

Jimmy Mullen, the defender whom Ashurst appointed Wednesday's captain, recalls:

Len was the first Wednesday manager to take the players camping on the moors in the middle of winter, and the venture inspired a famous Ralph Whitworth cartoon in the local paper showing two sheep out in the wilds. One sheep is saying to the other: "I've been roughing it on these moors for years, and I'm still no good at football!"

Anyway, we were out in the wilds and sleeping overnight with only groundsheets for covering – Len refused to let us have tents – and it was definitely a shock to the system.

Some of the Press lads decided they would come and join us so they could write about our experience at first hand. However, when they arrived with a tent, we felt they weren't exactly sharing our discomfort.

We looked on with envy while the journalists put their tent up, but, once we were sure they were settled and sleeping, two or three of us sneaked across and unhooked the canvas. It was a windy night, and I've never seen a tent disappear so quickly. It flew over the

hillside and out of view – amid loud protests from the victims and cheers from the footballers!

Rodger Wylde, also remembers the moors episode:

According to Tony Toms, the trainer, the club's directors were not very happy about the publicity our night on the moors generated, and, some time afterwards, he said that if we hadn't won our next match, against Chester, as comfortably as we did, Len Ashurst would have been sacked.

A Wednesdayite called Wilkinson: His era recalled

Howard Wilkinson was on Wednesday's books as an amateur while still at Abbeydale Grammar School and became a professional in 1962. Between September 1964 and March 1966 he made 22 appearances at outside-right before moving on to Brighton, then launching a career in coaching and management at Boston United in 1971. He had a spell as the Football Association's Sheffield-based regional coach, and managed England's semi-professional side and the England Under-21's. After guiding Notts County into Division One, he became Wednesday's manager in June 1983 and in his first season at Hillsborough led the the club

he'd supported as a boy back to the top-grade after a 14-year absence. He left in October 1988 and steered Leeds United from the bottom end of the old Division Two to the League Championship in three years. Shortly after leaving Elland Road in September 1996 he became the Football Association's Technical Director.

Alan Smith is one of the most respected "backroom boys" in modern football. He has worked on the international scene at various levels for 20 years, and, as England's full-time physiotherapist since February 1994, was on duty at the 1996 European championships and the 1998 World Cup. He worked for Wednesday from July 1983 to January 1994, witnessing at close range the remarkable and rapid progress which followed Howard Wilkinson's arrival at Hillsborough. Here he reflects on the Wilkinson era.

I look back on my 11 years at Sheffield Wednesday with much pleasure and great professional satisfaction because I was fortunate to be a member of a backroom team that helped re-establish the club in the top grade in five years under Howard Wilkinson and created the platform from which we went on to claim the club's first major trophy for 56 years under Ron Atkinson – then later qualified for European competition for the first time since the early 1960s.

It was very rewarding to be in at the

Howard Wilkinson's initial squad in 1983. Back row (left to right): Peter Shirtliff, Oliver, Hesford, Redfern, John Pearson, Lyons. Middle row: Blunstone (coach), Eustace (assistant manager), Mark Smith, Mossman, Megson, Mills, Heard, Simons, Matthewson, Morris, Sterland, Alan Smith (physiotherapist). Front row: Williamson, Taylor, Bailey, Wilkinson (manager), Bannister, Paul Shirtliff, Shelton.

beginning of something at Hillsborough, and the progress achieved in a very short time was remarkable. The transformation in that promotion season of 1983-84 is best confirmed by noting we had a 14,500 gate at our first home match and 36,700 at the last, with the 49,000 at the League Cup quarterfinal with Liverpool emphasising the dramatic revival in enthusiasm among supporters.

It was largely down to the leadership of Howard Wilkinson, who must rank as one of the great Wednesday managers. He was an outstanding technical manager, but there was always more to the man than tactical expertise, and he set such high standards. In many respects he was ahead of his time, for some of the things he introduced when he arrived are the norm in the game today. He recognised the merits of a professional approach in every area on the football side of the club.

Nowadays there's a greater awareness of the need for expertise and facilities in areas which were once neglected – and Howard had that awareness 16 years ago. Moreover, we operated with half the staff many clubs now consider the minimum necessary to do the job!

At the outset, apart from Howard, there were only three backroom staff – Peter Eustace, the first-team coach, Frank Blunstone, the Reserves and youth coach, and myself. Howard and Peter organised the management and coaching, while I was responsible for organising the medical and physiotherapy activities; and because we all had the same philosophy our separate roles were complimentary and created an environment and atmosphere geared for success.

The standard of fitness in the promotion season was excellent. It helped us win games. Within my own domain, where I had a set routine and a carefully planned daily programme which met the needs of each individual in my care, the response from the players was excellent. Injured players had the benefit of the best treatment and facilities at every stage of their recovery, but their days were much longer than those of the fit players – which was always great psychological aid to speeding their progress!

A typical day would start for me at 8.30am, and the players under treat-

Key men in the Wilkinson era: England defender Mel Sterland (left) and England physiotherapist Alan Smith.

ment had appointments from nine o'clock. By the time Howard was ready to start training at ten, he would have my report on the injured players, which enabled him to know what was wrong with them and how long each might take to get fit.

I'd be busy in the treatment room until around 11 o'clock, then we would devote the rest of morning to field work, gymnasium work etc., depending on the stage of recovery of each individual. After lunch we would resume at 1.30 or 2pm and repeat the sequence of events. While the fit players had already left the ground after a couple of hours training, players recovering from injury wouldn't be going home until 4.30 at the earliest. With much of the work put into rehabilitation very demanding (for instance the intensity of circuit training), and the days so long, players certainly didn't lack the motivation to get fit!

I believe I was the first full-time physio the club had ever engaged, and, at the time of my arrival at Hillsborough, I had been working in professional football for 11 years. As a youngster, I had aspired to a playing career in the game with my home-town club, Middlesbrough, but after breaking the same leg twice, those hopes were dashed at the age of 17. I then concentrated on qualifying as a chartered physiotherapist, and in 1972, aged 22, joined Rotherham and became the youngest physio in the Football League

– appointed, incidentally, by Jim McAnearney, the old Wednesday player.

I later spent six years at Blackpool, and in that period turned down an offer from Ron Atkinson, who wanted to take me to Manchester United. The clubs couldn't agree on compensation, but I was happy to honour my contract. How ironic that Ron would find me at Hillsborough when he came in 1989. It was when my contract at Bloomfield Road was about to expire that Howard Wilkinson, having just got the Wednesday job, invited me to join him.

I had worked with Howard with the England Non-League team, and knew I would enjoy working with him in a fulltime capacity – which, of course, I did. We shared many memorable days together at Hillsborough. One moment I especially remember was the day we learned that Wednesday's promotion in 1984 was assured. It was at Easter, and, ironically, Wednesday weren't playing that afternoon. However, after training, Howard, Peter Eustace and me were all in the referee's room at the ground, watching the results come in on television. The moment we saw the score which meant we were up, we launched into the first of many celebrations that were to follow in the next few weeks!

The pity was we didn't top a great season by winning the championship, but what mattered was we were back in Division One – and that was the prelude to some more memorable days.

Gary Megson, a member of the 1983-84 promotion team, comments:

Gary Megson, a member of the 1983-84 promotion team, comments:
Howard was very different from Jack Charlton in personality, but they were similar in that both were winners and each believed in the work ethic as the principal key to success.

Howard introduced a style of play which was designed to get us promotion – and it worked. We got a lot of criticism and Howard took some stick, because some people felt it wasn't the right way to play football; but most of the criticism stemmed from jealousy at our success. It was significant that the majority of those who had a go at us were with clubs who finished below us in the table!

We won promotion in 1984, not with a team of big-hitters but with lads who, in the main, had under-achieved elsewhere – and we profited from a system based on work-rate and organisation. Howard paid great attention to detail and tactical discipline.

A small incident which summed up Howard's approach came with a goal we scored in an FA Cup-tie against Barnsley in January 1984. We'd worked all week in training on a far-post corner-kick routine, and Howard, typically, kept us at it hour after hour until we got it right. You can't imagine the delight we felt when it paid off at virtually the first attempt in that Barnsley match – when John Pearson headed in Gary Bannister's cross, it was worth all the patient effort on the training pitch.

When you look back and note how many of the lads who played under Howard have gone into coaching and management, it says everything about how much the players learned from and were influenced by his philosophy.

Joe Ashton, an Owls' supporter since 1942 and a shareholder for 16 years before he joined the board in March 1990, comments:
I think Howard Wilkinson was the best manager we ever had when you consider what he achieved with the resources available to him. It's intriguing to speculate on how much we might

have done if the board at that time had tried to keep him – and Howard has suggested he would have stayed if Bert McGee, the chairman, had only said he didn't want him to leave.

One of my happiest memories is of the day we played at Liverpool soon after we finally regained our place in the top grade under Wilkinson in 1984.

The Labour Party conference was on at Blackpool, and, with me, my wife Maggie, our daughter Lucy, and Maggie's parents enjoying the experience of staying in the Gracie Fields suite at Butlin's Hotel, on the Saturday we topped up a working holiday with a trip across to Anfield for the big match.

It was the day when Imre Varadi punished a typical Bruce Grobbelaar dash from his goalmouth with a marvellous goal, and we won 2-0. I'll always remember how my father-in-law, a mad Wednesdayite, said as we drove back to Blackpool: "That's been one of the best days of my life – seeing the lads win at Liverpool."

It was certainly the sort of day you never forget, because everything about it went just right. The memory has always stayed with me because it wasn't long afterwards when Maggie's dad died.

Paul Hart

Paul Hart recalls two popular Wednesday colleagues called Smith – praising the professionalism of physio Alan, and reflecting on a misfortune which befell team-mate Mark, the Owls' long-serving defender, on a pre-season trip.

I had worked with Alan Smith at Blackpool, and so was familiar with the thoroughness and attention to detail for which he was renowned. Alan was always a great guy, but the treatment room was one place you wanted to avoid because, when you were recovering from injury, he made you work very hard and you knew every day would be a long one.

Believe me, you got fit as quickly as

you could. Alan would have you in at nine every morning and it would be four o'clock before you left the ground. You were sure to endure some gruelling sessions because Alan made you work really hard at whatever was necessary to aid your recovery.

The important thing, of course, was you knew that when you were ready for a return to the team after a lay-off, you'd feel pretty good. Alan had that knack of getting you into exactly the shape you'd been before the injury. That didn't happen at some of the places where I've played. I've known what it's like to get back into the side after three weeks out and feel knackered.

A story worth recording concerns my first summer at Hillsborough in 1985 when Howard Wilkinson took us all up to the Lakes for pre-season training. We were allowed to take our wives and children, but that didn't mean we weren't expected to work hard in training before relaxing with the family.

Indeed, if I remember, one day we went for a ten-mile run around Derwent Water, and me and Lawrie Madden, who were at the back, managed to get lost. We eventually caught up with the other lads to find Howard had everybody doing press-ups – in the water!

My daughter Caroline had contracted chicken pox around the time we went on that trip, but, as they do say it's not contagious once the spots come out, we didn't think there was any risk to anyone else.

It was only after we returned home and reported back to the ground that it emerged poor old Mark Smith had gone down – with chicken pox! The irony was he and I were rivals for the centre-half spot, and circumstances now meant he had no chance of being available for the start of the season.

In fact, we did subsequently play in the team together on a number of occasions, but I always kidded him I deliberately planted Caroline in our training camp to give myself a head start!

A Miscellany of Memories

Remembering Eric Taylor – "Mr Sheffield Wednesday"

Eric Taylor, who joined Wednesday as an office boy in 1929 and became the club's general manager and one of football's most respected administrators in an Owls' career spanning nearly 45 years, was in charge of team affairs at Hillsborough from 1942 to 1958. He died in September 1974 at the age of 62.

Frank Melling, who was a free-scoring amateur centre-forward with Wednesday in the early war years, remembers:
Eric Taylor took charge of team matters when Jimmy McMullan finished in 1942, and in his first season we reached the Final of the League North War Cup. At the time, of course, Eric had a full-time job in industry, at Howell's, and he used to do all his administration and other football work in his spare time.

Although Eric was the manager and invariably talked to individual players, he did not directly involve himself in tactics, and these were organised by Ted Catlin and the captain, Walter Millership.

In fact, we didn't have team talks as such. With the likes of Catlin, Millership, Joe Cockroft and Jackie Robinson, we weren't short of experience in the side, and they could stamp their influence on the others and give any guidance that was needed on the field. Eric was happy to let them get on with it.

Millership was probably not as polished a player as the other senior men, but he more than made up for it with his knowledge and example, and Eric always respected Walter's judgement. In the group, Cockroft was the thinker and as much a leader as Catlin and Millership.

Eric was always a very good organiser, and there was always a taxi laid on to meet the skip and the trainer and deliver them to away grounds from the railway station – and, when things were going well, we were always treated to taxis for the players as well!

Jackie Marriott, a Wednesday winger from 1947 to 1955, recalls:

Eric Taylor was a marvellous man. He was so straight with everyone and looked after his players well. He played everything by the book in the sense that he respected the rules and would never dream of even thinking about breaking them. But he ensured that we got the best of everything everywhere we went. When we played away, we always stayed in top hotels, and invariably went to the theatre. On foreign trips, to places like Switzerland and Denmark for instance, he would make sure you saw all the sights you were supposed to see – and, for players from very ordinary backgrounds, it was a wonderful experience in an era when going abroad was beyond the reach of most people.

The late Hugh Swift once recalled a prank that went wrong on an overnight stay in Newcastle in 1948 because the Wednesday players got the wrong man when their "victim" turned out to be Eric Taylor.
The lads had been taking a bit of stick from our coach driver on this particular journey to the North East, and, when we got to our hotel, we decided to pay him back by going to his room, where we stripped his bed, took the frame to pieces, and rolled up the carpet.

Unfortunately, we'd got the wrong room, and when Eric Taylor finally decided it was time to retire for the night, an hour or so after we had all settled down and were sleeping soundly, he walked up to his room and found it bare!

We were all roused from our slumbers and called to a team meeting. Eric said: "You've made a good job of it, and I enjoyed the joke. Now I'll give you five minutes to put it together again."

I think we lost 4-2 the next day, and our coach driver said he thought it must have been because our sleep had been disturbed. "I can't understand why," he added. "I've not had a more comfortable night's kip for years and slept like a log!"

Jack Sewell says Eric Taylor could always see the funny side and never lacked a sense of humour – even in adversity:

After we'd been relegated in 1951 despite beating Everton 6-0 in our final match, Eric came into the dressing room and said: "Never mind. I like celebrations, and we'll have one at the end of next season." He was as good as his word – we won the Second Division championship in 1952!

Eric England, who worked alongside Taylor from 1936 to 1974, comments:
I remember when we were fighting a desperate battle against relegation from the old Second Division in 1947, and Eric was watching the players relaxing in the club's snooker room. "Well," he said, "if we do go down, at least we'll be the only Third Division club with a snooker table."

I think the ability to always see the funny side of life was the quality which enabled Eric to overcome any problem. For instance, only Eric could have arranged for a recording of *You've Got To Have Heart* by Max Bygraves to be played over the public address system while the players were in training on the pitch the day after we'd suffered a heavy defeat!

Albert Quixall recalls there were were times when even Eric Taylor's sense of humour was severely tested as pranks went horribly wrong, and he remembers a famous occasion on a trip to Switzerland in May 1952 when he and Alan Finney played a trick on Redfern Froggatt which misfired – quite literally! Indeed, they set the hotel fire alarms ringing, prompted pandemonium in the middle of the night, and left some senior members of the Wednesday party embarrassed and rather hot under the collar!
When Alan Finney and I were youngsters together, we were always up to something by way of having a bit of fun at the expense of the older players, especially on away trips. We loved nothing more than pulling their legs, or, better still, catching them off-guard with our tricks. However, that time in Lucerne when we hid "Red" Froggatt's pyjamas, we caused more problems than we bargained for.

We played about five matches on that trip, and it was after one of these games that the rest of the lads were relaxing downstairs. Alan and I crept away and we went up to Redfern's room, where we put his pyjamas inside a chandelier over his bed. Then we carefully pulled some furniture behind the door so he would have to struggle to get into the room.

As "Red" tells it, he eventually went upstairs, and, as the room lights were on and he had a devil of a job pushing the door open, he knew we'd been there before him. He must have been very tired because, unable to immediately find his pyjamas, he jumped into bed without them and promptly fell into a deep sleep without putting out the light.

The next thing he knew, about two o'clock in the morning, he suddenly awoke and must have thought he was having a nightmare when he found his room full of people, including the hotel manager, a porter, a couple of Wednesday directors and Eric Taylor. As if that wasn't shock enough, someone was desperately trying to douse a fire in the chandelier – and, eventually, the charred remains of Red's pyjamas were removed!

I don't know how Red explained it, but I think we were rather more sheepish than him when we faced Eric Taylor and tried to tell him we hadn't really meant to cause an international incident!

Norma Lane, who worked alongside Isabel Brown in Eric Taylor's office for two years before switching in 1968 to become secretary to a succession of team managers, comments:
Eric Taylor was "Mr Sheffield Wednesday". He wanted the club to be the best and to have the best of everything. I remember he had a large map of the world in his office, and it was filled with lots of coloured pins which marked all the places where Wednesday had played – many of them in parts of the world where no other professional club had been.

He was a hard taskmaster in the sense that he wanted everything exactly right, and, every day, he would at some time visit every part of the ground. If he found things were not as they should be anywhere, he wanted to know why.

On a match day, he would sit in the directors' box but he didn't spend all the 90 minutes watching the match. He would be watching the stewards, knowing exactly where every one of them should be. He had his finger on everything, and nothing happened at Hillsborough without him knowing about it.

Yet, if he once knew you were a person who pulled your weight, he was never a stickler for insisting you had to be at work at nine or ten o'clock on the dot. He was well aware if women on the staff had such problems as getting children to school and suchlike.

Mr Taylor – we never called him Eric – invariably had his meals on the premises, and they were always cooked for him by Edie Adams in my early days at the club. Edie kept him supplied with cups of tea, and ensured he had exactly the food he wanted – always cooked to perfection. She was always running to the shop for fresh breadcakes.

One of Edie's job was to press the spare suit Mr Taylor always brought to the ground if he was going out or had to receive an important visitor.

Some Jack Charlton Stories

Jack Charlton, Wednesday's manager from 1977 to 1983, started a long-awaited Hillsborough revival when he led the Owls to promotion from Division Three in 1980, and he is remembered as one of the game's great characters.

Jimmy Mullen, the former Wednesday captain, recalls:
Not long after Big Jack took over from Len Ashurst, he was standing at the side of the pitch in his overcoat, drinking a cup of tea and smoking a cigarette as he watched the players practising free-kicks. I kept rolling the ball across for David Grant to hit it over the defensive wall and past Bob Bolder in goal.

Unfortunately, David kept missing the target, and I'm saying: "Come on, Granty, hit the ruddy target, the Gaffer's watching," when I see a sudden movement on the touchline, and Jack's shouting across: "Hang on a minute!"

Jack takes his overcoat off, sticks his cup on the ground, places his fag-end on the edge of the saucer, and strides across the pitch.

"Now," he says, "Play the free-kick to me." So I rolled the ball across, and, without hesitation, Big Jack meets it first time and whacks it with his left foot. The ball flew round the wall and curled past Bolder straight into the top corner of the net.

Jack turned to David Grant and said: "That's what I want!" Then he walked off the pitch, put his overcoat back on, took a sip of his tea and finished smoking his fag!

Rodger Wylde, the former Wednesday centre-forward, recalls a trip to Charlton's North Yorkshire farm:
One night all the lads went out for a drink, and, when we left the pub, Chris Turner and me decided it was too early to turn in, so we set off the walk the three or four miles from the village where we were staying up to Jack's house.

We got up there and decided to play a trick, and, for some stupid reason, we let down the tyres on Jack's Range Rover and Ian Porterfield's car – Ian was staying with Jack.

The next day Jack and Ian, very angry and annoyed, came down and confronted the players. They said they knew it was one of us because a local farmer had reported seeing two young men in his headlights as he passed Jack's place.

I think Jack had an idea that me and Chris were involved, but he couldn't prove anything. We didn't confess – and I don't think Jack knows to this day who the culprits were!

Ian Mellor, who played in the 1979-80 promotion side, remembers how the enthusiasm of "Big Jack" extended to even getting the right results in five-a-side games at the training ground.

Jack Charlton liked his fishing, and here he shows off a catch to Ian Mellor, who, at the time, was in temporary digs at the Charlton house near Barnsley.

There was one occasion when I was playing in goal in a five-a-side and somebody drove the ball hard towards me and several of the lads claimed it had gone in. But, of course, I disputed it. When Jack asked: "Did that go in?" I said: "Definitely not," and thought that was the end of it.

The next morning, however, Jack brought the club chaplain in to see me, and I had to swear on the Bible to tell the truth about what happened. I can't remember now what I said!

Gary Megson, who played under Charlton in his first spell at Hillsborough, comments:
Jack was a larger-than-life character, and things were never dull in his period at the club. There are stories suggesting he didn't spend a lot of time at the ground, and was often away fishing, but it's a bit of a myth. Jack was very committed to getting Wednesday back into the old First Division – and I think we would have done it in 1981-82 when we finished one point behind Norwich but would have ended up above them had the Football League not changed the points system from two to three for a win.

David Barber, now Wednesday's head groundsman, remembers an incident from the late 1970s:
One day Jack asked us to put a heavy roller on the pitch because he thought it was a bit bobbly. The trouble about doing as he wanted is that using the heavy roller can cause big problems. Derek Blunkett, who was then in charge, said: "Okay, Jack," but once the manager had gone, he turned to me and said: "I'm not putting the heavy roller on, it'll seal everything up."

At the finish, Derek got an old spare barrier off the Kop, put a piece of wood through it with a bit of string on, and we dragged that across the pitch. Turned upside down, it made a sort of mini six-foot roller, and it weighed only a few pounds. In the conditions, it left the surface perfectly flat.

When we'd finished, Jack came to have a look. "Aye," he said, "that's a lot better, I told you the heavy roller would do the trick!"

Norma Lane, secretary to every Owls' manager since 1968, recalls when Jack Charlton visited her in hospital:
I had an operation in 1979 and was recovering in the ward when, quite unexpectedly, in walked Jack Charlton, Maurice Setters and Tony Toms. They stood there looking a bit sheepish, and Jack said: "We were going to bring you some flowers, but found we'd left the ground without any money. Sorry." Then he added: "To be honest, I was going to bring you something – your typewriter. I've so much mail on my desk, I don't know what to do with it."

I was discharged the following Monday, and hadn't been home long when there was a knock on the door. John Harris, the chief scout, and Malcolm Denton, were standing on the step. "Jack's sent your typewriter – he wonders if you can deal with a few letters to pass the time until you're ready to come back to work!"

Peter Pollitt captures something of Big Jack's special qualities with this recollection of what he witnessed at the club's training ground:

Jack Charlton's mother, Cissie, pictured with a group of Wednesday lads when they visited the Charlton farm in North Yorkshire.

Jack Charlton pictured with Andy McCulloch on the day the striker's 100-goal career milestone was celebrated.

Jack Charlton's Wednesday squad in 1981. Back row (left to right): McCulloch, Mellor, Redfern, Bolder, Cox, Pearson, Grant. Middle row: Blunstone (coach), Setters (coach), Holton, Smith, Megson, Oliver, Sterland, Matthewson, Blackhall, Peter Shirtliff, Toms (trainer), Jon Honey (physiotherapist). Front row: Taylor, Owen, Curran, Hornsby, Mirocevic, Jack Charlton (manager), Leman, Williamson, Paul Shirtliff, King, Bannister.

Every Tuesday a group of old-timers used to collect their pension from the Post Office and spend the rest of the morning watching Wednesday in training. Most of them seldom saw a League match, perhaps because they couldn't afford it, or maybe because they were at an age when they wanted to avoid big crowds. But they loved their football, and watching these training sessions and meeting Jack Charlton was the highlight of their week. They wouldn't miss it for the world.

They knew Jack always made a point of going across to talk to them at the end of the session. They also knew his first words would invariably be: "Who's got a fag to spare?" Over the weeks, they shared the "honour" of producing a cigarette for the great man – and there was always a rush among the smokers to offer him a light.

I don't think Jack ever said anything to them that was really important or enlightening, but he had that ability to make them feel ten-feet tall.

James McKenna – from football to *A Touch Of Frost*

James McKenna was an Owls apprentice who turned to acting after dreams of becoming a professional footballer were dashed when Wednesday released him at the age of 18 in 1971. Now a regular in ITV's A Touch Of Frost *and the C4 soap*

Hollyoaks, *he looks back without regrets and says his Hillsborough years taught him principles which have stood him in good stead in the world of drama.*

One of the highlights of my early months as a Wednesday apprentice was a week in September 1969 when Sir Alf Ramsey, the England manager, brought some of his top internationals to Hillsborough for training. They were preparing for a Football League XI match against the League of Ireland at Oakwell, and, as the Wednesday first team was away playing in a League Cup game at Bournemouth, the young lads at the club were left to train with and look after the England boys as if they were our own professionals.

It was a marvellous experience, the sort you never forget. I suppose you could say it's the kind of thing certain to inspire a youngster to follow in the footsteps of those famous stars like Mike Summerbee, Francis Lee, Peter Bonetti, etc. Of course, I hoped I would emulate them, but, unfortunately, it wasn't to be.

Yet, if I was disappointed at the time I realised I wasn't going to make the grade, it was probably the best thing that happened to me. I had always hankered after doing what I'm doing now, and, had I gone on to spend ten or 15 years in football, by the time I finished playing it would have been too late for me to turn to acting. The way things

worked out, I've had two careers which most people can only dream about, and, if the football didn't last, those two years with Wednesday gave me self-discipline and a set of principles for which I have always been grateful.

Strange as it might seem, the parallel between the two professions are uncanny. There is so much that is the same whether you are preparing for a performance on the stage or on a football pitch: the training, rehearsals, the nerves before the kick-off or the curtain. It's all about work and dedication. Moreover, physical and mental fitness is so important. I still train five days a week and run 40 miles a week, and, wherever my work takes me in the world, I can always find an hour a day for exercise.

The things I remember about my time with Wednesday include chief scout Fred Scott inviting me down after seeing me play for Scotland Boys; travelling to Sheffield at the start of my apprenticeship on the same train as Tommy Craig, who had just moved from Aberdeen; and meeting coaches Ron Staniforth, Tommy McAnearney and Albert Broadbent, who talked about the importance of good habits and made such a big impression on me.

Albert Broadbent was a great character and a remarkable man, and I was especially sorry when he left. I missed him. George McCabe took over, but for me he never had the same influence. Things didn't work out as I wanted, and a back injury hampered my progress, but I wouldn't swap the time I had at Hillsborough for anything.

When I wasn't offered professional terms, it was a blow made all the harder to take because, at around the same time, my dad died. I had already met Beverley, who later became my wife, so I chose to stay in Sheffield. Then, once I was over the initial shock of being finished by Wednesday, I had a driving job and worked as an Izal rep before I got my head together and saw what had happened was meant to be.

I began to pick up the threads of what I really wanted to do, realising that, if I didn't give acting a go at that point in my life, I might always regret it. I didn't want to get to 40 and wonder what might have been, and knew that within six months of going to drama school I'd know if I had the potential. If

I hadn't got what it took, I could walk away and say at least I tried. I tried – and it worked!

Acting has given me a good living, and, if my career has meant I don't get much chance to see a lot of football, I often think about those years at Hillsborough, and especially recall some of the lads who were my pals – like Jimmy Mullen, Gordon Byron and Danny Cameron. Danny and I had a wonderful introduction to Sheffield hospitality when we were put into digs at Mrs Richardson's house in Grenoside.

An amusing coincidence occurred a few years ago while we were making the film *When Saturday Comes*, which starred Sean Bean and is set in Sheffield. I played the part of the team-manager, whose name, by one of those strange twists of fate, was George McCabe. Mind you, I put more of Ron Atkinson and Kenny Dalglish into the role! And at least when it came to the part of the script where I had to give the players a half-time rollicking, I could draw on personal experience. In fact, I was encouraged to re-write the scene – and doing so evoked a few memories of when football was my stage and I had been on the receiving end in a dressing room!

Eric Taylor, the Wednesday manager, seen here with referee Arthur Ellis following a pitch inspection at Hillsborough in 1956.

More Memories

In the early post-war era, Wednesday had a groundsman called Abel Garnett, who was sacked because he built a caravan-trailer in between doing his job.

In those days, staff working on the North Stand side of the ground seldom ventured across to the offices, and, by the same token, few people employed in the South Stand went over to the other side. However, Eric Taylor, the secretary, made a point of keeping an eye on things with regular spot checks. And one day he was astonished to see an almost-completed caravan under the back of the North Stand.

He asked Jim Smith, the joiner, who the caravan belonged to, and, ultimately discovering it was the work of Abel, said: "If he's been building himself a second home in the club's time, he can go and live in it – and take his cards with him!"

When Wednesday went on tour to Switzerland in the early 1950s, a young player who had never been abroad before arrived at breakfast one morning wearing a puzzled look.

"I don't know what's up with the toilet," he said, "but I can't flush away what I've done."

A senior colleague advised him to ask the hotel manager to look into the problem. He did, and later reported that the manager had said: "There's no wonder it won't flush. It's not a toilet, it's a bidet!"

* * * * * * * * * *

Joe Ashton, the Labour MP and former Sheffield City Councillor who has been an Owls director since 1990, likes to tell a tale about going on parade for the first time after starting his National Service. He says: "I was asked my religion, and when I said I was a Wednesdayite I was told to line up with the Other Denominations. For a few

days this meant I was excused church parades, but then someone realised the object of my worship was a football club!"

* * * * * * * * * *

A number of former Owls apprentices have mentioned the initiation rituals which were once a feature in the lives of every would-be professional at Hillsborough.

Some, like Dave Cusack, recalled the "cold-tub treatment" and the shaving and blacking of the groin area of a lad's anatomy ahead of being tied to barriers on the Kop and left for 20 minutes. Peter Fox remembered how new boys would be stripped naked and tied to a medical bench before being carried from the dressing room and placed in the centre-circle – then the female staff from the laundry and offices would be invited out to enjoy the spectacle!

Steve Eaton, a Merseyside product whose career as a Wednesday apprentice lasted only a few months in 1976, has never forgotten how, when attempting to escape being caught for the initiation ceremony, he ran so hard at an exit door he banged his head and needed two stitches in a deep cut.

Steve, who later played with Tranmere, Northwich Victoria and Telford, and is now a referee in the North-West Counties League and a Pontins League linesman, said: "I learned the hard way that the door was locked, but, despite my discomfort, I still had to go through the ceremony. With the stitches in my head, and urgently in need of a shower to remove the blacking, I thought I might be excused training that day – but I wasn't!"

The initiation ceremonies were banned after an incident in which one new apprentice was stripped and left on public display on a bench in the car park. Most of the people passing on their way to the ticket office were amused, but one woman was so shocked she lodged a formal complaint with the club's management. It was the end of an era!

* * * * * * * * * *

David Ford is one of several players who have mentioned the many foreign tours which are such an enjoyable part of a professional footballer's life.

Ford, a member of the 1966 FA Cup Final side, recalled one occasion when the Wednesday party arrived in Valencia to find a huge crowd of Spaniards outside their hotel. He said: "It was as if someone like the Beatles or, as we might say today, the Spice Girls were expected – and we were flattered that so many people had come just to welcome us to Spain.

"Only later did we discover the crowd was waiting for the famous matador El Cordobis, who was in town for a bull fight. In fact, after we had played our scheduled match that night, we got back to the hotel to find El Cordobis in the foyer, and he was plainly not in a very good temper. It seemed he'd been booed for failing to kill off the bull. One of our lads said someone should tell him you can't win them all!"

* * * * * * * * * *

There was another occasion in the 1960s when Wednesday went to Singapore, and, on coming out of the

Eric Taylor (left) and Derek Dooley outside the old main entrance at the time of Dooley's appointment as manager in 1971.

famous Raffles Hotel on the first morning, Peter Eustace, Wilf Smith and David Ford each hired a rickshaw. The trio offered the boys in charge of the rickshaws an extra cash prize for the one who got his passenger to the end of the street first. All the players remember 30 years later is the race caused havoc on the busiest and most crowded thoroughfare in town.

* * * * * * * * * *

Ian Branfoot is another player with fond memories of overseas trips. He comments: "I had a marvellous time in my first two years with Wednesday, what with the 1966 Cup Final and a string of foreign trips to places like Hong Kong, Singapore, Austria, Mexico and America. We had a lot of fun in between the football.

"One year we played in Mexico City, and, as John Ritchie had been injured in the match, manager Alan Brown stayed behind to visit John in hospital, so we went on to Acapulco for three days in the charge of Jack Marshall.

"It was while in Acapulco that I got arrested for driving a hired jeep the wrong way down a dual carriageway! To

be honest, I don't think it was my fault because there was a barrier preventing us from entering the road on the other side.

"Anyway, this policeman suddenly appeared on a motor bike, and, after telling us what we were doing wrong, he said we could either pay a small fine there and then or a larger one if we chose to go before a magistrate. As there was no way we wanted Alan Brown to learn we'd been in court, we said we'd pay up.

"Unfortunately, we didn't have enough cash with us, so me, Jack Whitham and Sam Ellis went back to the hotel to get the money – and we left poor old Colin Symm as a hostage to ensure we wouldn't run off!

"We never did have to explain what happened to Alan Brown, although, if I remember, that was the trip when we couldn't tell him the true reason why Peter Wicks had lost his false teeth. That had happened while we were out at a night club, but I had to tell Alan I'd knocked Peter's teeth out in a fight. He said he still couldn't understand why we'd not been able to find them afterwards!"

WEDNESDAY EVERY DAY OF THE WEEK

Graham Birks, a retired brewery sales manager who was on Wednesday's books from 1958 to 1964 but made the bulk of his 250 League appearances with Peterborough, Southend and Chester, remembers that when he went to Northern Nigeria with the Owls, he witnessed an amusing incident which a platoon of Nigerian soldiers didn't exactly regard as funny.

Birks recalls: "We were relaxing by a swimming pool in the army training camp which was our base when, suddenly, Alan Finney appeared with Derek Wilkinson's suit, shirt and underclothes – and he promptly threw them in the water.

"Derek, being the sort of lad who could laugh at anything, was quite undismayed, but he warned Finney he would get his revenge. Sure enough, less than half-an-hour later, Derek emerged from the changing room with a pile of clothes which were soon floating in the pool.

"Unfortunately, what Derek had thought were the lads' clothes turned out to belong to the Nigerian soldiers. He was horrified when the players emerged from the changing room all smartly dressed and realised the clothes in the pool had been taken from the wrong dressing room!"

* * * * * * * * * *

George McCabe tells the story of how, following the arrival of Roy Coyle from Glentoran in 1972, the Irish midfielder was puzzled to find himself being called "Bagga".

Said George: "He asked me about it, and I told him it was a nickname which you had to be a Sheffielder to appreciate. I explained that, in these parts, coal was often pronounced to sound like coil or Coyle!"

* * * * * * * * * *

Lily Shelton, the long-serving cleaner who retired in 1997 after 45 years on the full-time staff, tells the story of how she once inadvertently removed all the vital fingerprint evidence following a burglary at the ground.

"I went in one morning and was taken aback to see all this white stuff on the doors by the main entrance. I thought it was some workmen who had come in with dirty hands, and, as nobody said anything, I hurriedly got a duster and started removing the offending marks.

"Then this policeman came along and asked what I thought I was doing. I said that somebody had put white stuff all over the door and that it looked a mess, and he said: 'Yes, it's what we use to highlight the fingerprints. Didn't you know, there's been a burglary?'

"Apparently, the thieves had broken in during the night and blown open an old iron safe. 'Nobody told me,' I said. To add insult to injury, the policeman insisted I had to have my own fingerprints recorded, just like a criminal. Mine were the only prints left on the door I'd cleaned!"

* * * * * * * * * *

George McCabe, Wednesday's Youth Officer from 1970, had many successes in recruiting some outstanding schoolboys who went on to play in Wednesday's first team. However, he recalls that the best young player he ever signed, Kevin Spacie, never made the grade and walked out before his career had properly started.

Said George: "Kevin was a wonderful prospect whom we spotted playing with Chesterfield Boys, and, from the age of 11 up to him leaving school at 15, I had an arrangement with his parents whereby he spent every school holiday living with me and my wife, so I could take him to the ground for training and keep an eye on him.

"We knew Arsenal and Manchester United wanted him, but at 15 in 1972 he became a Wednesday apprentice, and, by the time he signed professional forms on his 18th birthday, he was a regular in the Reserves – a boy with the ability to go right to the top. Sadly, four months later he quite literally turned his back on the game.

"One day after he'd failed to report for training, I went to see him and found him working under a car outside his home. He remained under the vehicle all the time I was there and when I asked him why he hadn't turned up, he muttered something about not being able to live on the money he was earning at the time.

"I said well I've come to take you to the ground, and we'll discuss the matter there. But he said I'd have to hang on until he was able to break off from the work he was doing on the car. I told him he wasn't going to tell me to hang on – I was leaving now, preferably with him, but if I left alone, it would be the end of the story.

"He made no attempt to come from under the car, so I said cheerio and, drove alone to Hillsborough. Soon afterwards, we cancelled his contract, and, though the club retained his registration for a while and several attempts were made later to persuade him to resume his football career, Kevin was lost to the game.

"I haven't seen him since, and I often wonder what might have been if only he had stayed with us."

* * * * * * * * * *

Ian Mellor, who was with Wednesday from 1979 to 1982, comments: "All the players from my time at the club will remember the cafe we used to visit on Middlewood Road after training. Hazel and Glenys, who ran it, liked to chat with the lads, and I recall they invariably found that while they were talking the strings of their aprons had been tied to the chairs they were sitting on. This prevented them getting up quickly when called to serve a customer. It's a trivial memory, but these things amused us in those days!"

* * * * * * * * * *

Howard Wilkinson recalls that, having been an Owls fan from childhood and then a Wednesday professional in the early 1960s, it was a great moment in his life when he succeeded Jack Charlton as the club's manager in 1984 – and he savoured the occasion when he took his 12-year-old son Damian to the ground for the first time.

He said: "When we got to Hillsborough, Damian wasn't too bothered about touring the stadium – he was just very impatient to see my office, and I was pumped with pride at the thought of him wanting to see the place where his Dad was going to make so many important decisions.

"Once inside, he asked: 'Is that the manager's chair?' I said it was, and he said: 'Can I sit in it?' Then he beamed as he swivelled the chair and soaked up the feeling of being in the seat of power.

"I smiled when he remarked: 'I can't wait to get to school on Monday.' But he brought me down to earth as he added: 'My pals will all be very jealous when I tell them I've sat in Jack Charlton's chair!'"

Part Four – Matches, Goals and Heroes

Matches to Remember

Five Goals for Derek Dooley
Owls v Notts County
3 November 1951

Derek Dooley is best remembered as the red-haired scoring giant who shot to fame with a record tally of 47 goals in 1951-52, then saw his playing career shattered at the age of 23 in February 1953 when surgeons had to amputate his right leg, which had become infected after he broke it in a collision with Preston goalkeeper George Thompson at Deepdale. Here Dooley recalls an earlier and happier memory – the day he scored five goals and started to believe his place in Wednesday's team was finally secure with a haul of 22 in nine successive matches:

I shall always remember the Notts County match as marking a turning point in my playing career at Hillsborough. To score five goals in a game, and do so against Leon Leuty, who was then one of the best centre-halves in the country, was beyond my wildest dreams – but what really mattered was it settled me down and boosted my belief that I could make my first-team place permanent.

It was really a case of third time lucky. I hadn't had much joy on my League debut against Preston in March 1950, nor on my second outing at Charlton in January 1951, but, in the autumn of 1951, opportunity knocked again – and I was desperate to make this chance count. However, though I started off with a double against Barnsley in early October and earned the first decent senior run I'd been given, one goal in the next three games didn't exactly remove my fears of being

dropped. I still tended to look at the Reserves' line-up first when the teamsheets were pinned up in the dressing room on Fridays!

The day we played Notts County was wet and miserable, but it proved a golden afternoon for me, though, in fact, I wasted a chance in the first minute and, apart from when Jackie Sewell shot us in front, the first 45 minutes were frustrating.

The transformation started just after half-time when we were kicking towards the Kop end – and my five goals came in the space of 32 marvellous minutes. I think three were shots, one was a header, and the other was chested in. I also had an effort disallowed for offside. Meanwhile, at the other end of the pitch, the legendary Tommy Lawton didn't get a look-in!

After the game, incidentally, I learned that Roy Smith, the Notts goalkeeper, took a bit of stick from his team-mates because, as an old Wednesday man, he had been telling them

This picture of Derek Dooley was taken in the public practice match ahead of the campaign in which he shot to fame with 47 goals, including five against Notts County.

How the *Green 'Un* marked Dooley's five-goal feat.

I was unlikely to prove much of a threat!

Of course, about four years earlier my old pal Jimmy Dailey had notched five in a League game but it hadn't prevented his Wednesday career from falling away soon afterwards, so I knew I couldn't rest on my laurels. Yet I knew the experience would give me the confidence and determination to keep scoring, and, in fact, those goals inspired a run during which I bagged 22 in nine successive matches.

I finished up with 47 to claim the club record for a season which Jimmy Trotter had held for 25 years – and the local paper suggested the council should have a Dooley statue cast to replace Vulcan on the top of the Town Hall!

I always enjoyed kicking towards the Kop, and recall when I hit four goals against Everton just before Christmas, they were all at that end in the second half – the irony being I had missed two great first-half chances when I broke away and had only the goalkeeper to beat. I know I was feeling a bit upset about those misses as I sat in the dressing room at half-time, but Alan Brown, the coach, told me to concentrate on believing I could still make amends. I did, and it paid off.

When I think of the other occasion when I scored four, against Hull City in March, I am always reminded of our veteran Welsh wing-half, Duggie Witcomb. That day he was making his first appearance for four months, and, before we went out, he told me: "Get

cracking today, Derek, because I want us to win so I can be sure of staying in the team."

Noticing I was looking a bit pale, he asked what was wrong, and, when I replied: "Oh, I'm always very nervous before a game," he winked and whispered: "Shall I tell you something?" I thought he was going to offer me a cure for my problem, but he simply said: "I've played around 300 games and I still get nervous – when you stop being nervous you'll know it's time to pack up!"

Later, as we trooped off having won 6-0, he said: "You'll not be packing up yet, lad."

Too much Christmas goodwill
Owls v West Bromwich Albion
26 December 1952

Redfern Froggatt recalls a festive treat when Wednesday gifted their opponents the points:

This was a game in which we scored seven goals, led three times and were 4-2 up just after half-time, yet ended up losing 5-4 with three minutes left. It was an astonishing match which delighted a crowd of nearly 60,000 spectators.

I think Dennis Woodhead put us in front, West Brom equalised, and then I got one to make it 2-1 – and we'd only been playing about six minutes!

I remember the game wasn't 20 minutes old when Norman Curtis turned a shot that was going wide into our net to make the score 2-2, and later, when we were two goals in front with another Woodhead goal and one from Derek

Dooley, we again shot ourselves in the foot when Eddie Gannon managed to back-head a centre past Ron Capewell.

West Brom pulled level ten minutes from the end, and then snatched the points with a winner after 87 minutes. Both those goals were officially credited to Albion men, but I'm sure Mick Kenny put one in to become the third Wednesday player to score an own goal. I know it was Christmas, but it did rather seem we were taking the gifts a bit too far!

Cup triumph over the Blades
Owls v Sheffield United
13 January 1954

Ivor Seemley, a full-back who spent around ten years on Wednesday's books in the early post-war era, made all but five of his 23 senior appearances for the Owls in the 1953-54 season when the club's best FA Cup run since 1935 featured a famous third-round triumph in a Sheffield derby, which he recalls here:

That 1954 Cup run was the highlight of my career, and I remember it as a year when we seemed to make a habit of drawing at home and winning the replay. Three times we won at the second attempt, and our 3-1 victory against Sheffield United in a replay at Bramall Lane was especially satisfying because nobody expected us to win – yet we succeeded after coming from behind and despite having "Mick" Kenny sent off.

A particularly vivid memory about that January day is something which will probably seem quite novel to modern supporters familiar with professional footballers who earn thousands of pounds a week, drive expensive motor cars, and would never dream of using public transport. In my time, unfortunately, few players could afford to own a car, and most of us never gave it a thought.

After the game, I walked all the way from Bramall Lane to Bridge Street bus station. You can't imagine a player doing that today! Anyway, I caught a Shiregreen via Sicey Avenue bus (Route 151), and went home for a quiet evening with my wife at our house in Gregg House Road. I remember standing in the bus queue and listening to people talking excitedly about the match, but, not surprisingly, nobody recognised me as Wednesday's left-back.

In fact, it was only my fourth senior game, and I was elated just to be a part of it. At 24 I had been connected with the club from around 1944, being a full-time professional for nearly five years since finishing my National Service in the RAF. But I had made my first-team debut less than three weeks earlier – on 26 December 1953.

My family were all dyed-in-the-wool Wednesdayites, and it was a thrill simply being on the playing staff. My grandfather had often told me tales such as how he walked from Sheffield to Chesterfield to watch the Owls play at Saltergate when he was a youngster; and he and my father frequently recalled having eaten their Christmas dinner in the railway station buffet at Bradford when they went to watch Wednesday win 4-1 at Valley Parade on Christmas Day in the 1925-26 promotion season.

Grandfather took me to Hillsborough for the first time in September 1938 when I was nine years old. We stood on the terrace in front of the old North Stand and saw Wednesday beat Blackburn Rovers 3-0 with goals from Jackie Robinson, Charlie Napier and Bill Fallon. Today, 60 years later, I'm still a staunch Owls' fan and a regular in the South Stand.

It was because my father knew Sam Powell, the Wednesday trainer, that, at the age of 15, while still at Firth Park Grammar School, I was invited for training at Hillsborough on two evenings a week, and, when I started playing in the "A" team and then the Reserves, all the family were proud and pleased.

My enthusiasm knew no bounds, and Derek Dooley and I were so keen to get to the ground every day that we always caught the earliest possible Outer Circle (No.2) bus from Hatfield House Lane. Mind you, an added attraction was being able to get an hour on the snooker table before training – though neither of us was exactly a Joe Davis!

There was many a Christmas Day when, because there was no public transport, I walked to the ground from Shiregreen, played in an "A" team or reserve game, and then walked back. It

was never a hardship. You didn't think about it, and it's only in retrospect that it seems we lived in a very different world then!

Fortunately, there was a bus service operating on that Boxing Day in 1953 when I was unexpectedly called up for my first-team debut. I had gone down to the ground early expecting to travel with the Reserves, but ended up playing in the home First Division game with Manchester United.

I played in 18 of the remaining 25 games that season. Eight of those matches were in the run which took us to within one step of Wembley, and winning at Bramall Lane, Saltergate and Burnden Park were the high points of the most memorable few months of my Wednesday career.

Sadly, I think I only played about eight more times in the first team after Preston beat us in the Maine Road semi-final, and a year later I joined Stockport and later played with Chesterfield before ending my playing days at Sutton Town in the Midland League.

They called it "Quixall's Match"
Owls v Chesterfield
3 February 1954

Albert Quixall enjoyed one of his best seasons with Wednesday in the 1953-54 campaign when he gained his first England caps and helped Wednesday reach the FA Cup semi-final. He especially remembers the fourth-round replay at Saltergate:

I always enjoyed my football, but the season when we got to the semi-final and lost to Preston at Maine Road was one that gave me particular pleasure, I suppose because I was in good form. The only disappointment was that, having got so close to Wembley, we were finally beaten by a Preston side who, to put it kindly, were physically superior.

People often mention the midweek replay against Chesterfield on an afternoon in early February, when we won 4-2 and the newspapers called it "Quixall's match". I can only remember it as one of those days when everything I tried came off, especially in the last half-hour.

One thing I do recall is that Chesterfield's team included George Brown, who, like me was an old Meynell Road boy who had gone on to play for England Boys. George was an outstanding player at school, and he was at Liverpool before going on to Chesterfield.

In the first game, at Hillsborough, we had drawn 0-0. In the replay, I think Jack Shaw put us in front, but then Chesterfield equalised before half-time and went in front around the hour-mark. Jack Shaw pulled us level with about 20 minutes left, and Jackie Sewell and Dennis Woodhead clinched it for us with a couple of late goals. That win booked us a home tie with Everton.

Six of the best for watching Wednesday!
Owls v Everton
20 February 1954

Albert Clayton never forget the day in February 1954 when, with his newly-discovered passion for the Owls at a peak, he and his pals went to Hillsborough hoping to watch their favourites face Everton in the FA Cup and ended up finding an alternative means of catching up on the drama:

That was the day Wednesday beat Everton 3-1 in the fifth round with goals from Jack Shaw, Jackie Sewell and Dennis Woodhead, but me and my mates didn't see a thing. The only time we saw the ball was when it was kicked into the air!

It was a lovely sunny afternoon, and, when we started out we thought there would be plenty of room, but folks warned us that so many people wanted to be there, we'd be lucky to get into the ground. Indeed, when we reached Hillsborough, we were staggered to find queues a mile long everywhere you looked.

Anyway, we did get in, but most of the 65,000 people present had arrived before us, all the best places had been taken, and it seemed impossible to find anywhere to stand. Having tried and failed to find a decent vantage point at the Leppings Lane corner near the North Stand, we finally ended up on the Kop. But it was hopeless because we just couldn't see the pitch.

We were all a bit miffed at missing a famous victory, but then we discovered an unexpected silver lining. We learned that extended highlights of the match were being shown the following week at the News Theatre in Fitzalan Square. So we wagged it off school and went to watch the newsreel.

It was great. The programme was continuous, and I think we saw the extracts from the game at least five times. Unfortunately, the next morning our teacher didn't believe us when we said it was purely coincidental that so many of us had all been ill and unfit for school the previous afternoon. He insisted on caning us, which was painful. But it was worth it!

When the Doc caused the damage!
Owls v Preston North End
27 March 1954

Jackie Sewell has painful memories of the FA Cup semi-final in which Wednesday were beaten 2-0 by Preston North End at Maine Road, Manchester, on 27 March 1954:

We went into the 1954 semi-final believing that the only Preston man who was any real threat to us was Tom Finney, the England winger, but, at the finish, I was convinced the player who had the most influence on the game was Scottish wing-half Tommy Docherty. He certainly ruined the day for me, and I have always felt that the injury I suffered in that Cup-tie damaged my international career.

Docherty was giving me and Albert Quixall some terrible stick all afternoon, but the worst moment came in the second half, when I was just shaping up for a shot and suddenly my feet were whipped from under me. Docherty took my legs while completely ignoring the ball, and I ended up being carried off with a suspected broken right leg.

Fortunately, the leg wasn't broken, but the knee ligaments were badly damaged. Of course, there were no substitutes then, and, despite the pain and discomfort, I had to go back on and play as what we used to call "a passenger". But there was no way I could run around, and I don't suppose playing on did the knee much good.

Dave McIntosh, the Wednesday goalkeeper, is beaten by a shot from Preston's Jimmy Baxter, with Norman Curtis looking on.

McIntosh dives to make a save, with Gannon, Finney, Butler and Curtis looking on.

Preston won with a Charlie Wayman goal on the hour and another from Jimmy Baxter four minutes from the end, but I often think it might have been a different story.

I think I missed the next six games and was out for a month. I returned to the team for the last match of the season, at Cardiff, and was rather relieved to be able to play for the Football League against the Scottish League at Stamford Bridge at the end of April. The point was, I had been chosen to go on tour with England, and I probably rushed back sooner than I should.

Unfortunately, when England went to Budapest, nobody played well, and Hungary beat us 7-1. I could claim that, thanks to Mr Docherty, I wasn't as fit as I would have liked to have been. I never got called up again.

When Eckersley paid the penalty
Owls v Blackburn Rovers
27 December 1955

Keith Littlewood remembers a 5-1 win on a day Wednesday's goalkeeper was left smiling despite a reprimand from the referee:

An amusing incident I recall from this game occurred in the second half when Wednesday were leading 4-1 and Blackburn were awarded a penalty. Bill

Eckersley, the Rovers full-back, took it, but, as he stepped up, for some reason Les Williams, the Owls goalkeeper, started to advance from his goal-line.

The referee, Kevin Howley, ordered a re-take, first explaining to Williams that the laws of the game stated the goal-keeper had to remain on his line. I can't recall what happened with Eckersley's first kick, but his second one went wide.

It was the second penalty miss of the game because Roy Shiner had missed one for Wednesday. But we won 5-1.

The day they couldn't stop Broadbent
Owls v San Lorenzo
26 January 1956

Keith Littlewood has a special reason for recalling this friendly match – a hero called Albert Broadbent:

I remember this match not because we won 9-0 or the fact that both Alan Finney and Roy Shiner scored hat-tricks, but as a game in which Albert Broadbent was applauded off the field. Albert came to Hillsborough from Notts County, which might be why Wednesdayites used to sing the popular song of the day *Robin Hood* when he was in full flight.

He was a big lad, and that day in the friendly against the Argentinians he was absolutely unstoppable.

First game after Munich
Manchester United v Owls
19 February 1958

This famous FA Cup fifth-round tie, played in front of over 59,860 spectators at Old Trafford on an unforgettable Wednesday evening in February 1958, was one of the most emotional events in post-war soccer history, coming less than two weeks after the Munich air disaster which cost the lives of eight Manchester United players, four club officials and eight newspapermen. Wednesday lost 3-0, and here some of those who watched and played in that game recall their memories of an occasion they will never forget. Albert Clayton, a long-time Wednesday fan, has a vivid recollection of the day:

It just happened to be the first time I travelled away to watch Wednesday. I was 15 and had just started work as an apprentice to my father in the motor trimming trade. Even without the circumstances of the Munich disaster, it was a whole new experience for me. I went with a pal called Ken Griffiths, a terrific lad who always had a smile on his face. I remember on the train to Manchester that day in 1958 he kept laughing in between singing a new Buddy Holly hit *Peggy Sue*, which he said was going to go top of the charts within a week.

We'd arranged to meet at the top of Victoria Station Approach, and when I got there Ken, who was already waiting for me, took me by surprise because he was wearing a red and-white rosette trimmed in black by way of tribute to Manchester United.

He explained: "United need a bit of support."

I replied: "Need a bit of support? Have you heard everybody talking? Wednesday are going to be so over-whelmed by the sympathy everybody's feeling for United, it's us who'll need support!"

To be honest, I cursed Ken up hill and down dale all the way to Manchester, and, it being a normal service train packed with business people going home, some of the other passengers weren't impressed with me.

I didn't mean anything wrong. Once you got to Old Trafford and experienced that eerie atmosphere, you felt enormously sorry for United. What had happened was terrible. But I still wanted Wednesday to win and was more than a bit disappointed Ken didn't feel the same way.

In truth, Wednesday never had a chance. There were nearly 60,000 in the ground, and, with the vast majority willing United to win, I've never seen so many Wednesdayites so intimidated. A lot told me later that they felt they daren't even shout: "Come on the Owls". Some never muttered a word all through the game. I don't think the players really felt they should put them-selves about, either, although I'm sure some of them will dispute that.

About three or four minutes into the game, a ball went into the goalmouth at the Stretford End, where we were stand-ing, and Peter Johnson, our stand-in

centre-forward, headed it down and towards the net. It was going in. The bounce had beaten Harry Gregg, the goalkeeper – then, suddenly, Bill Foulke came from nowhere and hooked the ball straight into the terrace. The thing I'll never forget is that, when the ball beat Gregg and looked to be going in, there was a scream from all the women in the crowd like I'd never heard before at a football match. The floodlights somehow enhanced a feeling that was more ghostly than human.

Then, after about half-an-hour, United scored direct from a corner, and I hope Brian Ryalls, our goalkeeper that night, will forgive me for saying I still don't know if he pushed it in on pur-pose or because the atmosphere affected his nerves and judgement. He may have been caught napping because the defender at the front post didn't seem to react when the ball came over.

Anyway, we didn't need to wait for two more home goals in the second half to know we were going to lose.

A pal of mine from Frecheville, Mark Pearson, made his debut for United that night, and I remember being upset about his treatment of Redfern Froggatt in one incident. I thought Froggatt deserved more respect, but I suppose the only thing that mattered to most people was that United won.

Frank Ronksley, another long-time Owls' fan, also remembers that emotional night at Old Trafford.

I managed to get a two-bob (10p) ticket for that match, and, naturally, they were like gold. Before the game, we were in the Warwick pub when this chap came up to me and said: "I'll give you 15 for it."

I replied: "I'm not letting this go for 15 bob."

He said: "No, I mean £15."

I was staggered. At the time, it was nearly four weeks' wages. But I didn't hesitate and told him: "Sorry, pal, this is one match I'm not going to miss."

Brian Ryalls, Wednesday's goalkeeper on that February night at Old Trafford, recalls:

To say it was a very emotional night is an understatement, and I always remember that when we ran out before the game we were received in almost total silence. I don't think anybody in that crowd wanted us to win. We knew we were there just to make up the numbers, and I don't think any of us really wanted to play.

It is fair to suggest we had no chance, although I've sometimes thought that if we'd scored first we might have gone on to win. It would have been interesting to see what the reaction would have been if that had happened, but perhaps even if we'd got an early goal, Manchester United would still have come out on top. They played out of their skins that night, and you always felt there could be only one result.

People have mentioned the goal that Brennan scored direct from a corner. All I can remember is that Jack Martin, our right-back, was on the near post, and, when the ball came over, I thought he was going to go for it. But he didn't, and I ended up going for it late. I think the crowd blew it in!

I played only four more times in the first team, and in the following month Wednesday signed Ron Springett.

Jack Martin played in only three FA Cup-ties for the Owls. The second one just happened to be the trip to Old Trafford in 1958, and he comments:
I didn't think we played badly that night, but the emotion of the occasion gave Manchester United a great lift and we were always going to be up against it. I'll never forget the atmosphere, which was unique, but I don't remember much about travelling to the game, and my memory of a lot of the details is a bit vague.

I do know that Brennan, the United winger, scored direct from a corner-kick, and the ball swung in and went just inside the angle of the post and the crossbar. I was standing at the front post, and at first I thought Brian Ryalls, our goalkeeper, was going to come for it. I have a photograph which shows Brian stretching over me to try to reach it. I probably got in his way. I don't recall whether he got a hand to it or not. But the thing was that the ball came in very high and squeezed in at the very top corner of the goal where it was most difficult for both me and Brian to get to.

Ralph O'Donnell, Wednesday's centre-half, recalls:
An abiding memory of that night at Old Trafford is the shrillness of the crowd – the noise the spectators made was something I still find hard to describe. It was a shriek, a squeal …there was something feminine in the cry, and it wasn't the usual male-dominated sound that one then associated with big football match crowds. It served to emphasise that this was a long way from being an ordinary FA Cup-tie.

Peter Johnson, who had joined Wednesday as a full-back, was converted to centre-forward for the clash with Manchester United, and remembers:
The atmosphere was electric, and it was as though the crowd was putting 50,000 volts through every player – and the effect on every Wednesday lad was to be numbed by the emotion. I feel we could have been playing until now, 40 years later, and still wouldn't have won because everything was stacked against us. All the sympathy was with Manchester United, and we had neither sympathy or understanding.

We were on a hiding to nothing even before we kicked a ball. We were all shocked by what had happened at Munich, but it had reached a stage where the football had to resume. Life had to go on.

When we lined up in the tunnel ready to come out, I saw the referee, Alf Bond, had been crying, and, in fact, there were still tears running down his face. I thought then that we wouldn't get anything from him, and there is no doubt that Manchester United got away with a lot more that night than they would have done in any other circumstances.

I didn't begrudge them, but I remember an incident right at the start. Seconds after the kick-off, Mark Pearson, making his debut for United, kicked Froggatt. He didn't half whack him one. Even in those days it was worth a caution, or even a sending-off. But Mr Bond ignored it.

I played at centre-forward that night. I'm not a big lad, but I was always quick and busy. This high ball came across into the goalmouth and Harry Gregg, United's goalkeeper, caught it and pulled it to his chest. I knew I couldn't put in a challenge because I couldn't get into him shoulder to shoulder. But Harry, probably thinking I might hit him but making sure he got in first, flung himself at me shoulder-first, hitting me straight in the middle of the chest, and knocking me flat on my arse! In any other game, that would have been a penalty. But, again, there was no reaction.

Don't let anybody kid you that we had even a ghost of a chance that night.

Don McEvoy, the Wednesday captain, remembers how desperately he wanted to play in that 1958 FA Cup-tie, but, as he explains, it wasn't to be even though he was fit and available.
I made what proved to be my final first-team appearance for Wednesday against Chelsea four days before the FA Cup-tie at Old Trafford. Ahead of the game, I was having treatment for a knee strain, so I asked Eric Taylor if I could ease up on the training. But Eric and Jack Marshall, the coach, knew I was fit when the big day came.

The atmosphere on the Wednesday team bus on the way over the Pennines that day was the most sombre I can ever remember in all my time in football. There was no laughter, no joviality, just blank faces; and I sensed then that there were a few of our lads who didn't have the passion to go out that night and play to the best of their ability irrespective of what had happened in Munich.

That game was a tremendous occasion for some of our players, and, when we lost, that fact was just discarded in the euphoria of Manchester United winning. All the emotion and sympathy was with United. Nobody was interested in Wednesday. When we got to the ground, there were thousands of people around the entrance, but nobody was making any noise, nobody was thrusting autograph books in front of you. We just walked in, and nobody said a word.

Once inside, I said to Eric Taylor: "You're not going to play me, are you?" He replied: "No, I don't think I'd better risk you in a game like this."

I said: "A game like this is where you need me. I know Peter Swan is going to take my place permanently before long, because he's good enough and will get better. I know I'm on my way out, boss, but let me play."

I'm going cold just remembering this, it was such an emotional night. I got hold of Eric Taylor's arm and virtually dragged him into the middle of the pitch. There were 60,000 people in the ground, and there wasn't a sound of any sort. Eric and I stood on the centre spot, and if you dropped a pin you'd have heard it hit the turf.

There was no cheering until the ball was kicked to start the match, and, once the game was under way, it was quickly evident that we weren't going to win. There were six or seven lads in our side who shouldn't have been playing because they found the occasion too much.

When we were 2-0 down, I turned to Eric Taylor and said: "You've made a mistake, boss. You should have played me. I'm a senior player and it wouldn't have worried me at all playing against Manchester United today."

We were short of players who weren't worried about being in the first team to face Manchester after the disaster. Everybody was heartbroken about what had happened to those lads at Munich, and it was no disrespect to them to say we should have gone into that game really wanting to win it. I remember thinking that the Huddersfield team I played in would have won that game. They would have paid their respects, but, once the match was under way, they would have said we want to win it.

Tonic of victory over the Blades
Sheffield United v Owls
12 March 1960

Wednesday looked a fair bet to reach Wembley in 1960 when they beat Middlesbrough, Peterborough and Manchester United, then enjoyed some luck in defeating their Sheffield rivals in the Bramall Lane FA Cup quarter-final thanks to two Derek Wilkinson goals scored against the run of play. Frank Ronksley recalls:

I'm not one of those Wednesdayites who refuses to eat bacon because it's red and-white and reminds me of Sheffield United, and I'm certainly not one of those fans who won't be seen dead at United's ground even when our lads are playing there. In my view, when Wednesday enter the lion's den at Bramall Lane, it's every Owls' supporter's duty to be there to support them.

I always remember I felt very rough on the morning of the all-Sheffield sixth-round Cup-tie in 1960. When I woke up, I knew I'd caught that Asian 'flu that was going about, but I told my mother: "I've just got to get to that match." When I dressed, I put two shirts and a thick jumper over my pyjamas, and I wore my heaviest overcoat.

I trundled down Myrtle Road coughing and spluttering every step of the way, and, thinking it would warm me up, I called in at the Sheaf pub and had three pints of local ale. I felt very groggy as I stood behind the goal at the Bramall Lane end, but Derek Wilkinson's two goals made me feel better, even though I didn't have the energy to cheer.

I was in such a bad state, I collapsed halfway up Myrtle Road on the way home afterwards, and spent ten minutes sitting on the pavement trying to work out what day it was. I felt I was dying, honest, yet somehow I knew I'd survive because I had this warm glow inside – we'd beaten the Blades on their own mudheap, and I was sure we were bound to win the Cup that year!

Cheated so close to Wembley
Owls v Blackburn Rovers
26 March 1960

In the 1960 FA Cup semi-final the Owls faced Blackburn in front of 74,000 at Manchester City's ground. But it was a day when Wednesday's luck ran out and they lost 2-1, with Derek Dougan getting both Rovers' goals while John Fantham notched a late consolation for the men from Sheffield. Albert Clayton's memories of this match are no doubt typical of many supporters from that era:

We had a terrific side in 1960, well capable of winning the FA Cup, and they played unbelievably well at Maine Road in that semi-final. But the ball wouldn't go in the net for us. It was the biggest disappointment I experienced at a football match – bigger than some that came later because, at the time, I thought this was definitely our year.

As a schoolboy, I had discovered the magic and romance of the FA Cup when watching Newcastle triumph in those early Finals which were among the first screened on television. Frankly,

I wasn't bothered about Wednesday winning the League, I just wanted them to win the Cup.

I remember somebody predicting we'd beat Blackburn 4-1 in that 1960 semi-final, and it seemed a fair judgement. We not only had a good team, but, in that run, we'd had the kind of luck which makes you think your name is on the Cup.

In the previous rounds fortune had favoured us at Old Trafford, where we'd won with a Tom McAnearney penalty, and at Bramall Lane, where Wilkinson scored twice against the run of play. But our luck ran out with a vengeance at Maine Road. Dougan scored after ten minutes, but soon afterwards we looked to have pulled level when Alan Finney put the ball in the net.

When that one went in, I'm sure you could have heard the roar back in Sheffield. The din was unbelievable. Then it dawned on us that the referee, a Mr Williams from Nottingham, had disallowed it. Wilkinson, who was miles from the action, was alleged to be offside and interfering with play! I always thought we were cheated that day.

Wednesday hit seven at
Old Trafford
Manchester United v Owls
1 February 1961

This was the famous occasion when Wednesday thrashed Manchester United 7-2 at Old Trafford in an FA Cup fourth-round replay, with Keith Ellis bagging a hat-trick and John Fantham and Alan Finney both claiming doubles. Albert Clayton remembers it well:

We managed to get in before the gates were closed with nearly 65,000 packed in. Thousands were locked out. We were at the Warwick Road end, and we could look down on the less fortunate fans who couldn't gain admission. I've never seen so many people still outside a ground unable to get into a match. All through the game, those at the back were shouting to the fans outside how the game was progressing.

"Fantham's scored for Wednesday!" they called.

"Now it's 1-1."

"Wednesday have scored again!"

"It's 3-1 now!"

"It's 4-1!"

What a great night that was.

Anyhow, we came out at the end and made straight for a nearby pub where we knew Wednesdayites would gather. We were surprised to find some of the Hillsborough regulars already there, and obviously slightly intoxicated either by the result or the beer.

"How long have you been here?" we asked.

"How long have we been here …are you kidding? We couldn't get in the ground, so we stood outside, and when it got to 4-1 at half-time, we thought we might just as well start celebrating early. Anyway, what was the final result?"

Frank Ronksley recalls it as a night when pleasure was mixed with pain:

My pal Rod Slater was one of the thousands locked out that night, but me and "Railway" George Smith got in. Of course, we revelled in a magnificent Owls' victory, but we stood next to this elderly lady who kept hitting me and George with her umbrella. Every time we scored, she bashed us in turn, saying: "I don't like Sheffield Wednesday! And I don't like their fans either!"

I know we scored seven times because that was the number of bruises I went home with!

Never prouder of being a Wednesdayite
Owls v Tottenham Hotspur
13 April 1964

Supporter John Brodie recalls:
This was the first game Wednesday played after the newspaper revelations about the betting coup scandal involving three Owls players, and I remember it less for the fact that Derek Wilkinson scored twice in a 2-0 win as for the emotion of the occasion.

I'll never forget the absolute silence in which Eric Taylor, the general manager, addressed the crowd over the public address system at half-time. You could have heard a pin drop, and, somehow, you felt that every supporter in the ground was as heartbroken as Taylor himself.

The way the supporters rallied round the team that night was a superb expression of faith in the club, and, though what had happened was very upsetting, I was never prouder of being a Wednesdayite.

Baptism of fire for a youngster
Everton v Owls
9 January 1965

Andy Burgin, who is now caretaker at a private school in Blackburn, made over 300 appearances with four clubs between 1965 and 1976, but the former Sheffield Boys defender from Langsett Road school was limited to three senior outings with Wednesday, and has never forgotten his Owls debut at the age of 17 in a third-round FA Cup-tie at Goodison Park.

I got into the team at right-back because Brian Hill and Charlie Johnson were both injured, and I always remember that, as we travelled over to Everton on the team bus, Don Megson was giving me some encouragement. One of the things he said was: "If you make any mistakes, blame somebody else!"

Then, when we'd been playing about

Andy Burgin.

half-an-hour and the match was still at 0-0, I was just thinking how well I'd done to get into a good position to intercept a through pass when I went and put the ball into my own net! I recall turning to Meggie and shouting: "Who do I blame for that?"

I can smile about it now over 30 years later, but at the time it was a shattering experience to suffer such an ordeal in front of a 45,000 crowd. Not that any of the lads criticised me. Even Alan Brown, the manager, sympathised and said it could have happened to anybody. At the end of the day, we were unfortunate not to win, because goals from John Fantham and Johnny Quinn put us 2-1 up after about 65 minutes, and Everton only salvaged a replay with a Fred Pickering last-minute equaliser.

One thing I haven't forgotten about that afternoon is how our long-serving winger Alan Finney (he had made his senior debut two weeks before my fourth birthday!) went out of his way to look after me all through the game. But, of course, he couldn't help when that own-goal went in. One second I was attempting to put some pace on the ball to knock it towards the corner-flag, the next the ball somehow hit my heel and shot past Ron Springett.

I played in the replay four days later when, with over 50,000 in Hillsborough, we lost 3-0. The following weekend I made my Football League debut in another huge fixture, against Liverpool at Anfield. Alas, we lost 4-2.

Incidentally, I played only three times in the first team, and we had a different goalkeeper in each match. Roy McLaren stood in for Ron Springett in the Cup replay, and Peter Wicks, who was then still 16, made his debut at Anfield.

I never got another chance at senior level with Wednesday, and in 1967, after being given a free transfer, I played about ten games with Rotherham while waiting to join up with Detroit in America. When I returned to England, I started a run of about 250 games with Halifax and ended my League career at Blackburn in 1976 after two years at Ewood Park.

I settled in Blackburn, and today I don't see much football except on television, preferring to spend my Saturday afternoons fishing – a pastime I've pursued since I was a boy growing up in

Owlerton. But I have a lot of happy memories of my professional career, and will never forget the good times I had at Hillsborough with lads like Sam Ellis and my old Sheffield Boys team-mate Wilf Smith.

I still see Sam and we often reminisce about the old days. One story we invariably recall concerns a day when Sam's car was pinched from outside the cafe the players all used in Middlewood Road. When Sam first discovered it was missing, he thought some of the lads had pushed it back to the ground. That was a trick they sometimes played if you left your car unlocked.

He searched in vain for the vehicle for an hour, all the time insisting one of the lads had hidden it. Then he finally reported to the police that it was missing. It transpired someone had really nicked it and left it abandoned on some waste land opposite the Herries Road bus garage. Sam always kept his car locked after that!

A famous semi-final and other Cup memories
Owls v Chelsea
23 April 1966

This was the famous occasion when Wednesday defied the odds to register a memorable FA Cup semi-final triumph over Chelsea in the mud of Villa Park. Nobody gave them a chance against Tommy Docherty's star-studded side, and they were further handicapped when centre-half Vic Mobley suffered a serious injury in a clash with George Graham and had to play for an hour as a "passenger". But second-half goals from Graham Pugh and Jim McCalliog saw the Owls through.

Ian Branfoot, a defender then in his first season as a professional and destined to make 42 League and Cup appearances for the club between 1966 and 1969, was still ten days away from his Football League debut at the time of this epic semi-final victory. However, having joined the senior squad in special training at Lilleshall ahead of the big game, he remembers the mood in the Owls' camp:

When I went down to Sheffield from Gateshead at the age of 18, I loved everything about being a professional at Hillsborough, and what impressed me most was the great spirit in the dressing room. It was a wonderful environment in which to begin your career, and a memorable experience when my first season coincided with the club's run to Wembley.

Of course, I was never likely to be involved in the Cup team – but at least my boots were packed in the skip when the squad went off to the Final! Moreover, five days before the Wembley game with Everton, I made my debut in the First Division match against Burnley at Hillsborough.

The thing I remember about my debut was making the back-pass which led to Les Latcham scoring for Burnley. When I played the ball, the pass was 60-40 in goalkeeper Ron Springett's favour, but suddenly the balance swung to the striker's advantage. I was a bit upset about it, but, in the dressing room, Ron said: "Sorry, Ian, but you have to admit that wasn't a Cup Final ball." He was saying there was no way he was going to risk getting injured so close to Wembley – and he duffed it!

During the 1966 Cup run, the first-team went to Lilleshall for special training on several occasions, and, ahead of the semi-final, Alan Brown took the entire reserve team defence to assist in the preparations. Lilleshall, of course, is miles from anywhere, and, as there wasn't much to do in the evenings, we passed the time in a variety of ways.

Some of the things we did might seem pretty daft, but it was all good, lighthearted fun which generated a tremendous atmosphere. I recall a regular game of blind man's bluff which had us all in fits of laughter as we took it in turns to chase round a pitch-black room trying to find lads and hit them with a newspaper.

Graham Pugh, you'll remember, made his Cup debut in the semi-final at just turned 18. That week at Lilleshall he was rooming with me and Sam Ellis, and, one evening at dinner, he made arrangements to meet one of the waitresses outside the building at midnight. When he left to keep his date, we were all calling to the girl from our window, then we turned out the lights and got into bed.

Moments later, the door burst open, and in storms Alan Brown, the man-ager. He was carrying "Pughie"! The Gaffer literally threw the lad across the room, and I'll never forget how "Pughie" flew through the air and landed on his bed.

"Brownie" had the room next door, and, apparently, just as "Pughie" was creeping past with his shoes in his hands, the Gaffer stepped out and grabbed him by the scruff of the neck. The next morning after breakfast, "Brownie" stuck "Pughie" in the middle of a circle of players and absolutely destroyed him verbally. Poor "Pughie" was quickly reduced to tears!

Alan Brown could be tough, but he was one of the most decent people I ever knew. After the Final, we had a banquet at the Hotel Russell, and, naturally, the Gaffer was in big demand with so many guests around. Yet, when my Dad (he was staying in a nearby hotel) called to see me, "Brownie" made a point of having a word with him – a small gesture much appreciated by a young and obscure reserve in his first year at the club.

Paul Webster, then aged 12, was in his first season as an Owls fan when Wednesday went to the 1966 semi-final, and the kid from Oxspring, near Penistone, found it rather frustrating standing at the Chelsea end in the 61,000 Villa Park crowd:

I was devastated when my father only succeeded in getting a semi-final ticket for himself at the time they went on sale, but, to my great relief, a few days before the match he came home from work and said he'd managed to get a couple for me and my pal Mick Bramall. There was only one snag – we weren't going to be with him among the Wednesday supporters in the Holte End, but would have to stand behind the opposite goal among the Chelsea fans.

When I look back now, I can't remember one incident from the match because I didn't see anything. I was only a little 'un, and, no matter where I moved on that terracing, my view was obscured. The only time I saw the ball was when it was up in the air. If I'd been among Sheffield fans, you can be sure they would have pushed me down to the front, but the Chelsea supporters, spotting my Wednesday favours, were far from friendly.

The only way I knew Wednesday had scored was when I heard two roars from the fans at the other end of the ground. Naturally, I jumped up and down in delight – which didn't impress the Chelsea people around me!

Unfortunately, we couldn't get tickets for the Final, and I was in tears about it. Yet I was convinced we were going to go straight back to Wembley the following year, when, I felt sure, I'd find some way of getting a ticket.

I remember seeing us win 3-1 at Norwich in the fifth round in 1967 on an afternoon when I was in the Carrow Road ground nearly three hours before the kick-off; and I shan't forget the quarter-final match at Stamford Bridge a few weeks later, when, unfortunately, Chelsea had their revenge for the 1966 semi-final defeat.

Ironically, Chelsea won that day with just about the last kick of the game – and Tommy Baldwin would never have scored if he hadn't mis-hit his shot. Talk about our luck running out! Ron Springett went down anticipating a full-blooded drive, but the effort lacked power, the ball hit a divot, and all I can remember is the horror of seeing it bounce over Springett's hand and into the net.

Joe Ashton, a lifelong fan who was then a Sheffield City Councillor and still 24 years away from becoming an Owls director at the time of the 1966 semi-final, recalls:

Wednesday produced a terrific performance against Chelsea and triumphed despite a serious injury to Vic Mobley, but my most lasting memory of the weekend and the following few days was the coincidence of the inconvenience Mobley's damaged ankle caused my wife Maggie.

On the Tuesday after the game, Maggie, having spent three months on the NHS waiting list, was due to have an operation on a foot. She turned up on time at the hospital, and everything was set, but, unfortunately, just when she was bound for the theatre, she learned the surgeon had been called away to deal with "an emergency". We discovered later he had been busy operating on "Big Vic"!

Not that Maggie really minded. Coming from a family of mad Wednesdayites, she'd have waited another six months if it could have helped the club's cause.

Sadly, we didn't have the consolation of seeing Wednesday go on to win the Cup, but at least the Owls reaching Wembley contributed to a memorable year for Sheffield – what with Hillsborough staging some World Cup matches the following summer. I think the only negative note was, owing to the way the club organised the sale of Cup Final tickets, a lot of genuine supporters didn't get to the game while many people who weren't regulars did.

Nine-goal thriller at Hillsborough
Owls v Manchester United
31 August 1968

Ian McFarlane, the former Chelsea and Leicester defender who was a Wednesday coach from March 1967 to June 1969, has a special reason for remembering the Owls' famous 5-4 triumph over the European champions from Old Trafford:

Celebration – Jack Whitham (7) is hugged by Fantham and Ritchie after scoring Wednesday's fifth goal against Manchester United in August 1968, while Sam Ellis shows his elation.

When Jack Marshall, the manager, had to go into the Northern General Hospital for an appendix operation, I was put in temporary charge, and it just so happened that our next home match was against the mighty Manchester United, who had recently won the European Cup and boasted such great players as Bobby Charlton, Denis Law and George Best.

I can't recall all the details of the game, but have never forgotten that it was a lovely sunny August afternoon when, after taking an early lead, we went behind, hauled ourselves level, fell into arrears again, then hit back to win

Jack Whitham celebrates his hat-trick with a refreshing "cuppa".

5-4 in a sensational match which was surely one of the most memorable in the club's history.

Jack Whitham got a hat-trick for which he will always be remembered. Jack was the most inexperienced man in the team, but, despite having played in fewer than 30 games, he'd already claimed ten goals and shown a rare scoring knack.

Before the match, I told him to just go out and enjoy himself. "Be a free spirit and don't dwell on whatever role you're supposed to play," I said. But the look on his face told me he was definitely up for it, and I wasn't surprised he did so well. We created panic in the United defence, and it was probably Jack's threat which prompted Nobby Stiles to head one of the finest own-goals I ever saw!

I don't think I'll ever forget the joy on the face of Eric Taylor, the general manager, after the game. He came towards me and hugged me so hard I thought he was going to make love to me! Taylor and his assistant Eric England were like fathers to me in the spell when I was in charge, and I was delighted to see them savouring that moment of success.

That day I always wanted to give the credit to Alan Brown, and knew he would be pleased at the result. He had left the club and re-joined Sunderland the previous February, but he was my mentor and I owed so much to him. Barely 18 months earlier, Alan had plucked me from the obscurity of Bath City, where I was ending my playing days, and given me my first big break in coaching.

I had answered an advertisement, and was appointed to the staff following an interview which took place at the Hotel Russell in London a few hours before a game in which Wednesday beat Fulham 2-1 at Craven Cottage. Lawrie McMenemy arrived at Hillsborough at the same time having come to Brown's attention after sending Ian Branfoot and Colin Symm to Sheffield from Gateshead.

For a while the two of us alternated between the juniors and the Reserves, with Jack Marshall working as Brown's assistant until the "M" squad's arrangements changed when Jack became caretaker manager.

When Jack went into hospital and Eric Taylor summoned me to his office to say he was putting me in charge, I was so elated I honestly felt as if I was drugged. It all seemed such a long way from the Southern League I had so recently left. Yet if I was carried along by the adrenalin, I knew my playing experience with Aberdeen, Chelsea and Leicester, and the lessons I had learned under Alan Brown, equipped me to do the job.

I never had any problems with the players before or after my spell in charge. You can't kid them because they can see if you know what you're talking about, and they learn a lot about you from watching how you control and pass a ball in training. That the lads responded well is evident when you note we lost only four of 17 League games up to early November, and I was

at the helm most of that time. Ironically, our biggest disappointment happened within days of the Manchester United match, when we lost 3-1 at Fourth Division Exeter in the League Cup.

Unfortunately, a season which started so well turned a bit sour. Jack returned to duty, but he left in the following March when he was told his contract wasn't being renewed. In the meantime, Wednesday brought Tommy McAnearney back and appointed him first-team coach, which was a blow to me because I felt I had done well while Jack was away.

When I look back, I suppose one or two people in the boardroom thought I lacked experience, and they brought Tom in because Jack's health suggested he wasn't up to the job physically. Jack was a nice bloke, a lovely man, but, even when in the best of health, he could never be really tough with the players. Jack never used industrial language to get his point over.

Some people interpreted that as a lack of passion on Jack's part, but nobody could ever say I had no passion. I always said exactly what I felt because I cared, and I could never wrap things up in flannel. Some people had to use flannel with directors' to survive, but I couldn't do it.

McMenemy, of course, had also fancied the first-team job, but, at that time, the fact that he had never played League football did not help his cause. His reaction was to leave in December 1968 to join Doncaster Rovers, where he started on a managerial career in which he went much further than many people might have predicted.

Around this period, Alan Brown had recommended us both for the manager's job at Carlisle. I stayed at Hillsborough until the end of the season, but by the time Danny Williams was settling in as Wednesday's manager, I was on my way to re-join Alan Brown, who had offered me a job at Sunderland.

I think I hold some sort of record because I'm the only coach Alan ever appointed twice. In the event, however, I didn't stay with him long the second time, for, within three months, I was appointed manager of Carlisle.

I have now retired from football, but, when I reflect on my career in the game, I always recall my spell at Sheffield with a special affection, and remember that famous victory over Manchester United as a highlight to be treasured for ever.

David Ford, who claimed 37 goals in 135 games for Wednesday, wasn't on the scoresheet in this famous triumph, but the man who now has a central heating business and is a partner in the Champs restaurant and bar in Sheffield, has fond memories of the game:

I didn't score in this match, but was involved in making all our five goals, including the one Nobby Stiles headed into his own net.

A memory which sticks with me is that, in one newspaper, George Best praised my display and said what a good player I was. It was a nice compliment from a man who, along with his fellow legends Denis Law and Bobby Charlton, had helped Manchester United lead 4-2 at one stage. But I haven't forgotten that I should have made the score 6-4 in the last minute when I missed a chance from about three yards out. The ball finished halfway up the Kop!

It was great for Jack Whitham to score three. I'd enjoyed the experience the previous May against Burnley on the day Jack scored two on his debut after coming on as sub. In match reports, my first treble was a footnote to Jack's double, and now my contribution to his hat-trick hardly rated a mention, but, at the end of the day, the only thing that mattered was we won both games!

Jack Whitham's name will always be synonymous with that famous Manchester United match of 1968, and here he reflects on an unforgettable day in the context of fond memories of a Hillsborough career in which he scored 31 goals in 71 games between 1967 and 1970. He is now a leisure centre manager and club secretary with the South Yorkshire Police:

I came to Wednesday on a month's trial in late 1964, and was offered professional terms at the end of the first week after playing in two practice matches up at the Thorncliffe training ground. At the time I was coming up to my 18th birthday and had a good job with a promising future in accountancy, and I remember Johnny Logan, the trainer,

telling me to go home for the weekend and give my decision serious thought. He said the Gaffer [Alan Brown] felt I had the ability to make a career in the game, but I needed to be sure it was what I really wanted.

I spent the rest of that season playing in the juniors and became a regular in the Reserves in 1965-66 – the year when Wednesday went to Wembley and, if only substitutes had been allowed then, I might well have got a place on the bench at the Cup Final because I spent a lot of time working with the senior players around that time.

In fact, my first-team debut didn't come until near the end of the following season, and it was not without irony that it happened to be against my home-town club Burnley, for whom I'd played in the Lancashire League as an amateur. I remember ringing my parents on the Friday and inviting them and my uncle over for the game – although, as I was only a substitute, I said I was probably unlikely to play.

However, Brian Usher took a knock in the first half, and, at half-time in the dressing room, I saw Alan Brown consult with Bob Lyttle, the physio, before coming over to tell me I was starting the second half.

The score when I went on was 2-0, we finished up winning 7-0, and I scored twice. What a debut! I think what made the difference for me was getting a good first touch within a couple of minutes of going on. It settled me down, and the crowd's positive reaction when I ran on to David Ford's ball down the wing boosted my confidence.

Later, a ball came over from the left, somebody chested it down, and it bounced just right at knee height for me to swing my right foot at it and send it into the top corner. A second goal followed, and, at 7-0 we got a penalty which could have given me a debut hat-trick. I didn't ask if I could take it because, to be honest, I feared I might mar a memorable day by missing from the spot. In the event, Jim McCalliog failed to convert it!

Of course, when I did claim my first hat-trick it came in the famous game with Manchester United in 1968, and, 30 years later, it remains the occasion most people associate with my name. In fact, many still insist I scored four that day, but I've always said three will do for

me. Even now, Nobby Stiles often jokes that I became a four-goal star by claiming the one he headed into his own net.

After the game, I remember Eric Taylor, the club's general manager, crediting me with the Stiles goal because, he said, it was a case of cause and effect. The ball came over from the right, flicked my forehead as I got in front of Nobby and tried to glance it towards the back post, and Stiles, rising behind me, changed the direction of the ball, so, with goalkeeper Stepney committed, it flew into the roof of the net.

Taylor's theory was if I hadn't got the slightest of touches and forced the error, Nobby wouldn't have done what he did, so the credit was mine. My own theory is that if only I'd been able to make a firmer header, what Stiles did wouldn't have mattered; and, anyway, I've seen forwards credited with goals in those situations. If only the match had been recorded on film, I might have been able to prove it was my goal!

It was a lovely sunny afternoon when, frankly, there might have been 14 goals rather than nine. There were still 20 minutes left when it went to 5-4, and the only surprise was the scoreline remained unchanged in a late spell when United really went at us.

The scoring started after only two minutes when Dunne, the United back, suddenly went down with a pulled hamstring as he was running back intending to play the ball to his goalkeeper. I was following up, and, with the goalkeeper having advanced but still in his area, I nipped past Dunne, didn't break my stride and hit the ball in from 28 yards.

John Ritchie headed our second from Ford's cross; I got our third from a Ritchie knock-down; the fourth was the Stiles own goal; and I claimed the fifth when Ford's shot bounced back to me off Stepney's body.

The side that played that day was still Alan Brown's team, even though he had left six months earlier, and the spirit in our dressing room was still at a peak. In fact, the atmosphere among the lads remained high even when the club's fortunes began to wane after Danny Williams came.

Danny, unfortunately, parted with better players than he brought in. Yet, in the dressing room, the spirit and mutual feeling was such that, when we

The long and the short of it – giant-sized coaches Ian McFarlane (left) and Lawrie McMenemy, who were on the Hillsborough staff in the late 1960s, look down upon pint-sized apprentice Kevin Johnson in 1968.

Johnny Quinn's Over-35s. So I can say I have always felt at home on this side of the Pennines, and I'm certainly not short of fond memories!

Cup hat-trick for Brian Joicey Owls v Crystal Palace 19 February 1973

Former Wednesday striker Brian Joicey treasures memories of an unforgettable night at Villa Park when he scored a hat-trick in a 3-2 defeat of Crystal Palace in extra-time in a second replay of an FA Cup fourth-round tie:

I had some good times in football, but the night we twice came from behind to beat Palace has to be one of the most memorable of my career. There were just over 19,000 fans there, including about 10,000 from Sheffield, but so many people have said they were there, I think the gate must have topped 100,000!

I was suspended when we drew 1-1 in the first game at Hillsborough, where Tommy Craig scored our goal with a penalty, but returned for the first replay, in which we again finished level, with David Sunley on target on his 21st birthday. Palace were then in Division One but struggling. We were in Division Two, and, although we weren't doing as well as we wanted, there was a buzz in the team and we felt it wouldn't take much to set us on a good run.

I remember Palace led at half-time, and, just after the break, I got a simple equaliser. It was almost like a training ground goal in that John Sissons crossed the ball from the left and I was unmarked as I headed it in. Palace regained the lead, but, with about 12 minutes left, our persistence paid off when a corner from Willie Henderson enabled me to get a second equaliser with a header that went in off the goalkeeper. The extra-time winner came after Sunley had gone between four players and fed Sissons, who pushed the ball through for me to beat the goalkeeper as he came out. What a great moment!

It's intriguing to note that it was Mick Prendergast's turn to get a hat-trick against Palace the next time we met them, in a home League game in September 1973. Sadly, it was just after

were relegated in 1970, one of the lads made a valid point when he said: "This team without a manager could have stayed in the First Division."

Even after we went down, I didn't want to leave, and, in fact, did everything I could to get out of it when Wednesday decided to sell me to Liverpool. I didn't lose by the move because, having been on £35 a week at Hillsborough, it was quite an eye-opener to find myself on around £100 a week at Anfield. Yet I would have been content to stay in Sheffield.

At the time I was buying Don Megson's house in Butler Road. Josie and I got married on 6 June 1970 and were due to move into our new home on the 26th. Everything was going to plan until I got a call from Fred Scott, the chief scout, telling me I was wanted at the ground. When I went to see

Danny Williams, what persuaded me to join Liverpool was Danny saying he was selling me on the specific instructions of the board. If Wednesday didn't want me, I thought, I might as well go where I was wanted.

To be honest, I never knew the truth about why I was sold. Long after the event, I did hear Danny suggest it was his decision to let me go because he didn't think I'd be any good in the Second Division as it was "too physical" for me. It would have been nice to have had the chance to prove him wrong.

At least when my time in professional football came to an end, I was able to settle in Sheffield. For many years I had the Wadsley Jack pub, then I became a leisure centre manager responsible for what is now 43 sections, and, in the meantime, I have continued to play football for fun and charity with this that we were hit by a virus which affected just about every player on the staff, and our season collapsed. We won only three of our next 23 League and Cup games, and, in the meantime, Derek Dooley lost his job. Poor Derek was sacked on Christmas Eve.

Last-match escape from the ultimate failure
Owls v Southend United
29 April 1976

Rodger Wylde, who had finally gained a regular first-team place, remembers the emotion of the dramatic final game of the 1975-76 season:
People talk about pressure, but that night it was unbelievable. We needed to win or draw to stay in Division Three, and Southend had to win to save themselves. We were winning 2-0, then Southend scored towards the end, and the relief when the final whistle went was incredible.

The atmosphere at the finish, and the reaction of the supporters, was astonishing. We got back to the dressing room, and the staff were saying the fans were massed on the pitch, chanting and calling for us to appear in the directors' box.

I didn't feel it was quite the thing to be taking a bow when all we'd done was escape relegation to the Fourth Division. There was something a bit embarrassing about playing the role of conquering heroes when all we'd achieved was to avoid the ultimate failure.

John Brodie recalls a supporter's viewpoint:
I remember when Wednesday went into their final game of 1969-70 needing to win to stay in the old First Division, I couldn't bring myself to go to the game because I was so nervous about the outcome. However, when they were in a similar situation in 1975-76 and were in danger of dropping into the Fourth Division, I knew I had to be there.

But I was so nervous. I left work in Retford as early as 2pm and, after stopping for a meal in Sheffield, I was easily the first man into the ground when the gates opened long before the 7.30pm kick-off. I claimed a back-row seat on the uncovered terracing in front of the South Stand exactly level with the

halfway line, and sat back to endure a night of high tension.

In the event, Wednesday won 2-1 with goals from Mick Prendergast and Eric Potts, and the scenes at the end were astonishing. Most of the 25,000 spectators went on to the pitch, and the players appeared in the directors' box to accept the crowd's cheers. The joyful celebrations were such, you would have thought we had won the championship or the FA Cup rather than just saved our Third Division status!

But, naturally, I was as intoxicated as anyone by the sense of having clinched a vital victory, and my only regret about that evening is being one seat away from where Jimmy Mullen's shirt landed when he threw it into the crowd. What a treasured possession that would have been!

I think that was the only occasion when I went into the ground by an entrance in the South Stand and eventually left through the Kop exit. You see, amid all the emotional chanting and cheering, I couldn't resist venturing on to the hallowed pitch amid the celebrations …and, afterwards, it was easier to follow the throng back on to the Kop.

Dave Cusack, the Owls' defender, comments:
That Southend game came at the end of my first season in the first team, and, naturally, with so much at stake for both teams, things tended to get very tense. The incident I remember best came when Dave Worthington went in very hard on Peter Fox, our goalkeeper. I picked Worthington up by his hair and told him in no uncertain terms he shouldn't have done that because "Foxy" was my mate. The man didn't step out of line again!

Chris Turner, then 17, had been a trainee for just over a year when Wednesday avoided the drop to Division Four, and he had cause to remember both the night the Owls beat Southend and the morning after:
I was sweeping out the dressing rooms after the Southend game, and Dave Cusack asked if I fancied going to the Fiesta night club. He and the lads were celebrating staying up and Dave's 20th birthday bash. I thought: "I wouldn't mind a chance to mix with some of first-team boys." I was, of course,

under-age, but been able to get myself and girlfriend Debbie in at the Fiesta on several previous occasions by signing myself in as David Herbert, a young pro, at Hillsborough.

On this occasion I used David's name again, but had barely got through the door when I spotted Ken Knighton, my youth-team manager, standing at the other side of the room. Almost immediately, Ken came across, walked straight past me and out of the main entrance. He never looked at me, but I couldn't believe I hadn't been seen. Dave Cusack said: "Ken didn't notice you. He only popped in for one drink and then was going off home."

As apprentices we always used the away dressing room at the ground, but, as the season was now over, there was no training scheduled. However, when I reported for duty the morning after the Fiesta date, I saw a solitary set of kit hanging on a peg. One of the other apprentices looked in and said: "Ken's told me to tell you to get that kit on and start running round the track." I learned later that Ken had also asked Derek Blunkett, the groundsman, to keep an eye on me to ensure I ran at a decent pace and didn't attempt to slacken off.

I must have run for over an hour, and was all but out on my feet before Ken appeared at the end of the tunnel. He said: "If I ever catch you again in a night club, I'll report you to the manager – and you know what that'll mean." The following day my thighs were killing me, and it was two days before I could begin to walk without pain. But I took Ken Knighton's lesson to heart!

The Arsenal Cup 'Marathon'
Owls v Arsenal
January 1979

It took five matches and nine hours to settle the third-round FA Cup-tie between Third Division Wednesday and First Division Arsenal in January 1979. It was the kind of "marathon" which was not uncommon in the FA Cup in the days before penalty shoot-outs were introduced to prevent major delays in deciding ties after police forces around the country decided they needed ten days' notice to take on board replays.

Volunteers working on the Hillsborough pitch ahead of the first game with Arsenal in the extended FA Cup saga of January 1979.

David Barber, Wednesday's head groundsman, recalls how the first match, which ended 1-1 on 6 January 1979, only went ahead after an army of volunteers cleared the Hillsborough pitch of snow:

We had had snow on the pitch for about two weeks, and left it until the morning of the game to have it cleared, with scores of supporters turning up equipped to help us get it cleared in time for the kick-off.

Terry Neill, the Arsenal manager, wasn't really happy about the match being played, and, having arrived some hours before the scheduled start, he kept coming out to have a look at our progress, invariably muttering that he didn't think the pitch was fit. However, the referee was adamant that conditions would be playable. Where the snow had been cleared the surface was still icy, and with a thaw in progress the situation could only get better.

Big Jack Charlton came out and gave all the volunteers a boost, shouting: "Come on, let's show 'em we can get this pitch ready." But Neill appeared for about the fifth time and had another

grumble. Charlton, Neill and the referee were standing with me discussing things, and we were being closely watched by a small boy.

I had been working alongside this little lad mainly because I wanted to keep an eye on him. He had trudged along with a coal shovel, and I was scared he was going to seriously damage the pitch with that thing. In fact, quite a few of the volunteers were removing as much turf as snow!

Anyway, this lad was listening to every word the four of us were saying, and he was clearly unimpressed with Neill's comments. There was a break in the conversation and the boy looked straight at Neill and the referee.

Very seriously and deliberately, he said: "I wish you'd make your minds up – I'm missing *Tiswas* on television to be here!"

Terry Neill promptly departed, and never said another word about the pitch not being fit. The boy's words had clearly broken the ice – and even Arsenal realised they owed it to that kid and the others who had sacrificed their Saturday morning to help get the match on.

Rodger Wylde, the former Owls striker, remembers the first replay, at Highbury, which also ended 1-1:

This Highbury game sticks in my mind because, when I put Wednesday one-up after 50 minutes, the television cameramen were still at their half-time break, so it was the only one of the 16 goals scored in that marathon which wasn't captured on film!

I think it stemmed from a long through ball from Mark Smith, and I went past Willie Young and David O'Leary, the Arsenal centre-halves, and shot wide of goalkeeper Pat Jennings.

The big Highbury clock was showing that the final whistle was due when Arsenal got a corner, and I remember Willie Young saying to me: "I think we've had it." Then the ball got knocked back from the corner kick, and Liam Brady just whacked it goalwards. I think the ball squeezed into the net, possibly after taking a slight deflection off Mark Smith as he lunged forward in an attempt to block the shot.

We didn't know it then, but it was to be another 13 days and three more meetings before the tie was settled.

Arsenal went on to win the Cup that year.

Mark Smith, the former Wednesday central defender, recalls two memories relating to the Arsenal marathon.

A humorous incident occurred at the hotel we used for our pre-match meal ahead of the first of the three replays staged at Filbert Street. When we arrived, we went straight through to the main restaurant, and you can imagine the delighted reaction of our lads when they found there were two bars of chocolate placed on every side-plate at the table.

Some of the chocolate had been scoffed and some pocketed before a waiter came rushing in saying: "No, these tables are for Arsenal, not Sheffield Wednesday." Apparently the chocolate was there to boost our opponents' energy levels, but we inadvertently ensured they got short measure that day!

The dining area reserved for Wednesday was in a cramped room upstairs, where we had tea and toast in surroundings which I suppose reflected the fact that we were a Third Division club who didn't merit the luxury enjoyed by First Division Arsenal downstairs.

The pattern of the Arsenal marathon couldn't have been more dramatic if it had been scripted in advance, but, after sharing four goals in the second replay and six in the third replay, Arsenal finally beat us 2-0 at the fifth attempt on a night in late January when, frankly, I shouldn't have played.

I'd picked up an ankle injury in the previous game, and, unfortunately, physiotherapy in football then was not like it is today. Jon Honey, who was doing the job at Hillsborough in those days, only worked part-time. This is no criticism of Wednesday because that is how things were in football in the 1970s. Clubs might have top-class stadiums, but many aspects of the operation were not considered vital enough to justify extra expenditure.

We often used to joke that if you got injured in training after 11.30 in the morning, you had to wait until the next day for treatment. Things changed dramatically after Alan Smith came in 1983. Alan brought a professional and very disciplined attitude to the job. He

wouldn't have been impressed to find "Big Jack" keeping his fish in the ice machine in the treatment room, as happened in the Charlton era!

Anyway, ahead of our third trip to Leicester to face Arsenal, I had a fitness test in the gymnasium and, not wanting to miss out, declared myself available. My right ankle was strapped up, and, for the first 20 minutes of the game, everything was okay – until I felt something snap. I thought at first it might just be the strapping, but, in fact, the ligament had gone. In the end, I had no choice but to limp off.

That, alas, wasn't the end of my problems, because while the ankle gave me no trouble on the homeward journey, I ran into embarrassing difficulties when the coach dropped me off on Herries Road. Just as the team bus was shooting away in the direction of the Five Arches, I put my right foot down on the pavement – and the pain was excruciating.

Just to complicate matters, it was a bitterly cold night, and, with so much snow and ice about, the pavement was slippery. I stood there, unable to put any weight on my right foot while desperately trying to retain my balance standing on a left foot that was gently sliding on the ice!

Bear in mind, this was at about one o'clock in the morning, and there wasn't a soul in sight. For about half an hour, I just stood there helplessly wondering how I was going to move and start negotiating the steep incline which led to my parents' home. In the end, I decided there was no option but to crawl up the hill on my hands and knees.

All the houses I passed were in darkness, but at last I spotted one with the lights on and where the occupants were still up. I can't imagine what they thought when they heard this knocking and opened their front door to find someone standing there claiming to be a Sheffield Wednesday footballer! Happily, they let me use their phone to ring home. It didn't help that Dad was on nights. Mother had to go round to my uncle's house and knock him up, so he could get the car out and come to my rescue. We went home via the Royal Infirmary, and I ended up with a pot on my ankle. The injury put me out until late March.

An abiding memory of the next morning is a visit from Jack Charlton, who came to our house with Tony Toms and Maurice Setters. The snow was so bad, Jack couldn't get his car up our street. But I'll never forget how he stood warming his backside before the open fire in our front room, and he seemed more concerned with cadging a fag than listening to the story of how I'd struggled home after dropping off the bus!

The Boxing Day Massacre
Owls v Sheffield United
26 December 1979

A record Third Division crowd of 43,309 packed into Hillsborough for the 100th League and Cup derby between the Sheffield teams – a match with an 11am kick-off which saw Wednesday triumph 4-0 in what has passed into local football folklore as "the Boxing Day massacre".

Ian Mellor, who now works for the PFA's commercial department in Manchester, made over 350 League and Cup appearances with six clubs, including 80 for the Owls between 1979 and 1982. Here he remembers his first season at Hillsborough and reflects on the circumstances which prompted a turnabout in Wednesday's fortunes just around the time they met the Blades:

When I signed for Wednesday in the summer of 1979, I always remember telling John Harris, who was Jack Charlton's assistant, that I had a gut feeling I was coming to a club who were going to enjoy early success. In fact, it was not until around Christmas in my first season that the tide turned in our favour, and it happened because of a tactical change prompted by Jack's concern about the goals we were leaking.

Jack signed me from Chester as a striker, and we started that 1979-80 season with me playing wide on the left and Terry Curran wide on the right, with Andy McCulloch and Ian Fleming down the middle. Then Jack parted with Fleming, who only played about seven games, and we operated a 4-3-3 system up to just before Christmas. The turning point came when, to give the defence more support, he decided on a 4-4-2 formation to give us an extra man in front of the back four.

Terry Curran's headed goal in the Boxing Day defeat of Sheffield United.

This decision, which saw me dropped back to the left wing and leave McCulloch and Curran as the front pair, was immediately successful and suddenly made Curran really effective. Moreover, it coincided with the big Sheffield derby match against the lads from Bramall Lane.

The Blades were then top of the table, and, as it was the first time the clubs had met in the League for eight years, it was a very special occasion which the fans and local lads like Charlie Williamson and Mark Smith really savoured. I don't think the teams had ever played each other before in the Third Division, and the atmosphere was really tremendous. As a Mancunian raised on City-United derbies, I wasn't as emotionally involved as some, but I could hardly fail to appreciate what it meant to Sheffield people.

I remember how, a few minutes before half-time, I was going down the left wing and I could hear Mick Speight, the United captain, shouting to one of his colleagues: "Bring him inside, he hasn't got a right peg." So I was pushed on to my right side, and, about 25 yards out, I just whacked the ball goalwards. It might have gone anywhere off my weaker foot, but it actually sailed into the top corner!

We never looked back from that moment, both in terms of the game itself and all through the rest of the season. It was as if my goal had sparked

something which we kept going right until promotion was clinched. Meanwhile, Sheffield United's fortunes took a bit of a dip.

I often jest that, although I was at Hillsborough for over three years, I'm only remembered by Wednesdayites for two things – the first goal in "the Boxing Day massacre" and a diving header which sealed a 2-1 win at Blackburn to confirm promotion in April 1980. I like to think I did a few other good things, although it is pleas-

Ian Mellor was the man who set the Owls on course for a famous victory when he used his right foot instead of his more trusty left!

ing to think people associate me with the start of an upward climb that led Wednesday back to the top.

They were happy times, and I have lots of wonderful memories of so many good people – not least the laundry girls like Betty Pearson and the others, Dave Barber the groundsman, and, of course, some great characters in the dressing room.

It's a funny thing, really, but, about six years before I joined Wednesday, I was transferred from Manchester City to Norwich, and, in those days, the easiest way to travel by car from Lancashire to East Anglia involved going over Woodhead and via Stocksbridge in the early stages of the journey. Occasionally, the route took me straight past Hillsborough, and I used to look at the stadium and say to my wife: "I have a feeling I'll play for this club one day."

I did. I'm glad my hunch became reality – and my son remains as keen a Wednesdayite as any of the fans who cheered that 4-0 triumph of almost 20 years ago.

When Uncle Denis slept through the game!
Owls v Brighton & HA
16 April 1983

Long-time supporter Keith Littlewood recalls the April afternoon when Wednesday met Brighton in the FA Cup semi-final at Highbury as the day his Uncle Denis slept throughout the entire game:

I had a pal, Brian Robinson, who lived in London, and we used to meet up with him whenever we went down there to a Wednesday game. When the Owls reached the semi-final in 1983 and the match was staged at Highbury, Brian said he'd meet us at a pub which he assured us was not far from the ground and had the advantage of being a good place to park.

My Uncle Denis [Holmes] and his son were in our party, and, when we met up with Brian, we were in good time to have a few drinks after the long journey south. Brian said the ground was only a 20-minute walk, but by twenty-five to three I thought we were cutting it a bit fine. "Hadn't we better get going?" I asked.

The first shock came when Brian said he wasn't joining us on the walk. He'd got himself a lift to Highbury. The second shock was when we realised Uncle Denis, not having been satisfied to drink pints, had been popping brandies into his ale while propping up the bar. As soon as he went outside, the fresh air got to him – and it was clear he was drunk as a skunk!

Me and my cousin carried him all the way to Highbury, and a supposed 20-minute walk turned into a half-hour hike, which, to our embarrassment, meant we arrived late and missed the kick-off.

Our seats were on the front row at the extreme end of the West Stand, and we managed to prop Uncle Denis up in the corner seat. He spent the entire game leaning against a post, snoring and lost to the world. Even now, all these years later, he can't explain why Wednesday didn't play in the Final that year because he slept all through the game against Brighton and insists it was an event which didn't happen!

Two famous victories
Liverpool v Owls
29 September 1984
Manchester United v Owls
1 January 1985

Howard Wilkinson, the manager who led Wednesday back into the top grade in 1984, remembers famous victories at Anfield and Old Trafford in the context of a marvellous phase during which the Owls won promotion and quickly made an impact in the old First Division:

In the promotion season of 1983-84, we reached the quarter-finals of both the League Cup and the FA Cup, and that was probably the time when we began to appreciate what it meant to be starting to bring the big occasions back to Hillsborough.

When we played Liverpool in the League Cup in January 1984, there were over 49,000 in the ground to see us draw 2-2, and, though we lost 3-0 at Anfield in the replay, the enthusiasm of our fans knew no bounds. They kept up a constant chorus as they sang: "We'll be back! We'll be back!" – it was a marvellous moment.

The following September, after promotion, we returned to Liverpool for a First Division game, and, to the delight of our fans, we won 2-0 with goals from Gary Shelton and Imre Varadi. When our second goal went in they out-sang the famous Anfield Kop with an impromptu and continuous rendition of a song which had the words: "We said we'd be back, and now we are!" Another moment to savour.

To get promotion in 1984 was a fantastic feeling, and I treasured it all the more not just in a professional sense but as someone who had supported the club as a kid and come from a family of passionate Wednesdayites. Having been carried into the ground at the age of four on my Dad's shoulders and been a Hillsborough regular in my schooldays, I could relate to the ordinary supporter; and, as by 1984 I'd been in the game for 22 years, I could also enjoy a certain professional satisfaction.

Promotion year was very much a pressure season in that, after Jack Charlton left, it was imperative to achieve something because some people had generated a feeling that if Jack couldn't end Wednesday's long years in the wilderness, nobody could.

We had a team spirit that was unequalled. We didn't have a lot of money, most of the players at that time were probably classed as workmanlike, honest punters, and they achieved far more than many might have thought possible.

We took stick from some people for the way we played, which was totally unfair because what the team achieved was levels of performance which, really, they weren't entitled to attain with such consistency. But those lads had the determination to work and, with the sweat of their brows, make the best use of what talents they had within a system designed to help us win something.

They were great lads who revelled in being cast as anti-heroes. In recent times, when I've gone to Hillsborough and seen Peter Shreeves working at the ground, I'm reminded of the period when he was Tottenham's manager and we were travelling to White Hart Lane to play them.

The radio was on in the team bus and Peter was being interviewed. When the programme ended, the radio was switched off. Then, suddenly we heard a voice you would have sworn was that of Peter Shreeves pronounce: "We've got to get the ball to Hodders and Wadders, but, of course, we're playing Sheffield Wednesday today, and with them the ball's always in the air, innit? And that ain't fair 'cus when it's in the air we can't get it to Hodders and Wadders can we?"

Amid gales of laughter on the bus, we discovered it was our own Gary Shelton mimicking the Spurs manager in the guise of perpetrating the myth that Wednesday never played the ball on the ground. Nobody could ever say we couldn't poke fun at our false image!

Of course, there were times when the lads didn't see the funny side of things, and I remember one occasion in our first season back in Division One when they thought my attempts at psychology had sent me crazy. They certainly weren't amused on a cold, wet January day when I turned them out into the rain on the top of a windswept Woodhead.

We were travelling to play at Manchester United, and, before we left Hillsborough, I'd had a bit of a go at them in the dressing room. Now, on the team bus, they were all warm and comfortable, and, no doubt, quietly dwelling on the prospect of facing United. As we travelled over Woodhead I decided the best way to take their minds off the game was to stop the bus, make them get out and insist they walked around on the bleak hillside for a few minutes.

When we resumed the journey, the lads, brushing their wet suits and muttering, were too busy debating my mental state to think about the match at the end of our journey. Whether or not it was my psychology, I don't know, but we won 2-1 at Old Trafford. If I remember right, Imre Varadi got the goals and Martin Hodge saved a penalty.

Cup fame and frustration
for Andy Blair
Owls v Luton Town
20 November 1984

Andy Blair scored only seven goals in his 75 League and Cup games for Wednesday between August 1984 and March 1986, but a unique penalty treble earned him a special niche in the club's records and a

Andy Blair, seen here in the background, always said he was grateful that Mel Sterland took the crucial last-minute penalty in the famous 4-4 League Cup draw with Chelsea.

place in League Cup history. However, as he recalls here, some other Cup matches were less rewarding for the Scottish mid-fielder, who arrived from Aston Villa for £50,000 and returned there in a £120,000 deal 20 months later:

I have to admit it is still a source of pride to me to be remembered at Hillsborough, and I don't mind if the fact I'm not forgotten is entirely down to the night in November 1984 when I bagged a hat-trick of penalties in our 4-2 defeat of Luton in the fourth round of the League Cup.

It was one of those freak experiences that can occur in a player's career, but it might not have happened for me if Mel Sterland hadn't temporarily given up the task of taking penalties. I was nominated for the job, and, though I missed the first one I took for Wednesday, against Norwich, less than three weeks later I got another chance – well, I suppose you could say it was a treble chance! The feat inspired a lot of publicity at the time, and some of it was about the validity of the penalties. Luton's manager David Pleat wasn't very happy. However, as I said then, you have to accept the referee's decision, and I was grateful for the chance to achieve something no Owls' player had done before. I like to think that we wouldn't have complained if the spot-kicks had been awarded at the other end.

I can't recall the incidents that prompted Tom Fitzharris to point to the spot on 15, 51 and 70 minutes, but do remember beating goalkeeper Jake Findlay by varying the direction of my three kicks.

Our victory over Luton earned us a fifth-round date with Chelsea, which was a tie that went to three matches before ending in defeat at Stamford Bridge. However, the real disappointment came in the home game in late January when we were 3-0 up at half-time and looking a safe bet for the semi-finals until it all went wrong.

Chelsea pulled one back right at the start of the second half, and, incredibly, in the end we only salvaged a 4-4 draw with a last-minute penalty. The tension was tremendous, and I was grateful that Mel Sterland had resumed spot-kick duties. Mel kept his cool and his goal topped a very remarkable match.

The other knock-out game with which I am often associated was a 1-1 draw at Derby in the FA Cup in February 1986. It was, in fact, my 13th Cup appearance for Wednesday – but, sadly, my last. Howard Wilkinson, the manager, substituted me at half-time, and I never played in the first-team again. Soon afterwards, on transfer deadline day, I returned to Aston Villa.

I made the mistake which led to Derby's goal when my crossfield pass was intercepted by John Gregory. When I didn't reappear for the second half, the media made a lot of the incident. Though players don't always agree with a manager's decision, in this instance I went along with it, and, from that day to this, I have never once said a word against Howard Wilkinson because he had every right to do whatever he felt was right for the team.

In fact, I have nothing but admiration for Howard, even though, to be honest, I was heartbroken when he chose to sell me so soon after the Derby game. By the time of my transfer, Wednesday were in the FA Cup semi-final, and I was as sorry as anyone when my old colleagues lost to Everton at Villa Park.

Curiously, my very last game for Villa came against Wednesday when they came to the Midlands in November 1987 and beat us 2-1 in the League Cup despite having Gary Megson sent off. I had been out for some time with cruciate ligament trouble and was making a comeback. Sadly, it wasn't a happy night, for it signalled the end of my playing days. Nowadays, I run some retail sports shops in Coventry and seldom see Wednesday, but I often look back and invariably recall my Hillsborough days with affection and pleasure.

Big Ron's men beaten
Owls v Manchester United
9 November 1985

Paul Hart, who joined the Owls on a free transfer from Nottingham Forest in the summer of 1985 and went on to make 60 League and Cup appearances, recalls his arrival at Hillsborough, and especially remembers the day Wednesday achieved a famous 1-0 victory over Ron Atkinson's men from Old Trafford:

I was already 32 and a veteran of over 560 League and Cup games when I went to Wednesday, but the 18 months I spent at Hillsborough were among the most enjoyable of my career, and that Manchester United match in my first season was one of those brilliant experiences which served to show that, even after 15 years in professional football, a player never loses the sense of excitement at being involved in occasions he knows he'll always remember as extra-special.

Paul Hart savoured a memorable occasion.

I ought to explain that, when my contract was due to expire at Nottingham, Brian Clough gave me a "free" because he thought I was set to go into management. I think he was surprised when, subsequently, the goalposts were shifted and I ended up playing on in the old First Division with Wednesday.

In fact, I was interviewed for the job of player-manager at Tranmere, Stockport and Burnley. I also had the chance to join Lennie Lawrence at Charlton. But nothing came of those possibilities, then, one day, Howard Wilkinson got in touch and, when he invited me to move to Wednesday, I jumped at the chance.

That first season we reached the FA Cup semi-final and finished fifth in the old First Division – and, but for the ban on British clubs following the Heysel Stadium disaster the previous year, we would have qualified for a UEFA Cup place.

This was also the year when Howard began to formulate plans to start changing things in terms of the system, though, in the longer term, he lacked the financial resources to do it in the way he wanted.

It was actually after the 1986 semi-final when he took the first major step, and we switched to a back-four and started working on centre-halves coming to the line and joining in.

But Howard was conscious of what needed to be done even when I arrived. At our first meeting he told me he felt some players were abusing the long-ball game and hiding behind it, and said my brief was to use my experience to encourage a different approach. To a degree, it worked, but it was a culture shock for me when I came, because at Leeds and Forest we had defended deep, never played offside, and passed it.

Initially, I was one of three centre-backs, with Mick Lyons in the central role which controlled it all, and at first I didn't know whether I was coming or going. Later, after Mick left, I took the central spot, with Peter Shirtliff and Lawrie Madden or Mark Smith alongside. I remember playing a ball into Brian Marwood's feet, which surprised him because nobody had been doing that, and he said: "Great! Keep it coming."

Anyway, regarding the Manchester United match, it was a very big game because United were unbeaten in their first 15 outings and had 13 wins under their belt. The crowd that day was over 48,000, and the thing I'll never forget is the atmosphere. When we ran out, the ground seemed to be a sea of blue and-white, and the thousands packed into the Cantilever stand opposite stood as one man to cheer us on to the pitch.

I had played in front of big crowds at Elland Road, and appeared before 68,000 mainly hostile spectators at Celtic Park and 100,000-plus at the Nu Camp, but, honest, Hillsborough that day was a whole new experience. It made the blood tingle.

As for the game itself, I remember getting a kick when going into a tackle with Peter Barnes. He caught the top of my leg, and I must have trapped a nerve or something because I could hardly walk in the second half. I recall telling the manager at half-time: "Look, I'm struggling badly." But he insisted I stayed on.

I hobbled around for the next 45 minutes, and we emerged with a narrow victory thanks to Lee Chapman, who scored at the near-post from a corner. It was a triumph we all savoured – our fifth victory in an unbeaten run we went on to extend to nine matches.

"Chappie", by the way, was my big buddy and room-mate. He was a very brave centre-forward, and he's a great feller, but I know he'll not mind me saying he did rather like looking in the mirror – and was probably the most boring man I've ever met. So much so that we named him Mogadon after the sleeping pill. If I wanted to be sure of getting off to sleep, I'd ask him to tell me a story. He seldom got beyond: "Once upon a time", before I was snoozing sweetly!

Extra-time defeat
Owls v Everton
5 April 1986

Carl Shutt, who didn't make his first start in a Football League game until he was 24 years old, remembers his initial season as a full-time professional as one in which he made a dramatic impact, scoring 13 goals in 25 games and helping Wednesday reach an FA Cup semi-final with Everton which ended in an extra-time defeat. After 21 goals in 48 outings, he moved to Bristol City in October 1987 and later played with Leeds, Birmingham, Bradford City and Darlington:

I went to Waltheof Comprehensive with Mel Sterland and Charlie Williamson, but, while my two classmates joined Wednesday straight from school at 16, I had to wait seven years to follow in their footsteps – meanwhile completing an engineering apprenticeship at Moore & Wright's and learning a good deal about football far removed from the "big time".

To be honest, I had just about reached the stage where I thought the chance of a career in football was going to pass me by when, in the spring of 1985, things suddenly began moving in the right direction. I may have been a late starter, but at least I've gone on to manage around 400 games and 100 goals with half-a-dozen League clubs, while many better players who had an earlier start can't boast a League championship medal or claim to have played in the European Cup.

Of course, I had to wait until I went to Leeds to enjoy that pleasure, but, ironically, in my first season in the Football League, at Wednesday, we finished fifth in the old Division One and would have qualified to play in Europe but for the ban on English clubs. My consolation was in having finally reached the "big time" at Hillsborough.

The key figure in this development in my career was Mick Hennigan, who had been my boss at Spalding United in the North Eastern Counties League before Howard Wilkinson brought him back to Sheffield shortly after getting the Wednesday post. Mick, who was later with Howard at Leeds, is one of the game's great characters, and, but for him, I might never have got where I did.

Mick had come into my life about three years earlier when he watched me in Sunday football with the Earl of Arundel – one of many pubs for whom I played in those early days. Mick, who was then Spalding's assistant boss, saw me score twice in this match, and, after inviting me for a drink in the bar, he asked if I fancied playing for his club. I didn't even know where Spalding was, but saying "yes" was a step I never regretted.

In becoming a semi-pro, I started out playing on a match-fee basis for Spalding, which meant I could continue in Sunday football as well as turning out for them. In the following season I signed a contract which prevented me from playing for anyone else, but, later, I reverted to the old arrangement and rejected another contract after being upset to discover they had denied me the chance of joining Notts County by seeking a transfer fee of around £10,000.

The upshot of all this was that when I went to Wednesday, Spalding didn't get a fee, although, in fact, I think Howard Wilkinson did arrange to give them something.

The Wednesday link came about at a time when a number of Spalding players were training at Middlewood Road. Mick Hennigan asked me to pop into Hillsborough for a chat, and that was when he said him and Howard wanted to look at me in the Reserves. I don't remember who I played against in my first Reserves match, but do recall scoring with a tap-in after someone hit the bar. I managed 13 goals in 12 games which included matches against Sheffield United and Liverpool.

My workmates at Moore & Wright's were as pleased as me about my progress. One colleague, Walt Forrest, was so keen to help my cause that on days when I was due to play for the Reserves he used to get my boots out of my bag during the works lunch break and polish them with great care. Even the Unitedites in our shop started watching Wednesday Reserves, and everyone was sure that if the Owls didn't sign me, another League club would.

I shall never forget how I was at work one day when I was called to the phone, but, to be honest, I thought it was a wind-up when the caller announced himself as Howard Wilkinson. When he said he wanted to see me down at the ground, I asked: "What for?" He replied: "To discuss professional terms." I spent the rest of the day in a daze!

With a well-paid full-time job and what I was earning playing as a semi-pro, I was doing okay financially, but my wife and I had agreed that, should the chance to join a League club as a full-time pro ever arise, we had nothing to lose by giving it a go because I would always have my trade to fall back on.

The irony of accepting Wednesday's terms, although I didn't realise it right at the outset, was that in attaining my ambition and getting into League football, in the beginning I was actually about £50 a week out of pocket – even though Howard had promised I wouldn't lose by it!

After going on as a sub in a game at Oxford in August 1985, I made my first start in Wednesday's Division One side against Coventry in the following October. It was two days after my 24th birthday, and I celebrated with a goal – a diving header from my old school pal Mel Sterland's cross. Apart from the thrill of a scoring debut, the memory which stands out from that day is a gesture by Mick Lyons, our captain, before the game.

Mick had taken upon himself the job of putting me at ease, driving me to the ground and generally looking after me. When he noticed my boots weren't laid out, he fetched them from the boot room, then said: "You want some new laces in these," – and promptly set about removing the old ones and replacing them. It might seem a small thing, but the memory of such a big star doing that for me is something I've never forgotten.

I played three games because Garry Thompson, who had cost a record £450,000, was injured, and, naturally, when he was fit I went back to the Reserves. Then, although I had the pleasure of playing and scoring in a 2-2 draw at Liverpool on New Year's Day, I didn't get another decent run until March – when I captured a few headlines with six goals in three matches and

revelled in the feeling that I had finally arrived!

There was a sense in which the FA Cup fifth-round replay with Derby was like having my debut all over again, because, when we went to the Hallam Tower Hotel for the pre-match meal, I hadn't a clue I was going to play. I always remember I'd been after some new boots, and one of the backroom staff took me to try a pair on while the rest of the lads were having a team meeting at which (so I learned later) the manager had told them: "Carl's playing tonight, but don't let on just yet."

The funny thing was, I had told Mark Chamberlain how much I was looking forward to watching the game from the bench, and, when he said: "You never know, you might be playing," I laughed and remarked: "That's doubtful." Even when Garry Thompson didn't arrive in the dining room until after we'd had our tea and toast, I never suspected he wasn't playing – but I was.

Anyway, I got both goals in our 2-0 win, and three days later I bagged a hat-trick in the 5-1 defeat of Birmingham – a day when my second goal was a chance I snapped up after goalkeeper David Seaman let the ball slip through his hands, and the third followed a run when I just kept going from deep in our own half. Then I ended a wonderful week with the second goal in a 2-1 quarter-final success against West Ham.

To play in a semi-final in my first season was something special, but, unfortunately, the result, a 2-1 defeat against Everton in extra-time, spoiled the script. My only consolation was in scoring with a header, and at least I still possess one treasured memory of that goal in the form of a picture which one of my old Moore & Wright workmates took with his Instamatic as he stood behind the net at the Holte End.

I have never forgotten how, on the way to Villa Park before the semi-final, Lee Chapman played his favourite Tears for Fears tape on the team bus, and *Everybody Wants to Rule the World* seemed so appropriate – a great song for a great day. But we didn't rule, and I never hear the song now without recalling our disappointment.

Paul Hart has affectionate memories of his first season at Hillsborough when Wednesday not only reached the FA Cup semi-final but finished the 1985-86 campaign with a remarkable run-in which sealed their highest top-grade position since 1961:

After playing in the two third-round games against West Brom, I didn't figure in the 1986 FA Cup run again until the semi-final because of a hamstring injury. However, I remember a few incidents from the matches I missed – not least when Martin Hodge, our goalkeeper, got injured in the fifth-round tie at Derby, and when Nigel Worthington took a lot of ribbing after scoring with his right foot against West Ham in the quarter-final at Hillsborough.

"Hodgy" was an excellent goalkeeper whose form had put him on the brink of going to Mexico with England. He was unfortunate not to get a place on that trip after being on stand-by. He had a marvelously consistent run with Wednesday and went about 200 games without being absent.

That day at Derby he went for a high ball and fell head first on a bone-hard pitch. He did very well to carry on when he was obviously suffering from concussion, but that sort of bravery was typical of the man. He could even smile when we ribbed him that if he'd fallen on any other part of his anatomy, he might have felt it!

The semi-final, at Villa Park, brought us up against Everton, who were the reigning champions and holders of the European Cup-winners' Cup. They'd beaten us twice in the First Division that season – including a 5-1 drubbing at home. It didn't help that we were forced into a late re-jig when Brian Marwood suffered a hamstring injury in training ahead of the game. Moreover, I played that day with a broken toe.

In the end, we lost 2-1 in extra-time, but I remember it as a tight game which might have gone either way. We started very well and were so on top in the opening minutes that we should have scored.

Everton scored soon after the start of the second half against the run of play. We felt Harper, who had come on as a sub, was offside, but as Mountfield returned this ball towards our goalmouth from our clearance, "Hodgy" dashed out to dive at Harper's feet, and the Everton lad lobbed it over him into the net.

But we were level within about four minutes, when I got my head to Glyn Snodin's far-post cross and played the ball back to Carl Shutt, who nodded it in.

The winner, which came early in extra-time, was a stunning volley from Greame Sharp, who met a Paul Bracewell cross first-time and scored a great goal. "Hodgy" had no chance, and, at the final whistle, we could only accept defeat knowing we had done our best and not let anyone down.

The thing worth remembering about that semi-final defeat was the way we responded to it. Normally the bottom drops out of a club's season when they lose just one step from Wembley, but, remarkably, we won five and drew two of our last seven League matches. It served to emphasise the character and spirit in the club at that time, and, in finishing fifth in the old First Division, we claimed Wednesday's highest position for 25 years.

"Not the kind of goal I usually scored!"
Owls v Sheffield United
21 November 1989

John Sheridan recalls a memorable strike in only his fourth game for the Owls following his £500,000 move from Nottingham Forest. It brought his first Wednesday goal and sealed a 3-2 extra-time triumph in a Zenith Data Systems Cup game at Hillsborough.

I was new to Sheffield at the time, and, though this wasn't a major game on the fixture list, it was the first time the city's club had met at senior level for some years – and the clash attracted a crowd of over 30,000, which was a record for the competition.

The atmosphere was more like an FA Cup quarter-final than a ZDS match, and I think we led twice with goals from Dalian Atkinson and Carlton Palmer. But United got their second equaliser about a minute from the end of normal time.

I claimed the goal that proved to be the winner after about three minutes of extra-time, and what made it special was it wasn't the type of goal I very often scored. I just collected the ball and

started on a run in which I went past three or four men, then I whacked it towards the net – and it went in!

Sunday best at Wembley
Owls v Manchester United
21 April 1991

This was the famous occasion when Wednesday produced their Sunday best at Wembley and won the Rumbelows League Cup (the club's first major trophy since 1935) with a 1-0 defeat of Manchester United.
Alan Smith, Wednesday's physio from 1983 to 1994, has several special memories of the day when a John Sheridan strike sealed an unforgettable Owls' victory.

One thing I remember about that April afternoon in 1991 was the fantastic support we took to the game. As we travelled down Wembley Way in the team bus, the only colours we saw were Wednesday's, and, when we walked out to look at the pitch nearly two hours before the kick-off, the far end of the stadium was already a sea of blue and-white while the Manchester areas of the ground were still empty. You didn't need telling how much the occasion meant to the people of Sheffield.

Even at that early stage, it was a wonderful sight, and the reception the fans gave the players when they saw them was something very special. Carlton Palmer, you may remember, was suspended because he'd been sent off in a League match at Portsmouth. Now, when the fans saw him they started chanting: "There's only one Carlton Palmer" – and it brought tears to his eyes. Carlton being the tough character he is, making him weep takes some doing, but he was very moved.

We all felt very sorry Carlton couldn't play because he was such an inspiration to the team. You were seldom down for long when he was around. The other lads loved him, and everybody shared his disappointment at missing such a big match in the circumstances that had occurred. But was Carlton down? Not on your life.

If you've seen the group photograph that was taken on the pitch at the end, after we'd got the trophy, you'll see that

Carlton is standing next to me. There we are, all singing and chanting, and, considering Carlton had missed the game of the year, the thing I remember is he was the one who started everybody off singing. I heard him set the whole thing going. It emphasised his great character. Typically, he was too happy for the others to be sorry for himself.

Another thing I recall about the Rumbelows Cup Final is going on to the field near the end to give Peter Shirtliff some treatment. As I was coming off, I asked the referee, Ray Lewis, how long there was still to play. He told me and I ran back to the bench and said to Richie Barker: "He says there's two minutes left." Richie, in his dour way, replied: "They'll be the longest two minutes of our lives." And they were!

An all-Sheffield Wembley day
Owls v Sheffield United
3 April 1993

Mining engineer Keith Littlewood recalls he was away working in India when the Sheffield clubs met in the unique Wembley FA Cup semi-final in 1993, but distance only lent enchantment to the occasion:

Knowing I was going to miss the Wednesday-United semi-final because I was just starting a two-months stint in India, I took a short-wave radio with me and so was able to listen to the commentary. I always remember I was just finishing totting up my expenses when Mark Bright scored the extra-time winner. You could say I got a double bonus!

I was looking forward to reading about the game when the newspapers came from England, but, a couple of days later, another engineer arrived from home. He asked if I was Littlewood, and when I said yes he gave me a package containing a video recording of Sky TV's transmission for the entire afternoon of the Wembley match.

As you can imagine, I bored everyone to tears for the next few weeks replaying the match as often as possible. I was so familiar with the details of that game, I sometimes think I must have been there!

I got home for the Final against Arsenal, but have to say watching Wednesday in the flesh instead of on tape proved something of an anticlimax – well, the result, a last-minute defeat in extra-time in the replay, certainly was.

John Sheridan, Wednesday's Republic of Ireland midfielder, recalls Chris Waddle's memorable 30-yard strike from an early free-kick and a derby duel which was Sheffield's own Cup Final:
We couldn't believe it when Sheffield United wanted to have this game played at Wembley. We thought they would much rather have seen the match staged at Elland Road, where the pitch would have been more suited to their style. We knew Wembley was a pitch which would enable us to play to our strengths, and there's no doubt we went into that semi feeling very confident.

On the day, we outplayed United, and we could have won by a very big margin, though it made for a gripping afternoon when the game went into extra-time. The atmosphere that afternoon was probably the most memorable of all my time with Wednesday, and, when I look back, that was really our Cup Final.

Chris Waddle's early goal was unforgettable. The two of us used to share all the free-kicks, but I invariably took more than Chris. With this particular free-kick being where it was on the pitch, Chris said he felt he'd get more pace on it with a left-footer.

I was just about to ask him: "Do you want to hit it?" when he just ran up and hammered it – and before I could get the words out of my mouth, the ball flew into the top corner. It was a great strike, and the game had been in progress barely a minute.

Mark Bright, who went on to head Wednesday's extra-time winner in this famous Sheffield derby, also recalls Chris Waddle's fabulous early strike:
It was one of those coincidences which football often throws up that the free-kick from which Chris Waddle scored was conceded by my old Crystal Palace colleague John Pemberton when he pushed me as we went for a high ball together. John and I had played in an FA Cup Final together only three years earlier, against Manchester United, and he'd been involved when I scored in the semi-final defeat of Liverpool the same year.

Anyway, now, in 1993 I heard "Wadd" say to "Shez" Sheridan: "I'm going to hit it." It seemed to be a long way from goal, but I think Chris, having seen Paul Gascoigne score with a similar attempt the previous year, fancied anything "Gazza" could do he could do at least as well.

It being so soon after the kick-off, I doubt if anyone expected such a stunning strike, and, when the ball flew into the net, I don't suppose I'm alone when I say my reaction was one of utter disbelief – but tinged with joy!

It certainly shattered any game plan Sheffield United had made, though, to their credit, they subsequently pulled themselves level, and, despite the fact that we were much the better team, we had to wait until extra-time to get the winner.

The funny thing is, before the game manager Trevor Francis had said to me: "You'll get the winner today." He was right, and I remember feeling a terrific sense of relief when I headed the ball down and into the net from a John Harkes left-wing corner. I had scored in a semi-final before, but that had been at Villa Park, and getting the winner at Wembley on such a unique occasion was very special.

Cup Final heartbreak
Owls v Arsenal
20 May 1993

John Brodie, an engineer and surveyor who has followed Wednesday for 35 years, remembers his saddest moment – when the Owls lost in the last-minute of extra-time in the FA Cup Final replay in 1993:

The kick-off, you'll remember, was delayed on that Thursday night because of problems on the M1 which had delayed some Wednesday fans, and I recall making an urgent call home to my wife because I wanted her to re-set the video. I didn't want to miss being able to see the replay again later.

As it happened, it was a long time before I could bear to even think about that match, let alone watch it again. When Linighan's header went in, so desperately close to the end of extra-time, I saw grown men weep. I think the goal was scored with nearly a full minute of injury-time added, and a penalty shoot-out looked a certainty.

I didn't cry. I don't know why. It was something beyond tears, and I drove home in a state of shock. I just blanked that journey out, and it was probably the only way I could cope with what had happened. It must have been at least six months before that defeat was mentioned in our house.

John Sheridan, the Wednesday midfielder who had recovered from a knee operation in time to figure in the 1993 Cup runs, recalls:
My memory of the FA Cup Final replay is that we should have won it because we had the chances; and it was very disappointing when Arsenal snatched the winner in the last seconds of extra-time. There was nothing between the teams, really.

At the time the goal went in, I was turning my thoughts to the penalty shoot-out, because I had been designated to take our first spot-kick. I would rather have seen us lose on penalties than to be defeated in the way we were. It was very cruel.

Hammers were hammered for five
Owls v West Ham
18 December 1993

Mark Bright, the former Owls striker, remembers a 5-0 defeat of West Ham as one of the most satisfying games of his Hillsborough career, and recalls it as a match which will always be synonymous with Chris Waddle:

Chris Waddle gave the Wednesday fans many magical moments to savour, but the day we beat West Ham just before Christmas in 1993 has passed into club folklore as the definitive Waddle game. I think he had a hand in every goal and the fans thought Santa had arrived a week early!

"Wadd" scored one himself; his sheer brilliance induced Mike Marsh to turn the ball into his own net; and that afternoon Nigel Jemson, Carlton Palmer and myself all profited from his marvellous creative talents with goals. Poor old "Budgie" Burrows had the misfortune to be West Ham's left-back, and Chris went round him, past him, put the ball through his legs, and generally made Burrows wish he'd stayed at home.

It was one of the most enjoyable games I ever played in. You always like to win, and it's invariably very satisfying to win well; but some matches give you a special sense of fulfilment. Everything seemed to go for the team. The passing was good, the movement and touch excellent, and, with "Wadd" playing like a dream, the entertainment value for the fans was tremendous.

I was always a Waddle fan long before I ever came to play with him, and, when I had the chance to get to know him, I found that as a player and as a person Chris was out of the top drawer. He was different class – and Wednesday supporters worshipped him.

Goals to Remember

Charlie Tomlinson

Winger Charlie Tomlinson, affectionately known as "Shadows", had the distinction of scoring after only 12 seconds in a game at Preston in October 1949. He started playing for Wednesday at senior level in

Charlie Tomlinson – a brilliant goal at Bramall Lane.

1944, and scored 25 goals in 90 wartime games. In 1945 the Owls completed his formal transfer from Bradford (Park Avenue) for £1,000, which was ironic considering he'd had links with the club as a youngster. He made 77 peacetime League and Cup appearances and added 12 more goals to his tally before moving to Rotherham in 1951. Supporter Peter Pollitt remembers an unforgettable Tomlinson goal in Wednesday's 3-1 victory at Sheffield United in September 1945:

Old "Shadows" was what we'd call a character, a bit of a lad. But he was a very talented footballer and gave me a moment to treasure once at Bramall Lane. Wednesday were attacking the Shoreham Street end in the second half, and Tomlinson lifted this bouncing ball above Fred Furniss and into the air. As it came down, he headed it over Furniss

and another defender, then ran forward to meet it as it dropped for a second time with a marvellous volley which gave Jack Smith in the United goal absolutely no chance.

Jackie Robinson

Jackie Robinson, Wednesday's wartime goal-king, made only seven appearances for the Owls after "normal" football resumed in 1946-47 before he was transferred to Sunderland. In that spell he scored six goals, and his last double came in a 5-3 win at Leicester. Vin Kenny, the Wednesday full-back, recalls:

I made my first-team debut for Wednesday in a match at Filbert Street in September 1946 while on leave from the army, and there are two things I shall always remember about that game. One was the pitch, which was probably the worst I ever played on, and the other was a goal from Jackie Robinson which had to be the best I ever saw.

The conditions were terrible. In those days, Leicester's pitch was notorious for being heavy at the best of times, but now, after a downpour, it was dreadful. Within minutes of the kick-off the ball was like a lump of lead, and those 90 minutes were a hell of a stamina test for us all.

However, we won the match 5-3 in a real ding-dong battle. We went 2-0 down within half-an-hour, fought back to 2-2, and then trailed 3-2. But "Robbo" made it 3-3 on the hour when he scored from the rebound after Joe Calvert, the Leicester goalkeeper, had saved his penalty-kick. Then soon afterward, Tommy Ward shot us in front for the first time.

"Robbo" put the icing on the cake with about 20 minutes left when he made the score 5-3 with a marvellous goal. You have to remember that the ball, soaking and caked in mud, must have weighed a ton by that late stage of the game, but Jackie met it so sweetly on the volley that he might have been striking a tennis ball, and it shot 30

yards into the net to give Calvert no chance. One moment there had seemed to be nothing on, the next the ball was in the net.

Alf Rogers

The late Alf Rogers, a product of Birley Carr, scored 39 goals in 125 senior games between 1940 and 1950, but he always remembered the one he scored against Fulham at the Leppings Lane end in November 1947. This is how he recalled the incident:

It was a unique goal, not in the sense that it was a particularly memorable shot, but the ball finished up near the corner flag! In fact, it was a very ordinary cross-shot which I didn't hit especially hard. I don't recall who gave me the pass, and I have no memory of how far out I was. But I never forgot that the ball broke the net.

I saw the ball go in, and immediately turned, and, after the usual handshakes from colleagues, had reached the centre circle when I turned to look back, and was staggered to see the ball somewhere near the corner flag. I couldn't imagine how it had got there!

It transpired that the ball had hit a flaw in the netting and broken it open. The nets were new that day, and Eric Taylor, the manager, said later that he'd fit new nets before every game if I could be sure to find the flaw with a shot on target.

I scored a lot of better goals. I once scored three in a wartime game and recall hitting six in a reserve match, but that goal against Fulham was often the one people mentioned because it had the novelty of being different. All that mattered to me was that it helped us to a 2-0 win.

Edgar Packard

Edgar Packard was a centre-half who only scored once in 150 League and Cup games for the Owls between 1939 and 1952, but it was a goal which will always be remembered by supporters who witnessed the 2-1 defeat of West Ham at Hillsborough in December 1949. Frank Ronksley, a long-time Owls' fan recalls:

I've seen some cracking goals, but Packard's stands out because it was so unexpected and West Ham should never have let it happen. He ran with the ball from deep in Wednesday's half right to within a few yards of the opposition penalty area, and, perhaps

Edgar Packard – who can ever forget the day he caught the West Ham defence on the hop?

because they were sure he was going to pass it to someone, the defenders just kept backing off.

Packard seldom ventured far beyond his own penalty box, for in those days Wednesday's defenders were not encouraged to push forward. However, when he reached the halfway line and nobody went near him, he obviously thought: "I'll go into this strange area where only our forwards are allowed!" – and kept just toddling on and on.

West Ham seemed to be more concerned with who Packard was going to pass to than with stopping him, for his record didn't suggest he promised any threat as a potential marksman. Eventually, it dawned on one West Ham man that he ought to make a tackle, but, just as he lunged in, Packard swung his foot at the ball and – crack! It was in the back of the net.

That goal, scored at the Kop end and coming after about 20 minutes, was the one I recalled at the end of the season

when we clinched promotion – on goal-average!

Derek Dooley

Derek Dooley created an abundance of sweet memories when he established a post-war record with his 47 League and Cup goals in Wednesday's 1951-52 Second Division title triumph. Peter Pollitt recalls a great Dooley "goal that never was" – one of the best the giant centre-forward ever netted, but, alas, it didn't count:

In mid-February 1952, Wednesday played in a terrific game with Barnsley at Oakwell, and it was a great injustice that they lost 5-4.

When the score was 4-4, Dave McIntosh, the Wednesday goalkeeper, collected the ball, and though he was being hustled by a home forward, he managed to give it a good belt upfield. The ball just dropped nicely for Dooley near the halfway line, and he turned and set off like a great tank, powering down the middle of the field towards the home goal pursued by two Barnsley defenders.

When Dooley was in full flight, it was a sight to behold. He was big and awkward, but on these occasions he looked unstoppable. He only had one thing in mind – to slam that ball into the net. He was challenged, he was pulled this way and that, but he kept going and suddenly the ball left his boot and flew past the goalkeeper. What a goal!

The Wednesdayites roared, the other players surrounded Derek and congratulated him, and our lads were back at the halfway line before it dawned on everyone that the referee hadn't given the goal. He explained he had awarded Wednesday a free-kick for a foul on McIntosh as he was clearing the ball towards Dooley.

What an injustice! And just to rub salt in the wounds, McNeil, who was an injured passenger, went and nicked a winner for Barnsley in the last minute.

Redfern Froggatt

Redfern Froggatt scored 140 Football League goals for Wednesday between

October 1946 and April 1960, and more than a few were special. Here he remembers a goal that clinched promotion in the 1958-59 Second Division championship triumph as one of the most satisfying of his career:

I'm often reminded of a couple of hat-tricks I scored, one against Liverpool in the First Division and the other against Sunderland in Division Two.

My first treble, in October 1950, was particularly welcome because it brought only our third win in the opening 15 games of what proved to be a relegation season. That was to be the year when we went down despite winning our final game 6-0.

The second treble, in September of the 1958-59 promotion campaign when Harry Catterick was our new manager, is often recalled because we won the game 6-0 to make it six victories in our first eight matches, and it was Albert Quixall's last appearance before his record £45,000 transfer to Manchester United.

I'm sure both those occasions gave me a lot of pleasure, but it is a single goal in a game later in that 1958-59 run to the Second Division title which always sticks in my mind as perhaps the most rewarding. It was certainly a goal I had been waiting a long time to score.

A curious thing about my playing days with Wednesday was that I always seemed to do better in the months before Christmas than I did afterwards. I invariably excelled in the autumn, then, perhaps because I never really liked the cold months early in a new year, it always proved a struggle getting goals in the depths of winter.

That 1958-59 campaign, when I was captain and enjoyed my best tally in a season, illustrated the pattern. I finished with 26 goals, and, remarkably, 23 came in the first 25 matches. Then I went from January to April without finding the net, and didn't end my personal drought until we met Liverpool at home one Tuesday evening in mid-April.

It was a 7pm kick-off, and I'll never forget that it started to rain a couple of hours before the kick-off.

The rain poured down all through the match. You can tell how bad it was when I say that, by just after half-time, the open Spion Kop was virtually deserted because all the regulars had gradually moved to other parts of the ground in search of shelter.

After an hour, by which time we were kicking towards a Kop end occupied by a handful of drenched souls, we suddenly got away down the right. Tom McAnearney crossed the ball and I put it into the net. I was delighted, and remember being amused by the fact that there were so few people at that end to witness the goal.

It was good to score at last, but what made that goal extra special was it confirmed promotion. It also meant I had the added bonus of emulating my father, who had been captain of Wednesday when they went up from the Second Division 33 years earlier.

Ralph O'Donnell

Ralph O'Donnell scored only three goals in his 183 League and Cup appearances for the Owls between November 1951 and April 1962, and, as the former defender admits, they were all satisfying – although he always remembers them with a touch of amusement:

I don't imagine any of my three goals will have a special place in anybody's memory except mine, and, to be honest, I'm sometimes inclined to forget them!

The first one I ever scored in the Football League, against Port Vale in March 1956, was really quite amusing. It might be unfair to describe it as a thunderous shot, for it was probably travelling at about one mile an hour maximum. I hit the shot, and the goalkeeper, a chap called King, might have saved it if only he had realised that Roy Shiner was going to jump over the ball. Even I could hardly believe it as the ball just about made it across the line!

That day we beat Port Vale 4-0, but I remember we lost 5-2 when I scored at Sunderland in February 1957 – my first goal in Division One. One match report suggests I beat four players and scored with a low shot. My only memory is that, thankfully, the goalkeeper let it go because he thought the ball was going wide!

My final League goal was also at Sunderland, in March 1958, when we drew 3-3. I remember when I scored it put us 3-1 in front, but we couldn't hold

on. The goal came straight from the kick-off at the start of the second half. The ball was played to Quixall, Albert put his foot on it and waited until I dashed into the hole between the centre-half and the full-back, then he chipped it forward. I got to the ball first, but I seem to remember that, as I touched it goalwards, Billy Elliott, the Sunderland back, deflected it past his own goalkeeper. I claimed it, but some people would say the credit didn't belong to me!

Pele

In March 1962 the world-famous Brazilian team, Santos, paid the first of two visits to Hillsborough, when they produced a memorable display and won 4-2. Coutinho completed his hat-trick after Billy Griffin and David Layne had pulled Wednesday level at 2-2, but it was the final goal of the night, a penalty kick converted by the legendary Pele, which inspired a sense of wonder in the 49,058 crowd. The late Eric Taylor once recalled:

Pele did the fox-trot, a two-step and a tango as he stepped up to the ball. He then stopped dead and sent Ron Springett the wrong way. I felt sorry for our goalkeeper because, somehow, he was transfixed by Pele's trickery and nobody in the world could have saved that penalty. It was pure magic.

An intriguing footnote to this game is David Ford's memory of being a Wednesday apprentice at the time the Brazilians came to Sheffield. He recalled: As soon as I could after the match, I made the excuse of having to go into the visitors' dressing room to start sweeping up, but, really, all I wanted was to get a close-up view of Pele!

David Layne

More than a few of the 58 goals David "Bronco" Layne scored in 81 League and Cup matches for Wednesday between 1962 and 1964 still linger in the memory. Albert Clayton remembers:

"Bronco" got a double at Bramall Lane in the Sheffield derby match of October 1962, and one of them was something

to treasure. Yet, when I think of Layne, I'm always reminded of a crazy goal at Gay Meadow in February 1963 when we met Shrewsbury in the FA Cup.

Layne scored this perfectly good goal. In fact, it was the only one he got in his four FA Cup outings with Wednesday. However, he nearly didn't get it because the referee signalled a goal-kick! What happened was the ball went through a hole in the net, hit the wall behind, and rebounded on to the pitch. Shrewsbury's goalkeeper, the cheeky begger, compounded the initial injustice by picking the ball up and placing it ready to kick.

Fortunately, the linesman was flagging and we Wednesdayites standing behind that goal were shouting: "There's a hole in the net!" with such a vociferous sense of injustice that somebody had to take some notice.

The officials lifted the net up and saw the hole, and the referee finally signalled a goal. That gave us a 1-0 lead, but Shrewsbury equalised in the second half and we had to wait for the Hillsborough replay to win through.

Mark Pearson

"Pancho" Pearson was a Sheffield lad who joined Wednesday from Manchester United in October 1963 and went to Fulham in 1965 after scoring nine goals in 40 games. Albert Clayton comments:

Mark went to the same school as me, Frecheville Secondary Modern, but he was about three years in front of me. I think his best goal for Wednesday was a tremendous effort which earned us a point in a famous match at Stoke in November 1963. In that game we twice trailed by three goals but it finished 4-4, with the equaliser coming when this ball was knocked out by a defender and Pearson, who was making only about his eighth appearance for the club, met it on the volley to hit a beauty from just outside the penalty area.

Jackie Sinclair

Jackie Sinclair hit 16 goals in 109 games for Wednesday after arriving in the exchange deal which took David Ford to

Newcastle in December 1969, and the Scottish winger, who is now an assistant steward at Dunfermline Golf Club, remembers a late winner against Swindon in October 1971 as the best he scored in his time at Hillsborough:

We were all over Swindon that afternoon and doing everything but put the ball in the net, and when we hit the bar towards the end, I felt sure it was going to be one of those frustrating days when we'd have to settle for a 0-0 draw.

But then, with barely two minutes

Jack Sinclair.

left, Dave Clements, who had recently arrived with Brian Joicey from Coventry, hit a long cross from the left. Mick Prendergast got his head to the ball, and when it came towards me, I had my back to the goal. I threw myself at the ball and produced an overhead kick which sent it flashing past Roy Jones, the goalkeeper, into the net.

That spectacular effort meant we had won two League games on the trot for the first time that season, and, in fact, it was only our fourth win in 14 matches, but things were looking up because the victory extended what was our best unbeaten run in 1971-72.

Terry Curran

Terry Curran, who scored 39 goals in 138 games after joining Wednesday from

Southampton in March 1979, was one of the most popular players of his era – though he did dismay some Owls fans when he elected to negotiate a move to Sheffield United in 1982. Long-time supporter Paul Webster has no doubt that Curran claimed the best goal he ever saw from an Owls' player – a superb strike against Sheffield United at Bramall Lane in April 1980:

It was a goal which epitomised Terry Curran. When Terry had the ball at his feet, he was always positive, direct and capable of the unexpected. I can't recall where he got the ball from, but I have this abiding memory of him being by the corner flag on the left, then he cut in and went past two men before curling the ball into the top corner. It took your breath away, honest it did!

Gary Bannister

Gary Bannister scored 66 goals in 143 games for the Owls between 1981 and 1984, notching 22 in each of his three seasons at Hillsborough. Mel Sterland nominates a goal Bannister scored in the 1983-84 promotion run:

The one Gary Bannister got in the 2-1 win at Cambridge in March 1984 was unforgettable. He beat at least three players in a terrific dribble from the halfway line before sticking it past the goalkeeper, and it gave us an early lead

in a match we dominated. That was definitely a very special goal, a superb piece of individual skill.

Gary Shelton

Midfielder Gary Shelton, who joined the Owls from Aston Villa in 1982, made 240 appearances before moving to Oxford in 1987, scoring 24 goals. He was Player of the Year in 1983-84. Peter Shirtliff, the former Owls defender, recalls:

I shall always remember Gary Shelton's goal which gave us the points in a vital promotion game at Newcastle in April 1984. It was a match you knew was going to be settled by a single strike, and, happily, we got it – and in rather spectacular style. I think it stemmed from a Mel Sterland throw-in which Gary Megson headed on, and Shelton, with his back to the goal, launched into an overhead scissor kick. I don't think even Gary could believe it when he turned round and saw the ball nestling in the bottom corner!

Mel Sterland

Mel Sterland, known to the fans as "Zico", made 342 League and Cup appearances for the Owls between 1979 and 1989, and many of his 49 goals were special. Some were from the penalty spot,

Gary Shelton – a spectacular strike against Newcastle United in the 1983-84 promotion campaign.

David Hirst scoring one of his favourite goals, the equaliser against Sheffield United in 1992.

others were "crackers" from a distance. Howard Wilkinson, the former Wednesday manager, comments:

A lot of people still enthuse about a marvellous goal Mel got in a 3-3 draw with Arsenal at Hillsborough in April 1988, but for me the best I saw him score was in a 3-1 win at Oldham in September of the 1983-84 promotion season.

It sticks in my mind because, on the day after the match, Mel was due to join the England Under-21 squad. In the first half at Boundary Park, things hadn't exactly gone to plan for us, and I had a bit of a go at Mel in the dressing room at half-time. I warned him if he didn't get his finger out, he wouldn't be joining the England party.

He pulled his finger out all right! He walloped this volley from 25-30 yards and it flew into the net, transforming a game which had been slipping from us into one that we won comfortably.

David Hirst

David Hirst's 128 goals in 358 games for the Owls between 1986 and 1997 included more than a few which were

memorable. Phil King, a colleague of Hirst's in the 1990-91 Second Division promotion season, comments:

The thing I recall about the Wednesday team I played in was how many goals stemmed from great team effort and flowing moves which emphasised the quality in our side. However, for a great individual goal, the third of the four David Hirst scored against Hull in September 1990 takes some beating. David collected the ball just inside our half, in the centre circle, turned, and, with a terrific burst of pace, left a defender standing as he ran all the way to the edge of the Hull penalty area before rolling his shot past the advancing goalkeeper at the Kop end.

Many people often mention his swivel and terrific left-foot volley at the Leppings Lane end in the same game, and I know David himself felt his fourth goal was the one he enjoyed the most. This was one he dinked over the goalkeeper from eight yards, and, on the face if it, perhaps it looked the easiest of the four. But the tap-ins were the ones he'd been missing, and he was pleased to show he could score simple goals as well as the more spectacular.

To see David in full flight at his peak was a very thrilling experience, but we shouldn't forget that David could provide goal chances, too, and I have a memory of one he made for Paul Williams and another he set up for John Sheridan.

Late in that 1990-91 promotion season, I remember Hirsty getting away and crossing on the run with great skill in a match at West Ham – and Williams was there at the front post, flying through the air to score with a diving header.

On the day in August 1991 when Carlton Palmer claimed a hat-trick against QPR at Hillsborough, Hirsty set up the fourth goal when he whipped in a terrific cross from the right. Sheridan met it first time on the volley with the outside of his right boot. It was some goal, believe me, and I still have the image in my mind of John's delight as he ran towards a ball-boy behind the goal and they did a "high fives" – a moment that little lad will surely always cherish.

David Hirst himself comments on three goals he rates among his most satisfying:
My Dad's got the scrapbook which con-

tains my favourite photograph – the one taken just after I'd scored the equaliser against Arsenal at Wembley in 1993. I have lots of pictures showing me being pleased at having found the net in various matches, but that picture sums up the unique delight of scoring in an FA Cup Final. My eyes are closed, my head is back, and the gesture I'm making with my arms and clenched fists emphasise the sheer joy of that moment as Mark Bright lifts me up and John Harkes throws himself on to me from behind.

The goal stemmed from a lovely move started by "Shez" Sheridan, whose ball into the box was headed towards the far post by Brighty, and Harkesy nodded it back. I was half sliding on the turn and caught the ball sweetly with my left foot. Unforgettable!

Another favourite was one I scored against Sheffield United at Bramall Lane in November 1992. It was a goal I saw described as being taken with great economy of effort, but I recall it as a stab shot. I couldn't do any more than stab at the ball, really, because I'd just run 30 yards and felt knackered! I remember playing the ball to Chris Waddle, carrying on my run and shouting for the return. He played a great ball back, I hit it past Alan Kelly, and it added to my pleasure to score at the end where our fans were. We drew the game 1-1.

One of the first goals I scored after "Big Ron" came to Wednesday in 1989 was in a 3-1 win at Newcastle when we were pushing to pull away from the threat of relegation. I remember it because, at the time, I was literally out on my feet and standing by the touchline with the Gaffer just about to bring me off.

Then Greg Fee played the ball out to me, and I made one last effort, went past a couple of defenders and smashed a shot past Gary Kelly. I promptly returned to the touchline and said: "Right, I've emptied the tank now, I'm ready to come off!"

Paul Williams

Paul Williams is remembered as an inside-forward who was always a grafter – a player whose contribution cannot be measured by the 28 goals he scored in 114

games between August 1990 and September 1992. However, some of those strikes were memorable. Phil King, a former colleague comments:

Paul Williams scored some very important goals in his time with Wednesday. He was a busy, brave little player who was much appreciated by his teammates as well as by the fans.

The goal he scored at Crystal Palace in April 1992 was memorable because it typified Paul's knack of being in the right place at the right time, and his courage – while it also emphasised John Sheridan's brilliant control and ability to deliver the perfect pass.

The goal actually stemmed from a clearance by Nigel Martyn, the Palace goalkeeper. When he threw the ball out, Sheridan beat Gordon in the race for possession. The way John dinked the ball over Dean Gordon with deliberate

back-spin, then drove it into the goal-mouth on the half-volley, a bit flat and at head height, exhibited wonderful skill – and Williams met it at the front post with a flying header that flew into the net.

That was the day when, had we won, we would still have been in with a chance of winning the championship. In the event, Palace equalised through Mark Bright in the last minute, and, anyway, subsequent results meant we finished third in the table behind Leeds and Manchester United.

Ironically, Bright later came to Wednesday in the exchange deal that took Williams to Palace.

Nigel Pearson

Nigel Pearson, captain of the Owls' team that won promotion and the Rumbelows

Paul Williams (right) arrived at the same time as Danny Wilson, and they both made a big impact, with Williams not only scoring some vital goals but making a lot for David Hirst.

Cup in 1991, scored 20 goals in his time at Hillsborough – including a dozen in the famous "double" season. Here Pearson recalls how he suddenly became a goalscoring centre-back:

I don't think anybody now can believe I got 12 goals in 1990-91, but it came about because Ron Atkinson put me under a load of pressure to start scoring, and I got myself into good positions and had some good fortune in being in the right place at the right time.

The one I remember best was a spectacular overhead kick against Ipswich when we drew 2-2 at Hillsborough in December 1990. That was a game in which we went two-down in 21 minutes, and my goal was the equaliser. It followed a corner and came about 20 minutes from the end. Our other goal was a very good one from Trevor Francis.

I think I scored six in the League and five in the League Cup that year, and some of those goals were important – but I'm one of those people who wish I could enjoy scoring more than is usually the case. A lot of people must think I'm a miserable begger when I score, because I don't exactly get excited.

The trouble is, the moment I put the ball in the net, I immediately start thinking about getting back to my defensive duties and ensuring we don't slip up!
Author's note: Pearson retired as a player in the summer of 1998 after concluding his career with three memorable seasons at Middlesbrough.

Danny Wilson

Danny Wilson, who made 137 appearances for the Owls, already boasted over 530 League and Cup games before he joined Wednesday in 1990. A great favourite at Sheffield, the former Northern Ireland international was an instant hit when he turned to management as Viv Anderson's successor at Barnsley in 1994, leading them into the Premiership in 1997. Here he recalls two of his 14 goals for the Owls, whom he rejoined as team-boss in 1998:

Wednesdayites often tell me the volley with which I scored against Chelsea in the second leg of the Rumbelows Cup

Danny Wilson – seen here being tackled by Terry Butcher – scored some memorable goals in the 1990-91 promotion and cup "double" season.

semi-final in 1991 is the goal they remember best of the ones I got in my time with the club. Certainly it was both important and spectacular, but, to be honest, I think there were other goals I enjoyed better than that.

In the 1990-91 promotion season, for instance, I especially savoured a diving header of mine against Plymouth because it set us on the way to a 3-0 victory which put us top of the Second Division for the first time in that campaign.

We had only been playing about three minutes when Trevor Francis chipped a ball in from the right and, with the defence reading a volley, I went diving in and got it on an angle to put it

into the far corner. They had to be low ones for me to head them in!

One of the goals I got in the Cup runs of 1992-93 stands out, as well, because it was one of those you try over and over in training, and it's very satisfying to see it work out in a match. This was a drive from the edge of the box, hit first-time and hammered into the bottom corner. I think it was against Leicester and came after the match had already been won, but it was still a sweet experience!

John Sheridan

John Sheridan not only showed some sweet midfield skills, but scored 33 goals – many of them memorable – in over 240 games for Wednesday between late 1989 and 1997. Former colleague Phil King recalls his own favourite Sheridan goal:

John made and scored some wonderful goals, including, of course, the winner in the Rumbelows Cup Final in 1991. However, for pure genius, the one he got at Luton in October 1991 takes some beating. When we got a free-kick just outside the penalty area, I laid the ball back to him, and he flicked it up with one foot and volleyed it into the net with the other. Quite deservedly, it won a goal-of-the-season award.

John Sheridan – his first goal for Wednesday, in the ZDS Cup game against Sheffield United, was a foretaste of the superb quality which made "Shez" such a Hillsborough favourite.

Roland Nilsson

Roland Nilsson, Wednesday's Swedish international back, scored only two goals in his five seasons with the Owls, but long-time supporter Christine Norman has never forgotten the day he broke his "duck".

Roland has to be one of Wednesday's modern "greats", and few players were more popular with the fans. He created so many goals for the others with his runs down the right, and I always felt sure that one day he was certain to go all the way and score himself.

In fact, for most of the 1992-93 season I made a point of backing him for the first goal because, after about 80 games, he was definitely overdue. The irony was that when he did finally succeed, hitting the first in a 2-0 defeat of Norwich, I completely forgot to put a bet on!

Carlton Palmer

Carlton Palmer, who collected 18 England caps in his time with Wednesday, made 263 appearances for the Owls between 1989 and 1994, and many of his 18 goals were memorable. Danny Wilson, a Hillsborough colleague, has his own favourite Palmer strike:

Carlton Palmer's goal at Barnsley in October 1990 was spectacular in that it was a diving header and it came in the last minute of the match, but what was special was the importance of that goal. It saved us from defeat and salvaged a point. If I remember, it extended our unbeaten start to the season to 14 games, and, as our aim was to get promotion at the first attempt, that was the

Peter Atherton will always remember his first goal for Wednesday.

kind of result you valued.

I think Andy Rammell had put Barnsley in front with only 15 minutes left, and the final seconds were ticking away when Nigel Worthington crossed the ball, Paul Williams flicked it on, and Palmer threw himself full length to head a dramatic equaliser.

Peter Atherton

Peter Atherton, who cost Wednesday £800,000 from Coventry in 1994, made such an immediate impact with supporters that he won the club's Player of the Year award in his first season – a campaign he also remembers for a rare and spectacular strike in a 1-1 draw at Aston Villa:

When I was at Coventry, I took a bit of stick from the other lads because I didn't manage a single goal in about 120 games for the Sky Blues, but that was because I was never in a position to have a chance of scoring. When we had a corner or a set-piece in the opposition's half, I was always the one who stayed back.

So it was something special when I hit the target in only my 16th Premiership game for Wednesday at Villa Park in late November 1994. It was only the second goal I'd scored in 279 League matches and my first in 257. The previous one had come at Bramall Lane, against Sheffield United, in October 1988, when I was playing for Wigan in the Third Division.

What I remember about the one against Villa is their 'keeper Mark Bosnich hit his clearance towards me, which wasn't what he intended. I chested the ball down before shooting from about 25 yards. I caught it just right, and it flashed into the net off the underside of the bar. You always enjoy moments like that – especially when you've waited six years for it!

Author's footnote. The Owls' skipper had raised his goal tally for Wednesday to six in 166 games by the end of the 1997-98 campaign.

Hillsborough Heroes

Jackie Robinson

Jackie Robinson played for the Owls from 1934 to 1946, and is remembered as one of the club's all-time giants. He scored 39 goals in 119 peacetime games, but is best remembered as Hillsborough's great wartime goal-king with a tally of 90 in just over 100 outings – including 35 (featuring six hat-tricks) in the epic 1942-43 campaign when Wednesday reached the League North Wartime Cup Final and lost over two legs to Blackpool.

Frank Melling, an outstanding centre-forward who scored 35 goals in 55 wartime games for Wednesday, has fond memories of playing alongside Robinson. Melling, who always played as an amateur and later served as a Sheffield United director from 1954 to 1978, recalls:

Jackie was a brilliant footballer. He always played his own way, but there was nobody better, and when he was at his best he was breathtaking. He was ideally built, had a great turn of speed, marvellous ball control and skill, and a beautiful body swerve. Jackie could run with the ball as quickly as he did without it, and it always seemed as if the ball was tied to his toes. He had a terrific shot and I never saw a better finisher.

There is no doubt we would not have reached the League North Cup Final in 1943 but for him, and I especially remember one game in February of that year when we beat Sheffield United 8-2. Jackie scored three that day, and me and Jack Thompson claimed two apiece, with a chap called Reynolds getting the other. I think that season Robinson, Thompson and I shared about 72 goals, with Jackie leading the way by a mile.

If Jackie had a fault, it was that there were times when he tended to play for himself rather than the team. Eric Taylor used to say: "Give him an early goal and he'll play a blinder," because Jackie liked to be the man to score.

In fact, most people would agree that if Jackie had played for the team and not himself in the second-leg of the League North War Cup Final we might have had a chance of winning. Blackpool, who boasted a lot of guest stars, were perhaps the best team in the country then, but we could have won. We drew the first-leg 2-2 and lost the return 2-1.

However, in that game against Sheffield United, Jackie produced an unselfish and unforgettable display in which he showed all his great individual skills while doing everything necessary to benefit the team. His distribution was outstanding, and he absolutely took United apart. They never had a chance with Jackie in that form.

If it hadn't been for the war, Jackie might have become another Raich Carter or a Wilf Mannion, but, by the time normal football resumed in 1946, he was not the man he had been. His trouble was he didn't look after himself as he ought to have done. He was too fond of a drink. There were occasions when he would turn up obviously having been drinking, and I remember one instance when he was so drunk they wouldn't let him play. It was a great pity, because he had a rare talent.

Ivor Seemley, who watched Wednesday as a boy and later played for the Owls, remembers meeting his idol at a promotion celebration in the early 1950s:
Jackie Robinson was my original Wednesday hero, and I always remember he scored on the day I was taken to Hillsborough for the first time in 1938. I rated Derek Goodfellow, Harry Hanford and Albert "Jumbo" Ashley among my favourites, but "Robbo" was the tops!

I was thrilled when, after Wednesday won promotion during my time at the club and they held a celebration dinner at the Grand Hotel, I found myself sitting between Jackie Robinson and Jackie Thompson.

It transpired that "Robbo" could drink bottles of Guinness faster than he once scored goals, and, halfway through the evening, you couldn't see the table for empties – I had a hard time persuading people I was a non-drinker!

Charlie Napier

Charlie "Happy Feet" Napier made only 56 League and Cup appearances for Wednesday after arriving from Derby in 1938, and, because of the war and a fiery temperament which led to a long ban in 1943, the Scottish international inside-forward's subsequent outings were limited. However, he is remembered with affection as one of the Hillsborough greats. Fred Green, a long-time supporter, comments:

Charlie Napier was a brilliant footballer, one of the best I've ever seen. He gave us so much pleasure with his sheer talent, and, in terms of ability, he was an ideal captain. Unfortunately, he was also one of the dirtiest players I ever saw. Opponents didn't mess about with him, because if Charlie got kicked, he wouldn't hesitate to deal with the culprit!

I recall an FA Cup-tie with Yeovil in January 1939 when Wednesday were struggling to overcome a non-League side they were expected to beat with ease. During the game, which ended 1-1, Charlie clashed with Bill Kingdon, the Yeovil player-manager, and I have a vivid memory of seeing him thump Kingdon.

Dennis Woodhead

Dennis Woodhead, the Owls winger who scored 76 goals in 226 games between 1947 and 1955 and later became the club's commercial manager, is remembered not only as a fine player but as a man of ready wit. Derek Dooley, a former colleague, recalls:

When we drew 1-1 at Old Trafford in November 1952, there was some controversy when I shot us in front after half-an-hour. The Manchester United lads insisted I was offside, and, though the referee ignored their appeals, some of them were still complaining bitterly that "it wasn't a goal" as we lined up to re-start the game.

Dennis piped up: "Read tonight's

Green 'Un, pal, and you'll see it says we scored – and what's in black and green can't lie!"

The following month, we won 5-1 at Newcastle, and early in this match, Dennis got away and whacked in a shot to which goalkeeper Ronnie Simpson somehow got his fingers and deflected on to the bar. You can imagine how hard Dennis had hit it, because the ball rebounded to the edge of the penalty area, where I met it first time and thumped it into the net.

"That's right," said Dennis, "don't hit 'em, place 'em, Derek!"

Redfern Froggatt, who was so often Woodhead's partner on the Owls' left flank, said:
Dennis had some ferrets, and one day he brought them down to the ground. They were no problem until he released them in the dressing room. The situation was chaotic. Tommy Walker, the reserve-team manager, was certainly not amused, but Dennis couldn't understand why!

Dave McIntosh

Dave McIntosh, the Scottish goalkeeper who made over 300 appearances for Wednesday between 1947 and 1958, is another former Owl who is remembered as an outstanding performer on the field and a great character in the dressing room. Keith Bannister, who was captain of Wednesday's Second Division championship side in 1951-52, recalls:

McIntosh was a brave goalkeeper, but he couldn't land the ball over the halfway line from goal kicks and the other defenders had to take them for him.

He had a funny sense of humour. For instance, Derek Dooley, Ivor Seemley and me used to like to get down to the ground early to play a game of snooker before training. The game would just have reached a vital stage when "Mac" would appear on the scene. He'd waltz into the room, pick the balls off the table, and start chucking them about the room.

His favourite amusement was either spraying the lads with a hosepipe or drenching someone with a bucket of ice-cold water. It happened at least once

a day. On several occasions we got our own back by ganging up on him and throwing him into a cold bath. There was one time when we did this after he had dressed and was about to leave the ground. His suit was ruined, but he just laughed – and, the next day, he was back at his old tricks.

Gerry Henry

Gerry Henry, a wing-half or inside-forward who joined Wednesday from Bradford Park Avenue in 1950, is remembered as one of the "characters" of the period. Keith Bannister, a former Owls defender, recalls:

Gerry Henry was playing against us for Bradford one day in the 1949-50 season and he and Edgar Packard, our centre-half, were having a right set-to. They were a right pair of hard cases. I remember the referee had to separate them, and he managed to ease the tension for a time by making them smile when he offered to fight them both. However, at the final whistle, the pair were soon exchanging furious blows as we went up the tunnel.

Remarkably, it was soon afterwards that Wednesday signed Henry, and, surprising as it might seem, Henry and Packard immediately became the best of buddies. In fact, they were inseparable, and, if anyone was missing when we were due to catch the team bus, it was invariably those two. They could usually be found in the boozer.

Derek Dooley

Derek Dooley has passed into local football folklore as one of the greatest of Wednesday heroes – the giant centre-forward in the size 12 boots whose 63 goals in 63 games made him the best-known marksman in the Football League before his career came to a sudden end in February 1953 when, at the age of 23, he suffered a broken leg in a match at Preston, and a few days later the leg had to be amputated to save his life. Ivor Seemley, who played with Dooley in Wednesday's Yorkshire League and Central League teams, recalls:

Derek and I were good pals, and, as

we lived in the same area, we used to travel to Hillsborough together on the No.2 Outer Circle bus from Shiregreen. We were always very punctual and invariably tried to get to the ground at least an hour before we were due so that we could fit in a game of snooker ahead of training.

Ironically, the only time public transport let us down was one Christmas morning when we were playing for the "A" team and had to get to the ground to meet the coach taking us to some place in one of the South Yorkshire mining districts. The Outer Circle bus simply didn't arrive as scheduled, and, already certain to be late, Derek and I decided we had no alternative but to walk.

As luck would have it, the team bus (I think the driver had come looking for us) met us when we'd walked less than halfway to Hillsborough, so we still got to our match venue in good time. Unfortunately for Derek, first-team coach Alan Brown had chosen to go to that game, and, while he ignored me, he gave poor old Derek a right ear-bashing – as if it was Derek's fault!

Derek's physical style suited the way the game was played in those days, and, of course, he was absolutely fearless. But the thing people often forget is that, as well as being very strong, he was also exceptionally fast – and it was his speed which brought a lot of his goals.

Once, in November 1951, I travelled as 12th man with the first team when we played at Swansea. We stayed in Porthcawl for a couple of days, and Derek, who was then in the middle of an amazing scoring run, injured his knee during a players' snooker tournament.

Derek was very doubtful for the match, and, when we saw that the Vetch Field pitch was a quagmire, we didn't expect him to play with a dodgy knee. However, he insisted, and I was amazed at the way he defied the injury and still ran Don Weston, the Swansea centre-half, ragged. Dooley got two goals that day, both coming from typical down-the-middle dashes, and it was his sheer speed through the mud that created something out of nothing.

I remember playing with Derek in a Yorkshire League match at Owlerton Stadium in September 1950 when we beat Halifax Town "A" team 8-2 and he scored all eight. I saw him get some memorable goals, but I don't think there was a single good one among those that afternoon. It was simply a case of this big, awkward lad creating havoc in the goalmouth, and the ball went into the net off his backside, his knee, his thigh, his heel – every part of his anatomy!

Jackie Sewell, the England inside-forward who played alongside Dooley, reflects on his old team-mate's strengths and weaknesses:

When you had someone like Derek Dooley in your team, you had to adapt your tactics to suit his strengths. It was no use doing anything else. He was a big, awkward begger who created sheer panic in defences and wrought havoc in goalmouths. He didn't go around hitting people, he simply used his height and weight to maximum effect within the laws of the game. Once you knew what he was about, you made full use of that knowledge. We certainly profited from the attention he demanded from defenders as well as from his scoring ability.

The thing was, you had to get him facing the opposition goal before you gave him the ball. It's an understatement to say he wasn't a one-touch player. Derek liked to be facing the way he was going before he got the ball, because he couldn't flick it past a defender, then turn and run. There was nothing delicate about his style! If Derek was facing his own goal when I collected the ball, I used to hang on to it until he had time to turn and start running.

Once he was in full flight heading towards the goal he looked unstoppable. On heavy grounds, my goodness he used to plough through the middle, taking the ball with him, defenders floundering behind him.

I remember one game at Queen's Park Rangers, not long after he first got back into the team in that season when he finished with 46 goals. Derek and two defenders were chasing this ball down the middle, and he reached it first. Unfortunately, in that same instant, he trod on the damned thing, quite accidentally. He went flying forward, taking the defenders with him but not the ball. I happened to be running up behind him, and was able to get

in a hard shot which Reg Allen, the goalkeeper, saved superbly. I couldn't resist a tongue-in-cheek comment, so shouted: "Good ball, Derek!"

Derek would miss easy ones and score goals from impossible angles, and a classic example was at Brentford when he claimed a hat-trick in a 3-2 victory. He got this ball on the corner of the 18-yard box, right on the by-line, and came along the white line towards the front post. Then he just lashed at the ball, nobody (not even Derek!) knew whether it was a cross or a shot, but the ball flew into the goalmouth and, incredibly, flashed into the far corner of the net. A perfect fluke.

My old Notts County colleague, Tommy Lawton, was in the Brentford side that day. "Is that how he's scoring his goals?" he asked. I nodded. Tommy laughed: "Well, all I can say is he must have an angel on his back!"

Frank Ronksley, a long-time supporter, recalls a day when Dooley took some severe punishment at Bradford Park Avenue:

It was in that 1951-52 season when Derek was going great guns and couldn't seem to stop scoring. We were drawn at Bradford in the FA Cup, and, ahead of the match, their centre-half, a chap called Horseman, announced he was going to stop Dooley by any means, fair or foul.

What he did to Dooley that afternoon was honestly unbelievable – rabbit chops, elbows in the face, kicks up the backside. You name it, Horseman did it. Derek did score and, though we lost 2-1, he deserved a medal.

Norman Curtis, the defender who played in 46 of Dooley's 63 League and Cup games for the Owls, recalls that the giant in the No.9 shirt was heading for international recognition when his career was shattered by the accident at Preston:

I'm convinced Derek would have played for England. He was getting better all the time, and was always going to score goals. He was like a herd of elephants, absolutely fearless, and when he set off with the ball, there were no half-measures. He only had one thing in mind – and allowed nothing stop him getting to within shooting distance of the goal.

I was playing that day at Preston when it all came to an end. I think we all

thought that, with a broken leg, he'd probably miss the rest of the season. I shall never forget how shattered I was when, a day or two after the match, I got a telephone call from our coach, Alan Brown, at 6.30 in the morning with the news that Derek's leg had been amputated to save his life.

Derek's scoring feats in the 1951-52 season made him the most talked-about player in the game, and everybody wanted to have a look at him. At that stage, of course, there were a lot of First Division teams who had not seen him in action.

I remember that, in April 1952, a few days after we had completed our Second Division programme in that promotion season, we went to Kendal to play First Division Manchester City in the Westmorland Invitation Cup. The night before the game, with both teams staying in the same hotel, we organised a darts match for all the players.

City's German goalkeeper, Bert Trautmann, was telling one of our lads that he'd never seen Derek. "Who's this Dooley chap?" he kept asking, but none of us said anything.

Next day, early in the game Jackie Marriott centred from the left and, as Dooley went for it, he met the cross and Bert Trautmann at exactly the same time – and put both ball and man in the back of the net.

"That's him!" one of our lads shouted to Bert, who, just then, was in a sitting position wearing a rather surprised look on his face. We all laughed and the crowd joined in the laughter. Mind you, I don't think any of the spectators knew what the real joke was.

Trautmann did, but his consolation was that City were awarded a free-kick – not because of Derek's treatment of the goalkeeper – but because of an offside decision.

Incidentally, it is intriguing to note that, in the following season, Wednesday did not meet Manchester City until Easter – a few weeks after the ill-fated Preston game. So Bert Trautmann never played against Derek again.

Albert Clayton never saw Dooley play, but has a special memory of his first boyhood idol:

I was ten years old when Derek suffered the injury which led to him losing his leg, and I can remember getting very emotional when I read *The Star* on the night the paper reported Derek was fighting for his life in Preston Infirmary. I wept because my hero's career was over, and because I knew that now my dream of seeing him play would never be fulfilled.

For something like 18 months I had read every word written about Dooley in the local papers. On Saturday nights in the football season I was always one of the first in the queue for the *Green 'Un* at Rippon's shop at Frecheville. Derek was invariably in the headlines in every edition, and, to the small boy I was then, his feats made him very special.

At that time I had still not been to a Wednesday match, although this was not because I hadn't been agitating to go. Alas, Hillsborough was considered too far for me to go alone. I had almost made it on Christmas morning 1951, when a pal's father took me with his family, but, having got as far as the ground, to my dismay the gates had already been locked with the stadium filled to capacity.

Now, in 1953, I felt I had to show my support for Derek in his hour of need, and, while I can't recall how I got the money, I dashed off a 2s 6d (12½p) postal order direct to my hero in hospital at Preston. I explained it was my contribution to his testimonial fund. A few days later, I received a nice "thank you" letter from Dooley's wife, Sylvia.

The following summer, a group of us lads were playing cricket on the street in Frecheville when a boy brought the exciting news that Dooley had been spotted visiting a house on the nearby Birley Estate. "He's signing autographs, there's a big queue of kids at the door already," reported the boy.

We all dashed home to get some notepaper – we couldn't afford the luxury of autograph books then! – but, remembering the letter from Sylvia Dooley, still in its original envelope, I decided to take that with me.

It was, indeed, a long queue. Sylvia was patiently collecting a few bits of paper at a time from the autograph hunters and taking them inside for Derek to sign. I think my letter and envelope were collected in the fourth or fifth batch.

When Sylvia came out again, she wanted to know who the letter belong-ed to. I assume she had spotted her own handwriting and been prompted to read the note she had written six months earlier. When I said it was mine, I found myself invited to meet my hero – the envy of all my pals as I disappeared into the house.

It was a moment from my childhood that I will always treasure. Suddenly, there before me was the legendary Derek Dooley, sitting in a chair. He smiled and shook my hand, and I had never felt so proud as I told him how sorry all my pals were about his accident and explained that my ambition was to play for Wednesday.

When I returned to the street, I felt a bit of a star myself as the other boys surrounded me and asked what Dooley was like and what he had said. I don't recall what I told them, but, looking back across 45 years, I do remember thinking that he was just as I'd expected a hero to be – and I had no doubts he would always be my top favourite even though I never did see him in that famous No.9 shirt.

Albert Quixall

Albert Quixall, who made 260 appearances and scored 65 goals for Wednesday, was a great favourite with Owls fans in the 1950s before his record £45,000 transfer to Manchester United in September 1958. Jim McAnearney, who was with the Owls from 1951 to 1960, recalls:

I always remember the day Albert joined Manchester United. After the signing he came up to Hillsborough Golf Club and joined us for the last few holes. He was sick as a parrot. He didn't want to leave Sheffield Wednesday, and that's the truth. He was happy where he was, and I think he would have spent the rest of his career with Wednesday if he could. In fact, many people believe he would have been better off in the long term if he had stayed, because, though modern supporters probably don't appreciate it, Quixall was a very big idol at Hillsborough.

Unfortunately, Harry Catterick wanted rid of him because Albert was Eric Taylor's blue-eyed boy. Eric let him get away with murder. The irony was that, if Quixall had come under Catterick's influence earlier in his career, he might have been twice the player he was.

By the way, Albert was the best penalty taker at the club. He could side-foot them in with power, and I don't recall seeing him miss one.

Tom McAnearney, Wednesday's long-serving wing-half between 1952 and 1965, adds:

Albert Quixall was a likeable lad who always played with great confidence, and few people knew just how nervous he got in the dressing room before a game. He invariably developed a big rash across his body, and I often told him I couldn't understand how a lad with his abilities could get into such a state. He couldn't help it, it was the way he was.

Nobody who saw him in action could imagine he had been so nervous before the kick-off. He loved to entertain the crowd with his juggling during the kick-in, and, of course, with his extra-short shorts and his blond hair, he was worshipped by the fans.

And Albert loved to tease the crowd. I recall one game at Portsmouth when, early on, he went for a ball and slid into Jimmy Dickinson, the local hero. It was an accident, but for the rest of the match Albert was booed every time he touched the ball. At the final whistle, Albert caught the ball between his feet and lifted it on to his head – then walked off the pitch as if the ball was stuck to his forehead!

We happened to return to Fratton Park fairly soon after that, and it was typical of Albert that, when we walked out at the start, he went down the tunnel and on to the pitch with the ball on his head as if it had been there since the end of the previous match!

Albert was not a great dribbler, but he had a lot of instinctive ability and imagination. In recent times, people talk about a goal David Beckham scored for Manchester United from the halfway line as if it is something nobody ever tried before. But I remember one match when we were kicking off and Albert suddenly whispered: "Pass the ball sideways, the goalkeeper's off his line." He collected the ball and hit it half the length of the field, and, if the goalkeeper had been a split second later with his reaction, the ball would have gone into the net and the goal would have earned a place in the club's history.

Because he was the player everybody noticed, Albert sometimes got more credit that he deserved – or, at least, others didn't get the credit.

I shall never forget one game against Tottenham at Hillsborough, I was having a rare old tussle with Ronnie Burgess and Eddie Bailey, who were passing the ball backwards and forwards and making me chase this way and that. Albert was very amused: "Go on, Tom, you'll get it yet!" he called.

Anyway, I did a dummy and intercepted the ball at the third or fourth attempt. I promptly passed it to Albert, who in turn fed Alan Finney. After beating two players and going round the goalkeeper, Finney planted the ball in the net – a great goal. I'm not sure if Alan didn't get a hat-trick that day.

We were amazed when the headline in the local paper said something like "Quixall's pass sees Wednesday through", and Albert only chuckled when I reminded him that I'd won the ball, Finney had created a goal out of nothing, and yet he'd pinched all the glory.

Everybody remembers Finney and Quixall as a pair, but Finney was very under-rated. He was, without doubt, at one time the best uncapped winger in the game. He could run very fast with the ball, just like Steve McManaman in the 1990s. It's unfortunate he hasn't been remembered with the same acclaim as Quixall. And I have to say he was Albert's equal as a joker, too!

Don McEvoy, a Wednesday captain from 1954 to 1958 and a key figure in the 1955-56 promotion side, comments:
Albert Quixall was a wonderfully gifted two-footed footballer. He could do anything with a ball, and, in truth, I could hardly believe some of the things he could do with it. Albert was a lovable lad in many ways, and, when he wanted to play, he could be a great player, especially when the situation allowed him to do it his way. He tended to want to perform at home, where he was adored by the fans, but he was seldom as effective in away matches.

Tom McAnearney

Tom McAnearney was a Scottish-born wing-half back who made 382 League and Cup appearances for the Owls

between 1952 and 1965. Jack Mansell, who was Wednesday's coach from 1962 to 1964, recalls:

Tommy Mac was a very under-rated player who might have been a regular in the Scotland team if he hadn't looked a bit of a plodder when he was running. True, he was a little bit slow, but he was always in the game, always in the thick of things, and always wanted the ball. Whatever the situation in any game, he was always looking for the ball. In that sense he was a bit like Alan Ball – and I think he was a slightly better ball player than Ball.

Peter Johnson, the former Wednesday back, comments:
Tom was a true footballer. He always wanted the ball, even when there were four men round him. He would always try things, and he was always trying to place the ball with passes no one else would attempt. He could see situations that many others couldn't, and, being one step ahead in terms of vision, when he succeeded and found his man, the ball invariably finished in the back of the net.

Because some things he attempted didn't come off, a lot of fans failed to appreciate him, but I can tell you he was always appreciated by his fellow professionals. I did a lot of work for Tom in my time with Wednesday, but I knew he would always be there to help when I needed him – I can hear him shouting for the ball even now!

Peter Pollitt offers a veteran supporter's viewpoint:
I used to hear old-timers drool about the half-back line of Strange, Leach and Marsden. Well, I still drool about McAnearney, Swan and Kay. That was a half-back line! Tom had great vision, Peter was frightened of nobody, and Kay was tenacity personified – and all three had class.

Tommy Mac used to take a lot of unjustified stick from some fans because they got upset when he was sometimes caught in possession. But that was because Tommy was always looking to play that killer ball. Being a perfectionist, he knew exactly the moment when to make that pass, and, when it came, it invariably split the opposition defence wide open. I was

always ready to forgive him if, in pausing to look for the opening, he sometimes lost the ball.

Peter Swan

Centre-half Peter Swan played in over 300 games for Wednesday, including 17 in 1972-73 when he returned to Hillsborough following the lifting of the ban inflicted by the FA for his involvement in the notorious betting-coup scandal of the 1960s. He was capped 19 times by England. Peter Johnson, the former Wednesday back, comments:

I tipped Peter Swan as a future England player even before he became a regular in the first team. At the time I doubt if he'd played more than a dozen times in the Football League.

After I got injured at Blackpool in February 1958 during my first season with Wednesday, when I recovered I had a run in the Reserves, and I remember going home after my first game back. My wife, Jean, asked me how I'd gone on, and I said: "Everything's gone very well, and I'll tell you this – I've seen a kid today who'll play for England."

Peter had ability, but it was that bit of arrogance and self-assurance that made you feel there was something special about him. He was a good lad to have in your team, and he deserves to be remembered for what he achieved as a key player in a very good Wednesday team.

Keith Ellis, the former Owls centre-forward, adds:
If Peter hadn't been injured at the wrong time and then got caught up in that other misfortune which led to his ban, I'm sure Jack Charlton wouldn't have got a look-in – or, at least, Jack wouldn't have collected so many caps, while Peter would have earned a lot more.

Peter Pollitt, a long-time supporter, notes:
Swan had the lot – the looks, the physique, the ability. He had two good feet and always looked so fit, so in control. He strutted about the field boasting the best sun-tan you'll ever see, wearing very short shorts – which made him such a favourite with the ladies. The men simply admired his talent.

You were always glad he was on your side. In away games, he was so strong and firm, so determined. He was like a colossus at the heart of the defence. Opponents used to bounce off him, and it was unusual if the home fans weren't booing him almost as soon as the game started. If they weren't giving him some stick after 15 minutes, "Swanny" was having a bad day!

Peter Rodrigues, who was with Wednesday when Swan made his first-team comeback in 1972, says:

I always remember the day Peter Swan made his first appearance for Wednesday for eight years, on a lovely sunny August afternoon at Hillsborough when we beat Fulham 3-0. I was really pleased for Peter that day: he was so unbelievably happy, playing in a Wednesday shirt again in front of a big, enthusiastic crowd. I recall seeing him go to all four corners of the ground and punch the air with sheer joy.

In terms of his ability, it was almost as if he'd never been away. Make no mistake, he was in the team on merit.

Dave Cusack, who was an apprentice at the time Swan returned to League football, remembers:

I was Swanny's apprentice when he came back to Hillsborough, and he wasn't just an outstanding player who was still super fit despite his long lay-off – he was also a great character.

In fact, despite all that had happened to him, he had a sense of humour which enabled him to have a laugh at his own expense. David Layne, on the other hand, while he was a lovely guy, was rather more serious, and probably a bit more self-conscious about the circumstances which had kept them out of football.

One day soon after they returned to the club, Peter walked into the dressing room and removed his tracksuit top to reveal a vest covered in prison arrows. David didn't enjoy seeing Peter make fun in that way, and walked out of the room, but all the other players shared in a joke which put everyone at ease and prevented any embarrassment.

Peter, as everyone knows, liked to wear his shorts very short, while, at the same time, he always had his shirt outside his shorts – and he was particular about the length of the shirt. So, before every game, it was one of my jobs to turn up and tape Peter's No.5 shirt. I also had to put pegs in his boots to make the tongues stand up.

We also used to earn a few extra bob cleaning the senior players' cars every Friday, and I think the only time I saw Peter displeased was one occasion when he had a lovely new vehicle and, after cleaning it, we decided to delay his departure from the ground by hiding the car under a pile of cushions behind the North Stand.

Tony Kay

The red-haired Tony Kay, who made 203 appearances for Wednesday between April 1955 and December 1962 and then moved to Everton for a £55,000 fee to make him the game's most expensive

Tony Kay, seen here heading clear during a game at Arsenal in 1962. Other Wednesday men in the picture are goalkeeper Ron Springett and centre-half Peter Swan.

half-back, is remembered as a tenacious and outstanding player whose career was shattered through his involvement in the notorious betting coup scandal exposed in 1964. Jack Mansell, Wednesday's coach in the early 1960s, recalls:

Tony was a real character, a tough guy who might as well have worn a bandit's sign on his back – but an honest bandit and I loved the guy. I remember one game against Liverpool when he got a nasty kick in the privates a few minutes before half-time. We gave him treatment on the touchline, and, with help, he was just about able to walk to the dressing room at the interval. But when he went to the toilet for a pee, he discovered he was passing blood. We were a bit alarmed, and had the doctor look at him. Tony, however, insisted he felt all right, and went out for the second half and played as if nothing had happened.

In training he would scream and shout at anybody and loved taking the micky. I remember once in a practice match down at Owlerton Stadium he was giving Gerry Young some terrible stick. Gerry was such a quiet lad, it was unbelievable, and I told Tony to lay off him. When Tony responded by saying referees never stopped him abusing team-mates, I said: "I'm not the referee, I'm the coach!" And he promptly commented: "You could have fooled me!"

"Well," I said, "I'm not fooling you now!" – and promptly pulled Tony out of the game, replacing him with Wilf Smith, who was then an apprentice. Tony shrugged his shoulders, made it plain he wasn't pleased, and didn't just leave the field but went straight back to Hillsborough.

Long after the rest of us had jogged back to the ground and I had showered and returned to my room, there was a knock on the door. Tony appeared, gave me a friendly look and asked: "Are we reight?" I said: "Yes," and he disappeared calling: "See thee tomorrow!"

Typical Tony, never upset for long, always full of bounce.

Tom McAnearney, a former Wednesday captain, comments:
I remember an incident which summed up Tony's tendency to act first and think later – and which also says something about how his arrogant sense of humour could defuse a tense situation.

The game was at Burnley, and we were a goal in front with about a minute remaining. I was content to play for time, and wasn't tempted when, with Jimmy McIlroy and I standing over the ball near our goal-line, he was wanting me to put it out for a corner. In fact, the pair of us were refusing to be the first to do something.

Suddenly, Kay comes in from behind us like an express train, and me and McIlroy end up on the other side of the touchline in a heap. I can't remember where the ball went, but, anyway, the referee gives a free-kick, and, when it's taken, "Dusty" Miller meets it with his head. The final whistle went almost immediately, and it's 1-1 instead of 1-0 to us.

As captain, naturally, I gave Tony a right telling off when we got back to the dressing room. I felt so angry because his immaturity had cost us a point. Tony just smirked, and inquired: "Have you finished, Tom? Yes? Well, look, old lad, when I get to your age, I'll play like you."

I could only laugh, and so did everybody in the dressing room. Well, what else could you do? No good complaining that ignorance is bliss!

Don McEvoy, who was Wednesday's captain at the time Kay first got into the team, notes:
Tony was always going to be a quality player, but he was so jealous of Albert Quixall it was unbelievable. All he ever wanted to do was to be better than Quixall.

Albert Clayton, who has followed the Owls since 1954, gives a supporter's view:
My earliest heroes were Redfern Froggatt, Jackie Sewell and Albert Quixall, and I always liked Alan Finney and regarded Derek Wilkinson as a wonderful player. In more modern times, men such as Roland Nilsson stand out.

However, the best all-round player I've seen has to be Tony Kay. I never saw a man with a greater appetite for football. When he was in the team, you always felt they could get something out of a match, no matter what the circumstances. He was so arrogant, he just wanted that ball at his feet, so he could show everybody what he could do – which was plenty.

The story about how Tony became Wednesday's captain says a lot about his determination to do any job the team might need. When manager Harry Catterick wanted someone to sort out an opponent in the first five minutes, and one of the senior players refused to take on the task, Tony piped up: "I'll do it, boss."

Mind you, if Tony could give it, he didn't like it when anybody squared up to him. He'd back off a bit quick like, and when it came to a real confrontation, he tended to hide behind Peter Swan and Don Megson!

Roy Shiner

Roy Shiner, the Isle of Wight product who scored 96 goals in only 160 games for Wednesday between 1955 and 1960 after arriving in a swap deal from Huddersfield Town, was a great favourite with Hillsborough regulars because he was both an outstanding marksman and a 90-minute player who never gave less than his best. The centre-forward also had a sense of humour that the fans appreciated. Don McEvoy, the former Owls' captain, recalls his old pal and reveals how he took time off from a summer holiday to personally complete the transfer of his old Leeds Road colleague to Wednesday:

Roy Shiner was a good pal of mine, and, of course, we kept in touch after I left Huddersfield in December 1954. In fact, the following summer he persuaded our family to go on holiday with his family, and we spent six weeks in Ryde in the Isle of Wight, where his mum and dad ran the British Legion club.

One morning I got a phone call from Eric Taylor, who told me he had a chance to do a deal to take Shiner and Ron Staniforth, a classy back with several England caps, to Wednesday in exchange for Jackie Marriott and Tony Conwell. I knew Wednesday were getting a bargain when Eric said it was a straight swap with no cash involved. Shiner wouldn't let anybody down, and, as for Staniforth, he was one of the most gifted two-footed players I'd ever seen – a brilliant player in a tight situation.

I told Eric: "You sign Staniforth up

Roy Shiner – a 90-minute man who scored goals and was always a crowd favourite.

there, and send me the papers and I'll get Shiner to complete them here." The next day a package arrived from Sheffield containing the forms, and, taking them into the garden where Roy was sunning himself, I said: "Here, Roy, just sign these." Of course, he wanted to know what was involved, but when I said he'd get first-team football, the same money as the others, and a club house near the ground, he couldn't wait to sign. When everything was done, I shook his hand and said: "Congratulations, you're now a Sheffield Wednesday player!"

Roy did very well for Wednesday, just as I knew he would. I was well aware that he could score goals, for he got a good few with Huddersfield

reserves, and I saw him score a hat-trick against Plymouth in Town's 1953 promotion season. His misfortune was that he couldn't get a regular place in the first team because the senior centre-forward, Jimmy Glazzard, was such a brilliant player.

Roy always gave you everything, and it didn't need long for Owls' supporters to take to him. He scored 33 goals in the 1955-56 season when we won the Second Division title, and the rapport he had with the crowd was really remarkable.

They always forgave him even when he missed the easiest of chances.

When he wasted a golden opportunity, he had this habit of lifting up his foot and pointing to the studs in his

boots. He would hold a hand up to the crowd and point to his fingers, signalling that he had slipped or miskicked because he had only five studs on his boots. The crowd would yell towards the trainer's bench: "Get some studs in his boots, the poor lad can't stand up!"

At other times he would miss the target when it looked easier to score, then look at the ground. Wearing a puzzled look, he would stamp on the pitch as if to suggest loose turf had caused his misjudgment. Again the crowd would sympathise and start yelling: "Groundsman, get the ruddy pitch rolled properly!"

He had this knack of orchestrating the crowd and gaining their affection. I said to him one day: "You're a right lad, Shiner. I've played my guts out this afternoon, and all you've done is lift your ruddy boot up and make folks feel sorry for you because you've missed a goal!"

But I was always pleased to think that I was the one who had signed him for Wednesday – although my part in the story was something which very few people ever knew about. In fact, this might be the first time I've mentioned it for publication!

Ron Springett

Ron Springett, the goalkeeper who joined the Owls from QPR in 1958 and made 384 appearances before returning to Loftus Road in 1967, remains Wednesday's most capped England player with 33 international appearances between 1959 and 1966. Jack Mansell, the former Owls coach, comments:

You often hear stories of forwards selling dummies to defenders, but I recall one game at Tottenham when the roles were reversed and Ron Springett sold the legendary Jimmy Greaves the perfect dummy. Greaves was through with only the goalkeeper to beat, and, in those situations, you invariably felt he was certain to score. However, when Ron appeared set to throw himself one way, Greaves pushed the ball to the other side – only to find that was exactly what Ron had wanted him to do, and our goalkeeper picked up the ball and said: "Thank you very much!"

Ron was an outstanding goalkeeper

and a master of his craft. Yet he was always one of those players who came to the ground on match days, played for 90 minutes, and, when you looked round afterwards, he was washed and gone. He would never hang around to discuss the game or socialise. As far as he was concerned, he had done his work and that was that. If we were at home to a London club, his main interest at the end was ascertaining whether he could get a lift with them to the station, and, if possible, a place in their compartment (and with it free hospitality) on the train home.

Don Megson and Gerry Young

Don Megson and Gerry Young topped over 780 games for Wednesday between them, and they were two of the most respected players at Hillsborough in the 1960s. Here their former colleague Sam Ellis pays tribute:

Physically and mentally, Don Megson and Gerry Young were two of the hardest and most dedicated professionals I ever knew, and, in terms of example and encouragement, they were certainly the best senior colleagues a young player could meet at the start of his career.

"Meggie" was always looking after me, so helpful in such a lot of ways off and on the field. When I first arrived, for instance, he would run me home to Manchester on Saturday nights and bring me back on Sunday. He was an ideal captain, ever concerned for the rest of the lads.

When I got into the first team, he said: "If you have any trouble, tell me. If anybody's taking liberties with you, I want to know."

One day in the season after the 1966 Cup Final, we played Aston Villa at home, and I was getting knocked about a bit by Tony Hateley. I didn't say anything to "Meggie", but he'd noticed anyway.

Villa got a corner, and "Meggie" said: "Sam, stand in my place on the post, I'll mark Hateley." The ball came over, and the next thing I know, Hateley's flat out on the ground – I mean stone cold knocked out! To be honest, at the time I was scared someone might think I was

responsible, and I got away from the scene – fast!

I didn't have any more problems with Hateley in that match, and, a few months later, I read with interest a piece he wrote in a Sunday paper. He named the two hardest players he had ever met – one of them was Don Megson, and I knew why!

As for Gerry Young, a memory I have is of him sitting alone in the bath at Lilleshall after training during Cup Final week, singing over and over again *What a Day for a Daydream*. I don't think anyone was ever more content with his lot in life than Gerry.

Gerry was the best professional I ever knew – the epitome of consistency, the player who set such a terrific example in training and on the pitch, a man all the kids and young players looked up to. I never saw him have a bad game, and, in the eight years I played with him, he only ever made one mistake in a match – the one at Wembley in 1966 which, ironically, is still remembered.

Sometimes life is not fair, and fate picks on the wrong people. For me, Gerry was the best, and he deserves to be remembered for all the good things he did in around 350 games. Let's not forget that his qualities won him an England cap, and, but for an injury at the wrong time, he might have got a lot more. There has to be a positive place in the Hillsborough Hall of Fame for such a loyal and dependable guy.

Willie Henderson

Wee Willie Henderson was in the twilight of his career when he arrived in Sheffield in the summer of 1972, and he made only 56 appearances for the Owls, scoring five goals. However, the former Glasgow Rangers and Scotland winger proved an instant favourite at Hillsborough and the memory of his brilliance will always be treasured by supporters and colleagues. Derek Dooley, the manager who brought Henderson to Hillsborough, remembers:

Willie had a reputation as a rebel, and, when it emerged I was trying to sign him, a lot of people suggested I was inviting trouble. Willie knew what they were saying, and, when we met for the first time at the Grosvenor House Hotel in Sheffield, he said: "Don't believe all

Willie Henderson in action.

the stories you've heard about me." I told him: "I don't care what's happened in the past, it's what happens from now that matters."

He caused me no problems in his time here, and I never regretted signing him. He was a wonderful character whose enthusiasm was infectious and a great boon in the dressing room, and the fans loved him because he was an entertainer. He never asked for special treatment and expected the same discipline as the other lads.

For instance, I always fined players who arrived late for training, and, as Willie didn't drive and always took a taxi, he might have been expected to use this as an excuse. But, if he arrived even only a couple of minutes late, he'd walk straight into the dressing room and say to me "How much, boss?", put his hand in his pocket, and pay up before he'd even been asked.

I remember a match against Sunderland in early 1973 when we were find-

Willie Henderson is welcomed to Hillsborough by manager Derek Dooley.

ing the going difficult against a side inspired by the arrival of Bob Stokoe as manager. At the time they had gone nine games unbeaten, and, remember, that was the year they went on to win the FA Cup.

The scoreline was goalless at half-time, and Willie, who hadn't seen much of the ball, said: "Look, boss, if you get the ball to me in the second half, I'll win you the match." He was a joy to watch in the next 45 minutes, and, as he promised, he won us the game with a memorable goal.

I got back to the dressing room after the final whistle to find all the players lined up and waiting. Willie stood at the front with his hand outstretched. He laughed: "I knew you'd want to congratulate me on my second-half display and my winning goal!"

The fans loved him. I recall once when I went down to the bench late in a game in which we were struggling, and, as I walked down the tunnel, a supporter shouted: "It's about time you came down and got this lot sorted out, Dooley."

I spoke to Ron Staniforth, the coach, and we decided to bring off Willie, who was having a quiet game. As I went back up the tunnel, the same supporter called to me: "I don't know about sorting it out, Dooley, tha's made a bigger mess on it now – tha's taken off Willie, and he was our best player!"

Brian Joicey, who was Wednesday's cen-tre-forward in the early 1970s, recalls:
Willie Henderson was like a breath of fresh air when he came to the club in the summer of 1972, and we all loved

him from the moment he first walked into the dressing room. We knew he was in the building having talks with the manager, then, as we were getting changed, the door suddenly flew open and we saw this little man, 5ft 4ins tall, his hair thinning on the top, squinting across at us. He peered as if having trouble seeing us, produced a big cheesy grin, and said: "Hi ya, lads!"

He was a great character off the field, and a marvel on it – definitely the best winger I ever played with. The amazing thing was, he could barely see, his eye-sight was so bad. He used to set off down the wing with the ball at his feet and keep going until he saw that white line in front of him – then he knew it was time to deliver a pin-point cross, and he invariably did.

You always knew that when Willie got the ball, it was time to make your run into the penalty box, because he'd always take it to the by-line and get it into the goalmouth. He was so quick over five or ten yards, revelled in taking a man on, and, if he fell when chal-lenged, he was so small he never had any trouble bouncing back up and run-ning at defenders again.

He must have been a genius when he was at his peak, and, though he was at the veteran stage in his time at Hillsborough, he still had absolute faith in his abilities – and it was amusing to hear the way he used to talk incessantly to the opposing full-back. He'd taunt the man and say things like: "When I get past you, mate, you'll not catch me!"

I think Willie once said the first goal he ever scored at Hillsborough, in a 3-2 defeat of Huddersfield in September 1972, was his personal favourite, but I always remember when he got the win-ner against Sunderland the following February, because, after putting the ball in the net, he went down on his knees and saluted the Kop with raised arms. Somewhere there is a picture of this incident, and the sheer joy on his face is an image I'll never forget.

I'm on that photograph, just behind Willie, and you can see how happy I was for the little man. I think Willie had col-lected a ball which goalkeeper Peter Springett had thrown out to him, and Willie had set off running at the defence until he suddenly realised he was in sight of goal – and he put the ball into the top corner.

There was only one word to sum him up: magic!

Peter Rodrigues, the Welsh international back who played for the Owls between 1970 and 1975, comments:

Willie and I go back a long way because we first faced each other at schoolboy level when he clogged me in a game in which Scotland beat Wales 9-1, and I got my own back when we met many years later in a full international at Cardiff. We respected each other, and it was a happy twist of fate that we ended up together at Hillsborough.

He was a great little player, blind as a bat but a good old-fashioned winger who hugged the touchline – so much so that, after a game, he'd come into the dressing room, sit down, lift his foot in the air and say to Derek Dooley: "Hey, boss, is there enough white chalk on the soles of these boots to satisfy you?"

He used every ounce of his experience and skills to bamboozle defenders, and, though his stay in Sheffield was comparatively short, I think the Hillsborough fans treasured him because he put a smile on their faces.

Ken Knighton only had one season as a colleague of Henderson's at Hillsborough, but he has never forgotten the impression the little Scot made on him:

Willie was one of the most amazing characters I ever met. Of course, I knew him as a famous Scottish winger, but when I first met him at Hillsborough I couldn't believe what I saw. I remember him coming into the dressing room in the most outrageous jacket you've ever seen, but what really took me aback was the way he looked as if he was peering through a fog.

He was acting as if he was almost blind as he looked for his peg on the wall. Someone said: "It's over here, Willie!" – and when one of the apprentices acted as a guide, I honestly thought the whole thing was a wind up just for my benefit. Only later did I realise that Willie was, quite literally, as blind as a bat.

Yet he was the bravest player I've ever seen on a football field. He took some terrible stick from full-backs, but always bounced back and left them dazed with his dribbles. When a defender put him on the deck with an unfair challenge or tackle, Willie always wanted free-kicks played to him – and, the minute he had the ball at his feet, he'd run straight at the defender who'd just brought him down.

Terry Curran

Terry Curran, who scored 39 goals in 138 games between 1979 and 1982, including 24 in the promotion season of 1979-80, is remembered here by his former colleague Mark Smith:

There's not much doubt that Terry Curran got us out of the Third Division. Nobody could stop him, and he was not only the leading scorer with 24 goals, he also got me a lot of penalties. I scored 11 times from the spot that year.

Terry was a character, a real extrovert. He was a lad with plenty of rabbit, but could take it when people had a go back. He was into everything, and even cut a record, "Singing the Blues", which, of course, prompted us to take the mickey by playing it in the dressing room before matches.

I remember one day when he came into the dressing room after having his moustache dyed black. The rest of us wandered off into the boot room, found some black brushes, and returned with black hair stuck on our upper lips. Faced by so many imitators (some looked more like Charlie Chaplin than TC!), Terry joined in the joke and the place erupted with laughter.

On the field, of course, there was only one Terry Curran. Jack Charlton had brought him from Southampton as a winger, and he was very quick and a good runner with the ball. Jack decided to play him down the middle, and, of course, Terry was anything but an orthodox striker.

He was all over the place, and that is exactly what opposing defenders couldn't handle. Centre-halves didn't want to come out and follow Terry, so he'd pick up the ball and go down the middle doing just what he'd always done on the wing – running at defenders and creat-

Terry Curran – he always liked to run at defences.

ing havoc. Being so tricky and elusive, he was getting into the box and scoring, or, if he didn't score, he'd invariably get flattened and we'd be awarded a penalty. That season he was different class.

In the following year, Jack kept Terry in a striker's role, but, having been a free spirit, he now got to thinking about being a "proper" centre-forward. Terry decided he wanted everything to feet with his back to goal, and the upshot was he wasn't nearly so effective. He had become too self conscious about his role when he would have been better just being himself. In the end, to help boost his goal tally, he claimed the penalty-taking job.

Terry liked to be the centre of attention, but he was a great character, and one thing I liked about him was he always had plenty of time for the apprentices. He was constantly giving them tips about their game and enjoyed helping them.

Part Five – Working for Wednesday

Eric England

Eric England, who joined Wednesday as an office boy at the age of 16 in October 1936 and remained on the club's staff until his retirement in December 1983, formed a remarkable administrative double act with Eric Taylor for 38 of his 47 years at Hillsborough. It was in March 1974, on the retirement of his mentor and friend, that he was promoted to club secretary.

Billy Walker, the old Aston Villa and England inside-forward, had been the club's secretary-manager for about three years when I became a Sheffield Wednesday employee in the first week of October 1936.

However, it was Eric Taylor, then aged 24 and officially the assistant secretary, who dealt with all the administration. Walker, being a famous ex-international, was the football manager, and he was secretary in name only. It was the custom then for clubs to have secretary-managers who knew little or nothing about the non-football side of things, and these ex-players didn't want to be involved in the running of the club as a whole.

Anyway, it was Eric Taylor who interviewed me at the ground one Sunday morning after I had applied for the job of office boy, and I remember he gave me a shorthand and typing test which included him dictating a letter to Herbert Greenwood, who at that time was secretary of the Sheffield & Hallamshire FA. The terms Eric used were all foreign to me, and I discovered very quickly that football had a language and customs of its own far removed from normal business practice!

I lived at Shiregreen and had left school two years earlier, when I was 14. I had wanted to be an engineering draughtsman, but, with the effects of the Depression still evident even though the economic situation was picking up, openings were very limited.

So I ended up at a small cutlery concern called Bennett & Heron in Mary Street. Curiously enough, the boss was a man called John Bennett, who was well known in junior football circles for his connection with the YMCA. Indeed, in later years "Pop", as he was known to the boys, had links with a number of lads who went on to join Wednesday, including Keith Bannister and Derek Dooley.

Mr Bennett was a kindly man, so much so that, as he lived not far from us in Firth Park Crescent, he responded to my application for a job by turning up at our house in Gregg House Road one Sunday morning to ask me when I could start. As he was a bachelor with no family, he told my parents he was keen to teach me all he knew and help me learn about the trade, and I think he had in mind that, should I take to the work and make good progress, I might one day succeed him and take charge of the firm.

I enjoyed it there, and Mr Bennett was pleased to find me so enthusiastic about my evening classes in shorthand, typing and business methods. Unfortunately, like a lot of youngsters, I couldn't see where I was going, it was the present that mattered and the future seemed to stretch forever into the distance. In short, I didn't see a long-term career in cutlery.

So, after two years, I began looking around, and that's how I went to Wednesday. My first wage was 7s 6d (37½p) a week, which was increased to ten shillings (50p) after six months. From the outset, I got much satisfaction from the job. It was very different from normal office work, but it suited me. My initial duties included attending to correspondence, mainly typing replies, and dealing with the gate money and paperwork on Saturdays with a chap called Bulloss.

Bulloss collected the money from the gates, and I remember tuppence out of every shilling went in tax. I had to

Eric England, who worked for Wednesday from 1936 to 1983.

make out returns for the Customs & Excise and send a cheque for the appropriate sum by the following Thursday. I also kept records of match returns and similar essentials, and had a number of other regular tasks.

I worked in the same office as an old gentleman called "Tots" Baxter, who was actually the chief scout, though he was also my friend and guide. In those days there was not much contact between the junior staff and directors, and, when you did meet them, you tended to view them with awe. This especially applied to Sir Charles Clegg, a legendary giant of the game who was then not only top man of both the national Football Association and the Sheffield & Hallamshire FA, but the major and most influential figure when he chaired Wednesday's board meetings.

There was one occasion when Eric Taylor was ill, and I had to attend a board meeting held at the St James's Club in the city centre. It was all rather frightening, and "Tots" Baxter arranged to go with me to lend some moral support. Old "Tots" was a real character, a man old enough to be my grandfather, and it was a great comfort to have him with me.

Sir Charles, who was then a very old and distinguished man, was not the sort to take you aside and give you an encouraging word just because you were young and new. I doubt if he noticed how nervous I was. The whole episode was quite an education, for some of the other directors like Percy Bowker and Alderman Wardley were also larger-than-life characters. Mind you, it was amusing to see that they were also in awe of Sir Charles. When they knew his arrival was imminent, they made a desperate effort to clear the room of cigar smoke because the old man hated smoking and smokers!

Anyway, if it was an ordeal, at least I managed to get an accurate note for the minute book.

It was also an experience, though not one without pleasure, meeting the players for the first time as a member of staff. People like Ellis Rimmer and Mark Hooper, the first two I met, had long been my idols, and I had never expected to be close to the two great wingers who had given me so much pleasure as an ordinary supporter. But they and Joe Nibloe, Tommy Walker, and Walter Millership became good friends over the years.

We had some good times in the years I worked at the club. Before the war we used to have social nights for the staff and players in the old snooker room at the ground. These events were usually held on a Friday, not every week but regularly – and often on the eve of a big Cup game. We used to play snooker and solo.

I'd never played snooker before I went to Hillsborough, but Eric Taylor and Sam Powell soon taught me the rudiments. We'd play for tuppence and threepence. I remember one night being paired with Charlie Napier. He was a brilliant footballer, always known as "Happy Feet" – and a real character. I never played snooker with anyone quite like him. He said: "Eric, I just want you to play safe. I'll do all the potting." Anyway, we won the tournament, and then I topped the evening by winning at cards. I think I ended up with 12s 6d (62½p), which was a fair sum in those days.

Eric Taylor was my greatest friend and mentor at the club. He was always a big help and influence. Having been with Wednesday since 1929, when he, too, had started as an office boy, he taught me such a lot in those early days. At the same time, I think that later we learned a great deal more together, especially after I returned to the club following wartime service in the RAF – by which time Eric had become secretary-manager and I was promoted to assistant secretary.

Our great pride was the success we enjoyed in organising all-ticket FA Cup semi-finals in the early post-war era. Eric had made a success of organising a number of representative games staged at the ground during the war years, and in 1946 Hillsborough was put back on the big-match circuit when all-ticket matches were introduced for major football events in the wake of the Bolton disaster.

I remember I had just come home from Germany and was stationed in Norfolk when I learned Eric had persuaded the authorities to give me a 10-day pass. The irony was that it was hardly "leave" in the accepted sense, for my wife, Audrey, barely saw me and I virtually lived at the ground while Eric and I attended to ticket arrangements for a 65,000 crowd for the Birmingham-Derby FA Cup semi-final.

The tremendous surge in interest in football after the end of the war was staggering. So many people wanted to be at the big games, it was impossible to satisfy everybody. Remarkable as it might seem to anyone who was not around then, we had crowds ranging from 60,000 to 65,000 at those early post-war semi-finals, and, though there was no segregation and the majority of spectators were standing, we never had any trouble.

For those initial post-war semi-finals, we sold the bulk of our ticket allocation to people who queued all night waiting for them to go on sale at the turnstiles on a Sunday morning. The queues stretched for miles. Later we changed to a postal system, and the first time we did this the flood of letters we received was a sight to behold. Our allocation was 20,000 and we had over 150,000 applications – all piled high in an office which was packed to the ceiling with post!

What a job it was dealing with that lot, especially as so many cheques and postal orders had to be returned with a note saying: "Sorry, sold out."

Those occasions were invariably very exhausting. The hours were long, and we didn't have a fraction of the staff we had in later years. But we loved it. There were even times when we slept on the premises, not so much because we were too tired to go home as to protect the tickets from getting into wrong hands!

Eric and I were very different, but it was a happy blend of personalities and we complemented each other. He was the showman, always a man of ready wit – the public face of the club if you like. I was the quiet one, content to be in the background concentrating on the tasks which were of no interest to supporters.

We built a reputation for efficiency and got better because every year Eric and I learned something new. The club's progress in administrative terms coincided with ground developments which strengthened Hillsborough's status as a big-match venue, and Eric was the inspiration of those improvements. He was proud of what he achieved, and he would have been delighted with what has been done since his death.

Certainly he put the club on course to create the stadium we know today. He always dreamed of making Hillsborough an all-seater stadium. Yet there were just 5,700 seats when I started, and the figure was only 7,200 in 1949 when we made improvements in the South Stand.

The start of the real progress came when we put up up the Cantilever Stand. This replaced the old North Stand in which I had sat as a boy, and when the new structure, which cost £150,000 and was paid for by debenture, was opened by Sir Stanley Rous in August 1961 it meant our seating capacity was doubled overnight.

That was the development which put us on target for selection as a World Cup venue in 1966, and, of course, ahead of that milestone in English football history, we built the new West Stand and added seating on the terracing in front of the South Stand. Then, since I retired, there have been more major redevelopments which have further transformed the stadium, but it is often forgotten that the foundations for subsequent progress were laid in Eric Taylor's time.

I remember when Hillsborough was named as a 1966 World Cup venue, we said it would be just like us to get to the FA Cup Final the same year, and, remarkably, that is exactly what happened. In truth, the highlight in 1966 was seeing our own team get to Wembley. We lost to Everton after leading 2-0, but it was a great match and an unforgettable and such an enjoyable day – before, during and after the game.

Later, we had a lovely if hectic time during the World Cup games at Hillsborough, and we rounded it off by going back to Wembley to see England triumph over West Germany in the Final at the end of July, the day before my birthday.

It meant that in the space of a few weeks, I saw and savoured experiences that few enjoy in a lifetime, and it made me grateful to be doing the job I was.

Of course, the decline Wednesday endured in the 1970s proved a difficult phase. It is always harder when you have previously known nothing but stability. It is no exaggeration to say that for those of us who were at the club in those lean years, it was heartbreaking. You don't think it can happen to you, but it can happen to anybody if things are not right. It took us a long time to get things right again.

In the long run, it didn't do us any harm, but it was a painful experience and we had to learn some hard lessons

with new people at the helm. I was just pleased that, by the time I was ready to step down and into retirement, the club was well on the way back up. In my last full season we reached the FA Cup semi-final, and I bowed out halfway through the following season, which ended with us returning to the old First Division for the first time in 14 years.

As a retired employee and guest of the club, the trips to Wembley in 1991 and 1993 were occasions to savour, and winning the Rumbelows Cup in 1991, when we beat Manchester United to claim our first major trophy since 1935, was one of those days when you reflect that people can spend a lifetime in the game without enjoying that kind of moment.

I think Eric Taylor, who had died within a few months of his retirement in 1974, would have liked to have been with us that Sunday afternoon.

Ron Ward

Ron Ward worked full-time for Wednesday from May 1950 until his retirement at the age of 65 in November 1989 and then continued for another five years as a part-timer. He was the club's caretaker for the bulk of his 40 years at Hillsborough. His brother Ken was also employed by Wednesday for 27 years, and while one brother-in-law, Albert Morton, was an Owls goalkeeper from 1938 to 1953 another, Fred Smith, served as the Press Room steward for around 25 years.

It was just before Whitsuntide 1950 when my brother-in-law, Albert Morton, told me there was a job going at the ground as a joiner's labourer. The wage, £5 a week, was no better than I was already getting, but, as I was in a boring job and the chance to work at Hillsborough was too good to miss, I didn't need any persuasion to apply for the position.

When I told my mates I'd been set on, they thought I was the luckiest feller in the world. They were right. Wednesday had just won promotion and, within weeks of starting work, I dropped for a place at the big celebration banquet at the Grand Hotel. I thought I was in clover – all the more so as there were a few more promotion celebrations in the next few years!

I'd grown up in the Hillsborough district, and Dad had taken me and my brother Ken to watch Wednesday when we were kids. We used to go down and watch the players in training at the ground during the 1935 FA Cup run. I have vivid memories of the Cup Final that year, even though I didn't go to Wembley. I listened to it on the wireless, and it tells you how difficult times were then that we didn't own a wireless at home. I went to a pal's house to hear the commentary on Wednesday's 4-2 win against West Brom, and you could say I saw all the goals in my imagination.

My hero in those pre-war days was Jackie Robinson. He was definitely the best player I ever saw. While I was serving in the army from 1942 to 1947, one of my biggest thrills was meeting him when I was posted to Colchester after being wounded in Normandy. I couldn't believe my luck when I found Jackie was the lance-corporal on duty on the same cookhouse table as me!

After I came out of the army, I had a couple of jobs before joining Wednesday. I was set on by the joiner, old Jim Smith, and it was 18 months before I met Eric Taylor, the secretary-manager. In fact, in the early years I worked over on the North Stand side of the ground, and in those days you weren't allowed to wander over to the offices in the South Stand. Everybody knew their place. Joiner Jim used to bring my wages from the office – and, by the way, it was several years before I got my first pay rise.

I was offered the job of assistant

End of an era – presentations to Eric England on his retirement in December 1983, when a range of staff, including manager Howard Wilkinson, chief scout John Harris, scout Charlie Wain, manager's secretary Norma Lane, commercial manager Dennis Woodhead, and the players turned up to say goodbye.

caretaker after about three years, and later, when Harry Liversidge retired, I took over as caretaker. Harry was a bit of a character and something of a legend behind the scenes, and it was a challenge following in his footsteps. The job was mainly security, plus responsibility for the cleaning and maintenance of the stands and offices, and overseeing the laundry. One of the biggest annual tasks was the painting, which we always did ourselves, with everybody giving a hand.

I was supposed to work a 40-hour, five-day week, but it never turned out like that. On match-days you could never go home until everyone else had left, and you might not finish until midnight following an evening game – and it was sometimes well into the early hours before you got away when there was a midweek board meeting.

It was fortunate that I didn't live far from the ground, for I was often called out in the middle of the night by the police when an alarm went off, and there were many times when I had to return to the ground at 2am to let the team bus in after the players arrived home from a match at Southampton or Plymouth. There were no motorways then, and my sleep was often disturbed because someone had forgotten to take the keys.

For many years, I worked my summer holidays, mainly because at the time we couldn't afford to go away, and, of course, we were always on duty at times like Christmas and Easter. In all my 40 years, there was only once when I didn't work at Christmas – and that was a mistake which might have cost me my job!

It happened the first Christmas I was there. At the time I was courting my wife Florence, who lived at Shaw in Lancashire. I knew we had a home reserve match on Christmas Day and a home first-team game on Boxing Day, but, as I was only a joiner's labourer and nobody mentioned that I would have to work on those days, I assumed it was a holiday and went off to visit Florence.

Eric Taylor delivered a strong message when I went back to work: "Don't let it happen again!" When I got to know Eric, I found he was a stickler for discipline, and always wanted things done just so. But he was a great one for putting people at ease. He was exactly

Ron Ward, the Wednesday caretaker, saw his long service rewarded with a Football League award in 1986, and he is pictured here collecting his prize from chairman Bert McGee.

the same whether he was talking to the humblest employee or an important VIP.

There was a great atmosphere within the club, and everyone had a pride in working for Wednesday. There were strict rules, but there were no barriers to friendships within the staff, and there was always a good spirit. I never once had any trouble getting up in a morning and going to work, and, when I retired, I couldn't believe I'd been there 40 years because, honestly, it seemed to have passed so quickly.

We had a very good Supporters' Club in the early days, and they used to hold monthly dances at the Locarno ballroom, where players, staff and the fans would all mix and enjoy themselves. We always got along famously with the players because they belonged to the same generation and came from similar backgrounds to us.

In the 1950s, my wife and I had some great nights out with Ron Staniforth, Don McEvoy, Vin Kenny and Dennis Woodhead and their wives. Players didn't earn so much money then. Later, when they started commanding huge wages, you couldn't imagine them wanting to go out with the likes of us!

But, of course, the world has changed. In the old days you hardly saw anyone at the ground before matches until about an hour before the kick-off.

Now there's lots of visitors around from before mid-day, and, what with all the sponsorship and extensive catering facilities, it sometimes seems more like an hotel than a football ground.

I've had some wonderful times with Wednesday. The highlight was probably the 1966 FA Cup Final, when Eric Taylor organised an unforgettable weekend in London for all the staff. We went to the match, stayed in a big hotel, and, really, we had the time of our lives. The result, losing 3-2 to Everton, was very disappointing, but it was still an occasion we shall always remember.

We had some lean times over the years, and the 1970s were especially difficult. We went down to the Third Division, but we were always determined that our standards would not fall. We kept the ground and the offices up to the same old standards because we knew that one day we would be back at the top.

Wednesday were always a caring club. You always felt people mattered, even those who had left. I remember, for instance, that for many years every retired employee who had given long service was sent a hamper at Christmas. Unfortunately, the practice had stopped by the time I retired!

Author's footnote: One disappointment for Ron came just before the start of the 1997-98 season when he learned

Wednesday had withdrawn his complimentary season ticket – the custom of rewarding long-serving ex-employees in this way being stopped following financial reconstruction of the club.

Lily Shelton

Lily Shelton, a cleaner and supervisor who served on Wednesday's permanent staff for 45 years from 1952 to 1997 and continued to work at the ground on match days after her formal retirement, has long been one of the most popular figures behind the scenes at Hillsborough – a lady with a ready smile and a fund of memories.

There have been some big changes in my time at the club, and, compared with how it all looked when I started, it's very different today. But, as I walk about the place and see all the developments, I can still remember it as it used to be. It's very interesting to recall what was where before this change or that, and it brings back a lot of memories.

I've always lived within sight of the ground, but until I came to work here my only link with Hillsborough was when, as a youngster, I was one of a group of kids who used to get into the ground when the gates opened ten minutes from the end of a match – and I have to admit the big attraction was the chance to swing on the barriers on the Kop rather than the football!

I was married with two young children when the chance came to work for Wednesday. For many years I'd worked at Fletcher's Bakery, but, after the children arrived, I became a full-time housewife and hadn't seriously thought of getting a job until, around 1951, a friend called Edie Adams asked if I fancied earning a few bob helping out at the ground.

It was the close season, and Edie, who had been with Wednesday for a long time, said they needed someone to give them a hand to clean the stands. Later, the caretaker, Harry Liversidge, offered me a permanent job, and, as the hours fitted in with the children's school times, I accepted, never dreaming I'd stay for 45 years.

Wednesday became such an important part of my life, and mine was never a nine-to-five job, but there was such a

Lily Shelton (second from right) with her team of Hillsborough cleaners at the time of the 1966 World Cup matches at the Wednesday ground. Others in the picture include Dot Swan, Mrs Lavender, Jean Marriott, Flo Grant, Edie Adams, Lily Jones, Agnes Matthewson jnr, Ethel Baxter, Agnes Matthewson snr. Betty Pearson (née Matthewson) who is not in the picture, later joined her mother and sister and is still on the staff, working in the laundry.

lovely family atmosphere that working was like being at home. We worked hard, but it was so enjoyable because everybody pulled together and there was always time for a laugh. Eric Taylor, the boss, was a stickler for having things done exactly right, but he liked his staff to be happy, and I always remember how much he enjoyed the parties we had every Christmas when he revelled in the singing and entertainment.

As you know, the recent redevelopments have included extensive rebuilding of the South Stand, with a new main entrance which you reach by a bridge that has been built across the Don. When I look at that bridge, I remember it was something Eric Taylor talked about over 40 years ago. At the time, we used to wonder whether it would ever happen. I used to joke with Eric how it would be nice if he could arrange for the bridge to connect with our street, but he always said it would come out facing Hillsborough Park – and I'm sure he'd be delighted to think his dream had come true.

In the early 1950s, there wasn't the number of staff there is now. There was Edie, Agnes Matthewson and me on the South Stand side of the ground, with Dot Swann and May Marriott over on the other side. Agnes, by the way,

worked for the club for over 20 years until she retired in 1967, and her daughter, Betty, has been with Wednesday for over 30 years.

Edie, Agnes and me were not only responsible for all the cleaning on our side – the stand, the offices, lounges, dressing rooms, etc – but also did all the laundry. Each week we would concentrate on the washing until Tuesday; Wednesday would be devoted entirely to the ironing and darning; and Thursday and Friday were cleaning days – working in the stands, using wire wool to make the floors on the corridors sparkle, etc. Saturday, being a matchday, was always busy with hundreds of steps to be swept before the game. Of course, if there were midweek games, it increased the workload.

People forget that, in the early days before we had the luxury of washing machines, we had all the laundry to do by hand, using a brush to scrub the playing and training kit for five teams; and, because there were no spare shirts, shorts and tracksuits, you had to maintain running repairs and be very handy with a needle. Unfortunately, no amount of darning could save socks which tended to shrink!

Incidentally, a long day's ironing was all the harder because the stile room (used by the turnstile men on match-days) in which we ironed had a sloping roof – and that meant you had to work permanently bent forward. We were glad it wasn't Wednesday every day of the week!

There were very few jobs, if any, I didn't do in my time. I've even done some painting and decorating around the ground. On match days it's all about making tea for the directors' room, the dressing room, and taking a tray into the referee's room; then collecting the pots and washing them.

Over the years I became familiar with every one of the trophies at the club, knowing all their names and inscriptions by heart after polishing them every week for so long. Most of them used to be kept in cabinets in the old visitors' lounge, and, when that lounge was altered amid all the rebuilding, I knew exactly where each trophy found a new home.

Harry Liversidge, the caretaker, was a hard taskmaster and tended to be a bit domineering, but he knew his job and was so familiar with all our different tasks he could actually calculate where you would be at any given moment when you were cleaning the stand. His calculations even included time allowed for a smoke!

From the beginning, I found working at Hillsborough all the more interesting because seeing at close range how a football club was run was fascinating. Football people were such good company, and there was always a friendly atmosphere about the place. There were some wonderful characters on the playing and coaching staff.

Sam Powell, who had played for Wednesday in the late 1920s and been on the training staff for over 20 years when I started, was a grand chap, and a man who could always take a joke. I remember he would invariably come out of the dressing room in a track suit, wearing a white towel round his neck, and walk to the top of the tunnel leading to the pitch. If it should be raining, he'd say: "Oh, we'll train on the back corridor of the stand this morning." I used to kid him about being nesh and afraid of getting his hair wet!

One of the jobs Sam didn't like was stoking the stove we had in those days – because he had to go up and down some steps to get to the coke, and nearly always scraped his legs on the steps as he climbed out. Sam felt the system was antiquated even then, and, in these days when training staff would never dream of having to do their own fuelling up, I often wonder what Sam would have thought of today's "proper" central heating.

I remember in my very early days we had a trainer called Bill Knox, and I have never forgotten the last time I ever saw him. He was walking towards the old gym, which was then at the end of the corridor towards the players' entrance, and he stopped to talk to me as I stood on the wash-house steps. I told him he didn't look well, but he said he felt all right. It was late on, and I went home soon afterwards, still feeling worried about him. The next morning I arrived to learn Bill had collapsed and died soon after I'd left the ground.

When the players regularly trained on the corridors behind the stands, they would often be there while we were cleaning, and one image that often comes to me is of one player – I think it was Eddie Kilshaw – running up and down the steps for hours on end, and still finding the energy to keep singing *It's Magic!* It's funny the things you can remember.

Talking about singing, one of the managers, Vic Buckingham, was a bit stage-stuck, and, when you were down on your hands and knees scrubbing the corridor, he'd come up behind you whispering the words of a song. "That's very nice, Vic," I'd say, "but would you mind shifting – I've got work to do!"

Danny Williams was a manager with a sense of fun – always telling jokes and very dry in his humour. He never stopped asking me if I was going to have a bet. I'd say: "No, your horses don't win for me." He'd reply: "They can't win if you don't back 'em."

Of course, a lot of people have come and gone in my time at Hillsborough. That's the way football is, but you feel sorry when someone you've known for a long time leaves. You don't always have the chance to say a proper good-bye, and I have never forgotten the day Alan Brown left in 1968 because when I bumped into him as he was leaving the ground I didn't know he had packed in the manager's job.

Alan was just going out of the gate, and he surprised me by shaking my hand. I said: "I'll see you tomorrow." He didn't say yes, and he didn't say no, and his only words were: "Take care," which puzzled me because it wasn't the sort of thing he normally said. As Alan went one way and I went the other, I saw Eric Taylor, and, when I mentioned having spoken to Alan Brown and told him I'd see him tomorrow, he said: "You won't, he's just resigned."

Of course, a lot of the people who move on tend to come back from time to time, and one of the pleasures of many a matchday has been meeting up with them again. There's nothing nicer than hearing a familiar voice in the distance asking: "Where's Lily?" and knowing they haven't forgotten.

Norma Lane

Norma Lane, who has been secretary to every Wednesday manager since 1968, only expected to stay a few weeks when she joined the Owls' staff as a "temp" in 1966, but more than 30 years later she is still there – one of the club's longest-serving and most respected employees.

I started with Wednesday on the Monday after we beat Chelsea in the 1966 FA Cup semi-final, being one of three women recruited from a local bureau to help cope with the extra work in the run-up to the club's first Wembley appearance for 31 years. I was the only one of the trio kept on for a few further weeks to help with additional work concerned with the use of Hillsborough as a World Cup venue.

I worked part-time in general manager Eric Taylor's office, alongside his secretary Isabel Brown [Birks] and, once the World Cup games were over, it seemed my stay was finally at an end after a couple of months. Isabel thanked me and we said our goodbyes – then, just as I was walking out of the premises, Mr Taylor called me back. He asked me if I was interested in joining the permanent staff.

Funnily enough, I thought I'd blown my chances when I told him I couldn't work the following week anyway because my children were off school, but – and this was typical of the man – he said I could start when convenient to me. I didn't think then I'd still be here more than 32 years later!

WEDNESDAY EVERY DAY OF THE WEEK

When Alan Brown resigned as Wednesday's manager in February 1968, and Mary Faulkner, his secretary, left at the same time, I asked Mr Taylor if I could have the manager's secretary's job, and he agreed to let me give it a try, starting when Jack Marshall took charge. You might say 12 managers and several caretaker managers on, I'm still giving it a try!

Although the secretarial principles and practices are basically the same wherever you work, football is unlike any other world, and, initially, I didn't really know whether I would take to it, for some aspects of the job were a bit complicated, very different from the "norm". Fortunately, I was never short of help and advice from the football staff, and once I'd got to grips with everything, I wouldn't want to have worked anywhere else. I doubt if many people have enjoyed going to work more than I have over the years.

Every manager is different, but I've adapted to them all. They've included some great characters. Jack Charlton was first who was much more than just a football manager, but he was easy to work for. Ron Atkinson, who came back in 1997, is a very caring and knowledgeable man, so different from the image given him by the media. Jack and Ron are both "personalities" but they are also people with their feet very firmly on the ground.

The one thing most managers have in common is a dislike of office work and administration. Some don't even want to look at letters, but, once you've got to know the man, you have a good idea how he will want to word his reply. Danny Williams hadn't much of a clue about correspondence, and he told me: "Just get on with it as you see fit." Some, like Steve Burtenshaw and Howard Wilkinson, insisted on dictating replies, while others have tended to just give me a rough idea of what they wanted to say and left the rest to me.

Of course, the job is much more than dealing with the manager's correspondence. I also work for the chief scout, all the coaching staff, the physio, etc, and the work extends into helping administer the club's schoolboy and youth activities, organising accommodation for apprentices and new players, arranging hotel bookings for the teams on overnight trips – and lots of other duties directly or indirectly related to the football side of the business.

For instance, come August and the start of new season, I like to have the accommodation and travel fixed for all our four teams [Premiership, Pontins League, Northern Intermediate and FA Youth League] right up to Christmas. By October, I am finalising the details for the away games to the end of the season – always seeking to be several months ahead. Of course, everything is up-dated and confirmed closer to the time, but you have to ensure hotels are aware of the special food preferences of the players, and, of course, you have to know which players room together.

When new players arrive, it's not just a matter of organising hotel accommodation, but helping them find a house by liaising with estate agents; and having all manner of local knowledge at your fingertips is a useful thing. This is especially helpful when, as has been increasingly relevant in recent years, you are dealing with foreign players whose grasp of English and knowledge of British habits is limited. The lads from overseas often need that extra bit of help and consideration, especially those who have come from countries torn by civil unrest and find things here so different. I can't speak their language, but I can find someone who does!

Talking of useful knowledge, over the years I have compiled a set of records relating to every player who has passed through the club in my time. Eric England was always the expert, but when he retired someone had to start keeping records like he'd done. We don't only get asked about fairly modern players, we often get queries from the public about old players dating right-back to the club's beginnings in the 1860s, and, though it might seem far removed from the duties of a manager's secretary, answering them has become part of my job.

People tend to think you should know about every player and every match in Wednesday's history when, in reality, this is not possible. At the same time, when people ring up or write, you can't just say you don't know, and I have tried to improve my knowledge. I might not know all the answers, but I usually know where to find most of them – if they're available in published record books.

Norma Lane (right) with author Keith Farnsworth.

Attending to the needs of the apprentices is an important part of the job, for you not only have to arrange digs but keep in close contact with the landladies. Boys leaving home for the first time in their lives need a place to live where they're comfortable and cared for, and you have to keep in touch with landladies about food and other things.

Changes in attitudes and habits have affected the role of the landlady, and, in truth, accommodation for young boys has become harder to find for a number of reasons. Yet their welfare is still a top priority in making arrangements.

There is nothing more satisfying than to see a lad who has first come to the ground as a schoolboy start to progress through the teams and make the grade. Having been in the job so long, I've seen former apprentices, lads who I remember as shy youngsters, go on into management – and it's is very pleasing when they make a point of ringing or calling in to reminisce about how, as boys, they cured a dose of homesickness by popping into my office for a chat.

Over the years my office has always been a focal point for the players. Some of them may be big stars, but they are down-to-earth, ordinary people really – nice, decent lads with everyday interests and problems, and there's nothing they enjoy more than having a cuppa and a natter before starting training.

One thing I used to hate, but which fortunately doesn't happen these days, was seeing the annual ritual of apprentices and young pros discovering whether they were going to be kept on. From my room, I could see them turn up on a particular day every year and sit on a bench outside the manager's office waiting to learn their fate. You could always tell by the expression on their faces as they came out whether the news had been good or bad – and I always felt so sorry for those kids who had been told they were no longer wanted. It always seemed so cruel, because there is nothing worse than a young boy's dream of making the grade being shattered.

I was never a great football fan as a youngster. I came to a few games with some other girls, but we used to stand on the terracing in front of the old North Stand and admire the legs of players like Albert Quixall and Peter Swan rather than watch the games! Later, as a member of a local youth club, I recall performing in some gymnastic displays at Hillsborough before big matches. However, until I came to work here, I didn't really follow the club's fortunes closely.

Nowadays, of course, I'm very much affected by the team's overall results. People might think you are immune to the club's ups and downs, but you're not. On the occasions when we've been relegated, it's been terrible, you can't explain just how upset you get – and all the more so because the players, the football staff, are people you know so well, and you're more aware than most what it means to them.

Of course, there's been compensations, most notably the Rumbelows Cup win in 1991. Going to Wembley four times in 1993 was memorable. But losing in the two Cup Finals that year hurt, and, while all the staff enjoyed the trips and the club's hospitality, there was a sense of anticlimax which prompted a few tears.

I think the only time in my life I've ever had more to drink than I should was on the night after we had beaten Bolton with a goal from Ken Knighton to keep our place in Division Two. The relief was so great, I went into the Ozzie Owl club with my colleague Derek Knight – and two or three drinks proved enough to make me feel slightly intoxicated!

I remember, too, the night in 1976 when we avoided falling into the Fourth

Division, although I stayed sober on that occasion.

Until that season I had always worked on match days and made a point of seeing some if not all of every home game. Then Len Ashurst, who was a bit superstitious, said during a bad run of results: "I think it must be you who's bringing us bad luck – don't come to the match next week, and let's see if it makes any difference." I started finding something else to do when we were playing!

I didn't work on match days for some time after that, but Jack Charlton decided he wanted me there. Now, though I'm always around, I seldom see the matches because I can't sit still long enough to watch – and, anyway, these days there so many things to do which weren't part of the scene in previous years. In my old office, which backed on to the stand, I didn't need to be watching the game because I could hear the crowd and always knew how things were going from their reactions.

It was when Trevor Francis was manager that I started working full-time, which was something I'd not done since before I was married. It's a six-day week when we have a home match on Saturdays, and the days can be rather long. When there's a midweek game, I invariably work straight through from morning until around 11 at night, but, happily, I enjoy a life in which it's Wednesday every day of the week – except Sundays!

David Barber

David Barber is recognised as one of English football's top groundsmen, and won the national Groundsman of the Year award in 1991. He joined Wednesday in January 1977 as assistant to Derek Blunkett, whom he succeeded as head groundsman in 1979. He is, incidentally, the member of staff closest to the club's mascot, Ozzie Owl, who is thought to lodge in David's "den" in between matches.

I was a Wednesdayite from a very early age, and, having been a season-ticket holder for many years and being head groundsman up at Sheffield University's Goodwin Athletics Centre, I always fancied working at Hills-

borough. The chance came about through one of those happy coincidences that life sometimes throws up, for Ian Hicks, who had been with me at a local open-air school and remained a good pal afterwards, was assistant groundsman at the club.

Perhaps I should explain that, when I left school, I was advised to get an outdoors job for health reasons, so, after a brief spell in a warehouse at Stanley Tools, I became a garden lad with Sheffield Education Department. At 17 I moved to the university as assistant groundsman, and at 21 became the youngest head groundsman in the country. I stayed in charge for ten years.

The Wednesday link came about because I used to pop down to the ground to see Ian, and, as he and Derek Blunkett often had a lot on, I would sometimes give them an hour's labour. Derek, incidentally, had been at Hillsborough a long time, having come out of a steelworks to take on the job with no previous experience of pitch maintenance, but Ian had done a bit before he arrived, and between them they had pulled things round working on a very low budget.

Anyway, Ian asked me to help out on a match-day, and I also started coming down on some Sundays. It was all very casual and purely voluntary, and I never asked for anything because it was sufficient reward to be involved. Mind you, one incident, which is amusing to look back on, did put me off going on Sundays for quite a while.

Derek and Ian always had their lunch in the old Ozzie Owl club, but, being a non-drinker, it didn't appeal to me until one Sunday when I reluctantly agreed to join them – and soon wished I hadn't.

The place was so packed that dozens of people couldn't find a seat, but, as we went through the back door and I peered through the smoky atmosphere, I spotted a solitary vacant seat near the stage. "Go on," said Ian, "you'll be okay to sit there." I didn't think anything of it when everybody seemed to be looking at me. It only dawned on me very slowly that all those people had come to see a stripper – and I was sitting on the stooge's chair!

When Ian Hicks left to join Burnley, I started helping Derek Blunkett, who spent the next 18 months on his own, and, in the summer when he went on holiday, he asked me to cut the pitch for two weeks. At that time, the club relied a lot on people volunteering to come in and do such tasks for nothing.

I told Derek I wouldn't mind giving it a whirl if ever there was a permanent job at the ground, but nothing happened for a while. Then, at the back-end of 1976, I was invited to become Derek's assistant. Unfortunately, it all came about with such informality, I did have one moment of panic when, having given in my notice and confirmed I was giving up our tied-house, I feared I might be left both jobless and homeless!

There was never a formal interview, and I had only spoken very briefly with Len Ashurst, the manager, on the phone. Len told me to come to the ground and have a talk sometime, but the day I turned up coincided with the staff's Christmas party, and, apart from Julie in the office, the place was deserted.

I was sitting on the step outside the referee's room when, eventually, Eric England, the secretary, came along the corridor. As he had seen me when I'd been helping out, he had an idea who I was, but he just smiled and thought I was winding him up when I asked: "Is there any chance of me getting a contract?" As I explained I was starting as Derek's assistant a week the following Monday, Eric was quite clearly gobsmacked. When he said it was news to him, I began to wonder if I was mistaken in thinking I'd got the job!

When I went home that evening, I daren't tell my wife what had happened. Fortunately, a few days later Len confirmed my appointment in a letter which, ironically, mentioned an interview that had never taken place. I was probably the last person Len set on before he got the sack!

The first two weeks I was here, I was walking about in a daze. I'd been at the ground on match-days when there were lots of people knocking about, but, as Derek often said, the rest of the week it was like being buried alive in that you hardly saw a soul. Of course, there's a lot more activity around the premises nowadays, what with the sports hall and everything, but, then, it always seemed so quiet.

I shall never forget my first match as

Head groundsman David Barber (left) is seen here in his early days at Hillsborough, working alongside Derek Blunkett.

a member of the staff. Of course, I had told my pals I'd got a job at Hillsborough, and I felt very proud sitting with Derek and the others on the pitchside bench that cold, wet January evening. When Derek told me to be sure to check the penalty spots at half-time, I thought I'll not just check them, I'll give them a touch of white.

The big galvanised bucket was huge. Empty it must have weighed half-a-hundredweight. Filled with lime, most of which was stuck to the side, and a dried up brush, it felt like a ton. I'd taken off my overcoat, and, wearing a new army jumper with leather padded shoulders which was a gift from my mother, I stood ready to dash on to the field the moment the whistle went.

I had barely got beyond the touch-line when I tripped and fell full length, with the whitening splashing all over me and across the corner of the pitch. Fortunately, few of the spectators saw the incident because most were looking at the teams leaving the field, but I saw a nearby policeman crease up with laughter. Anyway, I regained my composure long enough to do the penalty spot. Then I ran to the garage, got some sand, which I used try to obliterate the lime piled on the pitch. Thankfully,

because it was muddy, my "accident" didn't really worsen the state of the pitch.

By the time I'd returned to the bench for the second half and sat for ten minutes, my lime-stained trousers and jumper were frozen stiff, and I looked quite a sight. Derek said: "What's thy been doing? I only told thee to put spots in. Didn't I say we normally use a brush not our clothes?"

Today we either own or hire modern machinery which enables us to do the job to a very high standard. Now we have machines which can rapidly complete work which once took us two weeks to do manually. However, in my early days we were very strapped for cash and the equipment was, quite frankly, in a terrible state. When I first came, the mower was the one we bought from the profits from winning the FA Cup in 1935, and the next major investment hadn't been until the time of the World Cup in 1966.

We did buy one machine, but, every time it broke down, we had to wait to get the money together before we could have it repaired. Once when I said it would cost £17 to repair it, Ernest Barron, the director, said we couldn't afford that much! Things are so much better now, and I think that is reflected in the standard of the pitch – although, as maintenance is a continuous operation, at any given time the situation is governed by a variety of circumstances, and you can still have problems.

In 1992 we had undersoil heating installed, with 18 miles of piping placed beneath the pitch, so frost isn't a problem. But the weather is still your boss, and conditions affect how you treat the pitch. Even things like the pitch being cooler on the South Stand side since the roof was raised have an influence, and, as you need two or three days to prepare the pitch for a match, if it's trained on in the meantime it can upset your calculations.

Different managers have different ideas. Jack Charlton, for instance, liked the lads to train on it once a week. Howard Wilkinson used it occasionally. Ron Atkinson was the best I've worked with because, if I was a bit iffy about training on it, he'd say: "Okay, we'll use the training ground." David Pleat liked to use it a lot – last year he used it 70 times for training, in addition to matches.

We were planning to have a new pitch laid in the summer of 1996, but, of course, it had to be postponed owing to the European championships, and, then, when the decision was finally taken in March 1997 to go ahead, it meant the contractors were five weeks late making a start in the summer – so we were always five weeks behind schedule, and the pitch wasn't as well established as I would have wished when the 1997-98 season started. In the early months, with being also used for training, it took a bit of a bashing when it needed a rest.

When I came, there were three of us. Today there's five – two at Hillsborough, two at the training ground (where we now have three grass pitches and an all-weather pitch), and myself. As the players spend over four hours at a time at Middlewood Road, the same standards have to be maintained at the training ground.

I have to admit I can't relax at matches, because I'm always watching the ball, and, when a goal is scored, I'm looking to see if a player has slipped or if the ball has hit a divot. When the opposition scores, I'm asking myself if it's the fault of the pitch.

It goes without saying that my saddest memory in my time here was the disaster at the 1989 FA Cup semi-final. That's something you can never forget. You never expect to go to work and have that kind of thing happen, and you don't think it can happen at your place. It's all a long time ago now, but it's still there, and it can still get to me in quiet, unexpected moments when I'm working on the pitch on a sunny afternoon.

Since then I've never had quite the same passion at matches, and I don't stand up and cheer like I once did when we score. In fact, though the groundstaff usually sit in front of the North Stand on match-days, because we now have in-house television I often prefer to watch the game in the garage.

Of course, I love my job, and it means a lot to be doing work that gives me a lot of satisfaction, and to do it with Wednesday.

There was a time, when I was about 15, when I dreamed of playing for the club, and I went so far as to write and ask for a trial. I was a goalkeeper, and recall my trial was in a game at Owlerton Stadium on a mudheap of a pitch. I only conceded one goal, but a weakness on goal-kicks probably proved my undoing. Anyway, the club sent me a letter saying I was too small and not quite up to the required standard.

I'm glad I passed my trial as a groundsman!

A Tale from "David's Den"

David Barber often recalls a match-day morning one February in the late 1970s when he and fellow groundsman Derek Blunkett arrived at Hillsborough to find one of the goalmouths on the pitch covered in a mysterious white powder. This is how David tells the story:

We couldn't work out what it was. Someone said it might simply be baking powder, but I said no, it's too gritty – and, in fact, I suspected it might be some kind of weed killer. Our fear was that, if it was weed killer, it would destroy the grass, and, in that case, it could be a serious case of sabotage on somebody's part.

We needed to do something about it quickly because, with a match due to kick-off in a few hours, the top priority was the safety of the players. Frankly, the heavy conditions were not conducive to hosing, but we decided the safest thing to do was to put the hosepipe on and wash away the mystery powder. We did that and were relieved there were no apparent ill-effects.

Ten or 15 minutes before the game, we were standing at the end of the players' tunnel and still debating the subject, wondering how someone had got into the ground overnight without being spotted, when Trevor Bayes, the sports hall manager, joined us.

Trevor said: "I had a right shock last night. I was just leaving, and, after locking the gates, I saw a taxi standing outside with its engine running. Then, all of a sudden, someone banged on the gates from the inside, and, when I re-opened them, there's a bloke standing there with a carrier bag in his hand.

"I asked him where he'd been, and he said: 'Oh, only on the pitch.' I asked what for. He said: 'Me Dad died a few weeks ago, and he wanted his ashes scattering on the pitch. I was told Wednesday wouldn't do it, so I thought I'd come and do it myself.'

Well, at least we could stop worrying. I don't remember whether we scored in that goalmouth that day, but if we did it may have been with a little help from the fan whose ashes had been washed away!

Part Six – Watching Wednesday

You Always Remember The First Time!

In Eric England's 47 years' service to the club, Hillsborough became a second home to him, but the former Owls' secretary has never forgotten the thrill of watching Wednesday for the first time in the early 1930s when he was a wide-eyed ten-year-old.

Although my Dad didn't go to every game, he was a keen Wednesday supporter, and had a great enthusiasm for football. From being a small boy, I often heard him talking for hours about some of the outstanding players of the day, and, as well as regaling me with frequent tales of those Wednesday favourites who had brought the League championship to Sheffield in 1929 and 1930, he invariably enthused about some of the big names at other First Division clubs.

Every visiting side then had at least one major personality, and three centre-forwards I recall Dad was always mentioning were Aston Villa's "Pongo" Waring, Newcastle's Hughie Gallacher and Everton's "Dixie" Dean. It seems quite probable that when he took me to my first Wednesday game, in May 1931, it was because the visitors were Aston Villa and he particularly wanted me to see Waring.

Of course, there was no television in those days. You couldn't see top players in action except when they came to Sheffield, although newspapers, magazines and cigarette cards ensured you knew something about them. Waring was fast, skilful and had a marvellous scoring knack, and that season when I saw him for the first time, I probably knew that he came to Hillsborough having already scored 49 League goals and boasting a new Villa record – though nobody would know then that it would still be standing over 60 years later.

I can't honestly say I remember too much about the match, but I do know Waring didn't score and Wednesday won 3-0. I think Mark Hooper got one of the goals.

No doubt, as we walked all the way from Shiregreen to see the game, Dad reminded me that "Pongo" would be wanting to lift his tally for the season to 50. But Hillsborough was apparently a ground where Waring often failed to find the net, and he was out of luck in this instance. I'm told he hit the post twice, missed two easy chances, and was also denied by good saves by Jack Breedon, who was deputising for Jack Brown in Wednesday's goal. Mind you, I have to admit I have no recollection of any of those incidents.

What I have never forgotten is how much I enjoyed the occasion, and, of course, I wanted to keep going back.

Dad took me in the old North Stand, and, though I didn't appreciate it until much later, by getting us places in what until 1914 had been the Press box, we had the best view available on that side of the ground in those days. If we had been seated anywhere else in that stand, our view would have been blighted by one of about 20 pillars and posts!

That wooden stand, as I learned later, had been brought to Hillsborough when Wednesday moved there from Olive Grove in 1899. It might have been a treasured link with the start of the club's professional era, but, frankly, it was already antiquated by the time I first started going to matches – yet it survived another 30 years! It was finally demolished to make way for the new cantilever stand in 1961.

It's interesting to note that, after I joined Wednesday in 1936, I discovered the old home dressing room in that Olive Grove stand had become a stable. I looked in on more than one occasion, and was intrigued to see that not only were the shirt pegs still positioned along the walls, but they still bore the names of some of the great pre-1914 players who were only names to me!

The groundsman when I arrived at the club was a man called Ted Smith, and the horse stabled in the old dressing room was used to pull the roller across the pitch.

Some supporters will recall that, behind the old stand, there was a practice pitch which was used for training, and a tennis court where the players staged five-a-sides. But I'll bet that only a few people now remember that the boundary wall which separated the ground from the backs of the houses in Vere Road featured a gate. That gate was created especially for the convenience of Ted Smith, and it led into his backyard. His home was so close, he had no excuse for being late for work!

The horse, by the way, didn't belong to the club. It was owned by a man called Vin Hardy, who had a fruit and vegetable round in the Wadsley Bridge area. Vin was one of the great characters in Hillsborough history, for he doubled as the club's odd-job man. One of his jobs was cleaning the drains, and it's no exaggeration to say that he had a great passion for the task. He absolutely loved it, and always revelled in getting filthy doing the job – especially when the time came round for him to deal with the toughest and dirtiest drains of all, those on the Spion Kop.

What a picture he made when he emerged from having completed the task, and he was oblivious to the smell that followed him everywhere! I think someone once said they ought to call him Pongo!

Peter Pollitt

When Peter Pollitt, now retired after a long career as a representative in the abrasives industry, was taken to watch Wednesday for the first time in October 1937, he was mystified by the brown paper parcel his Uncle Frank carried to the match... and even more intrigued when it turned out to contain a house brick. The brick, however, was put to a practical and quite legal use!

I was within a couple of weeks of my fifth birthday when my Uncle Frank gave me an early present which was probably the most influential I ever received. He introduced me to the wonder of watching Wednesday and inspired a lifelong passion.

I remember being puzzled by the brown paper parcel he carried as we walked from Wadsley Bridge to the ground, but the mystery was solved when, upon arrival on the terrace at Hillsborough, he unwrapped a house brick, placed it on the floor, and told me to stand on it to get a better view of the pitch! After the match he wrapped up the brick and took it back home.

I don't recall much about the game, but I'll never forget being mesmerised by the whole atmosphere. I had never seen so many people in one place, and the colourful scene on the field was intoxicating to a small boy. Wednesday beat West Ham 1-0 that day, and the goal was scored by Ellis Rimmer – the winger whose two late goals had won the FA Cup for Wednesday at Wembley two years earlier.

I don't know what happened to Uncle Frank's brick after I stopped needing to use it, but there soon came a time when I could go to Hillsborough without supervision. By then I preferred the Kop and the Leppings Lane ends to the terrace. We used to hang about before the match waiting to find out which way Wednesday were kicking in the first half. Then we'd dash around the back of the North Stand to get behind the goal the Owls were attacking.

Later, like the teams, we'd change ends at half-time!

When I was about 13, I got a bit too preoccupied with football and neglected my studies. It came as a shock when, one half-term, I finished third from bottom in my class at the Central Technical School – and a much greater blow was being told by my father that I was banned from watching Wednesday until things improved.

He kept me at home on Saturday afternoons, working on lessons provided by a teacher he knew. For three months, the nearest I got to watching the Owls was a long-distance view of the ground from the roof window of the attic of our house in Birley Rise Road. I could hear the crowd, but could only imagine what was happening!

However, at the end of that term I finished top of the class, and my privileges were restored. I was soon back with my pals on the Kop, singing about our hero Jackie Robinson. I remember we even sang the following words while queuing for hours to get tickets for the second leg of the League North (War) Cup Final with Blackpool in 1943:

Roll along Sheffield Wednesday,
Roll along,
Put the ball in the net
Where it belongs.
When Old Robbo gets the ball,
It is sure to be a goal,
Roll along Sheffield Wednesday,
Roll along

We've had our setbacks and suffered many frustrations, but I've enjoyed every game I've ever seen, and, to me, every player who has worn a Wednesday shirt has been a hero. Some may not always have deserved it, but I've always given them my loyalty.

I suppose the saddest night for me was in April 1975 when we came back from Nottingham Forest after a 1-0 defeat had condemned us to the Third Division for the first time in Wednesday's history. But I always knew we'd get back to the top grade, and, after a long struggle, we did.

Like many of my generation, I followed Wednesday all over the place for many years, but I stopped being a regular traveller in that period when away supporters started being segregated and began to be treated like second-class citizens at many grounds.

At my age, I don't like being kept in a ground for half-an-hour or more after a game, or being herded like cattle before and after a match. One experience at Newcastle in 1984, when there was some violence and aggression, made me question whether I could continue to put up with the trouble some home fans provoked – and which the methods of some of the people in authority didn't help us avoid.

It was a pity because I always loved going to away games. What's better than mixing with opposition supporters and talking football together? Renewing long-distance football friendships and getting more out of a trip than just watching the match was part of the fun.

I used to like going to Nottingham, for instance, because we made pals with some Forest fans. We had an arrangement whereby they got tickets for us at the City Ground, and we always sat with them there; and, when Forest came to Sheffield, we got tickets for them. We'd all meet up at the Abbeydale Sports Club a few hours before a game at Hillsborough, enjoy a glass of beer and a sandwich, and then go down to the ground together.

To me, that is how football should be. It's how my Uncle Frank liked it.

Albert Clayton

Albert Clayton remembers discovering the "special magic" of Hillsborough on the second day of January 1954 when Wednesday beat Burnley 2-0 and he was in a 34,040 crowd. Life, he says, was never quite the same again.

I was 11 years old when I finally got to see Wednesday for the first time, and the irony was that, three years earlier, on Christmas Day 1951, I'd been outside the ground and unable to get in for the game with Nottingham Forest because the gates were locked long before the 11.15am kick-off with over 61,000 inside and thousands more outside.

For months I'd been longing to see Derek Dooley, because everyone was talking about his goalscoring feats. In fact, it was a neighbour who organised what was going to be a Christmas treat for me. He turned up at our house and asked my parents if it was okay for him to take me to the match with his family. It was an experience just going to the ground, but an anticlimax not getting into the match.

It took a long while for me to get a second chance, and that was probably because although my father was a

Wednesdayite and had gone to matches regularly before the war, he wasn't quite as bothered about it when I was a boy. I think I only ever went once with my father, and that was to an FA Cup replay against Preston in 1957.

In fact, because we lived at Frecheville and it was more convenient, the group of kids I knocked about with started going to Bramall Lane before we decided it was time we extended our horizons and tried the longer journey to Hillsborough.

Lifelong Owls fan Albert Clayton and his wife Kathleen pictured on the Hillsborough pitch after their marriage in June 1968. Their wedding reception was held in the old Ozzie Owls Restaurant, and general manager Eric Taylor made special arrangements for photographs to be taken on the playing area – a privilege granted only rarely in those days.

The match was against Burnley in January 1954, and I stood behind the goal at the Leppings Lane end, where I had a perfect view when Albert Quixall had an effort deflected into the net off a defender and Dennis Woodhead made it 2-0 before half-time.

It was a major turning point in my life. The moment I went into the ground I felt a sense of wonder and knew instantly it was where I wanted to be. I'd discovered my spiritual home, and, though I continued going to Bramall Lane for a few years, it never again held the same attraction.

I remember at the end of that first season, knowing we wouldn't be back until August, our gang carved bits of turf from the edge of the pitch and took them home. I kept my piece in a plant pot at home for months. On the bus going home, the other passengers

thought I was mad holding this piece of grass in my hand. I explained: "This is no ordinary grass, it's come from Hillsborough"!

Author's Footnote: When Albert married his wife Kathleen in June 1968, their wedding reception was held at the Ozzie Owl Restaurant, and, although the Wednesday ground was officially closed down for the summer, general manager Eric Taylor made arrangements for caretaker Ron Ward to open up so Albert and Kathleen, and their guests, could stage a photo-call on the Hillsborough pitch. They may have been the first couple afforded that privilege – long before the practice became a regular part of the scene.

David Barber

Head groundsman David Barber, who has been on Wednesday's staff since 1977, recalls some boyhood visits to Hillsborough, and especially remembers a day when, at the age of nine or ten, he endured a painful experience and ruined his new Whitsuntide suit.

Dad started taking me to matches in the early 1950s when I was very young, and while I can't now recall the first game I saw, I have not forgotten how we used to walk over the top from Crookesmoor, always setting off very early so that Dad could call at the Park Hotel and have a pint before the match. I can still hear him saying: "Don't tell your mother!"

We always stood at the Leppings Lane end, and my favourite spot was in front of the railings in a raised area above the tunnel. It offered an undisturbed view of the game. However, as boys will, I did tend to try out various other vantage points.

One day when we went to the match, I had to wear the new suit I got at Whitsuntide because afterwards we were meeting my mother and going straight off to visit some family friends. I looked very smart in my green jacket and short trousers, and felt very dressed up wearing a tie. I can't remember why, but on this occasion, I chose to stand right behind the goal and took up my place half-an-hour before the scheduled kick-off.

There was a collection before the game, with a group of men walking

round the perimeter of the pitch carrying a huge sheet into which spectators were invited to throw coins. Nobody thought anything of that practice in those days, but, of course, it was fraught with danger. Coins can be pretty lethal, and it wouldn't be allowed today.

I didn't really feel it when a coin struck me on the back of the head, but, within minutes, it started to hurt, and when I felt blood running down my neck I feared the worst.

Someone called for an ambulanceman, and I ended up on the first-aid bench, where they cut away the hair from around the wound and stuck a large plaster on my head. To be honest, by now I was more concerned about reclaiming my place and watching the match – and more upsetting than my injury was seeing how the back of my lovely new jacket had been splattered with blood.

By the time the ambulanceman walked me back to my place, the teams were out and kicking in at both ends. All I remember is being just about to show the man where I wanted to get over the wall when "whack!" – this big greasy ball hit me straight in the chest. For a few seconds I could barely breathe.

The upshot was, I was promptly carried back to the first-aid bench, from where I watched the first half. At half-time I finally made it back to stand behind the goal, but I didn't find my Dad until after the end of the game. He took one look at my plastered head and blood and grease splattered jacket and quipped: "I didn't know you'd been playing!" Mother was not quite so amused.

The first time I went to a match with some pals independent of my Dad, I have to admit I ended up being thrown out of the ground. It was a trivial incident, but I was identified as a hooligan – and all because I threw a coil of wallpaper ends which dropped innocuously on to the track.

It was the time when fans had just started throwing toilet paper at matches, and, as we nine-year-olds wanted to be in fashion but couldn't afford to buy toilet rolls, one of the lads, whose family were decorating, came up with the idea of taking some wallpaper edgings to throw. The coils were barely the size of a 50-pence piece, and the one I threw plopped on the track about three feet away – and miles from Alan Finney, who was taking a corner at the time.

The next thing I knew, I could feel myself being lifted by the collar of my jacket, and the bobby didn't release me until we were outside the ground. I had a programme to prove I'd been at the match, but I couldn't describe the game to anyone because I'd missed most of it!

Keith Littlewood

Keith Littlewood, who spent most of his working life in mining engineering before a recent change of career, admits having no real interest in football until, in 1953 at the age of eight, he was taken to Hillsborough by his stepfather. It marked the beginning of a passion for the Owls which remains undiminished 45 years later.

I became a Wednesdayite in the autumn of 1953 when my stepfather took me to my first match, and I was instantly captivated by an atmosphere which was like nothing I had known before. As a quiet little eight-year-old, it was a revelation to hear the unique sounds of a football crowd, the shouting and cheering, and witness the uninhibited enthusiasm of grown-up people who would probably be very reserved if you met them in the street or in their homes on an ordinary day.

Saturday, 26 September 1953 marked a milestone in my life. The adventure began when we went to the Royal Oak public house at Chapeltown, and, while my stepfather popped in for a drink, I amused myself in the yard outside until it was time for us to board the supporters' bus which took us to Hillsborough. In those days few people had cars, and I still recall being astonished by the great throng of fans walking to the ground as our bus edged its way towards car parking space on Claywheels Lane, and, later, as we made our way on foot up Leppings Lane.

A trivial thing from those days which is worth mentioning is that, just along Leppings Lane there was an old cottage where an elderly lady used to sit on the doorstep and supervise operations as supporters left their pushbikes in her front yard. The sight of dozens of bikes and the lady on the step was a novelty which caught my imagination,

and I suppose it says much about social habits in the early 1950s. The cottage has long since disappeared, and so have the bikes!

There were over 45,000 people in the ground. I didn't know there were so many people in the whole world, and to hear them roar when the teams appeared was an experience I'll never forget. It made my blood tingle, and I wanted to keep going back to enjoy the thrill of that afternoon over and over again.

We sat in the old North Stand where, if you arrived early, you could claim a bench seat and avoid having to stand on the terracing in front.

Wednesday were playing West Brom, and I recall they pulled back to 2-2 after giving Albion a two-goal start, but then Albion snatched a late winner. Despite the defeat, I had already decided that Jackie Sewell, who had scored one of Wednesday's goals, was my first hero. Redfern Froggatt soon became the second.

A week later, incidentally, my stepfather took me to see Sheffield United draw 3-3 with Wolves, but, after Hillsborough, to a small boy the three-sided Bramall Lane didn't seem like a proper football ground, and, anyway, I was already hooked on Wednesday.

Mother, unfortunately, was unable to buy me a replica shirt (such things were unknown then, and there were no club shops), but an aunt did sew me two white strips on some black shorts, just like Wednesday had. I had to settle for a blue shirt with white sleeves, but, wearing a green jersey reminiscent of goalkeeper Dave McIntosh's, I could pretend to be a junior Owls' player!

I was always fond of goalkeepers. Brian Ryalls was on duty in the first game I saw, and I can remember him being brilliant on one occasion in that first season when I was taken to Blackpool to see Wednesday win 2-1. But McIntosh was the man in the green jersey whose bravery and agility earned him pride of place in my affections.

Hillsborough was already special, and there were so many little things about the ground as it was then which seemed so wonderful. For instance, the second time I went, when Wednesday beat Chelsea 2-0, I discovered the unusual scoreboard on the roof of the Leppings Lane Stand. It's a landmark which has long since disappeared, but it

will be forever synonymous with those early days.

I was amused not just by the man who watched the game through one of the small windows (he kept popping his head out to get a better view!) in the box, but by the crowd's preoccupation when he updated the score from Ninian Park. The reason, as my stepfather explained, was that our own Albert Quixall was making his England debut against Wales the same afternoon.

I continued to watch Wednesday from the old North Stand right up to it being demolished to make way for the new cantilver structure in 1961. Then I was a Leppings Lane regular until the fences went up, and, after a spell in the raised corner at that end until it was turned into an away fans' area, I removed to the South Stand.

The thing about watching from a regular place is the way you make friends with other regulars, and yet they're all people who you never see anywhere else but Hillsborough. There are some supporters I have known for 40 years, but, although we're on Christian name terms, I don't know their surnames or anything about them.

There was one chap I sat with for years. He was called Jack, and, when he died, his ashes were scattered on the pitch, but I never knew anything of his background. When we watched from Leppings Lane, there was a lad we knew as "Big Man" and I did discover his name was Doug Walters. It said a lot about the way we all used to mix without rancour that Doug was actually a staunch Unitedite, and he'd stand watching Wednesday with a radio glued to one ear so he could keep in touch with the Blades' progress!

It is true that you never forget your first matches, and I can recall almost every game I saw in that initial 1953-54 season. My first away trip was to Huddersfield, where our bus got stuck on a hillside overlooking the ground, and we ended up sliding down a muddy bank. I can still see Eddie Gannon, who started that game with a spotless white shirt, emerging caked from head to toe in mud within minutes of the kick-off.

A happier trip that year was to Bolton in an FA Cup replay in which the opposition camped in Wednesday's half for most of the afternoon, but the Owls nicked a famous victory when they got away twice, and first Sewell then Jack Shaw scored.

It was also in that initial season that I had my first sight of the legendary Stanley Matthews, and a Harry Heap cartoon in the *Green 'Un* reminds me that it was the day Norman Curtis, the Wednesday left-back, followed Matthews all over the pitch. Stan didn't get a kick all afternoon, but, unfortunately, goals from Jackie Mudie and Allan Brown gave Blackpool a 2-1 win.

Following Wednesday has given me more happy memories than sad ones, and I remember one occasion when the dismay of not being able to get into a match was tempered by the sheer pleasure of enjoying a famous victory at second hand. That was the evening in 1961 when we went to Old Trafford for an FA Cup replay, but found ourselves locked out.

I was only 16 at the time, but it didn't prevent me joining the others in the nearest public house – where I hid behind a raised newspaper for fear of being discovered as an under-age drinker. We could hardly believe our ears as someone kept relaying the news that Wednesday we're beating Manchester United – and ended up romping to a fantastic 7-2 success!

That wasn't the only time we went to an away match and couldn't get in. We suffered the same frustration at a Cup replay at Birmingham in 1969. Our consolation was that we missed a defeat.

I suppose the biggest disappointment was not being able to get a ticket for the 1966 FA Cup Final, which was Wednesday's first visit to Wembley in my lifetime. I might have got one by paying over the odds, but, as Josie and I were getting married that year and we were saving, I couldn't afford it. My stepfather and I watched the game on television, in black and white, and I suppose we could at least say we didn't have to make a long journey home after seeing us lose 3-2 when we'd led Everton 2-0.

In later years, my job as a mining service engineer took me all over the world and caused me to miss some very important games. I shan't forget that I was in India when Wednesday clinched promotion in 1984, and it was a totally unexpected surprise when I learned the news.

It was my first trip to India, and I hadn't thought I would have much chance of learning how Wednesday were going on against Crystal Palace. However, that day we were in the home of a local man, and he happened to have a short-wave radio which we persuaded him to put on. I was astonished when, after fiddling with the dial for only a few seconds, he quite accidentally located the BBC, and someone was commentating on a Liverpool match.

At the end of the commentary, they returned to the studio, and someone announced that Wednesday and Chelsea had won promotion – Wednesday doing so with a victory sealed by a Mel Sterland penalty. It made me very happy – and rather homesick!

I remember being abroad when Wednesday played at Chelsea in the Rumbelows Cup semi-final first leg in 1991, but made sure I was home in time to watch the Final at Wembley, where I savoured the joy of seeing the Owls beat Manchester United with John Sheridan's unforgettable goal. It compensated for 1966.

John Brodie

John Brodie, an engineer and surveyor now based at Loughborough, has been following Wednesday since 1963, and remembers savouring the special atmosphere of Hillsborough for the first time on a sunny August afternoon when the Owls shared a six-goal feast with Manchester United which provided the perfect introduction.

I was 11 years old and living in Retford, and, as nobody else in our family was then into football, it was a teenaged neighbour and pal called Joe Cox who first took me to watch Wednesday – 35 years later I still possess the ticket which got me into what was then the new North Stand, and it continues to remind me of the start of a lifetime's passion for the Owls.

Wednesday and Manchester United drew 3-3 that day, and it was a marvellous occasion, with Tom McAnearney (penalty), John Quinn and Eddie Holliday scoring our goals, and Bobby Charlton getting two for United; but what I remember best was the big crowd, the unique atmosphere and the sheer excitement of just being there. I was well and truly hooked!

We took an early train and looked around Sheffield before going on to the match, and I remember it as a great adventure. A curious incident I recall was, as we passed through the city centre after the match, Joe said: "Let's get a *Green 'Un*," and, when I asked what one of them was, he kidded me it was something to eat! I didn't realise it was a sports paper which, over the years, would become essential reading.

In fact, in later years, as well as collecting match programmes, I began searching through old copies of such papers as the *Green 'Un* when I started building records and reports of every League and Cup match Wednesday have ever played. From around 1985 it became my habit to travel to Sheffield on a Saturday early enough to spend the morning going through the newspaper files in the Central Library's local history department, have lunch in town, and then get to Hillsborough in time for the game.

I didn't really start getting involved in Owls' statistics until I was in my early 30s, but delving into the past and creating a full set of team line-ups has become a very enjoyable hobby, and it's certainly added to my appreciation of Sheffield Wednesday!

Going back to the beginning, I suppose I must have gone to matches with Joe for about three years, then, at 14 or 15, I was considered old enough to travel on my own, and those Saturday outings were invariably the highlight of the week.

I recall the train journey cost 3s 6d (17½p) return, a meal of egg and chips in Woolworth's restaurant set me back two-bob (10p), while the fare on the special bus to the ground was fourpence (about 2p) and I could get a match programme for sixpence (2½p). By then I was watching from the Kop, where admission was one shilling (5p). Seven shillings (35p) was the total outlay to enjoy the best day out a man could wish for!

I have, naturally, passed on my passion for the Owls to my son, Andrew, and my daughter, Jessica. Andrew, who is 12, was introduced to the delights of watching Wednesday about three years ago, and it was a joy to see him as wide-eyed and excited as I was back in 1963.

Christine Norman

Christine Norman, a legal secretary, has been following the Owls for over 40 years.

My Dad always used to tell a story about how his brothers took him to his first match when he was four years old and still too young to appreciate what was happening. They sat him on a wall, told him to stay there while they went to the front to get a better view, and promised to collect him at the end of the game. Unfortunately, after the final whistle they were so preoccupied with talking about the match, they dashed out of the ground – and had got home to Walkley before missing their little brother. They returned and were relieved to find him still sitting in a deserted Hillsborough – exactly where they'd left him!

Watching Wednesday

Jim Smith

Jim Smith is one of the most experienced and respected managers in the game, having worked in that capacity at every level from the old Fourth Division to the Premiership with eight clubs over more than 25 years. However, he has never forgotten his Sheffield roots nor lost his boyhood enthusiasm for Wednesday. Here he reflects on a passion for the Owls which started in his Shiregreen schooldays.

I doubt if anybody was more delighted than me when Wednesday won the Rumbelows Cup, their first major trophy for 56 years, by beating Manchester United 1-0 with that superb John Sheridan strike at Wembley in April 1991. Yet, daft as it might seem, for me the thing that really put the top on that great day was finally meeting an old favourite, Albert Quixall, in the reception room afterwards.

I was at the game as a guest of my old pal, Ron Atkinson, and it was when we were waiting to go back to the hotel in central London that I spotted Albert talking to Ron Springett. I couldn't

Jim Smith in full voice as the Derby manager. But he is still a Wednesdayite!

resist going up and introducing myself, and don't mind admitting it gave me a big kick to shake Albert's hand and talk to him.

Okay, I'm just an old romantic, but Quixall was one of my boyhood heroes, and, in all my years in football, until then I'd never met him face to face, and I suppose I wanted to tell him how much pleasure he had given me when I was a kid watching Wednesday from the Kop.

I grew up on the Shiregreen estate, and although my father was never a football fan and the game wasn't one of the organised sports at my first school, Hartley Brook, I developed an early interest and was soon regularly kicking a ball about with my pals.

After all these years, I've forgotten the details of the first professional match I ever saw, but must admit it was definitely at Bramall Lane, where Jimmy Hagan was in action with Sheffield United. However, soon after-

wards, the lads I knocked about with introduced me to Wednesday, and, once I'd been to Hillsborough, nowhere else ever held the same attraction – after that the men in the blue-and-white stripes were the only team that mattered.

I found a corner of the Kop, on the northern side, where the terracing was built up and there was a wall I could sit on, and that was my favourite spot for years. The funny thing is, I was only bothered about being there when Wednesday were playing: the FA Cup semi-finals and other games staged at the ground somehow never appealed to me.

I think the only time I deserted my place on the Kop was when Wednesday met Blackpool in an FA Cup-tie in 1953. I was actually taken to the match that day, and, in view of the 60,000 gate, it was considered safer for me to be at the Leppings Lane end.

Those were the days when small kids

were lifted down to the front, and I remember ending up watching while seated on the wall – getting a close view of the legendary Stanley Matthews, who, I'm sorry to say, spoiled my day by scoring in a 2-1 defeat of Wednesday.

The walk from Shiregreen was not a short one, and I often made the journey alone, but I can still remember the sense of excitement I always felt when I started out, and the pleasure it gave me to pass under the Five Arches in Herries Road and finally have sight of the Wednesday ground.

When I was at Firth Park Grammar School, I would play for the school in the morning, dash off for some fish and chips, and then make haste to get to Hillsborough, where I was invariably among the first to arrive.

I walked through rain and snow and, like most kids, thought nothing of it – though, of course, it was mostly downhill from Shiregreen. If you considered the return trip too testing, you could always get on one of the buses lined up and waiting at the end of the game!

There was always that extra sense of anticipation, something really special, about going to games on Christmas morning or a Boxing Day afternoon. They were unique occasions when everybody seemed to be going to the match on foot, and the combination of seasonal spirit and a big crowd full of banter made the games somehow different. One Christmas, I remember, Wednesday so got into the festive mood they scored three times for the opposition! That may have been the day, incidentally, when I discovered one of my non-Wednesday favourites, a West Brom wing-half called Ray Barlow.

My earliest heroes were probably Eddie Kilshaw and Eddie Quigley, and Dave McIntosh, the goalkeeper, was an instant favourite because, in his green jersey, he was not only distinctive but so acrobatic and brave. Goalkeepers then had to have courage because they got knocked all over the place, and nobody was more fearless than "Mac"!

When Quixall arrived on the scene with his blond hair and short shorts, he was always going to be a hero to every kid on the Kop because he was himself a youngster, and he was so clever with a ball. He used to do all sorts of tricks even when the teams were only kicking-in before the game, but I remember one

piece of skill which really caught my imagination.

It was in an evening game. McIntosh (but it might be that Ron Capewell or Brian Ryalls was in goal that day) cleared the ball towards the halfway line, and, as the ball came down, Quixall controlled it on his knee. I'd seen players collect a ball on their instep, but the way Albert could use his knee or thigh with such ease and skill was magic.

Some years later, by which time I had started my full-time professional career at Aldershot and could appreciate some of the finer points, I watched Albert give one of the best displays of his career on the day Manchester United beat Leicester City at Wembley in 1963. However, I'll never forget the pleasure he gave me in his Wednesday years.

I had so many Owls heroes in the 1950s and after. I always loved to watch Redfern Froggatt, and, as a budding wing-half, dreamed of emulating such players as Eddie Gannon and Doug Witcomb. Later, Tommy McAnearney and Tony Kay were the lads I wanted to play like.

Naturally, I always dreamed of following in the footsteps of some of those players, but, ironically, when I became a part-time professional in 1959, it was with Sheffield United. However, I still watched Wednesday as often as I could, and I still rate the 1960-61 side as the team which gave me the most pleasure as a supporter.

I appreciated their talents all the more, of course, by virtue of what I was learning from my own progress in the game, and there was so much to admire about the lads who were then playing under Harry Catterick. One game in which I saw Wednesday touch a marvellous peak was when they went to Old Trafford and beat Manchester United 7-2 in an FA Cup replay in February 1961.

Incidentally, it was only a few months after that when Sheffield United gave me a free transfer, and, until Aldershot offered me full-time terms, I wondered whether I really had a future as a professional.

Another great Wednesday memory came in April 1966. By then I was with Halifax, but I made sure I got to Villa Park for the FA Cup semi-final, and, on a very wet and muddy day, Don Megson and his lads turned the form-book

upside down by beating Chelsea – who were much-fancied – 2-0 despite having Vic Mobley injured and reduced to a passenger for an hour.

If I might have wished to have played for the Owls, the biggest regret I have is that I didn't even have the consolation of playing at least once at Hillsborough. There was one occasion, in my time at Sheffield United, when I was scheduled to be in action on the Wednesday ground in a Northern Intermediate League fixture. I was captain of that team, but it was sod's law that United just happened to choose that week to promote me to the Central League side!

As a manager, I've not been back to Hillsborough as often as I might have expected, but it was a happy coincidence that, in April 1986, when I qualified for the "92" club by managing a team on every Football League ground then in use, I reached the milestone in taking Queen's Park Rangers to play Wednesday. Well, at least I got on to the pitch for the presentation!

Of course, I suffered one of my heaviest defeats as a manager at Hillsborough when QPR lost 7-1 in May 1987, but at least when I returned with Newcastle on Boxing Day 1988 we won 2-1, and, as recently as September 1997, my Derby County side beat Wednesday 5-2 – which pleased me as a professional but left the Owls' fan within feeling almost as sorry as the kids who had succeeded me as Kop regulars.

On a couple of occasions, in 1983 and 1995, there was some talk of me being a candidate for the manager's job at Wednesday. Frankly, as far as I was concerned, it was always speculation, but it was an interesting thought and an intriguing possibility. For any genuine Wednesdayite, I suppose becoming manager would be considered the fulfilment of a dream. In my case, it didn't happen – and I'm not complaining because if you're fated to do it, you will, and obviously, it wasn't my fate.

At least I can still want the Owls to succeed, and, like thousands of other supporters, I know nobody can take away the many happy memories watching Wednesday has given me. I can even forgive them when they spoil my day as a visiting manager, although, to be honest, that hasn't happened very often!

This picture of Gary Shelton scoring for the Owls at Liverpool in the 1984-85 campaign is one of Joe Ashton's favourites because it evokes memories of a famous victory – and a family outing to Anfield during a Labour Party Conference up the road at Blackpool.

Joe Ashton

Joe Ashton, Labour MP for Bassetlaw since 1968 and a Wednesday director since 1990, began following the Owls as an eight-year-old, and recalls how, in the 1940s, he and his pals from Sheffield's East End found a novel way of making the long trek to Hillsborough on foot more interesting.

I first saw Wednesday play some time in 1942, and me and some other kids from Bodmin Street in Attercliffe had just started to get a real taste for it when my Dad refused to let me go to the biggest game the Owls played during the war years – the second leg of the League North Wartime Cup Final against Blackpool in 1943.

The reason he kept me at home was because, with 47,000 expected at Hillsborough, he didn't think a nine-

Joe Ashton.

year-old titch like me would be safe. I spent the afternoon in tears – and then wept some more when I learned our lads had lost 2-1.

Anyway, I was back on track the following season, worshipping the likes of Jackie Robinson, Alex Wands, Ted Catlin and a winger called Len Massarella. Len was a little, thick-set guy who came from a well-known family of ice-cream makers, and I always used to say he could lick any full-back in the League North! Being of Italian origin probably explained why, rather like Paolo Di Canio in modern times, he preferred to get winning goals as late as possible in a match. Di Canio says that's better for the crowd, but I don't know about Massarella's theory!

Hillsborough was a long way from the East End, and as kids we couldn't often afford the tram fare, so, more often than not, we walked. Well, we actually ran, because that was not only quicker but less boring – especially if we took a ball with us and kept up a passing game all through the back streets.

Kids couldn't do that nowadays even if they had the inclination, but, in the 1940s, there wasn't the volume of traffic because very few people in places like Pitsmoor, Woodside and Neepsend (which were the districts we ran through) could afford motor cars – and, anyway, petrol was in short supply.

Once you got to the Wednesday ground and went inside, long before the "proper" match, you could join dozens of other kids in a kickabout on the practice pitch which used to be behind the old North Stand. You'd get teams of 25-a-side with all 50 kids playing like lunatics in the hope of being spotted by an Owls scout!

If we couldn't get to a lot of Wednesday's away matches in those days, there was no local radio or teletext with which to keep in touch with the team's progress, so we had no choice but to join hundreds of other Owls fans who went to Bramall Lane – not to watch Sheffield United, but simply to keep an eye on the scoreboard.

You'll remember that at Bramall Lane then, the football scoreboard was in front of the old cricket pavilion, and, every 15 minutes or so, this little guy would climb up some steps at the end and walk along a gantry to update the score from Wednesday's match.

At half-time, when we were walking round the ground to change ends, we would often stand and gaze while he put up all the scores, and I remember one afternoon when, disappointed to note Wednesday were losing 1-0, I climbed on to the gantry and replaced the "0" with a "5"! The cheers it inspired confirmed there were at least several hundred Wednesdayites in the ground – but, unfortunately, their joy was short-lived because the little guy spotted what I'd done.

Fred Green

Lifelong Wednesdayite Fred Green, who had a six-month spell as manager of Rotherham United in 1967 after serving as Jack Mansell's assistant at Millmoor, is remembered in South Yorkshire sporting circles as a long-time secretary of the Atlas & Norfolk Sports Club. He held a similar position at Rotherham Golf Club for some years until the early 1990s after concluding his working life in Sheffield industry.

I well remember the 1935 FA Cup run, especially an amusing episode concerning my father which occurred on the day Wednesday beat West Brom 4-2 at Wembley to record their first triumph in the competition since 1907.

Dad was passionately devoted to Wednesday and followed them everywhere, but, having seen them in all the previous rounds, to his great dismay he was unable to get a ticket for the Final. Of course, there was no such thing as television then, and our only option was to listen to the match commentary on the wireless.

It might sound very unsophisticated more than 60 years later, but radio was a big thing at the time – indeed, it was a development regarded as one of the wonders of the age! Moreover, for the benefit of listeners who were football fans, the *Radio Times* used to carry a sketch of a pitch divided into eight numbered squares; and, during a match, while one man described the play, another called out a number which enabled you to identify where the action was taking place.

In those days we were living in Sheffield's East end, between Darnall and Attercliffe, and, on the morning of the Cup Final, there was a growing sense of anticipation in our little family newsagent's shop on Coleridge Road. My father could hardly contain his excitement, but then, just as we were gathering round the wireless shortly before the kick-off, the tension got too much for him. He suddenly stood up, put his coat on and walked out of the house!

He spent the next hour-and-a-half walking the streets, trying not to think what might be happening at Wembley. I always remember he popped his head round the door at about half-past four, and when mother and I told him the score was 2-2 with ten minutes left to play, he promptly went back out again!

By the time he returned, Ellis Rimmer had scored two goals in the last four minutes to seal a famous victory for Wednesday, and, at last, my father was able to relax and enjoy what was left of his Saturday afternoon.

When my father first took me to Hillsborough, in the early 1920s, I don't think I was old enough to walk, and I have no memory of the earliest matches at which I was present. My first vivid recollections are of the team that won the League championship in 1929, and my first hero was a full-back called Ted Catlin – not so much because of his ability as his very short haircut. I insisted on wearing my hair in the same style, thinking it would enable me to emulate Catlin and play for England!

Curiously, when I reflect on that period, it is an incident in a reserve match in 1930 which invariably springs to mind, and I think of Billy Marsden, a famous Wednesday half-back who suffered a very serious injury to his neck and spine while playing for England in Germany. It was feared Billy would never play again.

However, he launched an attempted comeback in a reserve game at Hillsborough, and the thing I remember was the sense of expectancy with which the crowd waited for Billy to head the ball for the first time. I don't know what we thought might happen, but we knew that was the great test of his fitness. When, at last, he got in a header, and especially as he showed no hint of any ill-effects, there was a terrific cheer which could not have been greater if he'd scored the winning goal.

Unfortunately, Billy never made it back to the first team and had to take early retirement.

My father and I had some great fun following Wednesday together, and I shall never forget the pleasure of going to matches with him. We always caught a tram from Attercliffe to town, and then travelled to the ground on one of the football specials lined up in Bridge Street. The same trams would form a seemingly never-ending line on Parkside Road and wait for the crowd to flood out at the end of the game, each tram filling up before gliding off in the direction of town.

As we queued six and seven deep in a long line waiting to board a tram after the game, all the supporters would discuss every incident and analyse the performance of every Wednesday player, and that in itself was as much a part of the entertainment and as great an education as reading the reports in the *Green 'Un* the same night.

One of my happiest afternoons at Hillsborough was during that 1935 FA Cup run. Tickets for the sixth-round tie with Arsenal were like gold, but my father managed to ensure that he and I, along with my mother, were in the 66,000 crowd that day, and we sat in the South Stand and witnessed an epic battle which ended with a dramatic 2-1 win for Wednesday.

Arsenal were top of the League at the time, and I recall feeling very upset when Ted Drake put them in front after only seven minutes but then jumping out of my seat in delight when Mark Hooper volleyed a wonderful equaliser. The crowd's reaction to that goal was a mixture of relief and enthusiasm which, to a 14-year-old, was intoxicating!

The winner came from Rimmer, the winger who scored in every round that year, but, before that, Drake missed a couple of easy chances, and the Green family weren't the only people pleased to hear the final whistle blow.

I have to admit that, in recent years, following two heart attacks, I don't get to Hillsborough as often as was once the case. Frankly, I can't cope with the excitement! However, I am often reminded of my father's great passion for Wednesday when I see my grandson Richard. Like his great-grandfather, Richard's enthusiasm knows no bounds. It's a family tradition.

Frank Ronksley

Frank Ronksley, a retired railway clerk who was brought up in Sheffield but has lived at Swinton, near Mexborough since 1974, started following Wednesday when he was five years old and insists that, at 59, he still gets the same buzz on match-day mornings as he did as a boy.

One Saturday in 1993 I missed my first home Wednesday match for 45 years. It was unavoidable, and came about because my mother-in-law died at dinner-time, just as I was getting ready to go to Hillsborough. The old girl had often threatened to find a way of stopping me from seeing the Owls one day, but I don't think she intended doing it in quite those circumstances. As you might expect, my regular mates at the ground made light of my excuse about a family bereavement, and at the next

game they greeted me with a notice on the electronic scoreboard which read: "Welcome Back, Part-timer Frank"!

They were even more amused when, in January 1998, I had to miss only my second home game since 1948 because my daughter was getting married. Here was I, a man who had placed great store on having a family in which everything was geared to my passion for Wednesday – yet my daughter decides to arrange her wedding on a Saturday in the football season.

Even when the Owls have been at their lowest ebb, I've never been tempted to deliberately give them a miss, and I watched every match, home and away, all the time they were in the Third Division. Well, to be honest, I missed the first seven minutes of a match at Mansfield.

The point is, I've never lost faith. And it is a religion. I feel the same now as I did as a small boy. When I leave our house and set off to watch Wednesday, I still get a buzz of excited anticipation.

Yet I've never been one to get too upset when we get beaten. We lost 8-0 at Middlesbrough once, and I consoled myself with my Grandad's old adage: "Win, draw or lose – always go on the booze!" We hadn't scored, so I had a pint for every throw-in, which wasn't enough to get me intoxicated!

If I'm honest, I can't remember my very first Wednesday match because I was barely five years old at the time, but the story was always told at home that

my reaction upon discovering Hillsborough was one of sheer pleasure. The previous week, my cousins had taken me to Bramall Lane, where they noticed a lack of enthusiasm as I watched the game. Yet, so they said, the minute I found myself on Wednesday's Kop, I was instantly animated and excited.

This was in 1944, and my earliest memory is that watching Wednesday meant travelling on a tram, which made it seem like a real adventure. Where we lived, we could walk to Bramall Lane, but I preferred a "proper" outing!

Curiously, from our house in Myrtle Road, the nearest tram stop was in Queen's Road, but we always went up to Shoreham Street and caught the Hillsborough tram outside the United ground. The reason was you had more chance of getting on at that stop, and, anyway, on that route the trams went straight through to Wadsley Bridge, so you didn't have to change in Fitzalan Square.

Within a few years I was making that journey on my own. Today, I don't think you would want to let a small boy wander off alone, but it was safer then. I used to reach Hillsborough, then nip up to the Park Hotel at the bottom of Wadsley Lane, where my Grandad Albert Ronksley would be waiting. He'd get me a bottle of pop, then go back inside to finish his drink before we walked down to the ground.

The first season of which I have vivid

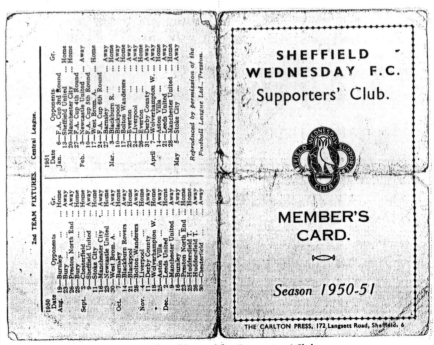

Frank Ronksley's 1950-51 membership card for Supporters' Club.

memories was 1945-46, when I think I had more fun following the Reserves because they were thrashing everybody and romped away with the Central League championship. It was not only much more exciting than watching the League North matches – there was so much room on the Kop at second-team games I could have my own personal crush barrier!

It was a different story when we met Stoke in the fifth-round of the FA Cup in February 1946. The Kop was packed and there were more than 62,700 spectators in the ground. I was astounded to see so many people. Everybody looked so tall, while I was so small. However, I had a marvellous view of the match because by then Grandad had discovered a raised ledge near the front at the North Stand side of the Kop – and it became my regular "seat".

I think a few grown-ups envied the kids who sat along that ledge at big matches when the ground was packed and some of the standing spectators found they couldn't see as well as they might wish. But, as all the kids wore short trousers in those days, we were often perished on cold afternoons. I recall when one old chap shouted: "It's all reight for you young 'uns up there, you can see better than me," one of kids called back: "Aye, but you won't get pneumonia like me – my legs are frozen blue!"

My first heroes were Frank Westlake and Frank Slynn, perhaps because they shared my Christian name, but later there were many others. For instance, there was Jimmy Dailey, a centre-forward who was known as "Horizontal Jim" because he'd dive into the goalmouth like Captain Marvel, defying flying boots to head in a knee-high cross. Cyril Turton was a commanding centre-half whose headed back passes were so powerful they inspired some of the best saves of goalkeeper Albert Morton's career.

Talking of goalkeepers, I remember the day we dubbed Dave McIntosh "Shingles". We played Bury in 1955 and drew 3-3, but we'd gone 2-0 down completely against the run of play. They were both down to "Mac", who, in one instance, made a diving save, suddenly winced, and the next moment the ball's slipped from his grasp into the net. The guy was obviously in pain, but only

later did we learn he was being troubled by shingles – and, as fans do, we thought it hugely funny.

Incidentally, another Wednesday goalkeeper, Ron Capewell, joined Wednesday from our local club, Midhill WMC, and the story went that the fee was £20 plus a set of those old blue-and-white hooped shirts the Owls wore at the back end of the war. What a transfer deal!

One special early hero was Alf Rogers. Remarkably, he became an instant favourite the day he mis-hit a shot so badly the ball knocked me off my perch on the Kop ledge! But I took to Alf in a flash when, after I'd been taken on to the running track and received attention from an ambulance man, he ran over, ruffled my hair, and said: "Are you alright, little 'un?" I couldn't get over the fact that a Wednesday player had actually spoken to me!

One of my first away trips was to Chesterfield in June 1947. I don't remember the details of how George Milburn scored a hat-trick of penalties against us that afternoon, but I have never forgotten the thrill of going to Heeley railway station and getting on a train pulled by an engine bearing the nameplate "Sheffield Wednesday". I was so proud that my club was important enough to have its own train!

To be honest, one of the things following Wednesday as a schoolboy gave me was a sense of pride. It might sound daft to a grown-up, and especially in modern times, but I always remember when Hillsborough staged a "B" international in 1950, and Hugh Swift was named as captain, I walked into school feeling so proud, and went round telling everybody who would listen that our left-back was going to lead England.

Until about 1980, for me everybody who wore a Wednesday shirt was a hero, but it's not quite the same now. It might sound silly, but, somehow, so many of the players today seem to look alike. Of course, it doesn't help that they now wear numbers nobody can read. Maybe I'm just getting old, but I can't form the same attachment to individuals when they so often lack the individuality which made some of my old favourites so easily recognisable.

But, anyway, it's the team that mat-

ters – the players as a group. I don't believe in anything but the team, because if you get involved with the people who run the club I sometimes think you might be tempted not to remain a Wednesdayite. They have a tendency to make you feel your passion for the club is misguided.

For instance, in 1991, when we met Sheffield United in the top division for the first time in over 20 years, my application for a match ticket was returned with a note attached to my cheque saying "Sold Out". The fact I had been a faithful fan for 47 years, was a long-time season-ticket holder and had invested in buying a share when the club was in deep financial trouble in 1976 – all this didn't seem to count. My sin was being so independent as to have failed to join the Travel Club.

The irony was that, as the game was at Bramall Lane, I went down to United's ground and got a ticket without any trouble. Unfortunately, United were cashing in on the situation because everyone who bought a ticket for the derby game had also to buy one for a match with Luton. So it cost me the price of two tickets to get the one I needed – but the important thing was to be able to see the Owls.

Audrey Barnes

Audrey Barnes, a retired cashier who worked for Hepworth Refractories for over 40 years, has been watching the Owls from the South Stand for more than half a century, since being introduced to the wonders of Wednesday by her father.

As an only child and the daughter of parents who were both keen football supporters (Dad was a shareholder at both Sheffield clubs), I suppose it was inevitable that I should be taken to a match as soon as they thought I was old enough to start sharing their enthusiasm. I'm glad they did, because I couldn't really imagine life without football.

Yet I must admit that when Dad took me to Hillsborough for the first time it was not an experience I enjoyed. I can't explain why, but, honestly, I hated it. I have forgotten everything about the game other than that Wednesday were playing Sheffield United, and it may have been in the last wartime season before "normal" League football was resumed.

After a few more visits with Mum and Dad, I found I liked football after all, and, although my parents took me to Hillsborough one week and Bramall Lane the next, I was soon a confirmed Wednesdayite. All these years later, I still go to both grounds, but, while I always want United to do well, my heart only belongs to Wednesday.

In all the 50 or more years that I've been going to Hillsborough, I have sat in virtually the same seat – on "B" row, behind where the hospital radio people used to sit and alongside the old Press box until this was moved nearer the back of the stand in the mid-1990s.

I had to move back a row myself when the club widened the gangways due to new safety regulations and improvements in the wake of the semi-final disaster of 1989, but I'm glad I've been able to remain in the same area of the stand from where my parents watched Wednesday for some years before they first took me.

Dad was a regular up to his death in 1963, and Mum only stopped going in 1987, a couple of years or so before she died; and what they liked about watching games from our regular seats was that you had a good view and also got to know a lot of people whom you only met at matches. Today, a great part of my enjoyment is knowing so many people who have been sitting in the South Stand for almost as many years as me!

It shows how times have changed when you think that, when I first went, my seat cost only a few shillings, and now, to sit in that seat for an "A" category match costs £21.

My first Wednesday favourite was Jackie Robinson, but he left soon after the end of the war, and later my heroes included Alan Finney, Albert Quixall and John Fantham. There have been many players I have admired over the years, but my all-time favourite is still Redfern Froggatt. Of course, there was a time when Redfern helped out with the hospital commentaries, and he was always as much a gentleman in that role as he was as a footballer.

I was always sorry my Dad didn't live to see Wednesday go to Wembley in 1966, but Mum and me went down on the train and had a lovely day which, if it ended up a bit of a disappointment

when we lost 3-2 after leading 2-0, was still very enjoyable.

The thing I remember is how civilised it all was. We had a meal on the train going down, and we walked down Wembley Way with all the comfort of a stroll in the park. Wednesday and Everton supporters were friendly to each other, and it was as if everyone simply wanted to enjoy the occasion. Even after the game, there was no aggravation, no hint of trouble, only happy banter.

I suppose the Rumbelows Cup win in 1991 was the highlight for me, because Wednesday brought a major trophy back to Sheffield for the first time in 56 years. I still treasure the memory of John Sheridan's winner, and Nigel Pearson and the other lads gave us a lot of success to cheer that year. In 1993, of course, we had the rare experience of going to Wembley four times in a few weeks, but, though we beat Sheffield United in that historic FA Cup semi-final, we lost both Cup Finals, and it was particularly disappointing to lose the FA Cup Final replay with Arsenal in the last minute of extra-time.

But, when I look back, I'm just glad I've been able to watch Wednesday at Wembley so many times. The supporters at some clubs never manage it once. Wednesday don't always enjoy the success we might like, but it's never dull supporting them.

Author's footnote: Audrey cannot identify the first game she saw, but it seems almost certain it was when Wednesday beat United 2-1 in September 1945, with Robinson scoring twice for the Owls.

Scott Sellars

Scott Sellars, who has played more than 500 games with Leeds, Blackburn, Newcastle and Bolton since launching his League career in 1983, was a Sheffield schoolboy star who followed in his father's footsteps in supporting Wednesday. The Wincobank product never saw his dream of playing for his boyhood favourites come true, but he remains a true-blue Wednesdayite.

Our entire family was always Wednesday mad, and I must have been about six years old when my father, Brian, first took me to Hillsborough,

and for the next ten years we seldom missed watching a home game together. We used to stand on the Kop among the same group of people. There was something about the place and the atmosphere that gripped me, and I loved it.

I would play for the school on Saturday mornings, then watch the Owls in the afternoon, and it never mattered to me that, at the time, the club wasn't doing as well as we might have liked. Everyone in a blue and-white shirt was a hero.

I can't recall my first game, but my earliest memories are of Willie Henderson, the little Scottish winger. There was a spell when Willie often seemed to be on the sub's bench, and, whenever he stood up ready to go on to the field, the whole stadium used to light up – there was this terrific air of expectancy, and you felt sure something good was going to happen.

Henderson, striker Mick Prendergast, winger Eric Potts, and goalkeeper Peter Springett are the players who were my first favourites.

I'll never forget the afternoon in 1974 when we beat Bolton 1-0 to ensure we didn't go down into the Third Division. Ken Knighton scored the goal, and everyone in the ground seemed to go mental with delight!

But, of course, the best day of all was probably what every Wednesdayite will always remember as "the Boxing Day massacre" in 1979 when we beat Sheffield United 4-0. United were really flying at the time, and that match, in the Third Division, attracted over 49,000 spectators. It was a game in which every Wednesday player seemed to be on top form at the same time, and I can still remember Ian Mellor's goal as something special.

I played with Hinde House School and Sheffield Boys, and, obviously, I imagined playing for Wednesday one day. But in terms of what I might do and which club I might join, I was open-minded. I felt I wanted to make the best choice for my career and kept my options open, feeling things would develop to help me make the right decision. I trained with Wednesday, and Charlie Wain, the club's scout, was always up at our house. But I also went to Manchester United, Leeds, Barnsley and Chesterfield.

In Wincobank I played with a team called Oakwell, who were associated with Barnsley, and, though I wasn't looking to sign for them, I went to Barnsley from the age of 12. Allan Clarke was their manager, and he had Martin Wilkinson with him looking after the youngsters. It was after they went to Leeds that Martin asked me to go up there for training.

I suppose the reason I plumped for starting my career at Elland Road when I left school was because the club, and Martin in particular, put a lot of time in with me, I really enjoyed it, and they worked at persuading me that signing for Leeds was the right thing.

Naturally, I have never lost my feeling for Wednesday, and I often think I would have loved to have had the chance to play for them. When I was at Newcastle, I could see what playing for the team they had supported as boys meant to lads like Lee Clark, Robbie Elliott and Steve Watson, and I suppose it made me wish I could have had the same experience.

There have been times, of course, when my name has been linked with Wednesday, but nothing ever came from it.

When I was 18 and starting to get into the team at Leeds, we played Wednesday at Elland Road and drew 1-1. It was the season in which Wednesday won promotion back into the old First Division, and Howard Wilkinson apparently tried to sign me as part of his team-strengthening the following summer.

I think Howard tried to get me several times, including once when I was at Blackburn. Then, in early 1993, when I was back at Leeds but things weren't working out, Wednesday were said to be in again. Newcastle were also trying to sign me, and that's where I ended up – with Wednesday having apparently dropped out of the race because Trevor Francis didn't feel I was strong enough for the Premiership!

I helped Newcastle win promotion in 1993, and, in the following year, we went to Hillsborough and won 1-0 with an Andy Cole goal. Wednesday hammered us that day – and, though I was grateful to be on the winning side, the Owls' fan in me felt a bit choked because they had not really deserved to lose!

On the Road with Wednesday

Nightmare ride from Tottenham, 1962

The things people will endure to follow their favourite football team! Albert Clayton never forgot the day in November 1962 when he travelled to Tottenham as a pillion passenger on the motor bike of his great pal Dave Rodgers, and mishaps on the homeward journey up the A1 included a puncture and a drive through freezing snow! This is how Albert told the story.

In over 40 years of supporting Wednesday, I never had a day quite like 17 November 1962 when Dave and I went to White Hart Lane and saw the Owls draw 1-1 in a terrific game in which Alan Finney scored our goal.

When I walked over the fields from Frecheville to Ridgeway to meet up with Dave, it was a beautiful autumn morning. There was a bit of frost on the ground, but the early sun was warm – it was lovely having that sun on our backs as we started the journey.

The first hitch, albeit a minor one, came when we were going on the then-new Grantham by-pass. A sharp breeze caught us, and Dave suddenly shouted: "I've lost me goggles, they've blown off!" Then he added: "Ne'er mind, I'll get some more in London."

When we reached London, it was drizzling, and, forgetting to make time to get Dave some new goggles, we parked up and made our way to the football ground. It was a real wintry scene, and the drizzle being highlighted by the Tottenham floodlights somehow made a pretty picture.

We were a bit damp as we started for home afterwards, but were oblivious to it. Unfortunately, we hadn't gone far when Dave stopped. "We've got a puncture," he announced.

We flagged down an AA man, but he didn't want to know about our problem when he realised we weren't members. At least he was good enough to point to

a garage at the top of the next hill, so we pushed the bike up there.

The bloke at the garage had obviously had a bad day. One look at the expression on his face told you that. When we explained we'd got a puncture and asked if he could help, he didn't hesitate: "No!" Then he added: "Sorry, but I've got to get away very soon, and I've another job on. You'll have to leave your vehicle and I'll do it tomorrow."

Naturally, we said that wasn't possible because we were from Sheffield and wanted to get home that night. "Blimey," he said. "Okay then, bring it in. You've got until six o'clock, then it's got to be out whether the job's done or not."

When we wheeled the bike in, he was mortified. He had expected a car, and wasn't impressed. But, fortunately, the chap working with him obviously felt sorry for us because, every time the boss went out to serve someone at the pumps, he dropped what he was doing and helped us repair the puncture. The boss also gave us a hand.

In fact, when the job was finished, the boss apologised for having been agitated earlier, and, when we offered to pay, he wouldn't take a penny. "Just make sure you get home," he said.

We thought that was the end of our problems, but we hadn't gone much further when it started snowing. We went through Huntingdon reduced to a speed of 20 mph with our feet hanging out to keep the bike balanced!

And it was getting colder by the minute. I was wearing a rubber mac over a crombie overcoat, a Wednesday scarf, and one of those Robin Hood hats. Dave, who was as tough as old boot leather and frightened of nothing, was in his motor bike gear and just as cold as me. He didn't have any goggles, of course, and was half blinded by the snow and cold. He complained his eyes were closing with ice.

We made it to some traffic lights in the middle of Newark, and I knew something was wrong when they changed from red to green and Dave made no effort to move. He said: "I can't go any further. I'm played out. I'm frozen stiff and I can't see!"

I persuaded him to make one last effort to push on for another couple of miles until we reached The Fox at Kelham, where I knew we could get a warm and a drink. We were so frozen when we reached the car park, I fell over trying to get off the bike. I scrambled to my feet and peered through the pub window.

Honest, the whole scene resembled something from a Christmas card, us out in the snow, and inside that pub, through the window, a huge welcoming fire in the grate. I shouted to Dave: "Come and look at this!" But poor old Dave was still stuck on the bike and couldn't move.

I ended up holding the bike while Dave got off it, and the next thing was the bike went over, I followed it to the ground, and, just at that moment, a chap came out of the pub. He walked past us on his way to the outside toilets, taking one look at us with an expression that said: "I wonder how much they've had to drink?"

Anyway, we eventually propped the bike up against a wall and went inside. We walked in, everything stopped, and everybody looked up at us. What a picture we must have made. It was just like the malamouke saloon job.

But it tells you something about what football was like in those days. We'd found ourselves in a room full of Forest fans. "Where've you been?" someone asked in surprise, and when we said we were on our way from Tottenham to Sheffield, they roared a welcome, made a great fuss of us, and started talking football.

It had stopped snowing by the time we came out and resumed our journey, but the roads were still very dicey. Our progress was slow, but, at last, just after midnight, we reached Marsh Lane, just through Eckington on the outskirts of Sheffield. By now we were again frozen with cold.

We used to go to a chip shop there. It belonged to a Unitedite, little Joe Glossop. The thought of some of Joe's chips was such a delightful prospect, we hardly dared to think we might still be in time for some that night. When we saw the lights were still on, we hoped he might still be open, but, once inside, our spirits fell when we saw Joe was cleaning up.

He took one look at us, and, knowing we were Wednesday fanatics, didn't need to ask where we'd been. "I've finished for the night, lads," he said, then he spoke those wonderful words: "Oh,

go on, I'll put t'ovens back on and cook you some chips."

We soon felt warm and human again, but there was still another twist to the story when we began the final lap of the journey home. Half-a-mile from Dave's house we ran out of petrol, so ended up pushing the bike up that last hill.

I'll tell you what, I wasn't half glad when I got home that night and saw there was still a good fire in the grate. I think I fell asleep dreaming about the point Wednesday had got at White Hart Lane. It seemed as if it had happened a week ago, not just yesterday afternoon!

Sometimes the Problem is Getting There!

Frank Ronksley, the retired railway clerk who has been following Wednesday since 1944, has missed only two home games since 1948 and only a handful of away matches, but, as he recalls here, there have been a few moments of acute frustration and some setbacks on the road with the Owls.

When I took early retirement in 1993 just before I reached the age of 54, I did so to ensure I would not be prevented from following Wednesday on their travels. Honest, there was no other reason. There had been two of us in the office where I worked, but the powers-that-be were moving my mate out as part of cutbacks, and my first thought was: "If I'm left on my own, I won't be able to get anybody to look after the shop when I want to go off in midweek to places like Southampton."

There was no way I was going to be sitting there with tears in my eyes while I watched other people boarding the train to follow Wednesday. The only solution was to accept redundancy.

Talking of away trips, it's appropriate to mention Tommy Gleadall and Rod Slater, two great Wednesdayites who were so often my travelling companions and mates at matches until their recent deaths. Tommy, who was 78, used to

take his son and all his son's pals all over the country in his old blue van for years, and I was often his passenger. Rod, who sold programmes at Hillsborough for 40 years, shared many escapades with me while following Wednesday.

The only complaint I had against Rod was that, when he asked me to be his best man, it meant we had to miss a match at Swindon. At least when I asked him to be my best man some years later, I had the sense to arrange my wedding so the date didn't conflict with watching Wednesday.

In fact, when I married at the age of 35, I made it plain to Gina that being my wife meant putting up with me having a drink every night and going to every Owls' match home and away. Happily, she is content to support the Wednesday cause in this way – although we were both left helpless when one of our daughters chose to get married on a day Wednesday had a home fixture!

I never missed a Wednesday game, home or away, all the time they were in the Third Division. Well, to be honest, I missed the first seven minutes at Mansfield once owing to transport problems. In fact, I maintained a 100 per cent record from October 1974 to April 1991 – although there was one appalling day in December 1990 when I got to Ashton Gate only in time to see the very last kick of a game which the Owls drew 1-1.

There was so much snow about that hundreds of supporters travelling by road never made it to Bristol. I thought I was being canny going by train. Unfortunately, on the way we ran into a major delay caused by some repairs to a bridge. I took a taxi from the station to the ground, but, seconds after I'd dashed through the gate, the referee blew for time. "Are you from Sheffield?" someone asked, and when I said yes he said: "Didn't you hear the half-time warning that the roads are so bad going north, you might struggle to get home?"

My pal Rod Slater was with me on the day we missed a game at Millwall – and weren't consoled by the knowledge that we were lucky to be alive after an amazing escape on the M1 going down to London. We were passengers in an estate van which, being driven by Bernard Wilson at 105mph because we were behind schedule, suddenly somersaulted off the fast lane when one of the tyres burst.

I was in the back seat, and all I remember is suddenly being upside down with the hundreds of bits and pieces in the back of the van flying all over the place. Miraculously, as I realised later, when the van finally came to rest, it finished upright on all four wheels a few feet from the grass verge.

Unfortunately, when I came to my senses, I couldn't see either Bernard or Rod, who had been occupying the front seats. I leaned over, grabbed the steering wheel, and managed to guide the van on to the verge. Next thing, Rod appeared from under the dashboard and scrambled through the passenger door, shouting back to me: "Jump out quick, it might blow up!" I didn't need telling twice!

Bernard, meanwhile, had somehow ended up on the grass on the central reservation, and the next few minutes were passed in a state of chaos and confusion, with the police, fire and ambulance services all on the scene with astonishing speed while the three of us tried to understand exactly what had happened.

The accident occurred about 55 yards above Trowell Services, and, eventually, after the van, which was in a right state, had been towed away to the nearby village, Bernard got underneath to see if he could do any repairs – he being as desperate as me to complete our journey.

Just then a couple of chaps came up and one of them said: "Hey, we've just seen a right accident involving a van. One poor begger was slung on to the fast lane, and we saw two bodies bouncing about inside the van. As we went past, it was upside down. I'll bet all three poor sods are dead. Did you see it?"

I said: "Aye, we didn't just see it, we were in it, and if you think we're dead, shake hands with a ghost. As for the driver who flew out into the road, well, he's underneath the van right now, trying to make the begger go so we can still get to a football match at Millwall!"

Of course, we never reached Millwall, and my only consolation was that, having lost my spectacles in the accident and given up hoping to find them, I wouldn't have been able to see any-

thing had we got to The Den anyway!

Curiously, one of the few other away games I've missed was also at Millwall. On that occasion, however, it was entirely my own fault, although I prefer to blame it on a bout of concussion. What actually happened was I had a few drinks and suffered a fall on my way home from the local pub one Friday night (or perhaps it was the early hours of Saturday morning) – and the upshot was I slept right through until Sunday.

I can remember waking up, looking at the clock, and, believing it was Saturday morning, saying to the wife: "I'll have to get moving or I'm not going to get to London." Gina replied: "I wouldn't bother – the match was yesterday, they lost 2-1, and, here, you can read about it in the *Sunday Express*."

There were two trips to Sunderland when we did get there, but only after a struggle.

One year we were going with Sheffield United Tours, but, when we got to Pond Street and took our places on the bus, the firm's clerk suddenly appeared and said: "Sorry, this bus isn't going to Roker. We need 18 passengers to make the journey profitable, and there's only 16 of you."

We ended up having a whip-round to raise the cost of the other two places, and, eventually, off we went. Whether or not it was because the bus was only half-full and didn't resemble a normal supporters' coach I don't know, but when we reached the outskirts of Sunderland, we were accorded a police escort right to the main entrance at Roker. Only when we trooped off and asked for the ticket office did the police realise we weren't the Wednesday players and officials!

Another time, five of us, including two women, missed the excursion coach to Sunderland, dashed to the railway station to find we had also missed the train, and ended up travelling all the way to Wearside by taxi.

When we found the train had gone, I rang Abbey Taxis, and, after the taxi pulled into the station entrance, the driver asked: "Where to?" I said: "Sunderland," Thinking I meant the old Sunderland Club on Ecclesall Road, he said: "It won't be open yet."

Naturally, I explained we meant Sunderland in the North East, and he said the charge would be £15. Now £3

each for the five of us might sound cheap in 1998, but in 1969 it was expensive. I think the train fare was about 15 shillings (75p). The bonus was that the driver said he'd wait and bring us back free – providing we paid for him to watch the match.

Ah, well, I thought, hang the expense. With a bit of luck, we may have converted him into a Wednesdayite anyway. Certainly he was quite enthusiastic on the way home.

Paul Webster

Paul Webster, a steelworks credit control manager who now works in the Hillsborough Press room at home matches and has been an Inter-City Owl travel steward on away trips since 1983, recalls an expensive trip to Southend in 1975.

Five of us went to Southend in 1975 (I think it was Wednesday's first match in the old Third Division) and, as if it wasn't enough to have seen the lads lose 2-1, we ran into serious problems soon after leaving Roots Hall when the battered old Peugeot car my pal was driving spluttered to a halt at a roundabout. This was the same vehicle which, after we'd left home at 10.30 that morning, had clocked 90mph most of the way from Sheffield and got us to the ground just before kick-off. Now it just "died" on us – and, in view of the hammer it had taken, perhaps it was no wonder.

We debated how to get home and decided the simple solution was to hire a taxi, but the first firms we rang refused to believe we really expected them to take us back to South Yorkshire. We finally found one cabbie who boasted: "I'll take you anywhere," but, until we were all aboard, we refrained from mentioning Sheffield.

This poor cabbie, who had never before in his life been north of London, thought Sheffield was a village a few miles up the road, but, on discovering it was a city some 200 miles away, he said he had always wanted to see the world. He switched his clock on – and off we went.

When he finally dropped us, the clock registered £88, and, with a £10 tip, it cost us £20 apiece, which was a lot more than any of us could really afford

– but it was worth it to be home in time to get to Hillsborough for the match with Brighton the following Wednesday!

In over 30 years of following Wednesday, I doubt if I've missed more than six or seven games, home or away, and the irony is that when my father first took me to watch the Owls I wasn't particularly interested. My "conversion" occurred after we had taken the train from Oxpring (near Penistone) to Wadsley Bridge one afternoon in February 1965 and watched Alan Finney and Peter Eustace score the goals in a 2-0 defeat of Sunderland.

By the end of the 90 minutes, I was hooked, and, even at the age of 12, simply had to be wherever Wednesday were playing whether or not my father could take me. Almost from the outset, despite our tender years me and a couple of mates thought nothing of travelling long distances to matches on our own – so by the time I was 14 I was a seasoned campaigner in dealing with the tribulations of getting across London on the Underground!

Some years ago, a spell out of work and a dramatic drop in my financial resources put my hopes of maintaining my regular attendance at away games at risk, but I solved the problem by volunteering my services as a steward on the Inter-City Owl. It means that for the past 15 years I've travelled in comfort – much better than using an old banger!

But did I say it was always comfortable? How can I forget a trip to Portsmouth when it rained the whole match, and 650 Wednesdayites were drenched to begin with, then returned to the train to find there was water everywhere in all the corridors and carriages. To add insult to injury, we hadn't gone more than four or five miles when the train stopped – and three hours later we still hadn't moved on.

On this occasion, nobody suggested taking a taxi, and it was two o'clock on Sunday morning before we reached Sheffield. I think we had seen the Owls win at Fratton Park, so any inconvenience was worth it.

Subscribers

1 David Edmondson
2 Peter Charlton
3 Gary Grimes
4 Paul Bentham
5 Richard Sharpe
6 Terence Kirk
7 Robert Howard Stephen Shaw
8 Cyril Ewart King
9 Michael Maskrey
10 Ian Gregory
11 Keith M Liddlelow
12 Ken Castley
13 Wayne Dalton
14 Tony Swift
15 James Shephard
16 Elliott Sam Coles
17 Adam Corner
18 Mark H Price
19 Bill O'Brien
20 Raymond H Smith
21 Robert A Smith
22 Stewart R Smith
23 Darryl Lomas
24 Thomas Lomas
25 Graham Lomas
26 Brian Whitehead
27 Garry Bennett
28 Alan Berisford
29 Dennis Millington
30 Ian Brownhill
31 Craig Radforth
32 Lee Craig Radforth
33 Mark James Radforth
34 David Sayers
35 Gerald Hinchliffe Harris
36 Adrian C Parkes
37 Brian Steers
38 Andrew John Brodie
39 John Bellamy
40 Martin C Andrews
41 M V West
42 Louise West
43 Nick West
44 Dave Levitt
45 Alan Denial
46 Ian Hunt
47 Terri Louise Button
48 Brenda Nicholson
49 Kevin Loy
50 Barrie James Earnshaw
51 Ken Price
52 John Robinson
53 Alan G Holmes
54 Brian A Holmes
55 Geoffrey Teasdale
56 Ryan James Lister
57 Alan Raymond Marshall
58 Robert Emmett
59 Stephen R Edwards
60 Maureen A Edwards
61 Janet E Edwards
62 Susan E Edwards
63 Derrick A Edwards
64 Arthur Edwards
65 Patrick Jospeh Ryan
66 Peter Wales
67 Geoff Clarke
68 Ailsa Brookes
69 D Barnett
70 John Andrew Saunders
71 David Sloboda
72 Paul Doherty

73 Paul Cooper
74 Scott Anthony Wilson
75 Jean Mary Taylor
76 Ian Taylor
77 Andrew Wood
78 Gary (Gaz) Millard
79 D R Davies
80 David Austin
81 Derek Tingle
82 Alan Kitridge
83 Mick Renshaw
84 Andrew David Hawley
85 Neville K Frost
86 Paul Lindley
87 Geoffrey Hunter
88 Robert Bingley
89 Malcolm Walter Wainwright
90 Charles J Fox
91 Dean A S Hedley
92 Jason Lee Otter
93 Richard W Taylor
94 Little Frank Ronksley of Swinton
95 Peter Otter
96 Trevor Vernon
97 Paul Kay
98 Anthony Trevor Bird
99 Barbara Ann Watson
100 Michael Grayson
101 Robin Caminow
102 John Martin Giles
103 Jack Barnett
104 Steven R Hallam
105 Andrew Neil Dalby
106 Mr Peter G Jones
107 F A Siddaway
108 Richard Sutcliffe BSc, Hons
109 Darren Lee Shepherd
110 David Mannion
111 Brett Carter
112 David L Mobley
113 John Clayton
114 Richard Adams
115 Ron Fearnley
116 John Mason
117 Fred Smith
118 Peter Webster
119 Rhys Luke Boughen
120 Dennis Gray
121 Adrian Kenneth Job
122 Derek James Fox
123 Robert A Ashton
124 Robert Moody
125 Ken Latham
126 Elaine Hargate
127 Audrey D Barnes
128 David B Turner
129 Graham R Akitt
130 Matthew Herbert
131 David James Illingworth
132 Martin G Mullane
133 Nicholas Paul Robinson
134 David North
135 F W Hobson
136 Alick Maltby
137 Richard Sykes
138 Michael James Thrussell
139 Peter Howard Pollitt
140 Daniel James Crowther
141 Jon Knight
142 Colin Fanshawe
143 Harry Lund
144 J L Walton

145 Darren Hawksworth
146 David Hawskworth
147 Ernest Hawksworth
148 Richard Eric Green
149 Thomas Alexander
150 Darren Hoggard
151 Wayne Hoggard
152 Ian Gregory Troops
153 Brian David Grayson
154 A Dyson
155 Ian Ardon
156 Michael Anthony Pearson
157 Alan N Cass
158 Pip Caselli
159 Richard Williams
160 David Parfitt
161 David Kevin Blagden
162 David Blagden
163 John Harrold
164 Stewart Robinson
165 Fred Priestley
166 Stephen Thompson
167 Martyn Sanderson
168 Richard Harrison
169 George C Hambleton
170 Vivien A Hambleton
171 C John Woolford
172 Patrick Widdowson
173 Andrew Cooper
174 Ian Robert Patterson
175 Brent Graham Hawksworth
176 Stephen Pond
177 Kenn Swallow, Happy 60th Birthday.
178 Simon D Trickett
179 J D Laude
180 Alan Barber
181 Alan S Thacker
182 Paul Antony Cooper
183 John Barrett
184 Daniel Hammond
185 Ian Hammond
186 Stephen Perry
187 Stephen Morrill
188 Russell Ian Davies
189 Robert H Carr
190 Garry Gabbitas
191 Colin Barry Wheeler
192 Terence Bownes
193 Richard W M Coe
194 Michael Bull
195 Gerry Hall
196 Linda Woodhead
197 Nicola Jane Wroe
198 Stephen James Rennie
199 Daniel Thomas Lewis
200 Ian Ford
201 John Slack
202 Steve Sampson
203 Michael John Hanagan
204 Geoff Cartledge
205 Rob Poulter
206 Colin Grant
207 Brian Derek Butcher
208 David Ashton
209 Mick Firth
210 Phelim Josef Cassidy
211 Charles Cope
212 Andrew Barden
213 Michael Warren
214 Alan Bower
215 Norman J Johnson
216 Terry Whitehead

217 Philip Corbridge
218 Ian Corbridge
219 David Richard Malcolmson
220 Russell England
221 Christopher J Wright
222 Leonard Thompson
223 Adrian Corner
224 Alan Methley
225 James Yule
226 Paul Garlick
227 Catherine A Hope
228 Brian Renshaw
229 Graham Thorpe
230 Mrs M Sharman
231 Graham Wassell
232 Christopher Marsh
233 Neale Andrew Parkin
234 Stephen D O'Shaughnessy
235 Steve Williamson
236 Danny McDonagh
237 John Hopkins
238 P Law
239 Keith Webster
240 David Cartwright
241 David J Nelmes
242 P S Pattinson
243 Frederick Robshaw
244 Dale Makey
245 Christine Anne Sanderson
246 Mr Alan Cobb
247 Mr Kevin Goss
248 Mr Michael Bancroft
249 Daniel Jones
250 Ashley Paul Lidster
251 Debbie Michelle Lidster
252 Eric Edgar Froggatt
253 Peter Bowell
254 Ian Durnan
255 Mike Franklin
256 David John Lee
257 David Alan Simmons
258 Craig Stevenson
259 Paul Robert Jacklin
260 Peter Thomas Bates
261 Peter Atkin
262 Christopher Atkin
263 Paul Atkin
264 David A Gaimster
265 Andrew Hellewell
266 Robert Foster
267 Stephen Phillips
268 Kevin Roebuck
269 William Henry Hubbard
270 F J H Brown
271 Ellen Rhead
272 Trevor Albert Glaves
273 Stanley Basford
274 Andrea Dunstan
275 Edward Blanchard
276 John Robert Hall
277 Adam Leighton Johnson
278 Wayne Garry Cutts
279 George Ernest Kompton
280 Vaughan Skirrey
281 John William Webster
282 Sharon Farquhar
283 Benjamin James Renshaw
284 John Emsen